was luther
a liberal or
conservative

Resilient Reformer

Resilient Reformer

The Life and Thought of Martin Luther

Timothy F. Lull and Derek R. Nelson

Fortress Press
Minneapolis

RESILIENT REFORMER

The Life and Thought of Martin Luther

Cover image: Painting: Resilient Reformer © Brad Holland 2015

Cover design: Joe Reinke

Library of Congress Cataloging-in-Publication Data

Print ISBN: 978-1-4514-9415-0

eBook ISBN: 978-1-5064-0025-9

Manufactured in the U.S.A.

This book was produced using PressBooks.com, and PDF rendering was done by PrinceXML.

To our parents, with love and gratitude:

Raymond Robert Lull and Ruth Cole Lull and Rodney and Mary Nelson.

Contents

Preface

The story behind the writing of this book is not as complicated as the story of its subject matter, but it is unusual. When Timothy Lull died very unexpectedly in May 2003, he left behind a shocked and mourning family, a grieving community, and untold numbers of in-the-works projects and plans. Some of his papers were collected and published as *On Being Lutheran* by Augsburg Fortress in 2006. But his biggest project was this one—an intellectual biography of Martin Luther. In various ways, he had been working on it for twenty years. I had the pleasure of being his research assistant for the project, and delighted in many conversations about the crucial decisions any interpreter of Luther must make, the paths taken by predecessors, and the needs and interests of present readers.

His widow Mary Carlton Lull and sister Patricia Lull entrusted the project to me to carry forward, and I am deeply grateful for their trust and support. Tim had finished most of the research, much of the outlining, and about half of the writing of this text. I hope that I was able to approach the inimitable style of his lively prose and to remain faithful to his general commitments and interests. In patterning myself after his voice, I gradually found my own. The first time we discussed the book, he proudly announced that he was going to call it *Luther: Six Crises*. He was shocked when I alerted him to the fact that *Six Crises* was the name of Richard Nixon's first memoir, and Tim, no sympathizer with Nixon's politics, quickly resolved to find a seventh crisis. The book's present title highlights, instead, the character traits of Luther that led him through so many crises.

The world is already filled with Luther books, and one feels slightly uneasy about presenting another. But it is an endless and joyful task to introduce Luther to new generations, and especially to general readers and beginning theological students. They will appreciate the gains of recent scholarship but may not find there the book they had been seeking. We are grateful for all the books that we have read and taught by other scholars that make this book possible. But despite their excellence, we found we also had something to say.

Often I have asked professors and others who know the Luther story well what the best *first* book on Luther is that people should read. There is no consensus, and in fact there is often confusion. Many books "tell the Luther story" as the compelling drama it is. Many books interpret Luther's theology, often in extraordinary detail. Yet it is hard to think of a book that tells the dramatic story *as* a theological story, giving due attention to both Luther's work and his context. And we have chosen *resilience* (modern popular psychology might say "grit") as the best way to understand both.

This version of Luther's life and thought reflects several of our convictions about the man. While he was a flawed thinker and leader ("sinner and righteous at the same time," as he taught us all to think about ourselves), he was also a wonderfully productive person over three decades, living for the last twenty-five years of his life under papal excommunication and imperial threat of death. Yet he found resources to keep rising to new challenges. There is inspiration for us all in such a life. But it means the whole story needs telling, not just the familiar and exciting early years but also the achievements and disasters of the older Luther. Only with a survey of the whole life can resilience be even partially understood.

We also came to believe that Luther was able to be Luther because he was surrounded by extraordinary people. These were not simply a circle of friends, but also a talented group of coworkers. They did not always work together easily or well, but they stuck together as long as Luther lived, continuing to remember their common purpose, and were held together in large part by Luther's own need for them and his ability to draw out the particular gifts of each. Hopefully, this introduction to Luther's life and thought has slighted neither Melanchthon nor Bugenhagen nor Spalatin at the court, nor the Cranachs in their studio, nor even the difficult but necessary Nicholas von Amsdorf. The princes of Saxony are here—Frederick and John and John Frederick—because, in the end, their support was decisive. Katherine von Bora Luther is here too, not only in the kitchen and the bedchamber, but also as the theological advisor and friend to her husband that she became.

We write as theologians first and historians second. We keep coming back to Luther because we continue to find in him fresh material for theological reflection in our time. That means writing with a bias and agenda, but readers have learned in recent decades to suspect that all biographies of Luther are "up to something." Luther by no means has all the answers, and in this self-critical ecumenical age we should be able to tell his story with great honesty. But the issues on which he was working are of continuing interest not only to Lutherans, but also to all Christians who wonder how an ancient faith can have current credibility, especially given the flaws and failures of every church. Those were by no means rooted out once and for all by the Reformation but continue to haunt us to this day.

We have not yet exhausted what we can learn from Luther about the grace of God, Christian freedom, the priesthood of all Christians, and especially the theology of the cross. Tim's work on Luther for twenty years was done less with a historical microscope (though this work is important, has been done well by many, and we have benefited from it) and more with the binoculars of theology and the life of the church. In other words, he sought to highlight both what was timeless about Luther and what was timely to say. Readers who, after finishing this book, want to know more about the debates over how to conceive of the Reformation and how Luther fits into it will find many resources here to guide their reading.

This introduction to Luther's life and thought is written in a traditional narrative form. For all the compromises that involves, it still seems closest to what readers of a Luther book might be seeking: to understand what happened to Luther in the course of his life and how he responded. We have tried especially to use Luther's own words when possible, for those wonderful (and sometimes terrible) words are still the reason that we read Luther today. He had a great gift for getting the attention of such a diverse range of people—not only fellow academics and religious leaders, but also those ordinary Christians whose presence he noticed, whose part in the church he celebrated, whose aspirations he understood. We have relished the opportunity to reread (and even read for the first time) much of what Luther wrote, and we hope this biography will point many readers back to direct engagement with Luther himself. The notes indicate many places where readers interested in finding more can begin, both in Luther's fifty-five-volume English translation *Luther's Works* (LW) from Fortress Press and Concordia Publishing House (with more volumes on the way from Concordia), and in the widely accessible single-volume *Martin Luther's Basic Theological Writings* (MLBTW3), edited by Timothy Lull, now in its third edition with Fortress Press. References to Luther's German and Latin writings are minimal because they are less widely available.

Much of this book was written in the first three months of 2001 while Tim and Mary Carlton were on sabbatical leave at the Faculty of Theology at the University of Stellenbosch in South Africa. Tim registered his gratitude to that school for doing everything possible to provide a comfortable and stimulating place for writing, and to Professor Dirk J. Smit, the faculty secretary Mrs. Wilma Riekert, and the library staff for their help in so many ways. Professor Smit was a good friend and most important colleague for twenty years. Special thanks also go to the management and staff of the Java Café for providing a wonderful home away from home, doses of caffeine, and access to the Internet.

Tim also thanked Pacific Lutheran Theological Seminary, its faculty, and its board of directors for granting him a sabbatical and for their support in his attempts to be a teaching and writing president. Pastor Steve McKinley, a member of the board of directors, took a leave from his own congregation to serve as acting president during the sabbatical, thus making him a kind of godfather to this book. Administrative colleagues Sharon Gruebmeyer, Paul Evenson, Ellen Peterson, and Dean Michael B. Aune deserve special thanks for extra burdens they carried during this absence.

The rest of the book was written while I was teaching at Wabash College and earlier at Thiel College, and I am glad to thank the administrations of both, especially Dean Gary Philips at Wabash, for their generous support. Oxford University and its Faculty of Theology and Religion graciously welcomed my wife Kelly and me for Trinity Term 2013 to use their wonderful libraries and benefit from lively conversation. St. Cross College, its Master Mark Jones, and Professor Diarmaid Macculloch helped arrange an ideal place in which to finish writing the book, and Johannes Zachhuber, Simeon Zahl, and Bill Wood were cherished conversation partners.

The cover art is a new portrait of Luther, specially commissioned for this biography, and created by acclaimed painter Brad Holland. Before achieving fame in the art world as illustrator for the New York Times op-ed section, Brad was Tim Lull's childhood friend in Fremont, Ohio. We are grateful for his contributions to this book, and to Tim's memory.

Many readers of the manuscript offered suggestions that made this a better book. These include Sharon Gruebmeyer, Mark Fisher, Daniel Peterson, Rob Saler, Lynne Miles-Morillo, David Blix, Kelly Nelson, Lowell Anderson, Martin Roth, and two anonymous readers. Students in courses at Wabash College and Thiel College read drafts of portions of the book, and I benefited from their good-heartedness in examining the argument: Stephen Batchelder, Joe Mount, Matthew Michaloski, Drew Breuckman, Patrick Wright, Grant Klembara, Kevin Kennedy, Sam Vaught, Cole Chapman, Ethan Groff, Abraham Hall, Harrison Schafer, Ashley Chase née Ahrens, Monica Smith, Ian Meakim, Abby Kusserow, Jamaal Dorsey, Marica Turan, Meredith Toth née Nagle, and James Beach. My thanks also go to Abraham Hall for his help in preparing the index. The team at Fortress Press, especially Will Bergkamp and Lisa Gruenisen, have been incredibly patient and helpful in bringing this book to the public. Tim's long-term conversation partner Mary-Carlton Lull once again accompanied him on this long and surprising journey, and her great spirit is probably evident wherever this book comes to life. My wife Kelly and I were blessed with the birth of our daughter Madeleine during the writing of these pages, which helped me understand Luther's writings on parenthood and Christian vocation.

This book is dedicated to Tim's parents, Raymond Robert Lull and Ruth Cole Lull and to my parents, Rodney and Mary Nelson in thanks for their strong faith and wonderful support all along the way. Both Tim and I had our parents' blessings to study theology, even though something a bit more lucrative might have been more attractive. That was one battle Luther fought that we are happy to have been spared.

For the Lull Family,

Derek R. Nelson
Oxford and Crawfordsville
May 20, 2015

Prologue: Here I Sit

The Crisis of Summer 1545

In the summer of 1545 Martin Luther was sixty-one years old and well-known throughout Europe. He was one of the five most famous people alive, three of the others being kings (Charles V of Spain and the Holy Roman Empire, Francis I of France, Henry VIII of England) and one a pope (Paul III). This was quite an achievement for a man whose grandfather had been a peasant and whose father had started out in life as a copper miner.

Luther was also a survivor. He had been living now for twenty-five years as a monk excommunicated by the Roman Catholic Church, and for twenty-four years as a person under the imperial ban, a death sentence if he came into the presence of the emperor or persons loyal to him. This death sentence—which Luther expected at any point to be carried out—greatly limited his ability to travel. At first, it had caused him to be very cautious about making any long-term commitments.

But in 1525, Luther had married a former nun named Katherine von Bora. They had become the parents of six children, four of whom were still living. Johannes, or Hans, the oldest son named for Luther's father and godfather, was now old enough to travel with his father on the trips he could make in the territory of Saxony. Marriage had surprised Luther; he said that he did it to spite the pope, but within a short time he was singing the praises both of marriage in general and of his remarkable wife Katie.

The reform set off by his protest had been reasonably successful. Supported by Luther's practical and warm theological work, the "Lutheran" version of the Christian faith had spread over northern Europe. Churches that stemmed from his teaching were now predominant in most of northern Germany and in Scandinavia. People were reading Luther these days even south of the Alps in places such as Venice.[1]

Daily life brought not only delights of family and many festivals, but also work and friendship. Luther had taught the Bible at Wittenberg since 1512, and he was now near completion of his largest project ever—*Lectures on Genesis*—which had taken over ten years to complete and would be published in many volumes.[2] A complete edition of his early Latin works was being published, and he was on his way to being "the most published author of the century."[3]

He had good, true, and long-standing friends in Wittenberg: the brilliant scholar and his frequent collaborator Philip Melanchthon, the town pastor and good friend John Bugenhagen, and the local painter and perennial Burgomeister Lucas Cranach the Elder. At a short distance lived old and trusted friends who now led the churches of the Reformation in major towns—Nicholas von Amsdorf, the bishop in Naumburg, and Justus Jonas, the pastor in Halle. Another friend, George Spalatin, had died that January. He had been Luther's go-between at the court in the early and dangerous days and in later

1. On this matter, see Thomas A. Brady and Heiko Oberman, eds., *Itinerarium Italicum: The Profile of the Italian Renaissance in the Mirror of Its European Transformations* (Leiden: Brill, 1976).
2. Martin Luther, *Lectures on Genesis* in *Luther's Works* (American Edition), Volumes 1–8, (St. Louis: Concordia, 1958–66). Hereafter cited as *LW*.
3. Martin Brecht, "Martin Luther" in Hans J. Hillerbrand, ed., *Oxford Encyclopedia of the Reformation* (New York: Oxford, 1996), 462.

life served as the pastor of Altenburg. Perhaps Spalatin's death seemed the beginning of the end of a circle that had worked so well and stood together so long.

But for all those blessings and achievements, Luther was deeply discouraged that summer. Some of this may have been physical; his health had been deteriorating since 1537. He suffered a terrible attack of kidney stones in late June, so intense that he told Amsdorf: "My torturer, the stone, would have killed me on St. John's Day, had God not decided differently. I prefer death to such a tyrant."[4]

Some cause for concern came from the news that reached Wittenberg about the plans of the pope and of the emperor. The long-awaited Council of Trent had opened early that year. It was clear that under Paul III the Roman Church had a serious and effective leader far more ready and competent to take on the Reformation than his predecessors had been. Luther at this time was ridiculing the council and the years that it had taken the Curia to agree to hold one, but he had no illusions that the issues he had raised would get a sympathetic hearing.

Charles V was in the process of making peace with Suleiman I, the Turkish sultan of the Ottoman Empire. The threat of expanding Turkish power (into Hungary in 1526 and even to the gates of Vienna in 1529) had often saved the Lutherans in the past. Charles needed the support of their princes for unified military action. But now it seemed that Charles—the most powerful ruler that Europe had seen in centuries—might finally be able to turn his attention to ending the religious divisions. This he was determined to do, by negotiated agreement if possible but by war if necessary. Others might have grown complacent about the danger in the past quarter

---

4. "Letter to Nicholas von Amsdorf" (July 9, 1545), in *LW* 50 (Philadelphia: Fortress Press, 1975), 267. St. John's day is not December 27 (St. John the Apostle) but June 24 (the Feast of John the Baptist).

century. Luther had stood face-to-face with the emperor in Worms in 1521 and never forgot the anger of that prince toward him nor underestimated his resolve to crush those who opposed him.

Despite threats from kings and the pope, the heart of Luther's discouragement was in Wittenberg itself. He had a stormy relationship with that town in the last years of his life. He had threatened to leave more than once. On June 14, he preached a harsh sermon in the town church—his frequent pulpit since 1514—attacking the stinginess of the church members, both toward the needs of the church and the care of the poor. "What are we preaching?" Luther said. "It would be better if we would quit. It seems that everything is lost."[5] He had hoped that once people were freed from religious rituals demanded by a controlling church, they would find new energy to care for their neighbors in need. A few responded in this way, but mostly Wittenberg experienced a growth of greed and indifference.

In his lectures on Genesis that summer, he was also speaking very critically of the way Wittenbergers lived. He contrasts the frugality of the ancient people of Egypt with reckless spending on liquor and luxuries in Saxony:

> For look what happens in our little town, where, after making calculations, the citizens have found that more than 4000 gulden are spent annually for barley. What, alas, is the meaning of such waste? Day and night we guzzle and fill our bellies with beer. But if we took as much pleasure in thrift, frugality, and temperance as we do in reckless wastefulness, we would be able to save and keep two or three thousand guldens every year. But how much wine the gluttons pour down in addition to the beer! How much is consumed by luxury in clothing and other useless things that are brought into our lands by the merchants![6]

---

5. Cited in Martin Brecht, *Martin Luther—The Preservation of the Church: 1532–46*, trans. James L. Schaaf (Minneapolis: Fortress Press, 1993), 262. Hereafter: Brecht III. Brecht's three-volume biography of Luther is the current standard; he is one of the few biographers to have explored the importance of this 1545 crisis.

On July 25, Luther set out on a journey that was expected to last at least two weeks. He accompanied his Wittenberg colleague Caspar Cruciger on a visit to Bishop Amsdorf in Zeitz. He was also planning to preach at a wedding some days later in nearby Merseburg. Luther's son Hans traveled with them. As often happened in his own region of Saxony late in life, Luther was welcomed warmly and entertained handsomely at each stop along the way.

Three days later, he wrote a very serious letter to his wife Katie. He told her that he had decided never to return to Wittenberg. He thought they should move to her farm in Zölsdorf, south of Leipzig, the one she had bought from her brother John as the last piece of the old von Bora estate. Luther believed they could live there comfortably, selling their properties in and near Wittenberg and giving their big house (the former monastery) back to the elector. He was prepared to ask that ruler, Duke John Frederick of Saxony, to continue Luther's professorial salary for a year. He said that he did not think he would live any longer than that.[7]

This was not a trial-balloon retirement scheme. Luther was really angry at Wittenberg and determined not to return. He told Katie that she should make all the arrangements and join him in Zeitz. She could, if she liked, ask the town pastor, John Bugenhagen, to say farewell for him and inform Master Philip Melanchthon as well. But he would not come back. "My heart has become cold, so that I do not like to be there any longer."[8]

The letter offers clues about what was wrong, but the whole story has to be pieced together. Luther said he had heard something shocking about Wittenberg on his travels, some piece of gossip that confirmed his sense of the low morals of the place. One of Luther's

---

6. "Lectures on Genesis 47" (1545) in LW 8:120.
7. Luther was right, as we shall see. He died about six months later on February 18, 1546.
8. "Letter to Mrs. Martin Luther" (July 28, 1545) in LW 50:278.

own maids, who had worked her way into their household with a phony story, was now pregnant and abandoned by her lover. He called the city "Sodom" after the biblical city that so displeased God.

But even more, his disappointment seems related to the hard-heartedness and greediness that Luther had been attacking in his sermons. He did not want Katie living there after his death. He warned her, "The four elements at Wittenberg certainly will not tolerate you."[9] He was a wise and experienced pastor, and he had always taught—against many of his Roman Catholic and radical Protestant opponents—that perfection eludes Christians in this earthly life. But it seemed increasingly true that his long work, especially his preaching, had been in vain in the very place where he had labored the longest and the hardest.

We do not know how his wife reacted, but the letter was a bombshell in the town of Wittenberg. The university had been built on the attraction of Luther and Melanchthon. If Luther left, students would stop coming, and Melanchthon himself might leave. This would be a blow to the university and to the town as well. Neither friends nor critics wanted things to end this way. A letter was drafted from the university to John Frederick, asking him to intervene. Professor Melanchthon himself traveled upriver to Torgau to deliver it to the prince.

At first, John Frederick was not available, but there was deep consternation at the Saxony court even before he returned. The chancellor, Gregor Brück, had been opposed for twenty years to Katherine Luther's property acquisitions. Now he was sure that he had been right, and it would not be easy to dispose of the properties they wanted to sell. Melanchthon himself worried that Luther's departure was caused by some differences between them on the

---

9. LW 50:278. The "four elements" refer to earth, air, fire and water. Luther is emphasizing that all imaginable forces may conspire against Katie.

teaching about the Lord's Supper that had arisen in recent years. Everyone saw the Luther crisis on his or her own terms.

That was true for John Frederick as well. He had been ruler of this part of Saxony since the death of his father, John the Steadfast, in 1532. He and his ally, Philip of Hesse, had become the leaders of the Lutheran movement within the empire. His wife, Princess Sybil, was a devoted friend of the Luther family. Luther's close friend George Spalatin had always supported Luther. The elector could imagine what the Roman Catholic enemies of Luther would make of the news of Luther's angry departure. He could visualize the harsh pamphlets and crude woodcuts that would circulate almost immediately. They would be a great source of mirth and encouragement for those assembled at the Council of Trent and in the emperor's court.

John Frederick also knew Luther could be very determined. For all the close ties that had bound them for decades, Luther could be stubborn. So John Frederick designed a three-prong plan. He sent his personal physician, Matthew Ratzeberger, to visit Luther. Luther had been ill so often recently, and the ruler sensed that Luther's own sense of impending death was a major factor in his decision. He also mobilized a group of Luther's friends—Melanchthon, Bugenhagen, and George Major—to go to him and reason with him. They were to enlist the help of Luther's other friends nearby, such as Amsdorf and Jonas. Finally, the elector wrote a personal and confidential message to Luther, asking that he visit him at the castle in Torgau. He knew Luther was not likely to ignore such a summons.

Luther had not been sitting depressed in Zeitz, however discouraged he may have been when he wrote to Katie. He had gone on with his work of visiting and preaching. On August 4, he preached a sermon at the marriage of Sigismund of Lindenau, the dean of the cathedral. This worthy man had been married for seven years, keeping it a secret for fear of the opponents of the Reformation.

Now it was to be made public. Luther gave a vigorous defense of marriage as God's good gift for men and women, and he attacked the false celibacy so insistently commended by the Roman Church but so frequently violated by their clergy.[10]

Then he went with his friend Justus Jonas to Halle for a day, so that he could preach there in the former home of his old opponent Archbishop Albrecht of Mainz—the one who started everything by hiring the monk John Tetzel to sell indulgences to help pay off his debts. Then Luther went back to Merseburg, where he ran into the delegation that had been sent to deal with the crisis. Ratzeberger and the others seem finally to have found him on August 6.

The negotiations went slowly, for Luther was at first determined not to return. Even when he agreed to go to Torgau to visit with John Frederick, they made their way slowly. The party paused in Leipzig so that Luther could preach there on Sunday, August 12. Finally, the next Friday, August 17, Luther met with John Frederick at the castle in Torgau. After that meeting, he agreed to go home.

Why did Luther change his mind? We have no account from him, but there are four likely reasons. First, Luther had been promised that things would be better in Wittenberg. There was an agreement by the leaders of the town, the university, and the elector to do something about the worse offenses to public morality—from the prostitutes that preyed on the students to the moneylenders who charged interest of up to 30 percent. At the end of 1545, a new ordinance tried to curb excesses, extravagance, even the amount of noise in the streets.

Second, Luther's friends were probably persuasive. The one who was railing against his longtime opponents at the wedding sermon

10. Luther's late-life crises are often seen as symptoms or manifestations of his psychological and physical problems, and there is some truth in that approach. However the sermon in Merseburg, just one week after the letter to Katie, is feisty and funny as ever and does not seem to be the work of an unduly discouraged or depressed man. The sermon can be found in LW 51:357–67.

in early August had not become indifferent to the outcome of the Reformation. Luther deeply trusted people such as Melanchthon and Bugenhagen, and he no doubt took to heart their warnings of the practical consequences that would result from his self-imposed exile.

Third, Luther took John Frederick seriously and was probably impressed by his arguments about the political blow that Luther's action would be to the Lutheran cause. Luther had always had good relationships with his princes and especially close ties with John Frederick and his father John before him. It would be hard for one who counseled obedience in all but the gravest circumstances to say no to a kindly and faithful prince.

Fourth and finally, on his travels Luther may well have remembered one crucial feature of his theology that was always slipping away. Among the greatest of Luther's formulations is his theology of the cross—his sense of hidden and surprising ways that God works in the world. You cannot jump to conclusions, Luther had been saying all his life, if you follow the God of the Bible. God's ways are hidden, and divine judgments not read from surface success or failure, strength or weakness.

When Luther went home on August 18, he wrote a poem in honor of Wittenberg and published it later that year with a wonderful woodcut of the town. It compared Wittenberg to Jerusalem—small among the cities of the ancient world and yet a place from which great things came forth. God had chosen a little, out-of-the-way place once again. A great renewal of Christianity had flowed from Wittenberg, from their work together. Luther hoped the Wittenbergers would not take for granted the astonishing things that had happened there, nor become complacently accustomed to a gospel that had radical implications when first preached to them. Perhaps the poem also implied that Luther would try not to jump to negative conclusions about the impact of the gospel. After all, such things can never be seen perfectly even by the best observer or the wisest pastor.[11]

So the summer crisis came to an end, although tensions remained between Luther and the town until he was buried in the castle church on February 22 of the next year. But several questions emerge from this incident that provide an opening to Luther, a way into understanding him after five hundred years.

There is a special challenge in approaching Luther because of his great communicative powers. He has many "sound bites" that cut through the centuries that separate us from him. These catch our attention and may make him seem more completely our contemporary than he is. For Luther is vast and complex enough that he can be read in many ways. Over the past centuries, people have raided the Luther story to make him all sorts of things, from the founder of the bourgeois family to the super-German patriot, from the ultimate advocate of prejudice and oppression to the father of public education and the Enlightenment.

Every Luther book ends up being partly a volume about its author, and everyone who reads Luther imposes a personal history on the Luther story.[12] Getting to know Luther in a balanced way requires taking his whole story into account, not just the thrilling early years of defying authority successfully, but also the middle years of constructing a new form of church life and the later years of living out the consequences of his good and bad decisions. Concentrating

---

11. A summary of the poem, which does not exist in English translation, can be found in Brecht III:265. Full text of the poem is in WA 35:593–95.
12. The most significant interpretation of Luther in recent decades comes from Heiko Oberman, *Luther: Man Between God and the Devil*, trans. Eileen Walliser-Schwarzbart (New Haven: Yale, 1989). Oberman is especially persuasive on the dangers of "modernizing" Luther. He puts one of Luther's strangest ideas to modern people at the heart of his study: Luther's conviction of the centrality of the devil in the troubles besetting the church and the world.

on Luther's most exciting and enduring ideas is strategic, but his foibles, missteps, and ugly or ghastly mistakes also need recounting.

Along the way, five questions raised by this prologue will endure:

- How did the grandson of a peasant and son of a miner become so important?
- What could he have taught to generate both such loyalty and such hostility?
- How did he survive the powerful forces of church government that were against him?
- Which were the key ideas in his multitude of writings that held his Reformation together?
- Above all, as Luther himself was pondering in the summer of 1545, had it all been worthwhile and would any of it survive his death?

1

A Family's Hopes

1483–1505

Once upon a time, there was an older son of a farmer from west of the Thuringian Forest. He had grown up in the village of Mohra, where there were about sixty families. Though the family lived simply, they were the second most prominent group in this town. This son, Johannes Luder, or Hans Luther as he came to be called, married Margarete Lindemann, a daughter of the even more prominent family. Her people originally came from the nearby town of Eisenach. But Hans and Margarete settled neither in Mohra nor in Eisenach, but went east to the region of Mansfeld where there was work in the copper mines. They could not stay on the farm: in the law of those days, Hans's brother, the youngest son, inherited the family farm.

"Once upon a time? I thought this was going to be theology, or at least history. Is this a fairy tale?" No, the story that begins with the young Luther couple moving to the east is not a fairy tale, but like a fable it has fabulous aspects, especially in its first stages, where the couple prospers and where their son Martin eventually becomes an educated person and then a famous person, a person dealing with kings and princes and popes. But all of that is far in the future. The beginning of the story, in the late 1400s, is the lure of economic opportunity for hard-working people in the German lands.[1]

Image 1: Hans and Margarete Luther, Martin Luther's parents, painted by Lucas Cranach

Upward Mobility, Sort Of

Many lives of Luther present him as a peasant who made good. They also paint his childhood as miserably unhappy—the precondition for his lifelong struggle with God. But there are reasons to challenge such versions of the Luther story. The family was not rich, not even comfortable at first, but the father came from a people who were well settled on the land, and the mother from people with connections in a prospering town. They were not the poorest of the

---

1. A classic place to begin to explore the economic and social factors on the eve of the Reformation is Steven Ozment, *The Reformation in the Cities* (New Haven: Yale University Press, 1980).

poor. They were the sort of people who could reasonably hope for a better life, which suddenly became a possibility with new economic opportunities available for some.

In the early 1480s the family was living in Eisleben, a good-sized town of four thousand people, most of them miners.[2] The largest German-speaking city in the world in those days was Augsburg, with fifty thousand, so after the sixty families in Mohra, a town of four thousand people was a considerable place. Hans Luther found work in the copper mines in that region—the County of Mansfeld. And there on November 10, 1483, or perhaps 1482, a first, or perhaps second, son was born to Hans and Margarete. He was baptized the next day in the neighborhood parish church of Saints Peter and Paul and was named Martin because that day, November 11, was the feast day of Saint Martin of Tours. This is the beginning of the story of Martin Luther.

"1483 or 1482? First or second son? Is this any way to tell a story?" The world has long settled on 1483 as the birth year; Luther's five-hundredth birthday was widely celebrated in 1983. The day—November 10—is much more certain than the year because, from the start, the story was told of how Luther came to be named for Saint Martin when he was baptized the next day. But neither Luther nor his mother could remember for sure which year it had been, and there are no surviving baptismal or birth records to settle the matter.[3]

2. Here begins much trouble with two towns easily confused: Eisleben and Eisenach. Eisleben is in the territory of Mansfeld; it is where Luther was born and, by a strange coincidence, where he also died. Eisenach, the town of his mother's people, is where he went to Latin school and where he was in 1521 and 1522 a prisoner for his own protection in the Wartburg Castle. (Some still debate whether Luther's mother was a Lindemann from Eisenach [his grandmother certainly was] or a Ziegler from Mohra.)

3. The best source for Luther's early years is Martin Brecht, *Martin Luther*, vol. 1: *His Road to Reformation, 1483–1521*, trans. James L. Schaaf (Philadelphia: Fortress Press, 1985), a translation of the 1981 German edition. Despite the remarkable achievement of this book, Brecht has changed his mind on some issues in recent decades, including the identity of Luther's mother. When Luther qualified for his MA in 1505, he admitted that he was not sure which year he had been born, and there was some question whether he was old enough to receive the degree.

The first definite written trace of Luther does not appear until 1501 when he signed the registry upon entering the University of Erfurt.

There is also no clear evidence of how many children the Luthers had; eight or nine seems most likely. Two boys and three girls survived to adulthood, and of these Luther himself was the oldest boy. His younger brother Jacob was his good friend and playmate in childhood. Jacob later became involved in the mining business in Mansfeld, and Luther's three sisters also married mine operators. Luther had continuing contact with his family all of his life. His brother came to visit in Wittenberg; after they were orphaned, several of one sister's children came to live with the Luthers; and Luther as a young man came to know his relatives in Mohra and Eisenach.

A few months after Luther's birth, the family moved to the nearby town of Mansfeld. Though this was smaller than Eisleben, it was a more important town because it was the residence of the local rulers: the counts of Mansfeld. There the Luthers prospered, and by 1491 Hans was one of the four town councillors, or representatives, who negotiated with the nobility. By 1507, they owned a house—although they owed money on it. Hans had moved from being a miner to being a small business contractor, renting mining equipment from the nobility, hiring others to do the actual mining, and in good years making a comfortable living.

Martin Luther's economic origins and social class standing are difficult to chart precisely. When he was fifty, he remembered his parents as poor and hardworking: "In my youth my father was a poor miner. My mother carried all her wood home on her back. It was in this way that they brought us up."[4] These reflections come from a

---

4. Luther, "Table Talk for January 1533," in LW 54:176. It is important to note that these "table talks" are not always especially reliable. Luther and his wife hosted many dinners, and guests and students frequently wrote down transcripts of things said at dinner. Sometimes they have been misremembered; other times fabricated. In this instance, as elsewhere, caution should be

time shortly after his parents had died. He seems to be remembering these sacrifices with appreciation. What he says here is probably true, but it is only part of the story.

The Luthers might be best described as people who were often strapped for cash. Hans Luther had considerable anxiety about how to support his many children and was famous for his irritation with monks and clergy who came begging. On several occasions, however, Hans gave money to rebuilding projects at the local Saint George's Church, which seemed to be plagued by fires in those years. When Luther was a university student, his parents were considerably more prosperous. Later, they seem to have reverted to a more modest, but still comfortable income. At Hans's death, he left an estate of 1,250 gulden—not a large amount, but double the value of the farm on which he had grown up in Mohra.

It was a hard-working world from start to finish. The Luther children were treated with considerable strictness, typical for that place and time. Martin remembered great seriousness, and he spoke of how attitudes had changed in his lifetime toward dancing, playing cards, and jousting—which used to be thought sins but had come to be regarded as amusements. Luther remembered being disciplined by his parents, sometimes rather severely for what seemed a small infraction. This has led to much speculation on a supposedly unhappy childhood, and even on Luther as an abused child, but this is probably to read modern standards into a very different world.[5]

exercised in taking their statements at face value, especially when they contradict more reliable sources of evidence.

5. For the stern father and childhood discipline as the source of Luther's later struggle with God, see most famously Eric Erickson, *Young Man Luther: A Study in Psychoanalysis and History* (New York: W. W. Norton, 1958). The Erickson thesis has stirred interesting other readings but has not carried the day with many Luther biographers. A noted exception is Richard Marius, *Martin Luther: The Christian between God and Death* (Cambridge, MA: Harvard University Press, 1999), whose focus is totally on the younger Luther and wholly interested in psychological explanations for Luther's pathologies. More typical is Bernard Lohse, who writes, "With all their seriousness, Luther's parents cared for their son and shared his journey." Bernard Lohse,

That world was changing dramatically in the years when Luther was growing up in Mansfeld. Columbus made his first voyage to the Western Hemisphere when Luther was almost nine. While this "new world" does not figure strongly in Luther's consciousness, he shows awareness of it all through his life, and the gold that poured into Spain from the Americas greatly upset the balance of power in Europe.

Luther grew up not in the rural world of his grandparents, but in the new world of towns, the source of much dynamism and change in central Europe.[6] There was no hint of democracy at the beginning of the sixteenth century, but princes—whose own power was growing—did have to take the opinion of town dwellers into account. Luther later came to think of himself as a "German" when he began to play his life on a larger stage. But from the time of his registration at the University in Erfurt until his death, he identified himself as Luther from Mansfeld. Larger towns such as Nuremberg had often achieved practical independence and were ruled by town councils rather than nobility. In all these towns, more and more people were literate—a remarkable change in the decades since Johan Gutenberg's first Bibles were printed in 1456.

Church Life

It was a world of deep spirituality, for all the flaws of the church in that period. Clergy and lay renewal movements had been underway for the last couple of centuries. They often had some success so

Martin Luther's Theology, trans. Roy Harrisville (Minneapolis: Fortress Press, 2011), 29. For a good airing of the promise and problems with Erickson, see Roger Johnson, ed. *Psychohistory and Religion: The Case of "Young Man Luther"* (Philadelphia: Fortress Press, 1977). Scott Hendrix has provided an intriguing and less pathological account of the issues in Luther's psychohistory in "Luther's Loyalties and the Augustinian Order," in *Augustine, the Harvest and Theology: 1300–1650*, ed. Kenneth Hagen (Leiden: Brill, 1990), 236–57.

6. The many works of Bernd Moeller are good starting places here, especially the older but still reliable *Imperial Cities and the Reformation: Three Essays*, ed. and trans. H. C. Erik Midelfort and Mark U. Edwards Jr. (Philadelphia: Fortress Press, 1972).

long as they did not challenge the power of church officials directly. The leaders who did challenge the church directly—John Wyclif in England (1320–1384), Jan Hus in Bohemia (ca. 1369–1415), Girolamo Savonarola in Florence (1452–1498)—had deep trouble with the authorities, the latter two being burned at the stake.[7]

There was an active life at Saint George's Church in town, with a full component of feast days and festivals observed in those years. But what Luther remembered was neither his first communion nor his confirmation; rather, he recalled stories about evil that lurked on the edge of all this spirituality—especially stories about witches. The adult Luther reported that his mother had been bothered by a neighbor woman who was a witch. Margarete had to "treat her neighbor with deference and try to conciliate her," for she was known to have real powers and had even poisoned a preacher who took her to task for her sorcery.[8] Luther's listeners in Wittenberg asked whether the Doctor thought such things could really happen "to godly people," and Luther insisted that they were possible. One learned scholar says that Luther was unusual in that, unlike most humanists, his "university education did not lead to a refining of his view."[9]

But neither the hardness of life nor preoccupation with the devil and with witches kept Luther's parents from having high ambitions for him. They seem not to have been literate, but they wanted education for their oldest son—apparently as much as he could get.

---

7. Richard Rex wisely urges caution in drawing too strong a line between Wycliffe, for instance, and later Reformation movements. *The Lollards* (New York: Palgrave Macmillan, 2002).

8. "Table Talk for February and March 1533," in LW 54:188. His relationship with witchcraft is complicated, though like all of his contemporaries Luther believed witches were real. In 1529, during a witch craze, he urged his parishioners in a sermon not to take the easy way out and blame their misfortunes on witchcraft. Late in life, Luther participated in a spectacle of witchcraft accusations in Wittenberg, where four women were burned in 1540. Perhaps the scene was too much: though he preached on the First Commandment ("You shall have no other gods"), Luther never discussed the matter again, even where tradition dictated a denunciation of witchcraft.

9. Lohse, *Martin Luther's Theology*, 29.

Access to learning was becoming much more widely available in the decades before the Reformation. Luther's education began at the Latin school in Mansfeld, which Luther entered sometime between his fifth and his eighth year. The little town was rough in many ways, despite the counts' castle across the valley, and the streets doubled as sewers. As a result, an older boy, Nicholas Oemler—who later became his brother-in-law—carried young Luther to school.

There was increased schooling for girls in those days, but mostly boys got to learn Latin. At the beginning stages, this did not seem like much of a privilege. The learning was rote, the teaching not very imaginative, and beatings at school far more common than those Luther remembers occasionally receiving at home. He did not forget these limitations of early schooling and tried to overcome them when he became an advocate of general education in the 1520s.

But things got more interesting as the students proceeded to read actual texts in Latin—first fragments of Scripture, hymns, and the Lord's Prayer, and then very soon a Latin translation of Aesop's fables. These stories of birds and beasts with their inevitable morals continued to delight Luther all of his life. In the Mansfeld years, the seed was planted for an appreciation of the classics, especially the Latin classics. He moved on with pleasure to Latin poets, dramatists, and historians. He became a great advocate of religious education but never had the narrow view that only Christian writings should be studied.[10] Later, when he entered the monastery, he sold all his books except those by the Latin poet Virgil and the playwright Terence.

10. For Luther's appreciation of Aesop, see "Table Talk" entries in LW 54:72, 210ff. Luther thought there was more genuine wisdom in Aesop than in all the writings of the admired Christian theologian St. Jerome (ca. 347–ca. 420).

Further Schooling

When he was thirteen or fourteen, the family decided to send Martin for further schooling. This must have been a great stretch for their resources, even with improving income. But if he was going to have a university education, Martin would need better preparation than he could get in Mansfeld. So as a young teenager (in 1497), Luther left home for the first time and traveled with another boy from Mansfeld, Hans Reinecke, to the great cathedral city of Magdeburg, some forty miles to the north.

The experience of leaving home must have been both thrilling and frightening, but the arrival in Magdeburg surely impressed a boy who knew only smaller towns like Mansfeld and Eisenach. Magdeburg was one of the larger cities in the Empire, with about thirty thousand people. At its center was the great cathedral of Saints Maurice and Catherine, the seat of the archbishop of Magdeburg. Built in the Gothic style, it was in 1209 and was in the final stages of completion in the years that Luther spent in the town. Inside, Luther could see the tomb of the famous German emperor Otto the Great (912–973).

The current archbishop was Ernst of Saxony (1476–1513), a brother of Luther's later prince and protector, Frederick the Wise. Ernst had been elected archbishop at the age of twelve, obviously more for his family connections than his spiritual achievements. Luther may have known something about the archbishop because, through connections of Hans Reinecke, the boys were able to visit the home of Paul Mosshauer, an official of the archdiocese who came from Mansfeld. This must have been the first opening into a very different social world from that of Luther's parents, and there would be much more such horizon-expanding contact in the next years in Eisenach.

The boys' living conditions were probably rather humble. Luther reports that he spent that year with the Brethren of the Common Life. The members of this renewal movement, which had started in the Netherlands about 1400, lived as monks and engaged both in teaching and in help with the local parishes. But unlike monks and priests, they refused to take vows, allowing members to come and go freely. And they did not beg, which provided full or partial support for many of the religious orders—the so-called mendicants—of Luther's time. They supported themselves in large part by becoming expert copyists, an occupation that, with the advancement of printing, was becoming obsolete in Luther's lifetime. There were houses of such brothers and of sisters spread over northern Europe.

The men with whom Luther lived in his Magdeburg year practiced an intense lay piety, something that certainly supplemented whatever religious instruction he received at home and in his local church in Mansfeld. They were deeply Christ-centered in their approach to Christian faith and put a strong emphasis on the need for practical good works. Since the brothers had no school in Magdeburg at that time, Luther and his friend likely attended the cathedral school. His musical interests and training, later to become such a delight for him, may have started at this point.

Luther stayed in Magdeburg only one year. For some reason, his father seemed dissatisfied, and the next year Luther was sent for further study to Eisenach—the town in western Thuringia that was the home of many of his mother's people. He made contact with some of them, including a cousin Conrad Hutter with whom he developed an ongoing friendship.

Eisenach was just one-tenth the size of Magdeburg. It had seen more glorious days when the nobility had lived in the now largely deserted Wartburg Castle that dominated the major hill overlooking the town. But there was a good school for Luther to attend, the Saint

George's School. Luther's Latin studies continued, and he seemed to have developed musically here as well. Students were expected to sing in the streets to earn money to pay part of their expenses. The strong musical traditions of Eisenach continued into the eighteenth century when it was the home of the Bach family and the birthplace of Johann Sebastian Bach, who was baptized in the same Saint George's Church where Luther had sung.

Luther became part of a circle of music and friendship that revolved around an older Franciscan priest, Johannes Braun. Luther stayed in touch with him and invited him to his first mass about a decade later. Luther had a good but rather high singing voice and was also able to play the lute. He spent time in the homes of prominent local families, such as the Schalbes and the Cottas, laypeople very interested in the church and very supportive of the local Franciscan monastery. Luther lived with one of these families and had such high regard for them that he hinted to Johannes Braun that he would have liked to invite them to his ordination but feared they might feel irritated by the burden of coming to Erfurt (or perhaps disappointed in his decision to become an Augustinian—a different order from the one they so generously supported).

In these years before he entered the University of Erfurt at age seventeen, Luther was not only improving his academic skills, but also learning new social skills and expanding his sense of the available varieties of Christian piety. Pious families such as those Luther knew in Eisenach were just the kind of the people who would be most excited by Luther's writings after 1517. He learned in Magdeburg and Eisenach enough of what their world was like to know how to communicate with them for the rest of his life. One of Luther's remarkable skills as an adult was the ability to move in a wider range of circles than most of his contemporaries—at home in the university, the monastic and churchly world, and the towns, yet still understanding the more humble social world of his parents and his extended family.[11]

University Life

When Luther was ready for university, his father (as the one paying the bills, he surely made the decision) chose the University of Erfurt—not far from Eisenach. Founded in 1392, it was already more than a century old when Luther began study there in May 1501. He was registered as a student by the newly elected rector (and later his important teacher) Jodokus Trutfetter of Eisenach. Luther was enrolled in the book as "Martinus ludher ex mansfelt"—Martin Luther from Mansfeld. The assessors considered his economic status as "wealthy," and he had to pay the full fee of one-third of a gulden.[12]

Both solemn and amusing activities marked the beginning of university study. There was a mass in the great Erfurt Cathedral. But in the *bursa* where Luther lived, new students were required to buy rounds of beer for everyone, and a certain amount of hazing took place. Luther later participated in such matriculation activities at Wittenberg and, on one occasion when he was releasing new students from their fledgling status, spoke in a way that recollected his own student days:

> This ceremony is intended to make you humble, so that you may not be haughty and arrogant and given to wickedness. Such vices are horns and other monstrous parts that are not becoming to a student. Therefore humble yourselves. Learn to be patient. You'll be subjected to hazing

11. Perhaps Luther first had access to a Bible in these Eisenach years. He tells the story: "Once when he was a young man he happened upon a Bible. In it he read the story about Samuel's mother in the books of Kings. The book pleased him immediately, and he thought that he would be happy if he could ever possess such a book. Shortly thereafter he bought a postil; it also pleased him greatly, for it contained more Gospels than it was customary to preach on in the course of a year." "Table Talk for November 1531," in LW 54:13–14. Martin Brecht finds the story charming but gives significant reasons to doubt its authenticity. Brecht, *Martin Luther*, 1:85.

12. For this and an extensive account of Luther's university training, see Brecht, *Martin Luther*, 1: ch. 2.

all your life. When you hold important offices in the future, burghers, peasants, nobles and your wives will harass you with various vexations. When this happens, don't go to pieces. . . . Remember that you first began to be hazed in Wittenberg when you were a young man, and that now that you have become a weightier person you have heavier vexations to bear. So this deposition of yours is only a symbol of human life in its misfortunes and castigations.[13]

Image 2: This illustration from the Nuremberg Chronicle shows the Cathedral and University town of Erfurt in 1493.

It was not all festivity at Erfurt University. The life of the young students was carefully controlled in the *bursa* or residence where they lived. No women were allowed. Student comings and goings were carefully noted. Students rose at four o'clock in the morning and went to bed at eight o'clock in the evening. There were large

---

13. "Table Talk for July 23, 1539," in LW 54:362–63. When Luther made these remarks, wine was poured on the heads of the students, and he released them from their probation.

sleeping and common study quarters. Two meals were served each day, with meat four times per week. There was some religious activity, including praying or singing the Psalter together every fifteen days. Many aspects of life in the monastery would later seem very familiar to Luther, more a continuation of what he had long experienced than a real hardship.

Luther worked very hard in his first year so that he could move as quickly as possible to the examination for the bachelor of arts. He had to attend about three lectures per day in the subjects that he had not yet completely mastered: more grammar, logic, rhetoric (persuasive communication, something at which Luther excelled as an adult), and natural philosophy—including physics, psychology, and astronomy. Of these, logic was the most important because it prepared those who continued beyond the bachelor's level for the study of philosophy proper. The writings of Aristotle were the general source, although very often the texts studied were reinterpretations of that philosopher by later and lesser figures.[14]

Another skill developed from the first stages of university education was the capacity to participate in a disputation. A scholar prepared theses or propositions for debate, and students were expected to respond after the initial discussion by their masters, attacking or defending various views as assigned. This sharpened Luther's debating powers and capacity to see the complexity of arguments. Fifteen years later, when Luther wanted to attack the sale of indulgences, he prepared a disputation, developing ninety-five theses or propositions for debate and discussion by his university colleagues and students. Even at the end of his career, in the 1540s, Luther was still presiding over and participating in disputations.[15]

---

14. Aristotle (384–322 BCE) was a student of Plato, and "the Philosopher" for Western Europe after about 1250 CE. His works had been reintroduced to universities in the later Middle Ages. Their emphasis on sense experience was a natural resource for the study of the physical world.

Luther moved quickly to the examinations for his bachelor of arts. Some might say too quickly, as he stood only thirteenth of the fifty-seven being examined—a rather undistinguished result. Perhaps it was a question of saving expenses. He seems to have visited his family in Mansfeld during holidays and certainly knew that the cost of his education was putting a strain on their living. Having received a BA in 1502, he spent the next couple of years preparing for the master of arts degree. This involved much more intensive study of philosophy, especially the ethics, politics, and metaphysics of Aristotle. Luther must have loved this material and been eager to get to it, for his nickname "the Philosopher" has survived from his Erfurt days.

What kind of philosopher was he? There was little simple and direct study of Aristotle himself through primary texts.[16] He was read according to the interpretation of one of the great schools—those of the Dominican Thomas Aquinas (1225–1274), the Franciscan John Duns Scotus (ca. 1270–1308), and the Franciscan William of Ockham (1285–1349). The great achievement of Thomas's era had been to integrate Aristotle into the Christian intellectual framework at a time when his major works, not available in the West until the middle of the thirteenth century, were being rediscovered and were a source of both excitement and panic for the church.[17]

The philosophical orientation of Erfurt was toward Ockham, but in a moderate sense. Ockham's more radical notions, particularly ideas critical of papal authority, could have been dangerous for a

---

15. An excellent resource exploring these late disputations as indicators of Luther's mature theological positions is Paul Hinlicky et al., *The Substance of the Faith: Luther's Doctrinal Theology for Today* (Minneapolis: Fortress Press, 2008).

16. The definitive work on Luther's relationship to Aristotle is Theodor Dieter, *Der Junge Luther und Aristoteles* (Berlin: Walter de Gruyter, 2001).

17. Until that time, the most important philosopher for Christians had been Plato. He was seen by theologians from Augustine to Bonaventure (1217–1274), Thomas's great contemporary, as more easily compatible with Christian faith than Aristotle, especially in his understanding of God.

university at the beginning of the sixteenth century. These were not taught at Erfurt. But Luther's teachers admired the crispness of Ockham's intellect, his skepticism about whether abstract notions had any reality in themselves (a view called nominalism), and his sense that philosophy and theology were quite different kinds of disciplines.[18]

By Luther's time, even Ockham was rather ancient history, and those who taught in his tradition or school were influenced by more recent thinkers such as Gregory of Rimini (d. 1358) and especially Gabriel Biel (1410–1495), the Tübingen professor who had only recently died. These issues became even more important for Luther in his theological studies after 1507, but he was already being exposed to them in his work for the master of arts.

Preparing to complete the master of arts was very hard work, with both perils and pressures along the way. Once, when returning to the university from a visit to his family, Luther cut an artery in his left leg on the short sword that he was wearing and almost bled to death a half mile outside Erfurt. A companion summoned a surgeon from town while Luther cried to the Virgin Mary for help. During his recuperation, Luther had more time to play music. Decades later, he spoke compassionately to his students about their hard work and encouraged them not to be too serious: "I absolve you of all pastimes through which you seek recreation, except such as are manifest sins, no matter whether they are eating, drinking, dancing, gaming or anything else."[19]

At the beginning of 1505, Luther stood for the master of arts degree. This time he did much better in the exams, coming in second of seventeen candidates. It was a remarkable achievement and

18. All these issues are presented in William C. Placher and Derek R. Nelson, *A History of Christian Theology* (Louisville: Westminster John Knox, 2013), 137–52.
19. "Table Talk for February 19, 1533," in LW 54:76. The story of the accident is in the same volume, 14–15.

a source of great pride to his family when he received the ring, the master's robe, and the master's hat. Luther sprang for a celebration feast and gave an inaugural address. At home, his father began to address him in the more formal *Sie* rather than the familiar *Du*. He was becoming someone important and was now ready for study in one of the advanced faculties. The family plan was for Luther to study law.

The whole story to this point does not sound like one of misery or depression, but a rather happy tale. As in a fairy tale, there were some difficulties to be overcome, but Luther dealt with them well and showed especially in his master's work the high promise that he had for achievement. The story is of Luther's rise, but also of his family working together so that one from the next generation could have an even better life—for the benefit of all of them.

In these early years, there are only faint traces of the man who would become the Reformer in Wittenberg, but there is a determination and sense of accomplishment that suggests deep personal strength. Some of this showed in the way that Luther benefited from the various schools that he attended, but even more of it would become clear later:

- in his courage to challenge his parents' plans for his life;
- in his even greater courage (or brashness) to defy princes and popes;
- in his capacity to make and sustain many friendships—and eventually a remarkable marriage;
- in his enormous productivity in writing, teaching, and preaching, despite living the last quarter century of his life under a hanging death sentence.

Image 3: Wittenberg is here depicted in 1556, a decade after Luther's death.

2

From Brother Martin to Doctor Luther

1505–1517

The Luther family celebration of Martin's achievements did not last long. The master's degree was awarded in January 1505. By the middle of May, he had begun his next level of study at the faculty of law. But six weeks later, Luther went through a crisis that changed his vocational direction from law to the church, much to the anger and deep disappointment of his family—especially his father.

A Sudden Vow

There may have been warning signs along the way. For the rest of his life, Luther had more than the usual amount of invective against lawyers. He may have heard enough in his first six weeks of study to become convinced that lawyers were not serious about the truth. The late June trip to Mansfeld may have been an occasion to express disappointment with his studies to his family. But the actual occasion came from outside—from another moment of intense physical danger. Caught in a thunderstorm outside Erfurt on his way back to school after a visit to his family, Luther was almost killed by a bolt of lightning. He cried out to Saint Anne—the mother of Mary, patron of travelers and miners (and therefore a great favorite in his native Eisleben), to save him, promising that if she did so, he would become a monk.[1] He thought she did, so he did.

Luther's friends were shocked and did their best to dissuade him. He spent two weeks trying to decide whether a vow made under duress was binding, but in the end he decided that it was. Much of his theology, as we shall see, depends on the reliability of a promise made and kept. Luther likely had been considering this course before—perhaps consciously, perhaps unconsciously. But on July 16, having sold his law books, he had a farewell dinner with his friends. The next day, they accompanied him to the gate of the Augustinian monastery in Erfurt—the house of the Order of Augustinian Hermits, a society with over two thousand chapters spread throughout Europe.

The disappointment for his family was considerable. They had sacrificed not only in the hope that Martin would do well, but also that he would make a good marriage, have a family, and be financially helpful to his parents and siblings. This would have been possible with Martin as a lawyer, perhaps as an official working with the counts of Mansfeld or as a town lawyer who could help the independent mining contractors like Luther's father with their affairs.[2] All of those prospects would come to an end when Luther took vows of obedience, chastity, and especially poverty. Hans is reported to have behaved like a crazy man for a time, but eventually

1. Luther and his friends must have remembered the occasion only a few years earlier in which he almost bled to death just outside Erfurt on his way back to the university.
2. There was a great increase in the need for lawyers at the beginning of the sixteenth century, given the rise of administration at both the many courts of the divided German principalities and in the new businesses that were prospering in the towns. It was a very plausible career choice for Luther. See J. A. M. Moran-Cruz, "Education," in *Oxford Encyclopedia of the Reformation*, ed. Hans J. Hillerbrand (New York: Oxford University Press, 1996), 2:20.

he sent word to Erfurt that he was giving his consent. If he had been arranging a very good marriage for his son, which some suppose was the occasion of Luther's trip home that month, his father's sense of loss would have been compounded. And his long-standing distaste for begging monks made it even harder to conceive of his son becoming one.

Image 4: Luther in 1520, depicted in this engraving by Cranach in his monk's cowl and tonsure.

It is not clear why Luther chose the Augustinians. They had a good reputation and were considered good theologians, but he may have known someone in his studies at Erfurt from that order or who spoke well of them. In any case, he entered a very different world at the monastery—another form of highly regulated life, especially for the first few years. It was a small community with perhaps fifty persons—priests and lay brothers—in residence. The day began with singing Matins while it was still dark. There were prayers all through the day, and mostly silence otherwise. He was on probationary status for some months and then became a novice. Final vows were taken after a year and a day as a novice. Life was very simple, with two meals per day and much fasting. Someone read from the lives of the saints during the meals. From all reports, Luther threw himself into the new disciplines with his characteristic energy.

Image 5: Life was simple and severe in the monastery; a small cell was the site of hours of prayer per day. Monks slept on the floor in the hallway.

He was given a Bible when he entered the monastery, and he studied this with great intensity, hoping here to find answers to many of his questions. When he first met the head of the order, John von Staupitz, in 1506, Staupitz had probably heard about this very "good catch" for the order—a promising young man with a good university degree and an unusual interest in the Bible. Staupitz ruled that Luther should continue with further study and should prepare for ordination as a priest.

Image 6: Luther lived in this Augustinian monastery in Erfurt after taking his vows.

Not all monks were ordained as priests; however, because the Augustinians had taken on considerable pastoral work in the various towns where they lived, they needed a good portion of their members to celebrate Mass and hear confession. Luther prepared for ordination by poring over *Exposition of the Sacred Canon of the Mass*, a long treatise by the theologian Gabriel Biel (ca. 1420–1495), who had once studied at Erfurt. It was a recent text, appearing in 1499 after Biel's death, and answered every possible question about the theology and practice of the sacrament in eighty-nine lessons. This reading both stimulated Luther and sensitized him to the possibility of doing something wrong. As a result, he experienced great trauma presiding at his first mass and long afterward.[3]

Sometime in the first months of 1507, Luther was ordained a deacon and then a priest in the great Erfurt Cathedral by Johann Bonemilch von Laasphe, the suffragan bishop of Mainz.[4] This allowed Luther to plan for his first mass, a great occasion for celebration and the time for inviting guests. He wrote to his old mentor Father Johannes Braun from Eisenach, inviting him to come and encouraging him to bring along Luther's cousin Conrad Hutter. This letter shows Luther's nervousness about the fact that his father Hans would be attending.[5]

The day had its difficulties. Luther's father did attend in a grand fashion. He brought with him twenty persons for whose lodging he paid. He also gave twenty gulden—a considerable sum—to the monastery for food and drink for the occasion. One of the monks said to Hans Luther, "You must have a good friend here that you should come to visit him with such a large company." But Hans was not completely reconciled to his son's decision. Luther reports that his father said he hoped it had not been the work of the devil leading Luther to the monastery and that he hoped Luther remembered that God had also said, "Honor your father and mother."[6]

The mass itself did not go well for Luther either. He admitted that he was so caught up in himself, worried about his own worthiness and proper action, that the critical aspect of faith was completely forgotten. He reports that in the middle of the service he almost broke down: "When at length I stood before the altar and was to consecrate, I was so terrified by the words *aeterno vivo vero Deo* ('to

---

3. For this anxiety and a comprehensive picture of Luther as a monk see Martin Brecht, *Martin Luther*, vol. 1: *His Road to Reformation, 1483–1521*, trans. James L. Schaaf (Philadelphia: Fortress Press, 1985), chapter 3.

4. A "suffragan" bishop would take care of the day-to-day local business of the diocese, while the archbishop attended to larger matters.

5. "Letter to Johannes Braun," in LW 48:3–5. As Luther's oldest letter, it is a fascinating document showing the young monk falling all over himself to be humble enough.

6. "Table Talk for May 20, 1532," in LW 54:156–57. See also "Table Talk for March, 1537," LW 54:234, and "Letter to Hans Luther," in LW 48:329–36, MLBTW3, 441–44.

Thee, the eternal, living and true God') that I thought of running away from the altar and said to my prior, 'Reverend Father, I'm afraid I must leave the altar.' He shouted at me, 'Keep going, faster, faster!'"[7] Luther reports that it was traditional for a new priest to dance with his mother, if she was still living, at the festivities after the mass, but we do not know whether Margarete Luther was present or whether Luther observed this custom himself.[8] Given the family tensions, it would have been a moment of forced gaiety at best.

Monastic Routine

Luther would not be completely reconciled with his parents for a few years, but his life in the monastery went well and he seemed to enjoy the same success he had known in his liberal arts degrees. By 1508—in only his third year in the monastery—Luther was one of the teaching faculty, in addition to continuing his studies. He came repeatedly to the notice of John von Staupitz, who became one of the most significant persons in Luther's life, both for advancing his career and for leading him toward the theology for which he would become so famous.

Staupitz—or rather von Staupitz—came from a family of the nobility in Meissen. From childhood, he had been a friend of Frederick of Saxony, and when the elector wanted help in founding a new university in Wittenberg in 1502, he turned to his old friend, the Augustinian priest who had recently finished his doctorate at Tübingen. Staupitz became the first professor of biblical theology there and also dean of the theological faculty.

In 1503, Staupitz was elected vicar-general of the German part of the Reformed Augustinians—Luther's branch of the order. This created continual problems: now he had two full-time jobs and could

7. LW 54:156, translation altered.
8. "Table Talk for December 5, 1538," in LW 54:325.

seldom devote the time to being in Wittenberg that the professorship demanded. The Augustinians were to supply not only the professor of biblical theology but also a second person to teach philosophy in the arts faculty. In the fall of 1508, Staupitz arranged to have Luther transferred to the monastery in Wittenberg, and in 1508–1509 Luther lived there, continuing his studies and teaching moral philosophy—mostly Aristotle—in the university.[9]

Luther's first stay in Wittenberg lasted only a year. It was an unimpressive place, with about two thousand people and ugly little houses, although Frederick was in the process of building an impressive palace and castle church at the east end of the town. But in the spring, Luther received his first theological degree, *baccalaureus biblicus*, from Wittenberg University. Perhaps Staupitz was already planning that Luther would eventually follow him as a professor of Bible and wanted to try him out as a teacher.

Luther was sent back to Erfurt in the summer of 1509 and there continued his theological studies, receiving the master of the sentences degree that fall. The *Sentences* were the work of Peter Lombard (ca. 1100–1160), a great medieval theologian whom Luther continued to respect. Lombard had assembled the basic textbook for theology as a collection of authoritative quotations (that is, sentences) from Scripture and the church fathers, arranged by topic. Luther was now qualified to lecture on these and continued to work toward his doctorate. For the next year, he seems to have engaged in an intensive

---

9. It shocks many people to know that Luther, who less than a decade later was saying "no one can become a theologian unless he becomes one without Aristotle," should have started out teaching the Philosopher's *Ethics*. Of course, Luther was changing his mind in these years. But it was Aristotle's view of God—distant, impersonal, the prime mover—that Luther thought was so contaminating for theology when it tried to build on those kinds of foundations. He continued to have some respect for Aristotle's ethical wisdom. See "Disputation against Scholastic Theology," in LW 31:12, MLBTW3 3–7. Late in his life, Luther says, "[Aristotle] doesn't believe that God cares about human affairs, or if he believes it, he thinks that God governs the world the way a sleepy maidservant rocks a child in a cradle." "Table Talk for Summer or Fall 1542," in LW 54:423.

study of Saint Augustine, the founder of the order, as well as study of the Bible.

Luther's rapid rise within the order may have caused some resentment in the Erfurt monastery by this, time. But in the fall of 1510, they asked him to undertake a journey to Rome to settle a dispute between the two German branches of the order—Luther's group, which followed a very strict rule of life, and the other group, which was backed by the powerful Augustinian monastery in Nuremburg. Staupitz was trying to bring these groups together, something the monks in Erfurt did not want to happen. Luther went as the representative of the protesting faction.

The journey must have expanded the horizons of the young Luther, who had never to this time been farther from his birthplace than Eisenach. He and another monk traveled through Switzerland and northern Italy, arriving in Rome near the end of the year. It was the Eternal City of the Romans, of Saints Peter and Paul, and, in Luther's time, of the Renaissance—but Luther seems not to have been impressed; in fact, he was perhaps disappointed.

In the early sixteenth century, Rome was a town of only about forty thousand people—smaller than the German city of Augsburg. Its churches, while impressive, were perhaps no grander than the great cathedrals Luther knew in Magdeburg and Erfurt. Many have bemoaned the fact that "Luther visited Rome and missed the Renaissance," but the great art of Michelangelo and Raphael was in private or papal palaces where the young monk would have not been admitted. Pope Julius II, the warrior for the independence of the Papal States, was off with his troops fighting the French. He had taken the name Julius to call to mind Julius Caesar, after whom the pope modeled his reign.

Luther's later reflections are of practical matters that he noticed and of his own spiritual struggles on his pilgrimage. It is hard to know how to take them because he recounted them after many years and many battles with the Roman authorities. He spent four weeks walking around and noted the ancient Roman ruins with interest. He admired the Italian tailors and considered their work vastly superior to the Germans. He often appreciated the hospitality that he received along the way. He praised the hospitals and orphans' homes in Florence as models of caring for the sick that everyone should copy.

But spiritually he was disappointed. He found the masses to be said quickly and without what seemed to him much reverence. The visits to sacred shrines and the prescribed spiritual disciplines left him wondering whether he had really freed his grandfather's soul from purgatory by a combination of prayers and fasting and masses attended. In the end, he said he would not have missed seeing Rome, even for a great deal of money, because "I wouldn't have believed it if I hadn't seen it for myself."[10]

In any case, their mission to appeal to the pope a decision of the head of the Augustinian Order was refused. Early in 1511, Luther and his companion started back for Germany, arriving in Erfurt in April. It was the longest journey he would ever make in his life. There were complex tensions after his return about the division between the two parts of the order. Luther now changed sides with Staupitz and argued that a compromise was necessary. This earned him the deeper enmity of the rest of the Erfurt leadership, and in the fall of 1511 both Luther and his good friend John Lang were transferred to the monastery at Wittenberg.

This may have seemed like a banishment and a way of getting back at Staupitz for those who arranged the reassignment, but it turned

---

10. "Table Talk for October to December 1536," in LW 54:208–9; "Table Talk for March to May 1537," in LW 54:237; and "Table Talk for August 1, 1538," in LW 54:296. All of these reminiscences are from decades later, so they may well have been textured with levels of interpretation, rather than simply being recollections.

out to be one of the turning points in Luther's life. Erfurt had seemed to be the center of everything and the source of opportunities—even though Luther the monk was not thinking much along those lines. But in fact, Wittenberg with its new university was open to change in a way that made it a far better habitat for Luther, who did not then realize that the Saxon town would be his primary residence for the rest of his life.[11] Staupitz put Luther in charge of the theological training of Augustinians in Wittenberg, and the size and quality of the program soared.

The Erfurt leadership did not realize that in Luther and Lang they were losing their best theologians. Luther was also assigned to be the monastery preacher. He traveled to Cologne the next May to attend the meeting of the Augustinian chapter, where he was confirmed as subprior of the monastery in Wittenberg. He was instructed to move toward his doctorate as quickly as possible, which he initially resisted. But Staupitz insisted, and Luther was qualified by 1512. However, there was a fee to be paid, and Luther did not have the required fifty gulden. His father was not likely to help him at this point.

Running in Power Circles

But Luther was now completely in the orbit of other figures—both of Staupitz and also of that monk's old friend Frederick of Saxony, who already in his lifetime was called Frederick the Wise (1465–1525). Frederick was among the most powerful princes in Germany, and, as an elector, he was one of seven who could elect a new emperor. He was also comparatively rich, as a result of revenues from silver and copper mining in his territories and his shrewd approach to finances. He was not married, although he had several children by his mistress Anna Weller. He intended that he would be succeeded by his brother

11. For example, from 1513 on Greek was taught at Wittenberg, which soon gave the students much deeper access to the original text of the New Testament.

John (with whom he already shared the rule in his lifetime) and then by John's young son John Frederick. The boy was receiving a good education, thanks to a well-educated priest named George Spalatin (1484–1545), who had been hired as his tutor and as an advisor to Frederick.

Spalatin and Luther quickly became close friends, but Luther had access to the prince only through Spalatin. At first, this was probably a question of social status; later, it was a deliberate policy on Frederick's part to keep his options open for handling the Luther situation. The amazing scholarly consensus is that these two key persons, who lived in a town of two thousand people, only met face-to-face when Luther was on trial at the Diet of Worms in 1521.

Frederick was a builder of castles and a collector of relics, art, and even professors. He had built the castle church to be a showplace for his collection, which eventually numbered more than nineteen thousand relics. A visit, with the right devotional spirit, to this collection on the one day it was open each year was said to earn the pilgrim an indulgence or forgiveness of almost two million days in purgatory. Frederick had deep roots in the traditions of the church of his time and earned a healthy sum from fees related to the relics.

But Frederick was also a man open to the new humanism that was sweeping northern Europe.[12] He knew Latin and French and had read some of the classics himself. He knew Erasmus, the greatest of the humanists. He bought from most of the famous artists of his day (including Albrecht Dürer) and convinced one of them, Lucas Cranach the Elder, to live in Wittenberg and serve as court painter. By the time Luther arrived, Cranach was one of the chief citizens of the town. He was also developing a pharmacy and printing business,

12. "Humanism" names the broad movement during the time of the Renaissance and Reformation that celebrated the possibilities of human reason and creativity. For a basic orientation to its import for the Luther story, see Alister McGrath, *The Intellectual Origins of the European Reformation* (Hoboken, NJ: Wiley-Blackwell, 2011), 34–66.

and was decorating the walls of the palace as well as painting for others on commission.

Elector Frederick was also becoming a collector of professors. His father and his uncle had divided the territory of Saxony, and while Frederick's line kept the status of elector, the Saxon university in Leipzig was part of the other territory—then ruled by Frederick's cousin George the Bearded (1471–1539). Frederick was willing to spend for buildings and professors to build up Wittenberg against its rival. When Staupitz told him that Luther was the best person in all of Germany to be his successor as Bible professor and that Luther had no ambitions and would probably stay for the rest of his life, Frederick agreed to pay the fifty-gulden fee for awarding the doctorate. Luther and Staupitz traveled together to Leipzig to pick up the money. Frederick got Luther for Wittenberg just as he would go out in 1518 and "collect" the linguist Philip Melanchthon, the most promising young scholar in all of Germany.

On October 18 and 19, 1512, there were two days of festivities for the doctorate, including a humorous speech by the theologian Andreas Carlstadt, the professor in charge of granting the degree. Members of the Erfurt monastery had been invited, but none came. In fact, they organized a protest against Luther's receiving the degree, since usually those who received lower degrees at Erfurt took an oath to take their doctorate only there and nowhere else. But no one had ever administered such an oath to Luther, and so the doctorate was awarded, although the Erfurt people disliked Luther and kept speaking ill of him. They kept this up for three years so that Luther seems to have had to preach against their malicious gossip at the closing of the chapter's general meeting in 1515. It was a first experience of being widely disliked and generally misunderstood.[13]

---

13. Many also simply considered Luther too young. He admits later, "In Erfurt only fifty-year-olds were made doctors of theology. Many took umbrage at my getting the doctorate at the age

Professor Luther

Though Luther was now to hold Staupitz's chair in theology, there was a year's delay before he started to lecture in 1513. In the world outside Wittenberg, great events were stirring that would later have a deep impact on Luther. Giovanni de' Medici—of the powerful Florentine family—was elected pope and took the name Leo X. Frederick's brother Ernst, the archbishop of Magdeburg, died and was succeeded by a member of a rival noble family, Albrecht of Brandenburg. These things were discussed at the castle, but Luther was focused on preparing to lecture on the Psalms.

Wittenberg had its own printing business operated by John Gruenenberg since 1508. Luther had him prepare an edition of the biblical book on which he would lecture (first Psalms, then Romans, then Galatians) with wide margins and space between the lines. Luther first read quite specific comments on the text itself (glosses) and then gave more general comments on the passage (scholia). This was the method for his first set of lectures, and it is part of what makes studying them so difficult.[14] We know from student notebooks, some of which have survived, that Luther stuck to the glosses he had prepared but ranged freely in the longer expositions. It could not have been easy for the students, since Luther's lecture hour in these first years was six o'clock in the morning on Mondays and Fridays, with seven o'clock in the winter. Later he moved to one o'clock in the afternoon.

of twenty-eight, when Staupitz drove me to it." "Table Talk for November 9, 1538," in LW 54:320.

14. There is another problem for the English-language student. The translations in LW of the early lectures (Psalms in vols. 10–11, Romans in vol. 25, and Galatians in vol. 27) are all of later revisions that Luther made for publication. This probably makes the texts more interesting as biblical commentaries but more difficult for understanding Luther's thought in this early period. The same is true of the fascinating "Seven Penitential Psalms," which Luther actually published in German in early 1517; the text in LW 14 is of a later revision.

Luther began his lecturing with the Psalms. This was a logical choice for his largely monastic students, since praying the Psalms shaped the daily worship of the religious community. Luther began with the traditional Christian assumption that the Psalms are to be read as the prayers of Christ unless their clear sense requires another interpretation.[15] At first, he used the traditional fourfold interpretation of these texts, with complex layers of meaning spelled out by means of allegory. But slowly the literal sense came to be most important to him, and he heard the Psalms not as the prayers of Christ but as the prayers of the humble and repentant person who is submitting to God. The influence of Staupitz's theology of humility is evident here, as is Luther's own monastic spirituality.

A passage from the later-published "Seven Penitential Psalms," which goes back to the original lectures, gives a flavor of what Luther was saying. In interpreting Ps. 130:3, "I wait for the Lord," Luther notes widespread human resistance to exercising such patience.

> Now there are some who want to set the goal, appoint the hour and measure, and prescribe to God how they are to be helped. And if they do not experience this, they despair; or, if possible, they seek help elsewhere. These do not tarry and wait for the Lord, God is supposed to wait for them, be ready at once, and help exactly as they themselves have designed. Those who wait for the Lord, however, ask for mercy; but they leave it to God's gracious will when, how, where and by what means he helps them.[16]

Luther's confidence that he had something to say was growing. It is hard to hear in these bold words the man who fought Staupitz's order that he should prepare for his doctorate. Perhaps this is why in 1514 Luther was assigned to be the preacher and pastoral administrator of the town church in addition to preaching in the monastery. From

15. On this, see the reliable exposition in Samuel Preus, *From Shadow to Promise* (Cambridge, MA: Harvard University Press, 1969).
16. "Seven Penitential Psalms" (1518), in LW 14:192.

that time until the end of his life, Luther would preach more often in Saint Mary's of Wittenberg than in any other place, but his close—and sometimes stormy—relationship with this congregation did not develop very deeply until his return from Wartburg in 1522. A sermon on Jesus' parable of the proud man and the humble man who went up to the temple to pray shows that Luther was already a powerful preacher of a message of humility and grace by the summer of 1516.[17]

He was also rising to higher responsibility in the order. He became district vicar in 1515, which actually put him in charge of his own local prior in Wittenberg and ten other monasteries from Dresden to Erfurt. The letters surviving about his administration show him to be both firm and quite pastoral. He visited each of the houses and noted every detail of their life, including their finances. His old friend John Lang was now prior of the monastery in Erfurt. How things had changed in the five years since Luther and Lang were sent into exile in Wittenberg in 1511! Luther does feel free to complain to Lang about the amount of work he is expected to do:

> I nearly need two copyists or secretaries. All day long I do almost nothing else than write letters; therefore I am sometimes not aware whether or not I constantly repeat myself, but you will see. I am a preacher at the monastery. I am a reader during mealtimes, I am asked daily to preach at the city church, I have to supervise the study [of novices and friars], I am a vicar (and that means I am eleven times prior), I am caretaker of the fish [pond] at Leitzkau, I represent the people of Herzberg at the court in Torgau, I lecture on Paul, and I am assembling [material for] a commentary on the Psalms. As I have already mentioned, the greater part of my time is filled with the job of letter writing. I hardly have any uninterrupted time to say the Hourly Prayers and celebrate [mass]. Besides all this there are my own struggles of the flesh, the world, and the devil. See what a lazy man I am![18]

17. "Sermon on Luke 18:9-14" (July 27, 1516), in LW 51:14–17.
18. "Letter to John Lang" (October 26, 1516), in LW 48:27–28. The style is reminiscent of Paul's catalog about his trials and "anxiety for the churches" in 2 Corinthians 11.

The ability to bear such burdens well and with a sense of humor shows what a good lawyer Luther would have made and why his star was rising in the order (the position of district vicar was an elected one). We should interpret the struggles that he mentions neither as obstructing his capacity to work hard nor as making him restless, gloomy, or depressed.

Encountering Paul

In these years between 1515 and 1517 he was chiefly occupied with Paul, lecturing first on the Epistle to the Romans (1515–1516) and then on the Epistle to the Galatians (1516–1517). In his *Lectures on Romans*, Luther's great theme was the righteousness of God—Luther was now celebrating not simply the sinfulness of humanity that he had learned from Augustine but also the glory of God who reaches out to Jews and gentiles, the proud and the humble, those far off and those who are near.

The phrase "righteousness of God" had once terrified Luther, for he had thought of it only in terms of God's judgment. All his monastic activities that were meant to reassure him had come more and more to frustrate and even terrify him. The mass could be spoiled by evil thoughts or even an involuntary nocturnal emission. Confession might be invalid if it were incomplete, and how could one ever remember all one's sins or even know what was sinful? Prayers might be a way to God, but if they were done in a routine way, could God be pleased? Living in community was a source of constant irritation, and yet one was to love all, always obey, and never complain.

But Luther was learning from Paul (as Staupitz had also been telling him) that he was making himself and his response too much the center of things. In Paul, he found something that had always been there in the church but that he had never been able to hear. The first and decisive move toward salvation comes from God, not from "doing what is in you" or "doing your best."

At the end of his life, Luther came to believe that even his entrance to the monastery had been an attempt to "do" something for God rather than to accept grace: "But against everyone's will I deserted my parents and relatives, rushed into a monastery and donned a cowl, because I was persuaded that with that kind of life and those severe hardships I was showing great allegiance to God."[19] But by the *Lectures on Romans* a decade later, Luther could speak of the "righteousness of God" as a source of joy and confidence for the struggling person: "In human teaching the righteousness of man is revealed and taught, that is, who is and becomes righteous before himself and before other people and how this takes place. Only in the Gospel is righteousness of God revealed (that is, who is and becomes righteous before God and how this takes place) by faith alone, by which the Word of God is believed. . . . For the righteousness of God is the cause of salvation. . . . This happens through faith in the Gospel."[20]

This important moment is the first of Luther's four great theological discoveries—or rediscoveries, as all of them are a sharpened formulation of the sense of Scripture. He would then deepen this insight about the free grace of God in his *Lectures on Galatians* (1516–1517), and together this would give him a Pauline base from which in the autumn of 1517 to attack the prevailing way of doing theology.

But it is not clear that Luther himself could accept the ideas he could deliver to others in lectures, nor that the ability to speak this doctrine meant he could believe it and hold to it in his struggles. Throughout the years in the monastery and early years in

---

19. "Lectures on Genesis—Chapter 49" (1545), in LW 8:276.
20. "Lectures on Romans 1:17," in LW 25:151.

Wittenberg, Luther had many serious bouts of anxiety mixed with depression and great fear about his salvation. He called this kind of internal attack on the self *Anfechtungen* (an untranslatable word meaning something like "bouts" or "afflictions") and came eventually to see them as the devil's inevitable assault on a person of faith, especially a theologian.[21]

Through many of these dark moments, Staupitz was Luther's confessor. He spent much time encouraging the young scholar to see God in another way. A particularly severe outburst took place when Luther was part of a procession at the Augustinian monastery in his birthplace of Eisleben. Staupitz worked with Luther afterward and said sharply to him, "Your thought is not of Christ." Luther had learned quickly that he must humble himself before God, but he could not—until he lectured on Paul—see that the decisive movement came from God in the life and death of Jesus Christ.[22] The struggles were terrible, almost life-threatening at times, and they dominate some biographies of Luther and dramatizations of his life.[23]

There is every reason to take Luther's reports of these attacks of doubt and despair seriously. In *Explanation of the Ninety-Five Theses* (1518), he gives one account of their intensity just after this period:

> I myself "know a man" (2 Corinthians 12:2) who claimed that he had often suffered these punishments, in fact over a very brief period of time.

---

21. See "Anfechtung" as the third and final aspect of the work of a theologian in "Preface to the Wittenberg Edition of Luther's German Writings" (1539), in LW 34:286–87, MLBTW3 39–42. The significance of this kind of experience for Luther's theology generally is brilliantly epitomized in Oswald Bayer, *Martin Luther's Theology: A Contemporary Interpretation*, trans. Thomas A. Trapp (Grand Rapids, MI: Eerdmans, 2008), 32–37.

22. "Table Talk for November and December 1531," in LW 54:19–20. On another occasion, Luther reports: "my good man Staupitz said, 'One must keep one's eyes fixed on that man who is called Christ.' Staupitz is the one who started the teaching [of the gospel in our time]." "Table Talk for Spring 1533," in LW 54:97.

23. See especially the play by John Osborne, *Luther* (New York: Signet, 1961), and the film *Martin Luther: Heretic*, a 1986 joint production of Concordia and the British Broadcasting System. Psychoanalyst Erik Erikson put a neurotic Luther on the couch in his *Young Man Luther: A Study in Psychoanalysis and History* (New York: Norton, 1958).

Yet they were so great and so much like hell that no tongue could adequately express them, no pen could describe them, and one who had not himself experienced them could not believe them. And so great were they that, if they had been sustained or had lasted for half an hour, even for one tenth of an hour, he would have perished completely and all his bones would have been reduced to ashes. At such a time God seems terribly angry, and with him the whole creation. At such a time there is no flight, no comfort, within or without, but all things accuse.[24]

Luther continued to have these attacks all his life with irregular frequency and intensity. His "breakthrough" on justification by faith did not mean an end to *Anfechtungen*. Rather, it meant that he had something, or rather someone—the person of Christ—to hold over against these shattering and life-dissolving experiences. And because many in his time had experienced a measure of the doubts and fears that Luther experienced, he was soon regarded as a great soul doctor, a spiritual director to a generation that had trouble believing the formal church teaching on the grace of God, given their own doubts and the church's far from grace-centered practice.

That is why the portrait here of the transitional years from law student to young professor is not of Luther in constant tears and anguish. These bouts were serious, but they did not define him. Rather, the achievements of these twelve years, punctuated by continuing struggles like these, gave him the basis for his double attack, which he launched in the fall of 1517, on the practice of theology and the practice of the church.

The rich community that surrounded him by the middle of 1517 provides further warning not to reduce Luther to a set of neuroses. He had broken ties with his family, particularly his father, but had found a mentor in Staupitz so congenial that scholars to this day

---

24. "Explanations of the Ninety Five Theses," in LW 31:129. Luther is speaking of himself when I says, "I know a man." The style imitates the apostle Paul's autobiographical reflections in 2 Corinthians 12.

still debate where Staupitz's insights end and Luther's begin.[25] He had some enemies in the Augustinian order, especially in Erfurt, but he had an impressive circle of friends in Wittenberg and beyond, including George Spalatin at the court; Luther's contemporary Nicholas von Amsdorf, a nephew of Staupitz and Wittenberg theology professor who was becoming one of Luther's close and lifelong friends; Wittenberg professor John Agricola from Eisleben, who was being won over to Luther's ideas; John Lang in Erfurt itself; and his former prior Wenceslas Link, now a preacher in the important city of Nuremburg.

Prominent people were noticing Luther's publications, especially his edition of the mystical classic *A German Theology*, first published in 1516. That book emphasized the way that a person's being was created from outside themselves (in Latin: *extra nos*) by an encounter with God rather than by the exertion of their own self-development (*in nos*). This approach to the creative powers of God's word leavened Luther's thinking about Paul all the more. Even the elector was noticing Luther, according to what Luther heard from Spalatin, although that made Luther very nervous. He may even by this time have made the acquaintance of his Wittenberg neighbor, the painter Lucas Cranach.

We get a sense of the joyful moments and Luther's ability to laugh at himself in a letter from August 1517 inviting Spalatin to join him and some others in a late dinner at the monastery that evening.[26] Spalatin is to bring with him Christopher Scheurl, the former law professor and now envoy from Saxony to Nuremberg. Scheurl had

---

25. For a sample of the theology of Staupitz that Luther found so helpful, see his "Eternal Predestination and Its Execution in Time" (1517), in *Forerunners of the Reformation*, ed. Heiko Oberman (Philadelphia: Fortress Press, 1981), 175–203. And for a critical examination, see David Steinmetz, *Luther and Staupitz: An Essay in the Intellectual Origins of the Protestant Reformation* (Durham, NC: Duke University Press, 1980).
26. LW 48:43.

been eager to meet Luther. Most importantly, Spalatin was to bring the wine. With superiors like Staupitz, obedience had not been too hard a vow for Luther. And in Luther's case, friendship and work that he loved took the edge off chastity. But the vow of poverty was still very real, and Luther knew that if they were going to have wine, the castle cellar would have to provide it.

3

Critic of the Church

1517–1519

In the years when Luther was becoming a monk and a professor, Desiderius Erasmus of Rotterdam (1469–1536) was the most famous scholar in Europe. This was surprising both because his background was not particularly distinguished and also because he had only temporarily held university positions.[1] Although he had not achieved prominence in any of the usual ways, Erasmus was an amazingly

---

1. Actually, Erasmus was the (illegitimate) son of a clergyman. This was a burden in the sixteenth century, but not an insurmountable one. Luther's close friend Spalatin was also illegitimate, and he made his way to a very distinguished career. Erasmus was for a time professor in Cambridge and earlier lived in London and Oxford where he was close to Thomas More, author of the famous *Utopia* and minister of Henry VIII. But it suited him best to live on the continent, and he spent the early years of the Reformation first in Louvain (1517–1521), then in Basel (where his printer was located), and finally, when Basel became a Protestant stronghold, in Freiburg, which was still safely Roman Catholic. An excellent short account of Erasmus is found in Hajo Holborn, *A History of Modern Germany: The Reformation* (New York: Knopf, 1964), 112–16. A classic biography written sympathetically is Roland Bainton, *Erasmus of Christendom* (New York: Scribner, 1969), and an updated, slightly more critical one is James D. Tracy, *Erasmus of the Low Countries* (Berkeley: University of California Press, 1997).

successful independent scholar, one who used his imagination and church connections to do the work he felt called to do.

Growing Courage to Protest

That work was mostly of a serious scholarly nature—editing a new critical edition of the Greek New Testament and new editions of the ancient church theologians. But Erasmus was also a popular writer, at least for the upper level of European society. He was a man of enormous wit, and he used that gift to poke fun at the various corrupt institutions of his day, including the church, monks and other clergy, pilgrimages, and even popes.

Yet Erasmus knew how to chide and scold without burning his bridges to either princes or popes. Charles V made him an advisor even before he was elected emperor in 1519, and Erasmus's celebrated edition of the Greek New Testament was dedicated to Pope Leo X. Like Luther, his Christian commitment was clear and moving to many, but he was radically different from Luther in his approach to both theology (much more centered on ethics) and change in the church (always cautious).

Erasmus had great influence on Luther's early thought in several ways. His scholarly work of editing provided Luther with a much more accurate text of the New Testament, which Luther used in his own lecturing after 1516 and in his translation of the New Testament beginning in 1521. Luther also ordered Erasmus's editions of the ancient fathers like Jerome (ca. 347–ca. 420), whom Erasmus admired. Luther learned a few things from Jerome but was already deeply committed to Augustine (354–430) in all the issues that had divided those theologians during their lifetimes. His knowledge of the texts of Augustine was fairly limited, but his allegiance was strong.

Luther was indebted to Erasmus in another way at the beginning of his public critique of the church in 1517; he had learned from Erasmus's brilliant use of satire that the way to bring about change might be through pointing out the incredible nature of how things were going in the name of religion and getting people to laugh. To the end of his life, for all his devout intensity and single-minded concentration on the issue of God, Luther could use laughter as a powerful persuasive tool and usually could laugh at himself as well.[2] Many of his opponents had trouble getting a hearing for their own good arguments because of the ponderous and self-important style in which they wrote and spoke.[3] One traditional Roman Catholic scholar, who concedes that Erasmus was in the end loyal to the Catholic Church, nonetheless blames Erasmus for lessening "respect for the authority of the Church and for faith itself among a large number of the highly-cultivated men of the day. Thus he did prepare the way for the impetuous and impassioned Luther."[4]

Luther discussed Erasmus in letters to his humanist friends at Frederick's court, especially George Spalatin. As early as 1516, Luther, while expressing gratitude for Erasmus's help in his own teaching, began to sense a deep difference between that scholar's moral, humane version of Christianity and the grace-centered version that Luther had found with Staupitz and in reading Augustine, a version being reinforced by lecturing on Paul. Luther offers his critique at first very apologetically, but by 1517 was speaking bluntly about a growing dislike for Erasmus's approach.[5]

---

2. A sympathetic look at this aspect of Luther's life and thought can be found in Eric Gritsch, *The Wit of Martin Luther* (Minneapolis: Fortress Press, 2006).
3. This "Luther advantage" hampered Tetzel, Prierias, and especially Eck in the early years of the Roman response to Luther.
4. Ludwig Pastor, *The History of the Popes*, vol. 7 (London: Routledge, 1950), 315–16. These translations of a late nineteenth-century multivolume work by a loyal Roman Catholic professor at the University of Innsbruck still are valuable for hearing the Luther story from the Roman side.

And in a letter the next year, Luther complained about him, writing that, for all his great gift in the use of language, Erasmus is "more violent" than his opponent, "though he makes a great effort to preserve friendship."[6]

What worried Spalatin, Luther, and most educated people in Northern Europe from 1513 forward was the bitter attack by the Dominican Order in Cologne on the great scholar Johannes Reuchlin (1455–1522). Reuchlin was one of the first Christians in this period to master Hebrew, and he was greatly admired for his scholarship. When he intervened to prevent the burning of certain Jewish books from the Kabbalah—a mystical text from the Middle Ages—he was reported to the Inquisition. For several years the authorities in Rome could not decide what to do with the case. The Dominicans were very powerful, as they would later be in their hostility to Luther.[7] On the other hand, Reuchlin also had many powerful friends, some of them in the Papal Court.

Luther even expressed relief in 1514 that the case had been sent to Rome, because he could not imagine a fair resolution of the case in Cologne with all the animosity that had been stirred up. He wrote Spalatin: "One thing, however, pleases me: namely, that this matter reached Rome and the Apostolic See. . . . Since Rome has the most learned people among the cardinals, Reuchlin's case will at least be considered more favorably there than those jealous people of Cologne—those beginners in grammar!—would ever allow."[8]

5. "Letter to George Spalatin" (October 19, 1516), in LW 48:23–26, and "Letter to George Spalatin" (March 1, 1517), in LW 48:39–40.
6. "Letter to George Spalatin" (January 18, 1518), in LW: 48:55. The friendship in question was between Erasmus and Lefèvre d'Etaples (also known as Faber Stapulensis); they were engaged in an academic brawl over the interpretation of Heb. 2:7.
7. In the early years of Luther's movement, much of the underlying tension was between the Dominicans and Augustinians and other orders, though this point is often missed.
8. "Letter to George Spalatin," in LW 48:10.

By the time of its resolution, the Reuchlin case had become a mass of conflicting pressures and fears, and it cast a shadow over the trouble that was to develop for Luther. The Roman officials would later see the complaints about Luther's Ninety-Five Theses as simply more trouble from Germany, and they would have difficulty reacting either swiftly or thoughtfully. But even more significant was the fallout among the educated public in Northern Europe. Their sympathies were with Reuchlin, and they were already set when Luther's case emerged to be skeptical of charges that any criticism of Rome was heresy. Luther said early in the case, "When such protests and opinions [as those of Reuchlin] can no longer be freely expressed, then we must fear that finally the inquisitors . . . will denounce someone a heretic on a whim."[9]

One Prong of the Attack: Teaching Theology

Luther was preparing to become publicly visible himself because his new theological orientation from teaching the Bible made him ready to complain about current conditions. However, he was a professor, and at the heart of his original complaint was not corruption in the church but concern about the way that theology was taught in monasteries and universities. A few weeks after his attack on the Scholastic method for teaching theology, he issued—almost as an afterthought—his critique of indulgences (the practice of paying a fee to the papacy or its agents for time off one's soul in purgatory), but that issue and the wide reading of his Ninety-Five Theses that quickly put Luther in the spotlight.

Once these battles were launched, Luther complained to Staupitz that he would have preferred to remain a private person, but there is something about this claim that does not quite ring true: "I have

9. Quoted in Bernhard Lohse, *Martin Luther's Theology* (Minneapolis: Fortress Press, 1999), 97, from a letter to Spalatin of February 1514.

45

always loved privacy and would much prefer to watch the splendid performance of the gifted people of my age than become a part of the show and be ridiculed."[10] He may have stumbled into the debate about indulgences, but he had been preparing his attack on Scholastic theology for some time.

For Luther, the study of the Bible had been a reorienting experience. He found in the Psalms and in Paul's letters something quite different than he had previously heard from the church, especially its professional theologians. The marriage of theology to philosophy had become a subordination, in Luther's view, and rather than casting the Christian faith in a bold way, it had obscured the basic message. The gospel did not, and could not, shine through as the "true treasure of the church" (as Luther was to call it in the Ninety-Five Theses) so long as theology worked within the Scholastic framework.[11] In this respect, all the schools—of Thomas, Scotus, and Ockham—were equally problematic.

Luther's mounting frustration with "the way things are done" in theology can be seen in successive letters to his friend John Lang in Erfurt. Luther was proud of the emerging success of the university in Wittenberg. He had written to their former teacher Jodokus Trutfetter to try to move him away from Aristotle. Luther kept up that unsuccessful campaign for years, and Trutfetter eventually considered Luther ignorant and a fool. Luther told Lang that he knows that modern people are supposed to "keep silent" in the presence of such great minds from the past as Aristotle and Peter Lombard. But he has come to think that Aristotle is not a fount of wisdom at all: "What will they not believe who have taken for granted everything which Aristotle, this chief of all charlatans,

---

10. "Letter to John von Staupitz" (May 20, 1518), in LW 48:69.
11. "Ninety-Five Theses," in LW 31:31, MLBTW3 11. Thesis 62 in its entirety reads: "The true treasure of the church is the most holy gospel of the glory and grace of God."

insinuates and imposes on others, things which are so absurd that not even an ass or stone could remain silent about them!"[12] In May, Luther wrote to Lang again, reporting that in Wittenberg, at least, "Aristotle is gradually falling from his throne, and his final doom is only a matter of time." Instead, students want lectures on the Bible, on Augustine, and on other ancient Christian writers.[13]

In September 1517, a disputation was held at the Wittenberg theology faculty. Luther prepared ninety-seven theses, or propositions for debate, concerning the prevalent Scholastic theology. There had been a series of increasingly sharp disputations over the previous year in Wittenberg, but for all the compactness of the arguments formulated in thesis form, the pointed nature of Luther's attack stands out. It can even be called a "declaration of war on Scholastic theology."[14]

The theses defend Augustine's view of the seriousness of human sin. They deny that human beings are free to choose the good or to choose God. All of this builds toward Luther's startling thesis 17: "Man is by nature unable to want God to be God. Indeed, he himself wants to be God, and does not want God to be God." From this it follows in thesis 29 that the only basis for salvation can be "the eternal election and predestination of God."[15]

The central part of the document is a frontal attack on Aristotle and especially his suitability as a source for Christian theology. Thesis 50 makes the bold claim, "Briefly, the whole Aristotle is to theology as darkness is to light. This is opposition to the scholastics."[16] Since

---

12. "Letter to John Lang" (February 8, 1517), in LW 48:37.
13. "Letter to John Lang" (May 18, 1517), in LW 48:42.
14. Martin Brecht, *Martin Luther*, vol. 1: *His Road to Reformation, 1483–1521*, trans. James L. Schaaf (Philadelphia: Fortress Press, 1985), 161.
15. "Disputation Concerning Scholastic Theology" (1517), in LW 31:9–16, MLBTW3 3–7. The claim about eternal election and predestination echoes a treatise of John von Staupitz published earlier that year, "Eternal Predestination and Its Execution in Time," in *Forerunners of the Reformation*, ed. Heiko Oberman (Philadelphia: Fortress Press, 1981), 175–203.
16. LW 31:12–13, MLBTW3, 5.

almost everyone in Western Europe at that time was using some version of Aristotle-dependent Scholastic theology, this was a very broad and fundamental attack on the whole discipline and one likely to stir great enmity (or to be dismissed as total madness). Before the theses are complete, they have attacked not only Aristotle but also such a wide range of respected Christian authorities that they were bound to offend almost anyone who took them seriously: John Duns Scotus, Gabriel Biel, Cardinal Pierre d'Ailly, and William of Ockham. If Luther wanted to sting, it would be hard to find a university anywhere not stung by this attack on how their basic work was done.

A Second Prong: Sale of Indulgences

These theses were stirring the University at Wittenberg but initially made little impact beyond it, despite their being sent to Erfurt and elsewhere. They were nonetheless the first and fundamental prong of Luther's emergence as a public voice in the church. Of course, he initially stirred a much greater hornet's nest with his theses questioning the sale of indulgences in the territory of Bishop Albrecht of Mainz.

Albrecht (1490–1545) was a younger son of the ruler of the powerful territory just to the north of Saxony—the Mark of Brandenburg. His father was marquis of Brandenburg and, along with Frederick the Wise, was one of the seven electors of the emperor. When Albrecht was twenty-three in 1513, he became bishop of Magdeburg and Halberstadt, following Ernst of Saxony, a brother of Frederick the Wise, who had been elected bishop at age twelve. Frederick surely took a dim view of this important ecclesiastical position passing from his family to rival neighbors. But the power dynamics were compounded when, in the next year, Albrecht was also elected archbishop of Mainz. That also gave him a vote as an elector and put two of the seven votes in the hands of the rulers of Brandenburg—the Hohenzollern family.

Image 7: In its earliest stages, the Reformation was protected by two savvy electors in Saxony, Frederick the Wise and his brother John the Steadfast.

Albrecht could not actually carry out the duties of being archbishop in both places, and in fact holding multiple offices was against the law of the church. But it had been known to happen, and things could be worked out with Rome in exchange for the payment of a very large fee. In Albrecht's case, because Mainz was such a prize—the largest archdiocese in all of Christendom—the fee was exorbitant: twenty-nine thousand gulden. Albrecht did not have this much cash in hand, so he did what was common in those days and borrowed the sum from the leading bankers of that period, the Fuggers of Augsburg.

In exchange, Albrecht was allowed to sell a special papal indulgence in his territory to earn the money to repay the Fuggers. Half the profits from these sales would go to him and half to Rome (the usual beneficiary of the sale of papal indulgences). The popes of this period were continually in debt, always needing money for their wars to protect the Papal States. The current pope, Leo X, had also undertaken the building of Saint Peter's, which was turning out to be a very expensive proposition. The arrangement seemed to offer something to everyone, except the faithful who knew nothing about it. At the beginning, among those faithful was Professor Luther in Wittenberg. It is interesting to speculate whether his approach might have changed had he known how much political power and financial complexity he was attacking.

Albrecht would turn out to be a constant in Luther's life, although not necessarily a dedicated enemy like John Eck. Magdeburg was some distance from Wittenberg, and Mainz was very far away. But Albrecht lived most of his life in neither of the cities where he was supposed to be bishop, residing instead in Halle, only a short distance from Wittenberg. There were regular flare-ups with Luther and the Saxon princes and then other periods that were very quiet. According to some, Albrecht at one point considered embracing the Reformation and marrying his mistress, whom he genuinely seemed to love. But in the turmoil during and after 1525, the lines of opposition hardened. Near the end of his life, Albrecht's efforts to keep Halle in the Roman Catholic camp failed, and he had to move to Mainz to the great cathedral where he is buried. He often bought paintings from the Wittenberg artist Lucas Cranach the Elder, even after Cranach became Luther's good friend and strong ally in the support for changes in the church.

The sale of indulgences was entrusted to a Dominican priest named John Tetzel (1465–1519). In the telling of Luther's story, he has often been presented as a very foolish person, but he seems to have been a competent priest, a supporter of the papacy, and one who genuinely believed in what he was doing. It is hard to know just what Tetzel and those under him may have said in their preaching of indulgences, but some were not very careful and gave the impression that forgiveness and salvation could be purchased for both the living and the dead.

The origin of indulgences can be found in a hard-to-understand distinction in the sacrament of penance, as it was articulated during this period, between forgiveness of sin, which can come only from God's grace, and the punishment for sin, which was considered a real consequence that could not be escaped. Forgiveness would mean that one's eventual destination was heaven, but it was impossible to come into the presence of the Holy God without having suffered the just punishment for sin, either in this life or after death in purgatory. Purgatory was not seen as a lighter form of hell but as a place of preparation—the forecourt to heaven—a destination that a baptized and forgiven Christian would reach eventually.[17]

The church argued that it had the power to announce both forgiveness as the gift of Christ and a release from the punishment or penalty accompanying sin. Indulgences were at first available only in Rome, at the Jubilee pilgrimage there in 1300, for example, but eventually they could also be obtained at shrines such as Assisi and Santiago de Compostela.[18] For some years they had been available from the castle church in Wittenberg on All Saints' Day. Luther had already had occasion in 1516 to preach about understanding indulgences correctly, and his colleague Andreas Carlstadt, the dean of the faculty of theology, had written some theses questioning them in the fall of 1516.

Perhaps in the end it was impossible to be careful enough in preaching about such a complex notion—not buying forgiveness but something very close to it. Skillful preachers preyed especially on the fear that one's dead loved ones were suffering in purgatory, and it was

17. Viewed biblically, as Luther quickly came to see, purgatory is an odd concept. Perhaps the best way to understand how it was visualized theologically is by reading the second part of Dante's *Divine Comedy*. Especially good theological notes are found in the older Penguin edition translated and edited by Dorothy L. Sayers.

18. Assisi was the home of beloved St. Francis of Assisi, and Santiago de Compostella in Spain is a popular pilgrimage site, said to be the resting place of the remains of St. James.

difficult not to buy indulgences for one's parents, just in case it might be of help after death.[19]

All through the summer of 1517, Tetzel was at work. He was in Eisleben and Mansfeld early in the year, and Luther may well have heard about this from his family. We can wonder whether Hans Luther, who did not like monks coming around and begging for money needed for the support of families, may also have taken offense at such sales.

By April, Tetzel was at work in Jüterbog, scarcely twenty miles from Wittenberg. People from the town were going out to buy indulgences, and Luther heard about this as he listened to confessions (the regular form of receiving forgiveness) and preached in the town church. Tetzel tried to set up shop in Leipzig, but this was under the jurisdiction of Duke George the Bearded, who would not allow it.[20]

Luther's Ninety-Five Theses were written in time for the eve of All Saints' Day, October 31, 1517—a major time of pilgrims coming to Wittenberg to venerate the relics in the castle church. The theses have become one of the most famous documents in the history of the world, but readers are often disappointed or deeply puzzled to understand what all the fuss was about. They are an invitation to university debate, but even with some understanding of penance in Luther's time, it can be hard to know what to make of certain individual theses. Luther himself presented a new version with explanations by the middle of 1518.

---

19. A reliable starting place for understanding the deeper issues of confession and forgiveness at this time is Thomas N. Tentler, *Sin and Confession on the Eve of the Reformation* (Princeton: Princeton University Press, 1997). A sequel of sorts to that book is the fascinating study of Ronald K. Rittgers on the later course of absolution in lands that embraced the Reformation. *Reformation of the Keys: Confession, Conscience and Authority in Sixteenth Century Germany* (Cambridge, MA: Harvard University Press, 2004).
20. Brecht, *Martin Luther*, 1:176–83. Brecht's treatment of the indulgence controversy is characteristically comprehensive and fascinating.

Luther begins with the Bible—arguing from his new biblical understanding against the contemporary practice of the church. Jesus meant for the whole life of his followers to be one of repentance, which the church has reduced to the sacrament of penance as they now practice it. By thesis 6 he is attacking the pope—a very dangerous strategy: "The pope cannot remit any guilt, except by declaring and showing that it has been remitted by God." Perhaps there are some church disciplinary penalties that come under the pope's power, and those he would be free to remit. But the preaching of indulgences gives "an indiscriminate and high-sounding promise" of release from penalties that only God could perform.[21]

In thesis 27, Luther continues by making fun of the popular saying "As soon as the money clinks into the money chest, the soul flies out of purgatory." No, he continues, what is sure is that when the money clinks, greed and avarice increase. At points, deep indignation at the whole sorry spectacle surges out: "Those who believe they can be certain of their salvation because they have indulgence letters will be eternally damned, together with their teachers." This commercialization of salvation not only flies in the face of the apostle Paul and Augustine's teaching, but also makes mockery of Luther—and many others—who wrestle with their sins and struggle to reform their lives. Even more radically undercutting the whole financial structure that is being served is the bold claim of thesis 36: "Any truly repentant Christian has a right to full remission of penalty and guilt, even without indulgence letters."[22]

Luther's rhetorical power seems to soar as he moves through the later theses, and the charges against the church become more and more memorable:

---

21. "Ninety-Five Theses" (1517), in LW 31:25–27, MLBTW3, 8–9.
22. LW 31:28, MLBTW3, 10.

Thesis 43: Christians are to be taught that if the pope knew the exactions of the indulgence preachers, he would rather that the basilica of St. Peter were burned to ashes than built up with the skin, flesh, and bones of his sheep.

Thesis 62: The true treasure of the church is the most holy gospel of the glory and grace of God.

Thesis 66: The treasures of indulgences are nets with which one now fishes for the wealth of men.

It builds to a very powerful climax near the end with a very subversive challenge:

Thesis 86: "Again, 'Why does not the pope, whose wealth is today greater than the richest Crassus, build this one basilica of St. Peter with his own money rather than with the money of poor believers?"[23]

Luther might have been astonished to know that the papacy under Leo X was constantly desperate for money and that the situation under his successor would be even worse, given the debts that he accumulated.

But were the Ninety-Five Theses really posted at all? Much of the Protestant world since the Reformation has celebrated the nailing of these propositions to the door of the castle church. Luther himself never mentions posting them, but the story goes back to the life of Luther written by his close friend Philip Melanchthon soon after his death. In 1961, a Roman Catholic Reformation scholar, Erwin Iserloh, raised the question of whether this had really happened.[24] Melanchthon was not yet in Wittenberg in 1517; he may not have had definite information about this event. There has been a scholarly

---

23. LW 31:29, 30, 31, 33, MLBTW3, 12–13. Some of these theses at the end are presented as hypothetical questions that laypeople might reasonably ask of indulgence preachers rather than arguments he is explicitly making. Reading the whole the document, however, one gets the sense that Luther is sympathetic to these views.

24. Erwin Iserloh, *The Theses Were Not Posted: Luther between Reform and Reformation*, trans. Jared Wicks (Boston: Beacon, 1968).

standoff for fifty years on this question, with no definite proof of the posting discovered. So Iserloh's question haunts, even if it spoils much later religious art and traditional reenactments.[25]

What Luther definitely did on October 31, 1517, was to write to Albrecht of Mainz complaining about the distortions of the sellers of indulgences. He enclosed a copy of the theses for disputation that he had already written. Later, according to Martin Brecht, perhaps in mid-November, Luther did post the theses, as was customary for documents prepared for university debate, and from that posting interest grew and copies began to circulate—first in manuscript and later in print. Brecht thinks that Melanchthon got the beginning date right (October 31) but conflated into that day events that took place over several weeks.[26] This interpretation seems to accord most with the available evidence.

In any case, Luther wrote to Albrecht asking not that the indulgence selling stop but that the preachers be exhorted to be more careful and that the instructions under which they operated, which Luther asserted promised falsely the entire remission of the punishments of purgatory without any need for contrition on the part of the purchaser, be amended. The letter is diplomatic but pointed, and it contains a warning at the end that if Albrecht does not act, someone will write against what is happening in a devastating way.[27]

25. Bernhard Lohse, *Martin Luther: An Introduction to His Life and Thought* (Philadelphia: Fortress Press, 1986), 43–4.
26. Brecht, *Martin Luther*, 1:200–202.
27. "Letter to Cardinal Albrecht, Archbishop of Mainz" (October 31, 1517), in LW 48:43–49. Lohse finds it significant that Luther for the first time in signing this letter uses the spelling "Luther" rather than "Luder." Very soon he will start using a Greek form of the name: "Eleutherius," meaning "free." He thought of himself as being free of the old way of doing theology, and perhaps also free to engage in public disputes. He did not long continue this usage, however. See Lohse, *Martin Luther's Theology*, 101.

Image 8: The church attached to the elector's castle in Wittenberg depicts the 95
Theses inscribed in bronze by the Prussians in 1858.

Luther probably did not realize that he had already written the
document that would cause an uproar not just about details of the
related preaching but about the whole practice of selling indulgences.

He wrote to his own ecclesiastical superior, Bishop Jerome Schulze, and he may also have written to other bishops in areas where Tetzel was preaching. The territory around Wittenberg belonged to several different jurisdictions—Magdeburg, Brandenburg, Merseburg, and Naumburg—so there were several people to approach. But even though Luther did not know the details of Albrecht's arrangements with Rome, he sensed that he was the key actor as the archbishop of Mainz and primate of Germany.

Within a few weeks, copies of the Ninety-Five Theses began to circulate widely. Someone translated them from their original Latin into more accessible German, and they were printed and circulated even more widely. By the end of 1517, many people had heard of Luther. In much of Germany, the reaction was very positive. Luther had been noticed. The long-standing German frustration with Roman taxes helped the theses receive a sympathetic reading. It was common among literate Germans at this time to spell out "the root of all evil is greed" as an acronym: ROMA (*radix omnia malorum avaritia*). Many suspected that, under the pious words of the preachers, indulgences were a scheme to send German money to Rome.

Luther soon made his argument much more pointed and available by publishing "Sermon on Indulgences and Grace," which was read even more widely than the Ninety-Five Theses. For all that he had distanced himself from Ockham's philosophy, Luther was arguing in his razor-sharp style, orienting the Christian life back to its New Testament foundations: "It cannot be proved from any Scripture that divine justice requires or desires any other punishment or satisfaction from the sinner than his hearty and true repentance and conversion, with a resolution henceforth to bear the cross of Christ and practice good works."[28]

But the negative reactions were also not long in coming. Tetzel and his fellow Dominicans, stung by Luther's attack and noticing a dramatic drop in business, responded with two sets of their own theses attacking Luther. These first responses do not defend indulgences but instead charge that at the heart of Luther's arguments was a refusal to submit to papal authority: "Christians should be taught that those who expose the Pope to jeers and slanders are marked with the stain of heresy and shut out from the hope of the kingdom of heaven."[29]

News of the uproar in Germany must have reached Rome by Christmas and in a variety of ways. Cardinal Albrecht himself sent Luther's letter and theses to Rome early in December with a suggestion that Luther be restrained. Not until February 3, 1518, did Pope Leo X instruct Gabriele della Volta, vicar-general of the Augustinian Order, to look into the case and find a way to end the turmoil. It was very difficult for Rome to take this fresh incident seriously; it sounded less important than the Reuchlin affair that had boiled for years. Luther was unknown, Wittenberg was a new university, and from the hills of Rome they both seemed on the very far edge of Germany.

It was also not possible at this time for the Curia to hear any serious criticism of indulgences, so deeply was the church tied to this practice by tradition and necessity. Roman minds were closed to such criticisms as Luther's and not prepared for the strong support that they would receive all over Germany. As a partisan of Rome laments, "At the court of the Medici Pope no account was taken of the deep-seated dissatisfaction caused by the Roman demands for money. With

---

28. Excerpts from "Luther's Sermon on Indulgence and Grace," in *Documents Illustrative of the Continental Reformation*, ed. B .J. Kidd (Oxford: Clarendon, 1911), 29. Amazingly, this key text of the early reformation is not part of LW.

29. "Tetzel's Counter Theses" in Clyde Manschreck, *A History of Christianity: Readings in the History of the Church from the Reformation to the Present* (New York: Prentice Hall, 1965), 18.

inconceivable thoughtlessness no attempt was made to leave the old beaten track. Quite regardless of the innumerable complaints which we lodged against it, the little official world lulled itself to sleep in false security. Misgivings expressed by a few individuals passed unheeded. Nothing was allowed to disturb the prevailing satisfaction with the actual state of ecclesiastical affairs."[30]

Back to Work: Lecturing on the Bible

The excitement continued for a long time, but in the meantime Luther was back at work—lecturing on the Epistle to the Hebrews and preaching in the town church. When Staupitz heard from the vicar-general, it was not clear what all he may have said or done. But one strange development was his asking Luther to prepare theological theses and to preside at the periodic meeting of the chapter that would be held in April 1518 in Heidelberg. These were not to be about indulgences or the pope; with the Augustinians he could go back to discussing something explosive enough but still safer than the authority of Rome—his first prong about how theology should be done.

So far Luther's program had been largely negative, critiquing the ways both the universities and the church were working. The prominent assignment at the forthcoming meeting in Heidelberg was an opportunity to show his real promise. All eyes would be on him, thanks to recent notoriety. But he would have a chance to vindicate the trust that Staupitz and others had in him by what he presented and how he conducted himself.

Luther was clarifying his understanding of both the method and content of theology in his preaching during Lent 1518. In two sermons from the month before Heidelberg, one sees his deepening

30. Pastor, *History of the Popes*, 7:328.

sense of Christ as the center of theology. In this there was nothing new, but Luther was building on his earlier work by developing a fresh articulation of how Christ and faith in Christ must be seen first and foremost as gift, as the grace of God. Luther commends Christ to those who find God terrifying:

> When we know and consider that Christ came down from heaven and loved sinners in obedience to the Father, then there springs up in us a bold approach to and firm hope in Christ. We learn that Christ is the real epistle, the golden book, in which we read and learn how he always kept before him the will of the Father. . . . Now we see that there is no shorter way to the Father except that we love Christ, hope and trust in him, boldly look to him for everything good, learn to know and praise him. For then it will be impossible that we should have a miserable, frightened, dejected conscience; in Christ it will be heartened and refreshed.[31]

Luther was preaching this just a few days after the Wittenberg students had stolen and burned eight hundred copies of Tetzel's defense of indulgences, but for all that turmoil he seems focused on the Bible texts for the day and the spiritual needs of the congregation.

This sense of Christ as gift is even more pronounced in a sermon that may have been given on Palm Sunday of that year. In "Two Kinds of Righteousness," Luther preaches on a classic Palm Sunday text—the second chapter of Paul's letter to the Philippians. Here Luther can now articulate the sequence of the Christian life. The church has drifted away from the gospel into teaching something like this: "Do what is in you, and God's grace will be added. Perhaps that will be enough. But by all means do what you can!" But Luther had seen, especially in Paul's theological connection between faith and obedience, that the sequence should be: "First take Christ as gift. God gives Christ to you freely, and without any merit or action on your

---

31. "Sermon on John 11:1–45" (March 19, 1518), in LW 51:46.

part. And then, in response, take Christ as example and be freed by his love for you to love your neighbor in the ways that the neighbor needs." It is a striking reversal of the approach taken by indulgence preachers and even Erasmus, who stressed what humans must do. By themselves, humans can do nothing, but freed from sin in Christ they may do much and will do it.[32]

A Theologian of the Cross

After Easter, Luther traveled to Heidelberg. For all the questions about his future fate, it must have been one of the most enjoyable journeys of his life. Most of the journey was made on foot, but he rode the last part of the way with Lang and others from Erfurt. It was certainly Luther's first moment in the sun, and many people were now eager to meet the monk from Wittenberg. The bishop of Würzburg received him politely and continued to speak well of him into 1519. At the impressive Heidelberg Castle, Count Wolfgang of the Palatinate entertained Luther, Staupitz, and Lang quite lavishly. Luther was impressed with his warm reception by this brother of another elector. A letter of introduction from Frederick probably helped open the door, although the count had studied at Wittenberg in 1515 and may have already known Luther.

The actual disputation took place not at the Augustinian monastery but at the university. Luther is very complimentary about the good reception they also had there.[33] Luther had written twenty-eight theological theses and another twelve philosophical ones on the themes he had first addressed in the *Disputation against Scholastic Theology* the previous September. But a new concept was introduced

32. "Two Kinds of Righteousness" (1519—or with Brecht 1518), in LW 31:297–306, MLBTW3, 119–25. Brecht's discussion of the writings from early 1518 is very helpful. See Brecht, *Martin Luther*, 1:229–31. He sees this as the true Reformation "breakthrough" for Luther—something most scholars put much earlier.
33. "Letter to George Spalatin" (May 18, 1518), in LW 48:60–63.

in the theological theses—the distinction between two ways of doing theology, which half the group found thrilling and the other half deeply troubling. Luther's *Heidelberg Disputation* theses contrast the old way of what Luther calls "theology of glory" with his new proposal of a "theology of the cross." Yet for Luther the new way was actually the older way, the approach of the Bible and of Augustine and most of the church fathers, that had been lost in the philosophical mazes of Scholasticism.[34]

The various schools (such as the followers of Thomas Aquinas or Bonaventure) that emerged in the later Middle Ages assumed that the theologian would use reason to establish the existence of God and anything else possible to explain with reason alone before proceeding to those distinctively Christian truths (the Trinity as God's nature, or the incarnation of the Son of God) that could be known only by divine revelation.[35]

One argument for this traditional insistence on the philosophical preliminaries before theology was taken from the apostle Paul. In Romans 1, Paul argued that all—both Jews and non-Jews—had sinned and stood in need of God's mercy. Gentiles did not have the law of Moses, but Paul considered that no excuse. They knew in any case what they should have done because the law was written on their hearts in creation, as conscience bore witness. God's reality was a part of creation itself. So Paul asserts: "Ever since the creation of the world, [God's] eternal power and divine nature, invisible though they are, have been understood and seen through the things [God] has made. So they are without excuse" (Rom. 1:20).

---

34. "Heidelberg Disputation" (1518), in LW 31:39–40, MLBTW3, 14–16.
35. An important strand of scholarship insists that Thomas did not, in fact, operate this way. See William C. Placher, *The Domestication of Transcendence: How Modern Thinking about God Went Wrong* (Louisville: Westminster John Knox, 1996), 21–36, for a summary of this minority opinion.

One might have thought that Luther would have been enthusiastic about this Scholastic use of Paul, but for him the very problem came in the result. The God who emerged in the theologies of Thomas, Scotus, and especially Ockham did not seem to be the God whose righteousness and mercy were celebrated in the main argument of Romans. Rather, theirs was a very abstract God, still largely unknown and inscrutable even after all the philosophical and theological work had been done. Thomas thought of God in terms of the categories of "being," whereas Luther needed to think of God in the categories of "person." The theologians of glory, as Luther calls them, had been led astray by Paul's side remark into a false way of thinking about God—with devastating results. They had read the surfaces—"the things God made"—and missed the deepest truth about God—"the theology of the cross."

For Luther, the most important things about God were what he had been finding while lecturing on Psalms, Romans, and Galatians: the mercy of God, the loving-kindness of God, the forgiveness of God for struggling sinners offered in Jesus Christ. These truths could not come from asking rationally what God must be like, because all of them confound human standards and expectations. The cross itself—judged from the world's standards—is the story of Jesus' failure, a tragic or heroic death at best. If the cross—so offensive to humanity as Paul well understood—is the heart of the Christian story, then all bets are off for what God is like or what God requires. Our notions of who God is and how God works will have to be radically recast with careful attention to what the Bible, not human reason, teaches about God.

This would turn out to be Luther's second great discovery, along with justification by faith, which he had come to in the Romans and Galatians lectures. The theology of the cross is, first and foremost, not a theory about how God uses the crucifixion for salvation. It starts with an understanding that God's ways are not our ways (Isa. 55:8) and that those who would speak of the Christian God must do so in "fear and trembling" (Phil. 2:13).

These theses are not easy to understand, and some of them raise issues that Luther had been pressing for some time. But in proposing that differences in the Augustinian Order stemmed from two different ways of doing theology, Luther put his finger on something very important. Most of the older Augustinians were shocked and displeased by Luther's theses. They felt attacked, which was a correct reading of Luther's intention. But many of the younger theologians were quite swayed by Luther's theology and also by his manner of presentation. We have an eyewitness account from someone who was there, Martin Bucer, who later became a major figure in the Reformation in Strasbourg and a recurring presence in Luther's life. Bucer reported:

> Although our chief men refuted him with all their might, their wiles were not able to make him move an inch from his propositions. His sweetness in answering is remarkable, his patience in listening is incomparable, in his explanations one would recognize the acumen of a Paul . . . his answers so brief, so wise, so drawn from the holy scriptures, easily made all his hearers his admirers. . . . He has brought it about that in Wittenberg the ordinary textbooks have all been abolished, while the Greeks and Jerome, Augustine and Paul, are publicly taught.[36]

Luther also reported this generational split to Spalatin at the court. He was happy for the good reception his ideas received among many but very concerned at the hostility of his former Erfurt professors, especially Jodokus Trutfetter, the major philosopher at Erfurt and the man who seventeen years earlier arrived at the university as its new rector. He had written a letter in which he accused Luther of being

---

36. Quoted in James Atkinson, *Martin Luther and the Birth of Protestantism* (London: Penguin, 1968), 161. This older book is still one of the finest introductions to Luther and his thought.

"an ignoramus in dialectic, not to mention theology."[37] But on the whole, Luther had done well, and had apparently steered clear of baiting the pope, as Staupitz had advised him.

Gaining Momentum and a Collaborator

The most significant "win" for Luther at Heidelberg was the positive effect his theology had on a most impressive scholar of the younger generation. This man would arrive in Wittenberg a few months later and in a matter of weeks would become Luther's close friend and most important collaborator. The University of Wittenberg had been hoping to add a professor of Greek, and Frederick the Wise became interested enough to promise money and help with the search for a suitable candidate through his humanistic contacts. The choice was a twenty-one-year-old very slightly built young man named Philip Melanchthon.[38] He had precociously earned degrees from Heidelberg and Tübingen, and his scholarship was already being noticed. It probably helped that he was a nephew of the famous scholar Johannes Reuchlin, who had recently been in trouble with Rome but whose reputation was very good in Germany. Philip's surname was originally Schwartzerd, which is German for "black earth." But like other humanists, he had taken a more elegant (and more difficult to spell) Greek version of the name.[39]

The new professor arrived in Wittenberg on August 24. For all the rumors of Melanchthon's brilliance, many must have attended his inaugural lecture on August 29 with some skepticism about whether this person could hold his own in a faculty with Luther, Carlstadt,

---

37. "Letter to George Spalatin" (May 18, 1518), in LW 48:62.
38. Some have understood Reuchlin to actually be the first choice but to have declined and suggested Melanchthon (who was his nephew) in his stead.
39. For Luther's hopes for a new professor, see the same "Letter to George Spalatin" (May 18, 1518), in LW 48:63. The best life of Melanchthon in English is still Clyde Manschreck, *Melanchthon: The Quiet Reformer* (New York: Abingdon, 1958).

Amsdorf, and many other talented persons. Luther was one of the many won over immediately. He wrote to Spalatin: "Four days after he had arrived, he delivered an extremely learned and absolutely faultless address. All esteemed and admired him greatly, so you need not worry on what grounds you should recommend him to us. We very quickly turned our minds and eyes from his appearance and person to the man himself. We congratulate ourselves on having this man and marvel at what he has in him. We thank the Most Illustrious Sovereign, as well as you, for your efforts."[40]

Luther and Melanchthon quickly became close friends. Though Luther was fourteen years older, from the beginning they worked as colleagues. Melanchthon may have been wary of coming to Wittenberg, and especially of Luther's reputation, but he soon became a powerful articulator of the theology that Luther was developing. Luther learned from Philip's unsurpassed linguistic skills and admired the way that he was soon attracting not only outstanding students but also average and even weak students to the study of Greek.[41] They shared a passion to reform the university away from Scholasticism and toward a combination of the ancient classics and the study of the Bible. By December, they had managed to replace a course in Thomistic logic with one on the Latin poet Ovid.[42]

The men were very different temperamentally. Luther was bold and sometimes rash, but he was a powerful communicator and relatively shrewd about the early political dimensions of the Reformation—both in terms of public opinion and working with the princes. Melanchthon was careful and precise. He was not a leader of others but could produce organized summaries of the faith in a way

---

40. "Letter to George Spalatin" (August 31, 1518), in LW 48:78.
41. It must have happened quickly. Luther reports this to Spalatin within five weeks of Philip's arrival. "Letter to George Spalatin" (October 2, 1518), in LW 48:83.
42. "Letter to George Spalatin" (December 9, 1518), in LW 48:95–96.

that usually eluded Luther. Philip was a far better negotiator. They made a wonderful pair, despite tensions at points later in their lives.[43] Luther had a great capacity for friendship, and whether or not Philip Melanchthon was his best friend cannot be determined. Melanchthon was surely his most important friend and proof that, even nearer its beginning, the movement in Wittenberg was not—as it has so often been portrayed—a one-man show.

Rome Mounts a Response

Luther was still in considerable danger for the sharp attack on Rome in the Ninety-Five Theses, but things were relatively quiet in the first half of 1518. Even into that summer, possibilities for a happy resolution of the complaints to Rome certainly existed. Luther had prepared an *Explanation of the Ninety-Five Theses* early in the year but publication had been forbidden by his ecclesiastical superior, Bishop Schulze of Brandenburg. It was finally printed in August 1518, apparently with encouragement from Staupitz who seemed to think the explanation might help clarify Luther's intentions. Copies were sent to Pope Leo X, to Bishop Schulze, and to Staupitz as Luther's three superiors.

It is hard to assess whether this much longer document could have helped Luther, even had it been read seriously and with openness in Rome. But it did give his opponents a much broader target with which to try to show his "errors," often a first step toward a charge of heresy. On some issues, like the existence of purgatory, Luther seems to be widening his earlier critique of church practice. But nothing like a plan for reformation can yet be found at this stage. Luther

---

43. Melanchthon was privately more honest with other people about his differences with Luther than he was with Luther himself. His correspondence with his friend the humanist Joachim Camerarius displays his concerns with Luther's temperament and even some theological positions.

insists that reform of the church will come but that it will be in God's way and at God's own time.[44]

During the summer, activity stepped up in Rome. In June, Sylvester Prierias, a Dominican theologian and advisor to the pope, was assigned the role of theological judge of Luther's case. He made a summary of possible false teachings in what Luther had written, including the ominous statement, "Whoever says of indulgences that the Roman Church cannot do what it actually does, is a heretic."[45] It is not surprising, then, that in July Luther was ordered to appear in Rome to defend himself against charges of heresy.

Word of this summons reached Wittenberg on August 7, and Luther realized the depth of his trouble. It was theoretically possible that he could go to Rome, come to an agreement, and return, but it was far more likely that his opponents there would have better connections and that he would be condemned as a heretic and either imprisoned or executed. In Germany, where the excesses he had attacked were better understood, he might fare better. So he began a campaign to get Frederick the Wise to arrange to have the hearing conducted in Germany. He wrote to Spalatin the next day, August 8, asking for his help in arranging this concession.[46]

Luther put the case to Spalatin not only on behalf of his personal welfare but also "the honor of almost our whole University." It was a shrewd way to approach Frederick, for few commitments mattered more to him than the fledgling university in Wittenberg. Frederick had paid for Luther's doctorate. He had not been happy about Luther's taking time to go to Heidelberg in April, and a trip to Rome could take a long time—in addition to having an uncertain outcome. Besides, Frederick had just arranged to bring Melanchthon

---

44. "Explanations of the Ninety-Five Theses" (1518), in LW 31:83–252. The comments about a coming reformation come near the end on 250.
45. Cited in Lohse, *Martin Luther's Theology*, 108.
46. "Letter to Spalatin" (August 8, 1518), in LW 48:70–73.

to Wittenberg. He was building something great and did not want it disrupted by unproven charges.

It is impossible to ascertain what degree of sympathy Frederick may have had toward Luther's theology at this point. He was a very traditional Roman Catholic in some ways, but he was also a very proud German. He loved the Bible and had learned a Bible-centered form of faith, likely in part from his friend Spalatin. So he worked to have Luther's examination take place in Germany as Luther had requested. Frederick was actually attending the Diet in Augsburg at this time (diets were regularly occurring meeting of the princes and other nobles of the Holy Roman Empire to conduct its business). The emperor Maximilian I had just written to Pope Leo X concerning Luther, whom he saw as a threat. But Maximilian was old and thought to be dying. Rome agreed to allow Luther's case to be heard by the papal legate Cardinal Cajetan, who was in Augsburg for this protracted meeting of the diet. They, too, were aware that Maximilian had not long to live. That meant a new emperor would soon be elected, and Rome cared desperately who it was. They could see in advance that Frederick's vote would be crucial. There was a chance Frederick himself would be elected. So the pope and his advisors had some willingness to accommodate Frederick—a far more important player than Luther.

It took some months for all these arrangements to be approved in Rome and Augsburg, and then for Wittenberg to be informed. As a result, Luther did not actually meet with the cardinal until October 12 through 14. It was a meeting of two great minds of the period, for Thomas Cajetan—originally Jacopo de Vio of Gaeta—was one of the most theologically astute members of the Roman hierarchy. He was an expert on Thomas Aquinas, having taken the name of that theologian in his honor, so one would expect from him no sympathy for Luther's critique of Scholasticism. And he was a Dominican, the order still smarting from the embarrassing Reuchlin affair. But he knew there were problems with indulgences, and he promised to give Luther a fatherly hearing.

The three days of talks were very difficult. The cardinal began with a demand that Luther recant—something he was not prepared to do. The cardinal felt he was being "fatherly," but Luther remembered a great many threats and much shouting. For Cajetan, the central issue was papal authority and Luther's refusal to acknowledge this absolutely. For Luther, the central issue was the lack of basis for indulgences in the Bible and the early church fathers. Though a good theologian, Cajetan was simply not prepared to debate the Bible with the professor. The debate widened into questions of possible papal error, of the superiority of councils to the pope, and of justification by faith—all key current topics for Luther but also dangerous expansions of the case. Luther finally made the cardinal so angry that he told Luther to recant or never come into his presence again.

Augsburg was full of rumors. Luther began to fear that if he would not recant he would be seized and taken to Rome. On the third day, Luther "borrowed" a horse from an old friend, Martin Glasser, and escaped. He wrote the cardinal saying that he was leaving for Wittenberg. It was a daring and probably shrewd decision on Luther's part. Staupitz was with Luther in Augsburg and on that day released him of his monastic vow, a drastic and dramatic step, so that Luther would not be bound by any order to stay.

Image 9: Cardinal Cajetan examines Luther in Augsburg to find out why he was challenging the papacy.

To defend his fleeing, Luther wrote and published *Proceedings at Augsburg* at the end of November. Luther stuck to his case and pleaded with his readers that, whatever happened to him, they should learn from him not to trust indulgences (as he had once done himself) but to trust only in the "merits of Christ." And in a parting shot, he accused the authorities of using Christ's free gifts "as a pretext for the filthiest and ugliest servitude to profit."[47] Having said that, he expected to be both condemned formally by Rome and banished from Wittenberg. He wrote Spalatin that he was "setting things in order and arranging everything so that if it comes I am prepared and girded to go, as Abraham, not knowing where, yet most sure of my way, because God is everywhere."[48]

47. "Proceedings at Augsburg" (1518), in LW 31:255–92. The quotation is from 291.
48. "Letter to George Spalatin" (November 25, 1518), in LW 48:94.

71

Things had changed by the end of the autumn of 1518. Possibilities for resolution were no longer wide open. The anger in Rome at the Luther case was mounting. Cajetan was insisting that Frederick turn over Luther so that he could be taken to Rome for a proper trial. But Frederick was still not willing to allow Luther to leave Germany. On December 7, 1518, Frederick formally refused the cardinal's request. He would not surrender Luther until he was convinced that he was a heretic; perhaps German scholars—rather than a Roman proceeding dominated by people who, Frederick worried, had personal grudges against Luther—would be best equipped to settle the matter.[49]

It had been an explosive fourteen months since the controversy over indulgences began, and no one in either Wittenberg or Rome knew just what would happen next. But even with Frederick's refusal, Luther had deeply challenged the church's practices and theology in a way that could not bode well for his survival.

49. For details of the legal situation and Frederick's thinking see Brecht, *Martin Luther*, 1:264–65.

4

Theologian for the Church

1519–1520

One's realization that death might well be imminent can be energizing or paralyzing. By the end of 1518, Luther understood the depth of his trouble with Rome and the strong possibility that he would have to flee or be taken prisoner. In Luther's case, the situation made him deeply aware of how much he still had to say. He plunged into the most amazing explosion of important theological writings in a two-year period that had ever been seen in Christendom. And when he was forced to admit his growing doubts about the papacy at the Leipzig Debate in the summer of 1519, he was set free to say all that he wanted to say, especially in anything he wrote, despite counsel and pressure from friends and princes to be restrained.

Mediators and Potential Allies

The new year of 1519 actually began on a more conciliatory note. Rome was determined that Luther recant, but there was not any hurry about the matter, especially with the emperor near death and with Luther's prince Frederick so important in the balance of power. So when Cajetan reported the failure of his attempt to deal with Luther in a firm but fatherly way, something else had to be tried. A minor Saxon noble, Karl von Miltitz (ca. 1490–1529), who had held a variety of lower positions in Rome, was allowed to try his hand at mediation. He could not make any settlement with Luther without the agreement of Cajetan, who continued as the papal legate in Germany. But little could be lost by seeing what he might find out in talking to all parties, especially to Frederick, whose intentions were hard to read. Miltitz was to award Frederick the papal Golden Rose—at the right time in negotiations and having warned him not to shelter heresy and thereby risk his own salvation.

Image 10: Emperor Maximilian I died just as the Luther situation was heating up.

Von Miltitz stopped in Nuremberg on his way to Saxony, and there he found many important people who were very supportive of Luther. The Nurembergers tried to play a double role. They cautioned Miltitz that Luther was not to be dismissed as a heretic priest but should be seen as one who spoke for many in Germany. But they also wrote to Luther and urged him to take the visitor seriously and not to dismiss out of hand his efforts toward a negotiated settlement.

Thus, very early in 1519 Luther found himself again talking to a papal representative, but this time with a very different tone. They met at Frederick's castle at Altenberg on January 4. Von Miltitz was surprised how young Luther was. They spent two days working out a four-point plan: Luther would keep silence (if his opponents would do the same); he would write to the pope a letter of humble submission; he would issue a little book "to admonish everyone to follow the Roman church, to be obedient and respect it"; and Luther's case would be referred to a bishop in the German lands—perhaps the archbishop of Salzburg—rather than be settled in Rome. Luther reported all this to Frederick, adding that von Miltitz did not think that these proposals went far enough but that they were a good start toward resolution.[1]

Luther never sent the humble letter of submission to the pope, but he did write a draft that has survived. The key paragraph shows both how far Luther was willing to go and why the effort was probably doomed from the outset:

> Most Holy Father, before God and all his creation, I testify that I have never wanted, nor do I today want, to touch in any way the authority of the Roman Church and of your Holiness or demolish it by any craftiness. On the contrary I confess the authority of this church to be supreme over all, and that nothing, be it in heaven or earth, is to be

---

1. "Letter to Frederick the Wise" (January 5 or 6, 1519), in LW 48:97–100.

preferred to it, save the one Lord Christ who is Lord of all—nor should Your Holiness believe the schemers who claim otherwise, plotting evil against this Martin.[2]

By mid-summer, as he spelled out the full significance for him of the phrase "save the one Jesus Christ who is Lord of all," Luther would be talking in a way that would make such submission impossible.

Image 11: Charles V was the most powerful ruler Europe had seen for centuries, and was Emperor for nearly all of Luther's career.

In a few days, it was all beside the point as news was received that Emperor Maximilian I had died on January 12. Looking back on these years near the end of his life, Luther admitted that with that news "the storm ceased to rage a bit."[3] Frederick was now one of two

2. "Letter to Pope Leo X" (written January 5 or 6, 1519, but not sent), in LW 48:102.
3. "Preface to the Complete Edition of Luther's Latin Writings" (1545), in LW 34:332.

imperial vicars to act until another emperor could be elected. Rome was for the next six months focused on efforts to prevent the likely candidate, Maximilian's grandson Charles V (1500–1558), king of Spain, from being elected. They preferred the king of France, or even Frederick himself, because of fear for the preponderance of power Charles would hold if elected.

This remarkable young heir of the House of Hapsburg was on his way to becoming the most powerful man in Europe in the last thousand years. He inherited the reign over the Low Countries, Austria, and parts of France from his father's side. As the grandson of Ferdinand and Isabella of Spain, Charles also ruled that vast kingdom—including the new possessions in the Americas from which gold was pouring in during the first decades of the sixteenth century. If he became emperor, he would be in a position to dominate Europe, to defeat his only rivals—the kings of France and England—and to put intense pressure on the papacy itself. Spain already controlled the southern part of the Italian peninsula, and Rome feared that the election of Charles would make the pope as dependent on him as the fourteenth-century popes had been on the king of France.

But von Miltitz went about his mission as if it still mattered. Contemporaries—including Luther himself, who was very put off when the noble flattered him and said farewell with an embrace and a kiss—could never quite decide whether or not to take him seriously.[4] But over the next few years, Luther again and again found himself having another conversation with von Miltitz, who would not give up on the notion that he personally could work something out. To that end, in March 1519 he visited Leipzig and made the Dominican monk Tetzel appear before him for a public scolding

---

4. Martin Brecht, *Martin Luther*, vol. 1: *His Road to Reformation, 1483–1521*, trans. James L. Schaaf (Philadelphia: Fortress Press, 1985), 269.

about his handling of the sale of indulgences. Von Miltitz hoped word of this would get back to Wittenberg, which of course is just what happened.[5]

For the next months and, as it eventually turned out, for most of the next two years, Luther was surprisingly free to do his theological work, to the extent that he could squeeze it in on top of his teaching, preaching, monastic obligations, and occasional polemics against his growing number of opponents. He did not follow the advice of the Nurembergers to be cautious in what he wrote, but he did make some attempts to reach out in this period, including an important first letter to Erasmus in March 1519.

Luther tried to humble himself appropriately to address the great man, setting aside his own reservations about Erasmus's theology (or lack of theology), which he had held for several years. The occasion was a visit to the scholar by Luther's old school friend Caspar Schalbe and Wittenberg colleague Justus Jonas. Luther wrote in the most flattering and humanistic style that he could manage, saluting Erasmus for his "outstanding spirit, which has enriched my own and that of all others." Noting that he heard that Erasmus had encountered Luther's work, Luther asks to be regarded as a "little brother in Christ." He also sent greeting from Melanchthon, who was better known in humanistic circles, and from Andreas Carlstadt.[6]

Erasmus did not immediately write back to Luther, waiting to send a letter with Schalbe and Jonas when they returned from Wittenberg. He did ask in a letter to Frederick the Wise in April that Frederick

---

5. Tetzel was very ill at this point and died not long afterward, largely deserted by those whom he had served. Luther wrote to him words of encouragement, noting that it was not Tetzel who had started all the fuss, "but the child has quite a different father." Cited in Ludwig Pastor, *History of the Popes*, vol. 7 (London: Routledge, 1950), 382. The letter is not extant, but Luther's early contemporary and opponent Jerome Emser describes its contents this way. Some have thought Luther implied that he himself was the father, but the more likely reading is that Luther thought God was stirring up a new movement against abuses.

6. "Letter to Erasmus of Rotterdam" (March 28, 1519), in LW 48:117–19.

protect learning against its enemies—a broad plea that would include scholars such as Reuchlin and Erasmus himself (who was beginning to experience his share of attacks from loyalist Roman Catholics), but also Luther and Melanchthon. In his eventual reply to Luther, written May 30, he combined a few reports of praise and the regard in which Luther was held with a broad scolding for Luther's lack of caution in attacking dangerous targets. If Luther would not practice more restraint, he would bring trouble on the whole enterprise of scholarship, including Erasmus. It was a chilly beginning to what would never be a friendship, but it would not break into open hostility until Erasmus's attack on Luther in 1524.

Ordinary Devotion

Those who wanted Luther to step cautiously would probably have approved of his first area of intense writing: a set of helps for spirituality and the devotional life. But for Luther this was a priority—not chosen only as a safe option—because he had come to see that *faith* in God was the central issue.[7] These next writings tended to be quite positive and free from polemic, and they do a great deal more to articulate Luther's understanding of the gospel, which was so central in all he did. The traditional piety had not worked for him, and his experience of pastoral work in Wittenberg continued to expose him to people who could not connect with the love and grace of God in Jesus under the medieval options.

He had a major opportunity to reach that audience in "A Meditation on Christ's Passion," which appeared in April 1519. Luther felt that the traditional Holy Week observance tended to confuse people rather than help them find the gospel. He speaks

---

7. For an excellent introduction to the migration of theology's center from love of God to faith in God, see Berndt Hamm, *The Early Luther: Stages in a Reformation Reorientation*, trans. Marcus Lohrmann (Grand Rapids, MI: Eerdmans, 2013), 1–25 and 59–84.

sharply against those who spend Holy Week "venting their anger on the Jews," which does nothing to bring them to the real point: "the sufferings of Christ."[8]

The right contemplation of the story of Christ leads to a twofold movement—of dying and rising, of humiliation and exaltation. You must stop blaming others and come to see that the story of Christ points toward your own sin, that you too have turned from God. "You must get this through your head and not doubt that you are the one who is torturing Christ thus, for your sins have surely wrought this."[9] You cannot escape this movement (as the proud might wish), but you also dare not become stuck in this awareness of sin, "for that would lead to sheer despair," as Luther knew personally and heard had happened to many others.

The glory of Holy Week and the destination of one who hears the story of Christ is to move beyond the sufferings of Christ and to see and be transformed by "his friendly heart and how this heart beats with . . . love for you." This will not only change your view of Christ from judge to savior, but if you follow the story to the end, it will change your understanding of who God is:

> Now continue and rise beyond Christ's heart to God's heart and you will see that Christ would not have shown this love for you if God in his eternal love had not wanted this, for Christ's love for you is due to his obedience to God. Thus you will find the divine and kind parental heart, and, as Christ says, you will be drawn to the Father through him. Then you will understand the words of Christ, "For God so loved the world that he gave his only Son, etc." (John 3:16) We know God aright when we grasp him not in his might or wisdom (for then he proves terrifying), but in his kindness and love. Then faith and confidence are able to exist, and then man is truly born anew in God.[10]

8. "Meditation on Christ's Passion" (1519), in LW 42:7, MLBTW3, 126.
9. LW 42:9, MLBTW3, 127.
10. LW 42:13, MLBTW3, 130.

This is the great discovery of the theology of the cross, which emerged in Heidelberg the previous April. But now Luther presents it not in terms attacking Scholasticism, but in moving language that speaks to the Christian struggling to find a coherent faith.

Two other pamphlets followed almost immediately, both dealing with prayer. "An Exposition of the Lord's Prayer for Simple Laymen" grew out of Luther's catechetical preaching in Wittenberg.[11] He wanted Christians to understand the basics of the faith, and no place was better to begin than the Lord's Prayer, which teaches us how to subordinate our needs and demands to God's priorities. This substantial pamphlet went through thirteen editions in the next three years and soon was known all over Europe. A Venetian printer exclaimed: "Blessed are the hands that wrote this," but not everyone was so satisfied.[12] Duke George, the ruler of the other part of Saxony, chided Luther that it had made his "simple laymen" so confused that they could no longer pray at all.

There was a tradition in the three days before Ascension Day of pilgrimages through the fields, praying for the crops that were soon to be planted. This observance of Rogationtide had originally started to counter and co-opt the Roman festival of Robigalia. But Luther knew that the processions had degenerated into an excuse for heavy drinking and immorality, so he wrote instructions for how one might properly pray for the harvest and have a procession that was truly solemn.[13]

Luther had another opportunity to write about spiritual matters in August 1519 when his prince and protector Frederick the Wise fell very ill after his return from the imperial election. Frederick held very traditional medieval beliefs about his relics and had a love of

---

11. "An Exposition of the Lord's Prayer for Simple Laymen," in LW 42:19–81.
12. WA 2:75.
13. "On Rogationtide Prayer and Procession," in LW 42:87–93.

the saints, including the Fourteen Holy Helpers, who had become a staple of Roman Catholic devotional life for a century. One of Lucas Cranach's earliest paintings was of these interceding saints—such as Christopher—for the grave of Frederick's sister-in-law.

Without attacking that tradition, Luther reformed it by writing *Fourteen Consolations*, a book initially intended for the prince alone but eventually published the next year at Spalatin's insistence. Luther wrote in Latin and asked Spalatin, the chaplain to Frederick, to translate it for him into German. Luther used a very visual approach—asking the elector to imagine first seven evils, then the seven comforts. Each had a location—one within, one before, one behind, one beneath, one on the left hand, one on the right hand, and one above. The evils allow the struggling person to face the realities of sin, death, and the devil, but these are driven out by the seven comforts that evoke the many promises of God. The final blessing or comfort is Christ about us, with us in life, who promises God's mercy and love at the hour of our death.[14]

Later that fall, Luther finished this round of spiritual writings with his remarkable "Sermon on Preparing to Die." The fear of death had been a major problem for many in Luther's time, and the church sometimes seemed to play on that fear for its own benefit rather than to provide any pastoral help. Many of Luther's devotional writings came from requests from persons with struggles, and in this case he wrote upon the repeated request of one of Frederick's counselors, Mark Schart, who experienced deep distress whenever he thought of death.[15]

Luther's advice was to immerse oneself in the gospel, in the promises of God that are one's only hope, but he was not unaware of practical considerations. His first point in the sermon was that those

---

14. "Fourteen Consolations," in LW 42:121–66.
15. "Sermon on Preparing to Die," in LW 42:99–115, MLBTW3, 392–402.

who are dying should put their own affairs in order, something that he did himself in 1542 when he began to think again that he would not live long. But that is only the preliminary stage. The real resource for dying is to have heard the gospel and lived it through long years, learning to trust God in all circumstances, so that fear—while real and understandable—is not the final word for Christians. "Love and praise make dying very much easier," says Luther, and while it is never too late to hear the gospel, love and praise are practices the Christian can learn in advance.[16]

Luther continued to write treatises on prayer and other spiritual matters through the 1520s. He was less concerned with such writing after 1530, but all his life he continued to write letters of spiritual advice and counsel to clergy, to princes, to town officials, to grieving persons, even to his barber. He did not have to change gears to address questions of faith and doubt, of life and death. These were Luther's own deepest questions, and his whole project of reorienting theology put such questions at the heart of its work.[17]

Dispute in Leipzig

Even though the Roman authorities were not dealing actively with Luther's case in the first half of 1519, his German opponents were hard at work trying to counter his sudden popularity and influence. Dr. Johannes Maier was generally called Eck for the name of his birthplace, a town in southern Germany. He was originally friendly with Luther but in 1518 wrote a blistering attack on the Ninety-Five Theses called *Obelisks*. Luther, never slow to respond in those days, countered with an equally sharp pamphlet called *Asterisks*. Eck

---

16. LW 42:115, MLBTW3, 402.
17. These letters that so splendidly complicate the picture of Luther's person have been collected in Theodore Tappers, ed., *Luther: Letters of Spiritual Counsel* (Philadelphia: Westminster, 1965).

was quickly established as Luther's chief critic and a fierce papal defender.[18]

But in the meantime, Luther's senior colleague at Wittenberg, Andreas Carlstadt, got into his own debate with Eck. He felt that some of the comments in Eck's writings were an attack on Wittenberg University, and he issued 370 theses in defense of the theological faculty. Eck tried to drop the whole thing at this point, but the arguments were out in the open and Carlstadt challenged Eck to a public disputation. The University of Leipzig, the proposed locale for the encounter, was not enthusiastic about having controversy about indulgences spill over into their university. But eventually, publicity got ahead of agreements to such an extent that a debate in July in Leipzig was now inevitable.

Many people in Germany would have enjoyed seeing Luther and Eck air the issues of the Ninety-Five Theses, but in the months before the debate Eck published a list of the propositions that he intended to defend—most on indulgences, but the final one on papal authority itself. This was the line that Tetzel and the Dominicans had immediately pursued against Luther, and it was a far more dangerous topic for Luther's case than the sale of indulgences—which even some powerful people in Rome criticized. But the debate was scheduled to be between Eck and Carlstadt; Duke George of Saxony, who intended to be present at the debate, had many reservations about giving Luther a platform in his territory.

Through the spring of 1519, Luther seemed resigned to debating Eck and at points even eager. He wrote to Staupitz in February that Leipzig University had now agreed to the debate but refused to allow Luther to participate. It was shaping up to be less an encounter of Luther versus Eck than of Wittenberg versus Leipzig. The older

18. For background to the Leipzig debate, see Brecht, *Martin Luther*, 1: ch. 9; and the introduction to Luther's account, "The Leipzig Debate," in LW 31:309–12.

university was quite confident of the outcome, despite the spectacular growth of Wittenberg at just that time. Luther reported that the town could hardly find lodging for all the students who were flocking in.[19]

Late in June, a great crowd traveled from Wittenberg to Leipzig for the debate, which actually lasted several weeks. In a bad omen, as they were coming into the city the cart in which Carlstadt was riding lost a wheel, and the theologian and his many books were scattered. It still was not clear whether Luther would be allowed to participate, but in the end something was worked out. Late in his life, Luther reported that Eck himself had taken the initiative:

> Here Eck came to me in my lodging and said that he had heard that I refused to debate. I replied, "How can I debate, since I cannot get a safe conduct from Duke George?" "If I cannot debate with you," he said, "neither do I want to with Karlstadt, for I have come here on your account, What if I obtain safe conduct for you? Would you then debate with me?" "Obtain," I said, "and it shall be." He left, and soon a safe conduct was given me too and the opportunity to debate.[20]

The occasion opened June 27 with solemn festivities, including music by the Saint Thomas Choir and a lecture by the Leipzig humanist Peter Mosellanus admonishing the participants to proceed gently and "avoid rancor." Eck and Carlstadt debated the rest of that day and the next, but June 29 was the festival of Saints Peter and Paul. Luther and Eck did not begin until July 4, with Eck and Carlstadt having a final two days at the end. It was an exhaustive and exhausting airing of the issues, and all three men impressed observers with their learning, which was able to fill so much time and to argue issues so closely.

Mosellanus himself has left rather candid portraits of the three debaters, and his account of Luther is fascinating evidence of how a rather neutral person saw the Augustinian at this point in his career.

19. "Letter to John von Staupitz" (February 28, 1519), LW 48:109–10. Luther reports on the growth of Wittenberg in "Letter to George Spalatin" (May 22, 1519), in LW 48:123–24.
20. "Preface to the Complete Edition of Luther's Latin Works" (1545), in LW 34:333.

Martin is of medium height with a gaunt body that has been so exhausted by studies and worries that one can almost count the bones under his skin; yet he is manly and vigorous, with a high, clear voice. He is full of learning and has an excellent knowledge of the Scriptures, so that he can refer to facts as if they were at his fingers' tips. He knows enough Greek and Hebrew to enable him to pass judgments on interpretations. He is also not lacking in subject material and has a large store of words and ideas. In his life and behavior he is very courteous and friendly, and there is nothing of the stern stoic or grumpy fellow about him. He can adjust to all occasions. In a social gathering he is gay, witty, lively, ever full of joy, always has a bright and happy face, no matter how seriously his adversaries threaten him. The only fault everyone criticizes in him is that he is somewhat too violent and cutting in his reprimands, in fact more than is proper for one seeking to find new trails in theology, and certainly also for a divine; this is probably a weakness of all those who have gained their learning somewhat late.[21]

This basically positive evaluation sounds much like Martin Bucer's report from the Heidelberg Disputation a year earlier, but perhaps the tendency toward polemic is now more pronounced.

On the festival of Peter and Paul, the duke of Pomerania had invited Luther to preach in the castle church, but the crowd was so great that the service had to be transferred to the debating hall. Luther took the Gospel for the day, Matt. 16:13-19, Peter's confession at Caesarea Philippi, as a way to preview the position he would take five days later when he finally was allowed to debate. The truth of the gospel is not a matter for reason or free will; Jesus tells Peter, who has confessed him to be the Christ, "Flesh and blood had not revealed this to you, but my father who is heaven." This is the deep Christian conviction that one must despair of one's own goodness and call upon the grace of God. This was another form of Luther's emphasis of faith as gift, and while controversial, it was not especially dangerous.[22]

---

21. Cited in Brecht, *Martin Luther*, 1:313, along with interesting portraits of Carlstadt and Eck.
22. "Sermon at the Castle Church in Leipzig" (June 29, 1519), in LW 51:56–59.

But Luther went on to speak of Jesus' promise to Peter, "I will give you the keys of the kingdom." This was the classic text for defending papal authority and primacy in the church. Luther insists that the matter is not very complicated:

> It is not necessary for the ordinary man to dispute much about the power of St. Peter or the pope. What is more important is to know how one should use it for salvation. It is true that the keys were given to St. Peter, but not to him personally, but rather to the person of the Christian church. They were actually given to me and to you for the comfort of our consciences. St. Peter, or a priest, is a servant of the keys. The church is the woman and the bride, whom he should serve with the power of the keys, just as we see in daily use that the sacrament is administered to all who desire it of the priest.[23]

This was not being careful, as Luther's humanist friends had hoped he would be in Leipzig.

During the debate, it did not take Eck long to turn the question from indulgences to that of the power of the pope. Like many Catholics who opposed Luther, he was not blind to the failings of individual popes or problems in the church. But he believed order could be maintained only if there were a central focus of authority. For such folk, memories of the humiliation of the papacy when it was the puppet of the French king in the fourteenth century acted as a warning against any dissent on this point. The church had finally gotten itself back together at the Council of Constance (1414–1418), and the way forward was not with a fresh assault on the papacy from Germany.

Constance was also the council that summoned John Hus (ca. 1369–1415), the Bohemian reformer, to appear, and where under somewhat complicated circumstances Hus was burned at the stake. Now a century later, part of the church in Bohemia was still split

---

23. LW 51:59.

from Rome. Prague—the city of Hus and the Hussites—was not far from the territory of Duke George, and he was no friend of that "heresy." So when Eck began to accuse Luther of being a Hussite himself, the duke took careful notice of Luther's reply.

Luther was sharply critical of the exaggerated claims for papal authority in the last four centuries that he felt went hand in hand with the decline of the church. He pointed to the Greek churches that had never been subordinate to Rome, although Eck was able to give some powerful counterexamples of his own. They were debating the history of the church and the classic biblical passages for the authority of Peter and his successors. But when Luther was challenged about Hus, he was puzzled, as he had always considered Hus a heretic. But Luther did remark in passing that not all the articles of Hus that the council had condemned were actually heretical. This showed that not only popes but also councils could err. Everything had to be tested by Scripture, just as they were doing now in asking about the biblical basis for papal authority. This seemed very radical to the Leipzig faculty and to Duke George, and it was not very well received.

In the end, Eck did a very good job of making clear that Luther was not only a critic of abuses in the church but of the very structure of the church itself. The winner of the debate was to be determined neither by Wittenberg nor Leipzig, but by an account of the debate submitted to the Universities of Erfurt and Paris for a decision. Luther knew that the citizens of Leipzig had been won over but that the result of the debate was far from a united front against Roman abuses. He wrote to Spalatin: "Since Eck and the people of Leipzig sought their own glory and not the truth at the debate, it is no wonder that it began badly and ended worse. Whereas we had hoped for harmony between the people of Wittenberg and Leipzig, they acted so hatefully that I fear that it will seem that discord and dislike were actually born here."[24] It is hard to know what Luther went into the debate expecting, but he came out of it exposed as a very deep critic of the church, one who questioned not only popes but also councils. And he came out of the debate with two determined enemies who worked against him as long as they lived: Duke George until his death in 1539 and John Eck until his death in 1543.

Frederick the Wise had missed the chance to hear his theologian debate in the presence of his cousin and rival, Duke George. Frederick had been all this time in Augsburg on imperial business, culminating in the election of Charles V as emperor on June 28—the day before Luther's sermon. Frederick had refused all the enticements of Leo X to become a candidate himself or to participate in blocking Maximilian's young grandson, who assumed this office at the very young age of nineteen. He heard an earful from Eck, who visited him after his return to complain of Luther and to inform Frederick that he intended to travel to Rome to help make the case against Frederick's professor.

Fortunately, there were other reports than just Eck's and Luther's. Philip Melanchthon had attended the debate; he came back to Wittenberg and wrote a glowing report of how well Luther had performed. This was widely circulated among the humanists who were nervous about Luther but trusted Melanchthon and had no particular use for Eck, who still supported Scholastic theology.

John Lang in Erfurt did his best to convince the university there that they should take no position at all. This made Duke George furious, and he insisted in a face-to-face meeting in Erfurt on December 29 that they reach a decision. They continued to refuse, which was itself something of a victory for Luther, since he had enough opponents in his old university that they were not likely to decide for him. The theologians of Paris delayed making their

---

24. "The Leipzig Debate," in LW 31:325.

decision until 1520 because they wanted payment to read the long accounts of the arguments.

Luther went back to Wittenberg and began to read Hus seriously. He also started a correspondence with people in Bohemia and soon realized that he was largely in agreement with what Hus had taught. "We are all Hussites and did not know it!" he wrote to Spalatin the next winter.[25] And in his Table Talk decades later, he could say that he was grateful to Eck for provoking him: "He made me wide awake."[26]

Image 12: Luther had always assumed that the Bohemian reformer Jan Hus' views were heretical. Once he read them for himself, he was not so sure.

25. "Letter to George Spalatin" (February 14, 1520), in LW 48:53.
26. "Table Talk for Winter of 1542–43," in LW 54:445.

Two years earlier, Luther was claiming to be "free." Now he was "awake." For the next eighteen months after Leipzig, he was able to spend most of his energy on his theological work, writing in an increasingly radical way as he followed his biblical and historical studies to their startling conclusions. Eck had set him free from pretending to be only a critic of abuses and had given him the energy and courage to write his great theological works of late 1519 and 1520.

Galatians, Sacraments, and the Nature of the Church

The first task was already completed before Leipzig—namely, putting before the public more of what made Luther tick: the biblical theology from his lecturing at Wittenberg. The Roman demands to submit to human traditions reminded Luther so powerfully of the obstacles that Paul faced with the Galatians. Luther had been revising his lectures from 1516–1517 both in light of the changing situation and of all that he had learned in the meantime. He now had Melanchthon for a colleague, a man with great linguistic and developing theological skills. Philip worked with Luther through the spring and summer of 1519 preparing this work for publication.

Luther dedicated *Lectures on Galatians* to his Wittenberg theological colleagues Andreas Carlstadt and Peter Lupinus. He noted that many wanted to correct him, saying: "I find almost as many teachers as readers, and free of charge at that." Correction is always possible unless the issue is the gospel, which is what Paul faced in Galatia. That apostle even had to stand up to Peter and confront him face-to-face when his behavior obscured the grace of God being shown to the gentiles. This had been his overriding goal from the beginning: "I have wanted to kindle the interest of others in Paul's theology, and this no good man will charge against me as a fault."[27]

But what an explosive epistle Galatians as interpreted by Luther turned out to be! It was full of a radical sense of the gospel as gift, of justification by faith, and above all of Christian freedom. Luther was probably the first Christian theologian to notice freedom as central to Paul, and he would return to that theme at the end of 1520 in his famous treatise, *Freedom of a Christian.* Though contemporary readers found Luther's exposition powerful—it was read widely beyond Germany in a very short time—he became dissatisfied with it almost as soon as it had been published. He returned to this letter in a much more massive way in his 1535 *Lectures on Galatians.* But he admitted near the end of the exposition that if this message could be heard in the church "outside the pale of danger, I would gladly and thankfully bear the reproach of being called a heretic."[28]

Luther turned to a fresh interpretation of the sacraments. He had begun with marriage in his "Sermon on Marriage" given in January of that year. Though it still shows many traces of his monkish attitudes (including marriage as a hospital for lust), it is surprisingly positive about marriage as a gift from God, with a refreshing sense of both the companionate nature of the relationship and the seriousness of the call to rearing children. Luther's own marriage was still seven years off, but this is one of the more positive interpretations of marriage—as opposed to celibacy—that had appeared in many centuries.

By the autumn of 1519, Luther had concluded that only two or three of the traditional seven sacraments really are sacraments—with an express biblical warrant. So he wrote a trilogy of sermons on these three—penance, Baptism, and the Lord's Supper—in which his new biblical and communal understanding of each begins to emerge. In all of these he is also stressing the importance of faith—the faith that

27. *Lectures on Galatians* (1519), in LW 27:153, 160.
28. LW 27:408.

receives the promises of God. This would lead some critics to say that Luther was making the promises depend on the faith of the person receiving it (which puts human work back in the center), and Luther would have to clarify this in future writings without backing down on the importance of faith as trust and reception of the gifts of grace.

The "Sermon on Penance" argues that while all the emphasis has been on reconciliation with the church and overcoming the church's penalties, the true meaning of penance is reconciliation with God and new life for the one who receives forgiveness. Christians should respect the authority of the church and of the priest but also remember that "in the New Testament every Christian had this authority to forgive sins, where a priest is not at hand." The heart of forgiveness is a new relationship with God and a fresh start in loving others.[29]

"The Holy and Blessed Sacrament of Baptism" followed the next month. This sacrament had not generated a Reformation dispute between Luther and his Roman opponents, and there is no sign yet of an attack on infant baptism that will distress Luther in the 1520s. He simply celebrates Baptism as something wonderful that has hardly been noticed because of the one-sided concentration on the Mass. But in Baptism, even if sin is not completely rooted out, God establishes a covenant with the baptized person. The whole life of a Christian is one of daily return to Baptism and confidence in the promise of God to love and to forgive.[30]

By the time he wrote "The Blessed Sacrament of the Holy and True Body of Christ, and the Brotherhoods," Luther was hitting his stride. The treatise quickly became famous because, in an aside near the beginning, Luther remarked:

For my part, however, I would consider it a good thing if the church

29. "The Sacrament of Penance" (1519), in LW 35: 9–22.
30. "Holy and Blessed Sacrament of Baptism" (1519), in LW 35:29–43.

should again decree in a general council that all persons be given both kinds, like the priests. Not because one kind is insufficient, since indeed the desire of faith is alone sufficient. . . . But it would be fitting and fine that the form, or sign, of the sacrament be given not in part only, but in its entirety, just as I said of baptism: it would be more fitting to immerse in the water than to pour with it, for the sake of completeness and perfection of the sign.[31]

Giving the laity the wine as well as the bread had been one of the chief demands of Hus and his followers. Even though Luther was not proposing to do this without the consent of a general council, he was reinforcing in the eyes of his opponents the sense that he was simply the new Hus.

The heart of the treatise, however, is one of Luther's finest descriptions of the meaning of the Lord's Supper. In this sacrament, he understands that a double exchange takes place. The primary thrust is vertical—our sins and burdens are cast on Christ, and we receive with Christ's body divine holiness and righteousness as a gift. With this comes a secondary but also important consequence—a horizontal exchange with members who share the body. Not only are they forgiven, but they also receive one another as a new community. Those who would share in the profit must also share in the costs.

Luther knows well enough that human beings want the gift without the responsibility, the forgiveness without the community. But this is to misunderstand what is happening in the supper. The sacrament draws us out of ourselves:

When you then have partaken of this sacrament . . . you must in turn share the misfortunes of the fellowship. . . . Here your heart must go out in love and learn that this is a sacrament of love. As love and support are given to you, you in turn must render love and support to Christ in his needy ones. You must feel with sorrow all the dishonor done to

31. "The Blessed Sacrament of the Holy and True Body of Christ, and the Brotherhoods" (1519), in LW 35:50, MLBTW3, 185–86.

Christ in his holy Work, all the misery of Christendom, all the unjust suffering of the innocent, with which the world is everywhere filled to overflowing. You must fight, work, pray, and—if you cannot do more—have heartfelt sympathy. . . . See, as you uphold all of them, so they all in turn uphold you; and all things are in common, both good and evil. Then all things become easy, and the evil spirit cannot stand up against the fellowship.[32]

Luther contrasts this community of mutual love and support with the behavior of the brotherhoods or "confraternities" that in his time were very popular lay organizations, originally organized for devotional and charitable purposes. There may have been good people in these groups originally, even some in Luther's time, but he felt the more common experience was that they served as a pretext for partying, just as the solemn processions through the fields had become an excuse for a day of heavy drinking in the countryside. Christians do not need other organizations for devotion or charity, for this is the heart of the church—a community gathered around the word and strengthened by the sacraments.

This is Luther's third great insight—the communal nature of the church set over against the hierarchical understanding of his Roman opponents. This concept was both exciting and frightening. It had a biblical note of authenticity. But if the church were simply the community gathered around the forms of God's gracious presence, what in the world would happen to the massive structures developed through the centuries? Luther was almost ready to answer that question at the beginning of 1520.

Good Works, Reform, Captivity

The writings of Luther from 1520 seem to many to be his most substantial contribution to Christian theology. In four long treatises,

---

32. LW 35:54, MLBTW3, 188.

he spelled out his understanding of Christian ethics, his program for the reformation of church and society, his deepest attack on the medieval sacramental system, and his developed notion of Christian freedom. These treatises were noticed in Luther's time and have been among the most widely read of his works. Concerns about his own legal situation did not become central again until the end of this year, so even with lecturing and some inevitable polemical pamphlets against his enemies, Luther still had time to prepare these four major theological works.[33]

Luther's strong emphasis on grace, Christ as gift, and justification by faith led many of his critics to complain from the beginning of his career that these teachings would undercut good works and lead to an erosion of the Christian life. Luther had an opportunity to address that charge in the first of the four, *Treatise on Good Works*, written during the first half of the year and published in June. Luther dedicated it to Frederick's brother and coruler Duke John of Saxony even though Frederick himself—through Spalatin—urged Luther to write on this topic and so reply to his critics.[34]

Luther's reformulation of good works has several aspects. They cannot be for him a road to praising God or earning salvation. They are instead the fruit of faith, the good things that a human being who has found peace with God and wants to serve God and neighbor freely will do. And they are also the result of Christians who understand the law, whose fulfillment is love of neighbor. But the writing also contains a powerful critique of the content of the works that were most popular in Luther's time—going on pilgrimages,

---

33. These writings are often seen as representing his developed theological position, but that is a more complex matter. He continued to develop his sacramental theology through the 1520s and changed his mind about a number of details about reform should take place both in church and in society. But the understanding of good works and of how freedom in the first and the last of these major works are fully developed positions for him. Later writings on these topics hone his 1520 positions without changing them.

34. "Treatise on Good Works" (1520), in LW 44:21–121.

buying indulgences, giving to religious beggars, paying for masses for the dead. These are not the things that God cares about, and they actually do little good.

The right understanding of good works is found in an evangelical reading of the Ten Commandments. Luther drew on sermons on this material that he had given in Wittenberg in the past five years. Each commandment gives clues about the kinds of things God cares about. Serving God turns out not to require leaving home or spending money, but simply serving in the ordinary relationships of life. Luther can interpret these commandments rather freely, however, so that keeping the Sabbath does not mean avoiding activity but rather means participating actively in the Mass and trying to get something for daily living out of the sermon.

During the summer, Luther assembled his own program for what should happen in Germany, his rhetorically powerful *To the Christian Nobility of the German Nation concerning the Reform of the Christian Estate*. This writing was designed to get the attention of the authorities, for Luther had come to believe that nothing helpful could come from Rome, which he saw as indifferent to the suffering of the church and blocking every attempt at reform. He called on the German rulers to become "emergency bishops" and set their hand to making the necessary changes in the church and also in the universities and society in general. He was building effectively on a tradition of *gravamina*, or grievances, that had been presented at almost every German diet in recent years.[35]

Luther was very much aware of the dramatic nature of such an appeal. His opening line reflects this emergency situation: "The time for silence is past, and the time to speak has come." Luther will no longer keep silent about what is wrong; he will say what everyone has

---

35. *To the Nobility of the German Nation Concerning the Reform of the Christian Estate* (1520), in LW 44:123–217.

been thinking but no one dared to say. Perhaps Luther the monk and professor is an unlikely person to take the lead in such great matters, as he admits early in the treatise. But he laughingly remembers that Abraham once had to listen to his wife, even though women were usually ignored, and, even more to the point, the prophet Balaam was rebuked by his donkey. "If God spoke then through an ass against a prophet, why should he not be able even now to speak through a righteous man against the pope?"[36]

The pope is the major target of this treatise, although Luther means not only Leo but the whole organizational structure of the Roman administration, including German bishops who, out of fearful loyalty to Rome, fail to do their duty to their people. In extremely sharp and memorable language, Luther argued that the popes had built three walls that prevented reformation—all of them based on lies. The first was that spiritual power was superior to temporal power. That clearly contrasted with the teaching of the New Testament that all Christians are priests together—the first strong statement of the Reformation concept of the priesthood of all the baptized.[37]

Anyone who has come out of the baptismal water, Luther asserts, is already a priest or a bishop, although it is good that certain persons exercise those offices on behalf of the entire community. "Because we are all priests of equal standing, no one must push himself forward and take it upon himself, without our consent and election, to do that for which we all have equal authority."[38] If popes and bishops do not tend to their task with integrity, instead getting distracted into war and immoral living, then it is right that the leaders of all

---

36. LW 44:135–36. For Abraham and Sarah, see Gen. 21:12. For Balaam and the ass, see Num. 22:21–35.
37. Though it is a minor point, Luther at no time mentions a "priesthood of all believers." See Timothy J. Wengert, *Priesthood, Pastors, Bishops* (Minneapolis: Fortress Press, 2008).
38. LW 44:129.

the people—Christian princes—take matters in hand until order and integrity can be restored in the church.

Image 13: This portrait of Pope Leo X (center) by
Raphael also shows Cardinal Giulio de' Medici,
who would later become Pope Clement VII.

From this powerful point, Luther is able to hammer at the other two Roman walls, the papal assertions that only the pope can interpret Scripture and only the pope can call a general council to deal with issues in the church. Princes themselves must now assemble and make the changes that are needed. For almost one hundred pages, Luther spells out in fascinating detail his program for reform. It includes the following:

- Stop paying the fees and taxes that Rome requires.
- Make appointments of bishops and other officials for Germany here in Germany.

- Let the popes continue to exist, but only as a court of appeals when consensus cannot be reached in Germany or any other nation.
- "Stop kissing the pope's feet!"[39]
- Allow clergy to marry and put an end to the abuses of celibacy.
- Abolish festivals or transfer them to the nearest Sunday.
- "Let the saints canonize themselves."[40]
- Abolish begging.
- Make peace with the Bohemians.
- Reform the monasteries—no binding vows from young persons.
- Limit the teaching of Aristotle to his *Logic*, *Rhetoric*, and *Poetics*.
- Providing schooling for all—both boys and girls.
- Control excesses in trade and luxury and control the Fugger family wealth.
- Abolish brothels.

There was much more, something to delight almost every German reader and something to enrage Luther's critics far beyond anything he had written to this date. He wove together his own biblical critique of the church with political frustrations and the program of the humanists into an impossible but wonderfully exciting document. Deep trouble was sure to come from its publication, but also profound support. In reading the treatises of 1520, the great Nuremberg artist Albrecht Dürer became himself a follower of Luther and even prayed for God to protect him.

This treatise alone would have kept Germany buzzing for years to come, but Luther was just warming up and had much more to say. In the early autumn, he was busy recasting his earlier writings on the sacraments into another great attack on Rome, *The Babylonian Captivity of the Church*. In this third long writing of the year, Luther

39. LW 44:168.
40. LW 44:187.

argued that the system of the seven sacraments, which had been the organizational principle for human life in Christendom for centuries, was in fact an enormous distortion or captivity of their true meaning that obscured the gospel, led people to trust in themselves, and kept the Roman Church all-powerful. Here Luther was able to argue that only two or three of the sacraments really were sacraments and, above all, to criticize the Mass as its practice in recent centuries had obscured the true and gracious meaning of the Lord's Supper.[41]

How does the Mass keep the people of God captive? First, Luther argues, by unjustly withholding the wine from the people and having only the priests receive it. (Here Luther was siding completely with the heretic Hus and the schismatic Bohemians.) Second, the theory of transubstantiation uses categories from Aristotle to try to explain the mystery of Christ's presence. Third, the understanding of the Mass as sacrifice makes the sacrament a work of the priest, obscuring the gift character of the sacrament and the sufficiency of Christ's death once and for all. Luther believes that the gospel is finally lost when the Mass is seen as the work of the priest; it is no wonder, then, that the people commune infrequently and pay little attention to the action of the service.

These matters were also of very great interest, and the positions he was embracing were equally dangerous for Luther's future, but they would not stir the public in the same way that the *Appeal to the German Nobility* had. But here, too, Luther gained new supporters and new opponents. Johannes Bugenhagen, a pastor from Pomerania in the far northeast of Germany, was shocked when he initially read this treatise and considered Luther the worst heretic ever. But he came to Wittenberg the next spring, studied with Luther, and

41. *The Babylonian Captivity of the Church* (1520), in LW 36:11–126; part 1 is found in MLBTW3, 196–223. Luther thought that only baptism, holy communion, and, perhaps, absolution of sin were truly sacraments. He later dropped absolution because it lacked an earthly "element" like water, bread, or wine, but he continued to value the practice of private confession.

became convinced that his views were sound interpretations of the word of God.[42] In fact, Bugenhagen stayed and became the town pastor and one of Luther's most important coworkers.

On the other hand, King Henry VIII of England was shocked and enraged at the treatise and wrote (or had someone write in his name, which seems more likely) a learned rebuttal of Luther that he titled *Defense of the Seven Sacraments*. Pope Leo X was so delighted with the English king's work that he granted him the title "Defender of the Faith," something Leo's successors in the later years would regret when Henry came to his own break with Rome. But that was many years in the future. For now, Luther had another powerful enemy, and they would tangle in print several times during Henry's lifetime.

Staupitz was drawing back and had recently stepped down as vicar-general of the order. Luther's good friend Wenceslas Link had replaced Staupitz. Link now wrote to him with personal concern. Luther admitted that he had a "stinging tone" but cited the sharpness of Paul's letters as a precedent. Luther knew Staupitz was unhappy with the *Appeal to the German Nobility* and wanted Luther not to publish it, but it was too late. So Luther urged Link to do what he could to placate their common mentor.[43] It would have been a remarkable year for any writer or theologian, but Luther was not quite finished—he had saved his best work for last.

Freedom

Suddenly, after many months of quiet, Rome was acting again. A bull threatening excommunication had been published June 20 and was in the slow process of being delivered to Wittenberg. At that

---

42. Bugenhagen's theological work can be found in two hefty volumes: Kurt Hendel, ed., *Johannes Bugenhagen: Selected Writings* (Minneapolis: Fortress Press, 2015). A brief biographical sketch is David Steinmetz, *Reformers in the Wings* (New York: Oxford University Press, 2001), 58–63.

43. "Letter to Wenceslas Link" (August 19, 1520), in LW 48:170–71.

moment, Karl von Miltitz appeared again and made one last attempt at mediation. It seems impossible to imagine this after the very harsh words already published in 1520, but Luther was urged to listen to him and to take his proposals seriously. What Miltitz wanted was for Luther now, even now, to write a letter of apology to Leo and, as a sign of good will, to dedicate some work to him, preferably something devotional and noncontroversial.[44] Luther reported to Spalatin, and through him to Frederick at court, that he would do as Miltitz advised, adding: "If it turns out the way we hope, it is well; if it turns out differently, it will also be well, because this is the will of the Lord."[45]

Luther's letter to Leo is quite an amazing document after the *Appeal to the German Nobility* and the *Babylonian Captivity*. The opening tries to set Luther's continuing respect for and even loyalty to Leo against those "flatterers" who have tried to drive a wedge between them. Luther affirms that he has not intended to speak against Leo personally, and he begs Leo to give him a hearing. He will prostrate himself before the pope and submit to him in every matter save those involving the word of God itself. But he will not recant and asks that this not be required of him. And as a sign of goodwill, he encloses a writing dedicated to Leo "as a token of peace and good hope." Luther believes that it presents "the whole of Christian life in a brief form."[46] Of course, Leo could only have been shocked that the rude German does not know how to address a pope

---

44. Bernard Lohse argues against seeing this as "simple political expediency." We should not read Luther's story backward from the standpoint of how it came out. Other results were not impossible, even at this late date. See Lohse, *Martin Luther: An Introduction to His Life and Work* (Philadelphia: Fortress Press, 1986), 49.

45. "Letter to George Spalatin" (October 12, 1520), in LW 48:180–81.

46. "An Open Letter to Pope Leo X" (written in October 1520 but predated September 6), in LW 31:334–43. It was dated earlier, on von Miltitz's advice, so that it would not seem to be occasioned by the publication of Leo's bull threatening excommunication in sixty days, which had recently been published in Germany. For a fuller understanding of the very complex situation in which this treatise was written, see chapter 5.

and speaks to him as if they were equals, even as if Luther was his father confessor. So the new insights of the past year are muted, but hardly abandoned.

The treatise Luther enclosed became one of his most famous, *The Freedom of a Christian*. It had already been dedicated to the mayor of the town of Zwickau, but Luther was willing to override that with the dedication to Leo. Freedom seems an odd and dangerous theme for a gesture of reconciliation and partial submission, but this treatise has disappointed readers through the centuries who went to it seeking the call to arms that can be found in *Appeal to the German Nobility*. Luther, drawing especially on his work on the book of Galatians, spells out the meaning of freedom for a Christian not as a call to cast off burdens but, paradoxically, to take them on gladly.

The heart of the argument is Luther's statement of the nature of freedom for a Christian, one that has two parts: "A Christian is a perfectly free lord of all, subject to none. A Christian is a perfectly dutiful servant of all, subject to all."[47] It would seem to human reason that the second half cancels the first, but Christian freedom takes its distinctive cast from Jesus, who, though in the form of God, as Paul explains, did not exploit that fact but humbled himself, taking the form of a servant—obedient even unto death (Phil. 2:5-8).

This means that the heart of Christian freedom is not physical or political, but spiritual. No one can take freedom from a Christian by prison or even by death, but Christ conveys true freedom without cost, as a gift. The Christian has been raised to communion with Christ and all other Christians and comes to know this as the highest dignity that anyone could ever receive.

But one who has been shaped into Christ's story does not consider this freedom something to hoard or to exploit. One's heart is opened,

47. *The Freedom of a Christian* (1520), in LW 31:344, MLBTW3, 407.

as Luther had been arguing so eloquently in other writings, in service to others—which no longer seems like slavery in the negative sense, nor even a means to some other end, but rather the path of following Jesus. He uses the image of a marriage, where a bride and groom exchange rings, to evoke the passionate sense in which the exchange of faith happens.

The concept of Christian freedom is the fourth of Luther's seminal theological ideas—following justification by grace through faith, the theology of the cross, and the communal understanding of a church gathered under word and sacraments. It had an explosive power beyond Luther's own attempts to limit it to the spiritual realm. Unrest was stirring all over Europe in 1520, some of those involved were taking Luther's own writings and example as the occasion to question authority.

A student rebellion in Wittenberg that very year provided a preview of how difficult this would become for Luther himself. There had been a series of brawls between students and the apprentice painters who worked in the studio of Lucas Cranach. The students resented the fact that the painters could carry swords while they could not. At one point in August, things got so stormy that the imperial army had to be moved to just outside the town. Luther was completely opposed to the action of the students, which he saw as unwarranted rebellion. He was even more disgusted by faculty colleagues who expressed some sympathy for the students, and he stormed out of one faculty meeting exclaiming that the devil himself seemed to be presiding.[48]

Order was eventually restored, but the problem it exemplified was to haunt Luther for the rest of his life. He had challenged the church

48. Brecht, *Martin Luther*, 1:295–96. Luther wrote to Spalatin during the crisis: "This disorder in our University infuriates me; it will bring us real disgrace." See "Letter to George Spalatin" (July 14, 1520), in LW 48:168–69.

sharply and even made suggestions for the improvement of society. But when others rebelled, he tended to be as offended by their actions as the Roman Curia had been by his. Luther had splendidly articulated the freedom of a Christian, but it was not clear that he had the exclusive right to control it or could confine it to spiritual matters alone. And late in 1520, with excommunication pending, it was far from clear that Luther would survive long enough to see how things turned out.

5

The Trial of Martin Luther

1520–1521

The excommunication of Martin Luther by the pope and Luther's appearance before Emperor Charles at the Diet of Worms are among the best-known parts of Luther's story. Yet events unfolded in such a way that no one could have predicted the outcome (which was not evident for many years), and scarcely anyone knew what would happen next at any point. Luther's own mood swung from exhilaration to calm trust in God to sheer fear and back again. Yet he continued to write and preach, even though he was now not just a widely read author but at the center of power and politics in Europe, playing a role in shaping the events in which he was a part.

Ultimatum from Rome

The Roman officials had been very distracted from Luther's case by their attempts to prevent the election of Charles V. Not until the pope's dynamic young nephew, Cardinal Giulio de' Medici (later

Pope Clement VII), returned to Rome in October 1519 and sounded the alarm about Luther did the Curia begin to develop a strategy for the trial of Luther. On January 9, 1520, the case against Luther was formally opened, and for the next few months a committee drafted a careful condemnation of Luther based on his writings of 1517 and 1518. In this process, Cardinal Cajetan was deeply involved. This was good in that he had actually met Luther and had some comprehension of the issues, although Luther's views had greatly shifted in 1519, and his antipathy to Rome was increasing at the very time his warning was being drafted.

It was also decided at this time that much more pressure should be applied to Frederick the Wise and that, if necessary, a threat of excommunication should be made against him. The Augustinian Order was instructed to make another attempt through Staupitz to prevent Luther from writing anything else and to get him to Rome. These pressures may have led Staupitz to resign as vicar-general of the order that May and to move to Salzburg—as far away from Luther and his friends as possible within the German-speaking territory.[1]

John Eck had vowed to go to Rome and pursue charges against Luther when the Leipzig Debate ended in July 1519, but for some reason he was delayed in making the journey. It is not clear when he arrived in the spring of 1520, but once he did, things changed considerably. Eck was able to paint an even more horrifying picture of Luther's errors, stressing now not indulgences and the bondage of the will but his support for Jan Hus and critiques of papal authority, which Luther expressed at the debate and in his later writings of 1519. Eck became deeply involved in the process of drafting the bull (the name for an official document bearing the papal seal, or *bulla*) against Luther. The forty-one statements of error that it eventually contained

---

1. For a fine brief portrait of Staupitz see David Steinmetz, *Reformers in the Wings* (New York: Oxford University Press, 2001), 15–22.

were not yet listed carefully; at this point the document included a range from outright heresies to statements possibly offensive to pious ears.[2]

On June 15, 1520, the decree, called *Exsurge Domine* after its first words in Latin, "Arise O Lord," was issued by Pope Leo X. It spoke at first of errors that had arisen recently in Germany and listed these, but the bull was pointed directly at Luther himself, who is named eventually. His books were to be seized and burned. He was given sixty days to recant from the time that the bull had been posted in three cathedral cities in his part of Germany. He was then to submit completely to the pope and come to Rome. If the sixty days expired without such submission, he was then automatically excommunicated.

The document showed every sign of trying to make up for lost time in stamping out the spread of something very dangerous to the Roman understanding of faith. But it was based on a very superficial reading of the way Luther's support was growing daily in Germany. Eck himself admitted that it was a mistake not to have condemned Luther on his own terms, arguing from Scripture and the church fathers. The decree's belligerent tone struck most readers as reflecting only power and control, not comprehension of the serious issues that Luther had raised.

To take the bull to Germany and see that its provisions were carried out, two men were chosen. Jerome Aleander, a good theologian who had taught at the University of Paris, was to go to Charles V in the Netherlands and to see that the bull was enforced in the western part of Germany, especially in the cathedral cities of the Rhine, including Cologne and Mainz. Eck himself was charged with

---

2. For all issues treated in this chapter, the reader is referred to Martin Brecht, *Martin Luther*, vol. 1: *His Road to Reformation, 1483–1521*, trans. James L. Schaaf (Philadelphia: Fortress Press, 1985), chs. 11–12. The detail of Brecht's treatment here makes it one of the finest sections of his much acclaimed three-volume life of Luther.

taking the bull through the southern parts of Germany and on into Saxony. This was logical from Rome's point of view but probably another strategic mistake. Eck was known to be bitterly opposed to Luther, and many saw him not as an instrument of Catholic faith but as a one being vindictive toward his Leipzig opponent.

Eck had mixed success on his journey. He was able to have the bull posted in the cathedrals of Meissen (September 21), Merseburg (September 25), and Brandenburg (September 29). These were the three places necessary for the sixty-day time period to begin. In Leipzig, which had supported him well in the debate a year earlier, his reception was very stormy, and the university refused to post the bull at all. He met the same resistance in Erfurt. He sent copies by messenger to the town of Wittenberg and the university there, and to Weimar for Duke John of Saxony, Frederick's brother and coruler, knowing well enough what a poor reception he would receive in both those places.

The letter accompanying the bull listed six other persons, supporters of Luther, who were to be excommunicated unless they submitted to Eck within the same time period. These included Carlstadt at Wittenberg and several of Luther's friends in Augsburg and Nuremberg. On the whole, the announcement that Luther was on the verge of excommunication did nothing to slow the strong interest in his writings and the support that was growing in the second half of 1520. Even the very piously Roman Catholic dukes of Bavaria were reluctant to get involved.

Image 14: Jerome Aleander was the gifted theologian sent from Rome to oversee legal proceedings related to Luther's excommunication.

Luther knew about the bull from October 1 and had a copy by October 11. He was not shocked or surprised, although its tone was so harsh that he (like Erasmus) wondered whether it was authentic or whether Eck had written it himself. At the end of August, Luther had already written to Charles V asking his protection and assurance of a fair hearing for any charges that might come against him.[3] But it is not clear that Charles ever received his letter or would have had any sympathy with it, in any case.

Aleander made his way to the emperor in Antwerp at the end of September and was having an easier time than Eck. The emperor promptly ordered all of Luther's books burned throughout the

---

3. "Letter to Charles V" (August 30, 1520), in LW 48:175–79.

Netherlands, and the first burning took place in Louvain on October 8 in the presence of the theologians. Late in the previous year, these theologians had condemned Luther, along with their colleagues at Cologne, on the basis of written reports of the Leipzig Debate. But burning books was another matter, and they seemed to have attended with some reluctance.

The pope's representative was delighted but a little surprised at Charles's quick agreement with the pope's instructions. But the twenty-year-old Charles was a devout Roman Catholic, the grandson of Ferdinand and Isabella of Spain, who had been known as "the Catholic monarchs." His childhood tutor had been Adrian of Utrecht—a fine scholar who would eventually become the next pope with Charles's strong support.

Charles was at this time on his way to Aachen, to the great cathedral of Charlemagne, to be crowned king of the Germans. This took place on October 23 and was followed by Charles's announcement that the first diet of his reign would be convened in Worms on January 6, 1521. The terms of his election had designated Nuremberg as the place for the first diet, but this was overruled, as there was an outbreak of the plague in that city. Charles began to make his way up the Rhine toward Worms and reached Cologne in early November.

Wittenberg's Response

In the meantime, Frederick the Wise had not attended the coronation because of illness, but he was waiting in Cologne to meet the emperor. There, on November 5, Frederick had a visit from Erasmus, an old and trusted friend. They discussed the Luther situation at some length. Erasmus was at this stage always careful not to commit himself about Luther. He had a certain sympathy for the monk but was appalled by his recklessness and blunt language. He feared that

Luther would bring catastrophe on all of them. Erasmus had written a letter a year earlier to Albrecht of Mainz full of reservations about Luther but hoping "that heart, which seems to hold certain bright sparks of evangelical doctrine, be not crushed but rather corrected and called to preach the glory of Christ."[4]

Frederick pressed hard for advice, as he was clearly struggling about what attitude to take with Charles toward the Luther affair. Finally, Erasmus was drawn into a sharp critique of Leo X and his language in the bull. He wrote out some instructions for Frederick, urging him to do all that he could to protect Luther.[5]

Soon Erasmus asked for the notes back. He too was wise about politics and wanted to cover his tracks. But this advice to Frederick—from Erasmus of all people—may well have saved Luther's life. Frederick worked tirelessly, and finally successfully, to avoid a condemnation of Luther at the forthcoming diet without a personal appearance and a hearing. This was the line he took when he first met with Charles V. Frederick was perhaps the most powerful and certainly the richest of the electors. Charles had no wish to hear Luther, and Aleander had clear instructions from the pope that there was to be no hearing and that the diet was not even to take up the Luther question. If Luther wanted a hearing, Leo would offer a promise of safe-conduct to Rome.

---

4. Erasmus of Rotterdam, "Letter to Albrecht of Mainz" (October 19, 1519), in *Christian Humanism and the Reformation: Selected Writings of Erasmus*, ed. John Olin (New York: Fordham University Press, 1987), 134.

5. Roland Bainton, *Erasmus of Christendom* (New York: Scribner, 1969), 166–67. See also Brecht, *Martin Luther*, 1:416–17. The account is also found in the classic life of Charles V by Karl Brandi, *The Emperor Charles V* (London: Jonathan Cape, 1939), 127. For a more up-to-date version of Charles's life, focusing on social history, see James D. Tracy, *Emperor Charles V, Impresario of War: Campaign Strategy, International Finance, and Domestic Politics* (Cambridge: Cambridge University Press, 2002).

ALBERTVS ARCHIEPISCOPVS MOGVNTINENSIS.

ALbertus ex illuſtriſsima familia Brandenbur
geſium natus, frater Ioachimi ſenioris electo
ris & Iohannis filius extitit. natus eſt anno 1490. die
28 Iunij. Eū parentes à teneris annis in literis ac om
nis generis uirtutib us inſtituerunt, ita ut in uirum
maximū euaſerit. Vnde primò canonicus Mogun
tinenſis & Treuerenſis conſtitutus fuit. In ea fun-
ctiōe ſua pietate & uitæ integritate talem ſe decla
rauit, ut omnes magnam de eo ſpem conciperent.
Vnde cum Magdenburgenſis ſedes uacaret, anno
1513 in eius loci Archiepiſcopum electus eſt. Mox
etiam Halberſtatenſis Epiſcopatus adminiſtratio
committitur. In ijs locis adeò moderatè ſeſe geſsit,
ut omnibus gratiſsimus exiſteret. Sequēti uerò anno 1514, cum Vriel Mogun-
tinenſis præſul uita functus eſſet, ei ob plurimas corporis & animi uirtutes e-
tiam eius loci eccleſia cum Electoratus dignitate committitur. id quod hacte
nus nemini aut paucſsimis contigerat. Pontifex quoqʒ Leo huiuſmodi ele-
ctiones confirmauit.

Image 15: Albrecht of the Hohenzollern family (rivals to Charles V's Hapsburg and
Frederick's Wettin families) was simultaneously archbishop of Brandenburg and
Mainz.

Frederick was in no hurry to meet Aleander, but the papal
representative found him. In a respectful conversation, he made it
very clear that Frederick must turn over Luther to Rome or risk the
charge of heresy himself. Frederick was so responsive that Aleander
thought for a time he had convinced him. But in the end, he would
not turn over Luther until he had received a proper hearing.

Then, surprisingly, Charles gave in to Frederick's request. On
November 28, he promised Luther a hearing at the diet, but then
withdrew this offer December 17 under great pressure from
Aleander. Frederick, for his part, said that he had exchanged "only
twenty words" with Luther and that he would support the decision
of the diet so long as the hearing had been a fair one. Whether or not
Luther would appear was an undecided question at the end of 1520.

In the meantime, things were uncertain in Wittenberg with Frederick absent for a prolonged period. About 150 students left the university that fall; most were from territories ruled by bishops who thought that studying with a potential heretic might not be good for their future careers. The city was also threatened in the bull against Luther and was not sure how to proceed.

But Luther was finding support in surprisingly many places, not only from Erasmus behind the scenes but also from Frederick's nephew, Prince John Frederick. This seventeen-year-old was being groomed as Frederick's eventual successor, after his father, John of Saxony. Spalatin had been his tutor, and he was well acquainted with Luther and well disposed to him. At this time he wrote to the monk, offering his support in strong terms. Luther was delighted and wrote back, praising John Frederick's "enthusiasm for the holy and divine truth." Luther went on to report about his own attitude and activities:

> As the bull has in no way frightened me, I intend to preach, lecture, and write in spite of it. I suspect, however, that the people of Leipzig, if they could, would drive me out of Wittenberg with the help of Duke George and the Bishop of Merseburg, who have developed toward me a hatred defying description. But I have commended all this to the divine will. I well realize that they try to destroy not me but rather Your Grace's small university at Wittenberg. They have played with this thought for some time, and now they rejoice that they have found a "just" reason.[6]

It was always a good tactical move with Frederick, John, and John Frederick to wave the flag of the University at Wittenberg because it was a cherished cause for these three successive electors.

John Frederick's support would be very important for Luther in the long run. But in the immediate crisis, a far more significant correspondence was undertaken with Ulrich von Hutten. This knight was one of the most complex figures of the Reformation, but

---

6. "Letter to Duke John Frederick" (October 30, 1520), in LW 48:182–83.

he was a real force by the second half of 1520. Poet laureate for Emperor Maximilian, sometime courtier for Albrecht of Mainz, and friend of Erasmus, he seemed an unlikely ally for Luther.

In the early stages of the struggle about indulgences, Hutten was dismissive of Luther as a person engaged in a monk's quarrel. But he began to notice Luther in reports of the Leipzig Debate, particularly Luther's increasingly critical stance toward Rome. Hutten had great plans for the righting of wrongs done against Germans, and his partial authorship of *Letters of Obscure Men* received attention in the same nationalist circles that admired Luther's *Appeal to the German Nobility*. Hutten offered protection for Luther, and at the Diet of Worms he helped stir support for Luther and opposition to the pope.

Daily Life amid Danger

It was clear both that Luther was in danger in the fall of 1520 and that he had friends who would try to protect him. He was in Wittenberg, lecturing and preaching and continuing to write in response to the situation, sometimes in a conciliatory way but often harshly critical of the pope and his emissaries. If Luther had any reason to be cautious other than his accountability to Frederick, it may have come from pressure within his order. It appears that Staupitz and Wenceslas Link, his new superior, may have visited Wittenberg in September and urged Luther to do what he could in a conciliatory way for all their sakes.

Perhaps that is why Luther was willing to work one last time with Miltitz, writing the October letter to Pope Leo and dedicating *The Freedom of a Christian* to him. But those activities in October, at about the same time as the receipt of the bull, were last gestures in that direction. For Luther, the bull was really the last straw, the confirmation that the pope was the antichrist. The one person who should have praised Luther for championing the gospel instead condemned him and was about to cast him out of the church. Luther looked to the experience of the prophets of Israel to find an example that helped him understand what was happening to him—with the threats coming not from princes but from the supposedly highest religious leadership in Christendom.

Four times in quick succession, Luther wrote responses to the papal bull—twice in November, again in December, and in a more considered way in March 1521.[7] But the sixty days allotted for submitting to Rome had expired November 28, and Luther responded to the situation in a very dramatic way. On December 10, a great bonfire was constructed outside one of the town gates. Students and other interested persons gathered at nine o' clock in the morning, and there Luther threw on the fire his volumes of canon law, the papal decretals, and volumes of Scholastic theology. Then he stepped forward from the crowd and threw a small document on the fire—a copy of the papal bull. This was not simply a refusal to submit but an act of outrageous defiance.[8]

Why did Luther do this? The burning of his own books in the Netherlands, the Rhineland, and southern Germany had offended him deeply, especially the papal failure to make any distinction between works of controversy and such devotional books as even his enemies had admired and praised. He soon wrote an interpretation of the event: "Why the Books of the Pope and His Disciples Were Burned," and it was in print within a few weeks. In it, he cited biblical precedent—the burning of pagan books reported in Acts 19. Still, the overwhelming motivation was to respond in kind to the burning of his own writings: "Since, then, through their kind of book

---

7. For the last of these, see "Defense and Explanation of All the Articles" (1521), in LW 32:3–99.
8. For details of the book burning, see LW 31:381–82. Brecht adds that they had also hoped to burn a copy of works by Thomas Aquinas, but none of the scholars would part with their own edition. Brecht, Martin Luther, 1:423–26.

burning great damage to the truth and a false delusion among the plain common people might result, to the destruction of many souls, I have on the prompting of the Spirit (as I hope), in order to strengthen and preserve the same, burned the books of the adversaries in turn, since their improvement is not to be hoped for."[9] The language and the action both parody in a deadly serious way the actions of the pope, taken against Luther.

Luther also paralleled the list of forty-one of his teachings in the papal bill by listing and discussing thirty false teachings of the papacy: being above the church, above secular authority, beyond any human accountability, having the power to make law for all parts of the church, forbidding clerical marriage, holding the sole power to interpret Scripture, and others. These were familiar charges to those who had been reading Luther for the past year especially, but their form as condemnations of false teachings must have been especially striking to the readers of the pamphlet. He concluded with the charge that would later be at the heart of his defense at the Diet of Worms:

> I am willing to let everyone have his own opinion. I am moved most by the fact that the pope has never once refuted with Scripture or reason anyone who has spoken, written, or acted against him, but has at all times suppressed, exiled, burned or otherwise strangled him with force and bans, through kings, and other partisans, or with deceit and false words, or which I shall convince him from history. Nor has he ever been willing to submit to a court of justice or judgments, but at all times bawled that he was above Scripture, judgment, and authority.[10]

In the fight for control of public opinion that was being waged in the bull and in Luther's response, Leo was trying to stick the term *heretic* on Luther, and Luther was trying to stick the term *tyrant* on Leo.

---

9. "Why the Books of the Pope and His Disciples Were Burned," in LW 31:384.
10. Ibid., 394–95.

It is not clear that Rome knew about the burning of the bull when, on January 3, 1521, Leo issued a second bull, *Decet Romanum Pontificem* (It Pleases the Roman Pontiff), which made Luther's excommunication final. Albrecht of Mainz, Eck, and Aleander were to proceed not only against Luther but also against all those who supported him. They could absolve those who submitted except for Luther, Hutten, and the two Nurembergers—Spengler and Pirkheimer—who could be absolved only by the pope.[11] Soon this was implementated, and priests even in Saxony began asking people in the confessional whether they owned or had read books by Luther. Luther had to write quickly an opinion, "An Instruction for Penitents concerning the Forbidden Books of Dr. Martin Luther," in which he advised them to leave the confessional and even forgo receiving the Eucharist for a time rather than submit to such harassment.[12]

Drama before the Diet

The Diet of Worms, which had been called for January 6, finally opened January 25, 1521. Frederick was now wavering about whether there was any point in bringing Luther there, although he still seemed committed to do all that he could to protect him. Luther was not on the original agenda, which included the emperor's financial needs, what to do in his absence (frequent over the next tumultuous decade), the war with the Turks, and diplomatic issues with both France and the Papal States. Duke George of Saxony, no friend of Luther's, was distressed that the *gravamina*—the list of complaints of the Germans against the pope—were not included. Frederick was determined that they needed to deal with Luther in some way, and Aleander's instructions made it clear that this was to

11. See Harold J. Grimm, *Lazarus Spengler: A Lay Leader of the Reformation* (Columbus: Ohio State University Press, 1978), 43.
12. Brecht, *Martin Luther*, 1:429.

be avoided at all costs. The pope had dealt with Luther, and only mischief could come from this kind of group—many of them laity, for that matter—dabbling in theological matters where they had neither jurisdiction nor competence.

At the end of 1520, Luther had written one of his most important letters ever to Spalatin on the question of his possible appearance before the diet. He knew the dangers clearly enough from the story of Hus. But he also sensed that a moment for courage and confession was probably looming for him:

> Of course I would by all means come, if called, in so far as it would be up to me, even if I could not come by my own power and instead would have to be driven there as a sick man. For it would not be right to doubt that I am called by the Lord if the Emperor summons. Further, if they should employ force in this matter, which is most probable (for they do not want me called there because they want me to learn something), then this matter can only be commended to the Lord. For He who saved the three men in the furnace of the Babylonian king still lives and rules. If he does not want to preserve me, then my head is of slight importance compared with Christ, who was put to death in greatest ignominy—a stumbling block to all, and the ruin of many. We must rather take care that we do not expose the gospel (which we have finally begun to promote) to the derision of the godless and thus give our enemies a reason for boasting over us because we do not dare confess what we have taught and are afraid to shed our blood for it. May the merciful Christ prevent such cowardice on our part and such boasting on their part. Amen.[13]

At the end of January, Luther wrote to the elector himself, repeating his willingness to appear, hoping that Charles would provide a promise of safe-conduct.[14]

Aleander was very fearful about the situation, especially given the great crowds in Worms that seemed to support Luther. But

---

13. "Letter to George Spalatin" (December 29, 1520), in LW 48:188–89. Brecht calls it one of Luther's greatest statements. Brecht, *Martin Luther*, 1:422–23.
14. "Letter to Frederick the Wise" (January 25, 1521), in LW 48:195–97.

he gave a great speech to the diet on February 13, arguing that Luther had already received every consideration and that they were risking the encouragement of heresy even to consider calling him to appear. That led Charles's councillors to introduce a simple measure to condemn Luther, but no consensus could be reached about this, given the opposition that was led by Frederick and by the Count Palatine.

After lengthy behind-the-scenes negotiations, on March 6 Charles changed his mind and again agreed to summon Luther to Worms with a safe-conduct. He had promised in the conditions of his election not to send any German away without a hearing, and he stuck to that promise despite the unhappiness of the papal party.[15] To show that he had not tilted toward Luther, on March 26 he issued an order for all of Luther's books to be destroyed throughout the empire.

In Worms, pictures were being sold of Luther with a halo and with the Holy Spirit over his head in the form of a dove. Aleander said in one of his dispatches to Rome that three quarters of the Germans seemed to be Lutheran, although it is hard to know what that could have meant. Perhaps some large majority of Germans did enjoy the hard time Luther was giving the papacy, but only a handful could have been very familiar with his teachings at this early date. Ulrich von Hutten was hard at work stirring the crowds with his writings, and in an attempt to silence him Charles offered him an imperial pension. Concern for public opinion was great enough that Aleander dared not publish the bull of excommunication in Worms.

In Wittenberg, people were buying pictures as well. Lucas Cranach had teamed up with someone, possibly Philip Melanchthon, to produce a series of woodcuts that contrasted Christ with the antichrist—that is, the pope. Christ was shown driving the

---

15. Brandi, *The Emperor Charles V*, 129.

moneychangers out of the temple, while the pope welcomed people bringing him bags of gold. Christ was shown washing the feet of his disciples, while followers of the pope were kissing his feet.[16]

Luther was now preparing to leave Wittenberg for Worms with the imperial herald Casper Sturm, who had been sent to accompany him and see to the safe-conduct. On Maundy Thursday, he preached for what could have been one of the last times in Wittenberg, a very calm and moving sermon on the worthy reception of the sacrament. There is no direct reference to his coming trip, but Luther continues to explore his theology of freedom and how the church's requirement of communion at least once a year has given the wrong motivation for coming to the table: "Such hunger and thirst are created not by compelling a man, but by showing him his frailty and his need so that he will see his wretched condition and feel the desire to be delivered from it. This happens, for instance, when you recognize that you are weak in faith, cold in love, and faint in hope . . . the greater and more fervent this desire is in you, the better fit you are to receive the sacrament." [17]

They left Wittenberg on April 3, the Wednesday after Easter. Luther had already been absolved of his obedience to the Augustinian Order, but they continued to follow the tradition that a monk should not travel alone. A rather obscure brother, Johann Petzensteiner, was assigned to be Luther's companion. Nicholas von Amsdorf also went with him, and Justus Jonas joined the party in Erfurt. Melanchthon wanted to go but could not be spared from teaching because, after all, Wittenberg had become a famous center of learning practically overnight, and someone needed to be there. Spalatin was already in

---

16. Brecht, *Martin Luther*, 1:432.
17. "Sermon on the Worthy Reception of the Sacrament" (1521), in LW 41:172–73. On the very same day, Pope Leo X, quite agitated by developments in Worms, was issuing a third bull, called *In Coena Domini* (At the table of the Lord), against Luther.

Worms with the elector, so Luther would have several trusted friends to advise him.

They traveled through Leipzig and Naumburg to Weimar where Duke John, who gave Luther additional money for the trip, entertained them. The expenses of such a party were considerable. Luther was very ill at stages along the journey and at times quite distressed. But he was also greeted at almost every point by those who wished him well. In Erfurt, he preached at the Augustinian church to an overflowing crowd on some of the first words of the Gospel for the Sunday after Easter, "Peace be with you." It was a powerful invitation to trust not in oneself, but in the gospel freely given by God. Luther contrasted God's generosity with the demands of the church: "Everything that comes from the Pope cries out, 'Give, give; if you refuse, you are of the devil.'"[18]

He also preached in Gotha and Eisenach—in Saint George's Church, where he had been a choirboy. Luther was revisiting places that he knew well, the scenes of his youth, his education, and his monastic formation. The crowds continued to cheer him, although he reminded his companions of Jesus' experience of Palm Sunday and how quickly the crowds changed their allegiance. Heiko Oberman, noting Luther's fears and distress, insists, "Luther did not travel through Germany to Worms in a mood of stoic equanimity and unshakable resolve. . . . It was Luther's contemporaries who turned his journey into a triumphal procession."[19]

From Frankfurt am Main, near Worms, Luther wrote to Spalatin of his pending arrival:

To my friend in the Lord, Master George Spalatin, Saxon court

18. "Sermon in Erfurt" (April 7, 1521), in LW 51:63.
19. Heiko Oberman, *Luther: Man Between God and the Devil*, trans. Eileen Walliser-Schwarzbart (New Haven: Yale University Press, 1989), 198. Oberman includes a drawing by Albrecht Dürer of a tough-looking Sturm, the imperial herald, who accompanied them. One gets a sense that he was well suited to the role.

chaplain, honored in Christ Jesus: Greetings. I am coming, my Spalatin, although Satan has done everything to hinder me with more than one disease. All the way from Eisenach I have been sick; I am still sick in a way which previously has been unknown to me. Of course I realize that the mandate of Charles has also been published to frighten me. But Christ lives and we shall enter Worms in spite of all the Emperor's letters. It is not wise to write further letters until I first see in person what has to be done, so that we may not encourage Satan, whom I have made up my mind to frighten and despise. So, prepare the lodging.[20]

There was one last decision before they arrived in Worms, and it was Luther's to make. Ulrich von Hutten had been negotiating with the emperor's confessor, Jean Glapion. They both thought some compromise might be worked out if they could negotiate with Luther away from the diet. They sent Martin Bucer to bring Luther to them in the Ehrenberg Castle. Luther did not trust this last-minute change of plans, which he later learned could have jeopardized his safe-conduct. So the party went on, and Luther entered Worms on April 16, two weeks after they had left Wittenberg.[21]

The crowds were not only waiting for Luther along the way. Visitors came to his lodgings after his arrival, some from curiosity, many to wish him well. One was the young Landgrave Philip of Hesse (1504–1567), only seventeen years old when he met Luther at Worms for the first time.[22] But as Luther had written to the young John Frederick of Saxony, so he took time to talk with Philip, who was not yet a supporter of the evangelical cause.[23] In the last part of Luther's life, John Frederick and Philip would be his two most important supporters, and they would both spend years in the prisons

---

20. "Letter to George Spalatin" (April 14, 1521), in LW 48:198.
21. Brecht, *Martin Luther*, 1:450–52.
22. "Landgrave" is a title of the nobility, roughly equivalent to a duke.
23. "Evangelical" here and elsewhere in this book, refers to the view that the "good news" (Gk: *euangelion*) of the gospel, the central claim of the Bible, was to be the superior authority for Christian life and faith.

of Charles V after Luther's death because of their refusal to renounce his teachings.[24]

Drama at the Diet

Luther was scheduled to appear before the diet on the afternoon following his arrival. He was called at four o'clock and taken into the hall by a back way to shield him from the many spectators who lined the streets. It was a dramatic moment that none of the principal players would ever forget. As he wrote his memoirs at the end of his life, Charles was still offended at the rudeness of a mere monk who refused to recant, thinking that he knew better than the "whole church." Luther knew that he was in a situation of extreme danger to his person, but one of great opportunity to his cause.

All eyes were on him, and many in the imperial and papal parties were extremely offended by Luther's appearance and manners. It was said that he was grinning, even laughing, when he walked into the presence of the emperor. It was said that he looked around and even spoke words of greeting to those he knew. This was clearly a provincial person who did not know how to behave in court. Aleander wrote to Rome, "The fool entered with a smile on his face and kept moving his head back and forth, up and down, in the presence of the emperor."[25] When asked to speak the first day, Luther's voice was so low that he could hardly be heard.

Luther was questioned by a man named Johann Eck—but this was not his old opponent from Leipzig. The spokesman for the diet was the highly respected Johann von der Eck, secretary to the elector archbishop of Trier. Luther was asked two questions: whether he acknowledged the books as his and whether he wished "to retract and recall them and their contents or to cling to them henceforth and

24. Ibid., 1:451–52.
25. Quoted in Oberman, *Luther*, 199.

insist on them." The Wittenberg lawyer Jerome Schurff, who was functioning as Luther's advocate, insisted that the names of the books be read. This was done, and it included not only the early books but also the recent ones, including *The Babylonian Captivity*, that were offensive even to some who had sympathy for Luther. Luther admitted that these were his books and that he had also written others.[26]

In regard to the second question, Luther shocked the assembly by asking for more time. He noted that what was asked here, about affirming or denying these writings, was "a question of faith and the salvation of souls, because it concerns the divine Word." He asked for "time to think" so that he might "satisfactorily answer the question without violence to the divine Word and danger to my own soul." Answering this request required consultation among the princes, and especially the consent of Charles. Was it evidence that Luther was finally crumbling before the powers present at Worms? Or was it a Saxon trick to stall for time? While Luther waited, there were expressions of goodwill toward him from many in the crowd.[27]

Von Eck then gave Luther both a scolding and a reply to his request: "Although you, Martin, have been able to learn well enough from the imperial order why you have been summoned, and, therefore, do not deserve to be granted a longer time for consideration, yet, out of innate clemency, his imperial majesty grants one day for your deliberation so that you may furnish an answer openly tomorrow at this hour—on this condition: that you do not present your opinion in writings, but declare it by word of mouth."[28] This was already an attempt to spin public perceptions of

---

26. See "Luther at the Diet of Worms," in LW 32:131, for a listing of the books and more on this dramatic setting.
27. LW 32:107. The authorship of "Luther at the Diet of Worms" is unknown, but it is included in LW, and Luther seems to have had some part in assembling it.
28. LW 32:107–8.

the event, as the imperial party knew the power of Luther's writings to sway opinion. They did not want another Luther publication in the making.

In the next twenty-four hours, Luther had ample time to consult not only with his legal advisors but also with his friends Amsdorf, Jonas, and Spalatin. That evening, Luther took time to write a note to Vienna, to an official of the Hapsburg Court there whose brother was in Worms. Luther thanked John Cuspinian for the sympathy he had shown to Luther's work thus far and shared with him a summary of the first day's events, including the very short time given him to prepare his answer. But he vowed, "With Christ's help, however, I shall not in all eternity recant the least particle."[29] Ever the pastor, early in the morning Luther rose and heard confession from three soldiers with heavy consciences.

The second day Luther was again scheduled to appear at four o'clock in the afternoon, but he was kept waiting for two hours as the diet considered other business. The meeting this time was in a very large hall illuminated with torches because it was now dark. Many guests not ordinarily attending the diet were also present. Luther had to stand to speak in the midst of the princes. He was chided by von Eck for asking for additional time but then made his reply—first in German and then repeated in Latin. Charles V, among whose titles was "king of the Germans," could not speak the language well; he is reported to have said, "I speak Spanish to God, Italian to women, French to men, and German to my horse."[30]

Luther began by apologizing for any discourtesy in his behavior of the previous day. Perhaps he had been informed by the Saxon

---

29. "Letter to John Cuspinian" (April 17, 1521), in LW 48:199–200. Cuspinian, who had strongly supported the Reformation's early stages, drew back after the Wittenberg troubles of 1521–1522 and the Peasants' War of 1525.

30. Quoted in Fred Shapiro, ed., *Yale Book of Quotations* (New Haven: Yale University Press, 2006), 144. There is reason to dispute the reliability of this statement, however.

advisors that his manners seemed inappropriate to some: "If through inexperience I have either not given the proper titles to some, or have offended in some manner against court customs and etiquette, I beseech you to kindly pardon me, as a man accustomed not to courts but to the cells of monks."[31] His apology underscored the unprecedented nature of someone of Luther's status appearing and speaking before the nobility of the German lands. He seemed quite confident this second day, and his voice was louder and clearer.

As to the question of his books, he divided them into three categories. First, there were works "in which I have discussed religious faith and morals simply and evangelically, so that even my enemies themselves are compelled to admit that these are useful, harmless, and clearly worthy to be read by Christians." Even the first bull against him had admitted that some of his works were inoffensive, but all were condemned together. He would under no circumstances disavow such books. This was a shrewd distinction at the beginning of his address, for even many opponents were willing to admit that Luther at times had written well on the Bible and devotional subjects.[32]

A second set of books, Luther argued, "attacks the papacy and the affairs of the papists as those who both by their doctrines and very wicked examples have laid waste the Christian world with evil that afflicts the body and spirit." This kind of speaking was not likely to reassure Charles, but Luther reminded the diet that "property and possessions, especially in this illustrious nation of Germany, have been devoured by an unbelievable tyranny." This was Luther's clear conviction on such matters, but he would have found part of the audience sympathetic here too. If he renounced those books, he would become "a cover for wickedness and tyranny."

31. "Luther at the Diet of Worms," in LW 32:109.
32. LW 32:109–10.

That left a third group "against some private and (as they say) distinguished individuals." Here Luther could admit that he had been "more violent than my religion or profession demands. But then, I do not set myself up as a saint; neither am I disputing about my life, but about the teaching of Christ." So here too Luther could not retract, lest he feed the very tyranny that raged not only against him but also against a whole people of God as it obscured the gospel message.[33]

So far Luther had taken a very hard line, and his supporters must have been quite uneasy. But he came now to name his alternative to recanting. He admitted that he was a man, not God, and that he was willing to be instructed of his errors. Having been shown them, he would lead the procession to cast his books into the fire. But the standard for that showing had to be "the prophets and the evangelists." For only from them and not from the sheer assertion of church authority of pope or councils would he be able to make a sincere and genuine change of mind.

It was a powerful and impossible demand at the same time. In a way, it made perfect sense. Luther was a professor of Scripture, and he had written on controversial subjects from what he had learned in the Psalms and Paul and the rest of the Bible. He wanted to be shown how he was wrong by scholarly argumentation, not by a simple quotation of a biblical verse. Luther was showing that Pope Leo was right in one way, that the diet was not equipped to respond to him. They were not experts in the Scriptures. But neither were Leo and his court, at least from the evidence of the two papal bulls. Nor had Eck shown his capacity in Leipzig. Only a long discussion with other scholars could truly and fairly settle the objections to Luther that had been raised.

Luther concluded his speech with an acknowledgment that he had introduced division and debate. But this, said Luther, is what

33. LW 32:110–11.

the word of God always does, and for his part he considered the current debates "the joyful aspect of all these matters." Human beings, especially rulers, often like peace and reassurance, but the mirror of the Bible suggests that it is often wrong to cover things over at the expense of truth.

The room was very hot. Luther was sweating profusely. There was a question as to whether they could really stand to listen to the speech repeated in Latin, but Luther insisted. He probably had good instincts in this, because of Charles's poor German, and Frederick the Wise later reported how especially pleased he was with the Latin version. Then von Eck expressed irritation that Luther had spoken a great deal but not really answered the question at all. He wanted an answer without horns—without ambiguity.[34]

So Luther, who seemed prepared for this demand, also spoke these widely quoted words in summary:

> Since then your serene majesty and your lordships seek a simple answer, I will give it in this manner, neither horned nor toothed: Unless I am convinced by the testimony of the Scriptures or by clear reason (for I do not trust either in the pope or councils alone, since it is well known that they have often erred and contradicted themselves), I am bound by the Scriptures I have quoted and my conscience is captive to the Word of God. I cannot and I will not retract anything, since it is neither safe nor right to go against conscience. I cannot do otherwise, here I stand, may God help me. Amen.[35]

It would suit the needs of filmmakers and dramatists had the session ended there, but actually it continued for some time. The princes consulted. Luther was chided for the inadequacy of his response. Luther was challenged on details of his address, such as that councils

---

34. On the particulars of how things were going see Brecht, *Martin Luther*, 1:459. On von Eck's demands, see LW 32:112.

35. LW 32:112–13. Some early official transcripts of this portion of the speech omit "I cannot do otherwise, here I stand" but the first printed record contains the line. It would be natural for early editors to omit so brazen a comment made by a mere friar in the presence of an emperor.

had erred, but he said he would be happy to prove it. Not wanting to give him that opportunity, the session ended. Luther was followed back to his lodgings by a group of Spaniards in the service of the emperor who jeered him and cried out that he should be sent to the flames. But when he joined his friends, he raised his arms as German athletes did at the end of a contest, saying, "I have come through." He had not given way to fear and had been able to make the bold confession that he intended.

Lutherans and other Protestants make much of their confessions—documents that were produced in the subsequent Reformation struggles that defined their identity over against the Roman Church, and sometimes against each other. Luther would play a part in writing many of those confessions in the next twenty-five years. But the prototype of the act of confessing was Luther before Charles V in Worms, and from his courage others in later encounters took great comfort. Frederick was pleased and told Spalatin: "Father Martinus spoke well before the Lord Emperor, all the princes, and the estates," but added, "he is much too bold for me."[36] It still had to be determined what price Luther would pay for his boldness and whether the Spanish cries of "to the flames" were predictions of how the journey to Worms would end.

If Luther could give a powerful speech, Charles could write a powerful letter. The next morning when the estates met, they were read a response to Luther's appearance that Charles had composed in French:

My predecessors, the most Christian Emperors of the German race, the Austrian archdukes, and the dukes of Burgundy, were truest sons of the Catholic Church until they died, defending and extending their belief to the glory of God, the propagation of the faith, and the salvation of their souls. Behind them they have left the holy Catholic rites so that I should

36. Brecht, *Martin Luther*, 1:461–62.

live and die in them. Until now I have lived with the help of God as a Christian Emperor. It is my privilege to maintain what my forefather established at Constance and other councils.

A single monk, led astray by private judgment, has set himself against the faith held by all Christians for more than a thousand years. He believes that all Christians up to now have erred. Therefore, I have resolved to stake upon this cause all my dominions, my friends, my body and blood, my life and soul.

We are sprung from the holy German nation and appointed by peculiar privilege to be defenders of the faith. It would be disgraceful, as well as an eternal stain upon us and our posterity, if in this day and age not only heresy but also the very suspicion of it were to result from our neglect.

After Luther's stiff-necked reply in my presence yesterday, I am now very sorry that I have so long delayed moving against him and his false doctrines. I have made up my mind never again, under any circumstances, to listen to him. Under protection of his safe-conduct he shall be escorted home. But he is forbidden to preach and to seduce men with his evil beliefs and incite them to rebellion. I warn you to give witness to your beliefs as good Christians and in consonance with your vows.[37]

Such a speech might have put an end to the Luther affair rather quickly, but that was not how things worked in German diets. The views of Charles were now clear, but the others present wanted to continue debating what to do about the situation. A few were still quite sympathetic to Luther; others—including Albrecht of Mainz—were not but feared an uprising of the people if Luther were put to death. Eventually, they decided to appoint a Committee of Ten to meet with Luther and see if anything more satisfactory than a simple no could be worked out. In the meantime, many people, some of them quite threatening, were coming to visit Luther's rooms. The papal theologian Cochlaeus challenged Luther to renounce the safe-conduct and debate him immediately on the issues. Luther declined.

37. Quoted in Clyde Manschreck, *A History of Christianity: Readings in the History of the Church from the Reformation to the Present* (Grand Rapids, MI: Baker, 1964), 31–32.

Attempts to pressure Luther through the Saxon delegation also continued.

The committee met with Luther at six o'clock in the morning on April 24—one week after his first appearance at the diet. The meeting was chaired by the widely trusted archbishop of Trier but included such strong opponents of Luther as Duke George of Saxony. When their threats and compromises failed to satisfy Luther, they asked what he could suggest. Luther was shrewd, but he had no plan, no political compromise that would get them out of their dilemma. He advised the path suggested by the great Rabbi Gamaliel in Acts 5, who told the Jewish council that they must wait to see whether the new movement was simply human or from God. This did not satisfy the committee.

There were still more conversations over the next two days, and some made threats that Luther by refusing to recant would bring destruction on Melanchthon and spoil his promising career. But no compromise could be found. Finally, Luther asked that he be allowed to leave Worms, and this permission was granted by Charles, allowing him three weeks to return home under the safe-conduct that he had promised. He was not to preach.

Kidnapped!

At some point before he left Worms, Luther received a tip from Frederick that he was planning to arrange for Luther to be hidden away for a time. It was widely assumed that Luther would flee to Denmark or Bohemia, both beyond the immediate jurisdiction of the emperor at that time. Amsdorf was among the few who were aware of plans that Luther would not return to Wittenberg. Frederick gave him forty gulden for the journey, and many came to say farewell, including Philip of Hesse, who must have been impressed.

The party traveled back through Frankfurt, where Luther wrote to his Wittenberg neighbor, the artist Lucas Cranach. He thanked the town for the cart they had provided for his transportation and hinted to Lucas that he would be disappearing for a while into friendly custody. From this letter, we get a sense of what Luther might have hoped for in Worms—however unrealistically. He writes: "I thought His Imperial Majesty would have assembled one or fifty scholars and overcome this monk in a straightforward manner. But nothing else was done there than this: Are these your books? Yes. Do you want to renounce them or not? No. Then go away! O we blind Germans, how childishly we act and allow the Romanists to mock and fool us in such a pitiful way."[38]

Luther also wrote to Charles V at that time, probably as he had been instructed through Frederick. He reviewed his sense of what had happened at Worms and expressed both thanks for the safe-conduct and openness to future discussion with other scholars. The letter was never sent.[39] The party had been to the great abbey in Hersfeld, where the abott received them warmly and had Luther preach. He preached again in Eisenach, over the objection of the local official who summoned a notary to record his dissent. Then the company parted ways. Luther had already sent the imperial herald back once they reached Hesse, which was considered friendly territory. He now sent Jonas, Schurff, and the others back toward Erfurt and Wittenberg, and set out with only Amsdorf and his Augustinian brother Petzensteiner to visit his relatives in Mohra, which they did. It was a perfect location for "disappearing." On May 4 the party was attacked, and Luther was seized so forcefully that he was only able to grab a New Testament and a Hebrew Bible from

38. "Letter to Lucas Cranach" (April 28, 1521), in LW 48:202. It is not clear when Luther became acquainted with the Cranachs, but the personal touches in this letter make his friendship with both Lucas and his wife Barbara seem well-established.
39. "Letter to Charles V" (April 28, 1521), in LW 48:203–9.

his possessions. By late that evening, he was safely hidden in the Wartburg Castle that towered above Eisenach. Frederick had staged the abduction of Luther. He could therefore plausibly deny that he needed to solve the Luther problem immediately.

Back in Worms, some princes, including Luther's supporters Frederick and the Count Palatine, began to leave before the end of the diet (which had been running for four months). This cleared the way for those remaining to adopt the Edict of Worms unanimously on May 8. Charles signed it on May 25. It declared Luther an outlaw of the empire and called on all to assist in his capture and delivery to the authorities. Charles declared: "We enjoin you all not to take the aforementioned Martin Luther into your houses, not to receive him at court, to give him neither food nor drink, not to hide him, to afford him no help, following, support, or encouragement, either clandestinely or publicly, through words or works. Where you can get him, seize him and overpower him, you should capture him and send him to us under tightest security."[40] The effect of this edict haunted Luther for the rest of his life. It limited his movement to within Electoral Saxony and, after it instituted the Reformation, also to Hesse. In the very last years, this also included Ducal Saxony, Brandenburg, and even Halle, but by that time Luther was not venturing far from Wittenberg. It kept Luther from ever coming into Charles's presence again—on pain of death—though on at least one occasion, when the Augsburg Confession was presented in 1530, Luther would have liked to be there.

More seriously, it meant that for the next twenty-five years until his death Luther lived under daily worry about whether he would survive. At times the threat may have seemed remote, as when Charles was off fighting against Tunis in the Mediterranean or even

---

40. Cited in Oberman, *Luther*, 203.

having a war with the pope later that decade. But Luther was always in danger from treachery, from a lone assassin or a supposed friend actually in the service of the empire. The strain was considerable and has much to do with Luther's exhaustion later in life, but those who know how the story comes out—that Luther died a natural death at a good age—knew something that the Reformer himself could not know.

Image 16: This painting by Hans Holbein depicts Luther as the "German Hercules" slaying the powers of his time.

Luther had made his testimony before princes, but it seemed that Charles would have the last word. The emperor asked Aleander whether he was content, and he replied that he was. Rome was pleased too, and the response to Aleander's final report from Worms was very gratifying to Leo and his court. They had opposed Charles's election as emperor, but that had to do with the protection of the

Papal States. Charles knew of that opposition but was not being vindictive. He was proving in the Luther case what a good friend and loyal son of the church he could be. He also seemed determined to bring Luther to trial very soon; they expected that, barring some accident along the way, the heretic monk would be brought to Rome. This good news was shared with all the cardinals in a consistory July 7, after which Luther's books and picture were burned in the Piazza Navona.[41]

We do not know about Eck's feelings at the end of the diet, but Aleander was delighted in what he had accomplished. He felt secure enough about the outcome that he could even be generous to his opponent Luther. He wrote to Cardinal Giulio de' Medici that they should take a lesson from the way that Luther, Hutten, and their friends had built public support. He said, "Would that the Pope, through the intercession of your Eminence, would by praise and reward, encourage men of talent to make an intelligent study of Scripture and put their pens to work, after the example of the German, in defense of the faith."[42] Perhaps something was starting, after all. Later that year, Luther would write of faith in general words that seem apt for his particular situation. The ends of important processes—be they matters of high politics or personal faith—could rarely be known in advance. After all, "This life, therefore, is not righteousness but growth in righteousness, not health but healing, not being but becoming, not rest but exercise. We are not now what we shall be, but we are on the way. The process is not yet finished, but it is actively going on. This is not the end but it is the right road. At present, everything does not gleam and sparkle, but everything is being cleansed."[43]

41. Ludwig Pastor, *History of the Popes*, vol. 7 (London: Routledge, 1950), 37.
42. Pastor, *History of the Popes*, 7:440.
43. *Defense and Explanation of All the Articles*, in LW 32:24. Translation altered.

6

Luther the Prisoner

1521–1522

For the second time in his life, Luther had escaped from a situation of extreme personal danger. There had been an active debate among Charles's advisors at Worms whether to ignore the safe-conduct and either put Luther to death or send him to Rome as a prisoner. But the emperor was also aware of the delicate situation both with the German nobility and the general public and decided that he could deal with Luther at a more opportune time.

In a letter to Spalatin at the Electoral Court, Luther describes the situation of his capture:

> After a short while, close to the Altenstein Castle, I was captured. Amsdorf knew of course that I was to be captured by someone but does not know where I am in custody. My fellow-friar, seeing the horsemen in time, jumped off the wagon and is said to have arrived in Waltershausen in the evening, unseen and on foot.
>
> Here I was stripped of my own clothes and dressed in a knight's cloak. I am letting my hair grow and beard grow, so that you would hardly

know me; I can't even recognize myself any longer. Now I am living in Christian liberty and am free of all the laws of that tyrant.[1]

In another letter to Amsdorf, Luther recalled that it took many hours to get to the Wartburg Castle, where he would be held for the next several months, because they took a winding trail to confuse any who might pursue them, not arriving at the castle until eleven o'clock. It was quite an experience for Luther to spend most of the day on a horse, as his custom was either to walk or to ride in a cart.[2]

Luther was safe, but his life began to change in dramatic ways even beyond the efforts at disguise with a beard, a full head of hair, and a knight's clothing. He was without two of his greatest resources: his books and his friends. He did not know what was happening in the larger world of which he had been a central player for the past few years. He began to eat at the table of the master of the castle, and this rich food of the nobility, so different from what was served in the Augustinian Cloister in Wittenberg, soon led to Luther filling out his bony frame.

He could write to Spalatin that he was free, but in another sense he was a prisoner in the Wartburg. He began to speak of the castle as his Patmos, a comparison to the small island off Asia Minor where the author of Revelation was imprisoned when he had his vision of the Apocalypse. In mid-July, he fantasized that he would not return to Wittenberg but would go to teach at Erfurt or Cologne. He did not want to cause trouble for his friends.[3]

---

1. "Letter to George Spalatin" (May 14, 1521), in LW 48:227–28.
2. "Letter to Nicholas von Amsdorf" (May 12, 1521), in LW 48:219.
3. "Letter to George Spalatin" (July 31, 1521), in LW 48:274.

Image 17: The Wartburg Castle, perched high above the city of Eisenach, is a watershed of German history. Luther lived here in hiding for many months in 1521–1522.

Luther's health was poor for the first five months, and even when constipation and attendant bleeding left him weak and helpless, he was not free to go to nearby Erfurt—as he repeatedly requested—for medical attention. The elector wanted Luther out of circulation, and so he remained for some time. Spalatin sent pills from the court that do seem to have helped, although Luther does not report good health until October 7.[4]

The physical struggles were severe, but the spiritual difficulties from fear and isolation were even worse. He was always a person whose energy came from conversations with those who surrounded him—colleagues, students, and family. Both in his personal life and

4. "Letter to George Spalatin" (October 7, 1521), in LW 48:316.

his professional achievements, Luther owed much to the contributions of others. Luther remembered these struggles years later in his Table Talk when advising a pastor on how to deal with specters and evil visions: "I was often pestered [by the devil] when I was imprisoned in my Patmos, high up in the fortress in the kingdom of the birds. I resisted him in faith and confronted him with this verse: God, who created man, is mine, and all things are under his feet! If you have any power over him, try it."[5] As his health improved, the spiritual afflictions seemed to increase, with a particularly severe experience around All Saints' Day, November 1. He told Spalatin at that time the "evil and astute demons" were amusing him, "but in a disturbing way." He asked for his friend's prayer that "Christ does not desert me in the end."[6]

Contemporary visitors to the breathtakingly beautiful Wartburg Castle may have trouble imagining how Luther suffered in his ten months' confinement there. But the dangers that he faced were considerable. One of the greatest was that news of his whereabouts would leak out. Only a handful of people knew that Luther was in that particular castle, one of many in Frederick's possession. In July, he also conspired with Spalatin to lead people astray by writing a letter, suggesting that he was in Bohemia, to be "lost" where opponents could find it.[7] The general gossip among Luther's opponents was that he had gone to either Denmark, where the king was Frederick's nephew, or Bohemia, the land of Hus and opposition to Rome.

Official hostility to Luther was growing in many of the places where he might have sought refuge. Francis I of France was burning Luther's books in Paris, despite his many disagreements on other

---

5. "Table Talk for April 5, 1538," in LW 54:280.
6. "Letter to George Spalatin" (November 1, 1521), in LW 48:324. See also "Letter to Nicholas Gerbel" (November 1, 1521), in LW 48:319.
7. "Letter to George Spalatin" (ca. July 15, 1521), in LW 48:272–73.

matters with the pope. On May 12 in London, the papal bull condemning Luther was posted publicly and his books were burned. Most of the monarchs of Europe were rallying around the pope and the emperor against Luther. Henry VIII personally began to write *The Defense of the Seven Sacraments*, an attack on Luther's *Babylonian Captivity*. A splendidly bound copy was presented to Pope Leo X on September 14. In July, King Sigismund of Poland issued a severe edict against the spread of Lutheranism.

But the greatest danger to Luther came not from these monarchs, but from the emperor himself. His strong language in the Edict of Worms had led to rejoicing in Rome, as well as a burning of Luther's writings and his picture on June 7. But when the Diet of Worms was concluded late in May, Charles turned to other matters. He went to Austria to confer those territories on his brother Ferdinand. He saw his sister Mary married to the king of Hungary. By September 18, Pope Leo X was quite discouraged with his emperor. He had Aleander write to Charles complaining that unless he took action immediately, the elector of Saxony might be emboldened to take even more terrible steps than his current protection of the heretic Luther.

What neither Charles nor Luther could have known at the time was that Charles was on the verge of travels and wars that would keep him from dealing with Germany very directly for a decade. If hostility to Luther was increasing among rulers surrounding Germany, support for Luther was increasing rapidly in Germany at the same time. By the time of the Diet of Nuremberg in 1522, it had become clear that there could be no wholesale enforcement of the Edict of Worms. Luther's books might be burned and his followers harassed in one territory, but in another any movement against Luther would have brought the government itself into danger. Impatience with the papal church was rising throughout

Germany, and increasingly this dissatisfaction was being linked to demands for social reform. These demands would boil over into widespread conflict in the Peasants' War of 1524–1525.

Concern for Friends

Luther's struggles in Wartburg were real enough, but we should think of them more as periodic bouts of great intensity than as nonstop unhappiness. Luther's previous resilience was evident again in the way he spent these ten months. If he missed his friends, he would write to them. If he lacked books, he could write them. Luther never believed that work overcame discouragement and the devil; only the help of Christ could do this. But Luther quickly went to writing letters and articulating the things that he wished yet to say, perhaps now more strongly than ever.

Of the forty-two letters from these ten months in the American edition of *Luther's Works*, thirty-six are to close friends, including eighteen to Spalatin, nine to Melanchthon, and four to Amsdorf. The case of Spalatin is somewhat special, as he functioned as Luther's advocate at Frederick's court. Yet these letters also testify to Luther's capacity for friendship. He was able both to seek help, prayers, and support from these coworkers and to express great affirmation to them for what they were able to accomplish in his absence.

In the very first letter to Melanchthon, soon after his arrival at the Wartburg, Luther expresses concern that news of his whereabouts will leak out. Yet he can also take courage from the support that he experienced from the crowds at Worms and even joke that, before it is all over, even Albrecht of Mainz may wish Luther would come back because it would be easier to deal with him than with the common people. At the same time, he understood the ambiguity of this popular support and is quite distressed to hear of students in Erfurt rioting and threatening the houses of priests. Taking this direct and unwarranted action "creates disgrace and just repulsion for our gospel."[8]

Though Luther writes most often to Spalatin, his deepest concern seems to be for his young colleague Philip Melanchthon, who is only twenty-four years old at this time. From the beginning, he exhorts Philip to provide leadership in his absence but not to do too much. Near the beginning of his time in the Wartburg, he wrote: "You, therefore, as minister of the Word, be steadfast in the meantime and fortify the walls and towers of Jerusalem until [the enemy] also attacks you. You know your calls and your gifts. I pray for you as for no one else, if my prayer can accomplish something—which I do not doubt. Return, therefore, this service so that we carry this burden together."[9]

In July, he gave Melanchthon a very candid report of his situation in this friendly confinement. After scolding his younger colleague for being too gentle and for thinking too highly of Luther, he pours out his heart to his friend. He has not been able to work for eight days. Nor can he pray or study. His body is ill, but he is also experiencing "temptation of the flesh." He vows to go to Erfurt to seek medical help and to appear in public, knowing as he says it that this will not be allowed by the elector.[10]

At the beginning of August in one of his most famous letters, Luther again urges Melanchthon toward greater courage in his person: "If you are a preacher of grace, then preach a true and not a fictitious grace; if grace is true, you must bear a true and not a fictitious sin. God does not save people who are only fictitious sinners. Be a sinner and sin boldly, but believe and rejoice in Christ more boldly, for he is victorious over sin, death, and the world. . . . Pray boldly, you too are a mighty sinner."[11] The letter does not

---

8. "Two Letters to Philip Melanchthon" (May 8, 1521), in LW 48:210–14.
9. "Letter to Philip Melanchthon" (May 12, 1521), in LW 48:216.
10. "Letter to Philip Melanchthon" (July 10, 1521), in LW 48:257.
11. "Letter to Philip Melanchthon" (August 1, 1521), in LW 48:281–82.

make any sense as general advice. Luther would never have written this to Henry VIII or Philip of Hesse, who in their own ways were as bold as Luther. But his careful, fearful young colleague needed just this kind of encouragement not to worry himself to death over small things. This is Luther practicing individualized pastoral care in a way that might surprise those who knew only the writer of the sharp pamphlets and treatises. Luther was offering this kind of deeply personal guidance, visible only in his thousands of letters, all through his career.

Luther also knew that Philip worried about him, and he took this friend seriously enough to admit in his next letter that he thinks he may be dying. Perhaps, Luther admits, this may be the end of his ministry. "Have I not stirred up enough disturbance single-handedly? I have not lived in vain."[12] He seems to have genuine confidence that Wittenberg is in good hands. He tells Amsdorf that he would love to be a student there now, rather than a teacher, so that he could take Hebrews with Amsdorf and Corinthians with Philip.[13]

But while sharing his joys and his struggles with these friends, again and again his concern returns to Philip. This escalated in September when Luther received a copy of Melanchthon's *Loci Communes*—the first summary of their common Reformation teaching.[14] He had taken the major themes of theology and organized them as clues for reading the Scriptures properly. It was a stunning work that Luther valued highly from the beginning, partly because of its usefulness and partly because it was the kind of work that Luther could not have written. This publication raised Melanchthon even another notch in Luther's estimation. He said in his Table Talk that

12. "Letter to Philip Melanchthon" (August 3, 1521), in LW 48:288.
13. "Letter to Nicholas von Amsdorf" (July 15, 1521), in LW 48:267.
14. "Letter to Philip Melanchthon" (September 9, 1521), in LW 48:296–97. *Loci Communes* can be found in Wilhelm Pauck, ed., *Melanchthon and Bucer*, Library of Christian Classics 19 (Philadelphia: Westminster, 1969).

the *Loci* was the one book in addition to the Bible necessary for learning to be a theologian.[15]

On the whole, Luther was a good mentor for Melanchthon, but his high estimation of his young colleague sometimes led Luther to push Melanchthon into more work while at the same time urging him to rest and not do too much. Melanchthon regarded Luther with immense respect but also worried about Luther's bombastic side, and he complained frequently in correspondence with humanist friends like Joachim Camerarius that Luther could be difficult to work with. For his part, dissatisfied with the arrangements for preaching in Wittenberg in his absence, Luther campaigned with Spalatin and Amsdorf to get the town council to permit Melanchthon to preach in the evening in his home in the German language for the edification of the common people.[16] Philip was not ordained and the arrangement was unusual, but it was finally approved. We have no record of whether this was a task Philip actually wanted to assume.

Luther could also be protective of his brilliant young colleague. In the same letter in which he reported on the restoration of his own health, Luther said that he had heard reports of the plague in Wittenberg. Luther ordered Spalatin to force Philip to leave if there was any danger. "That head must be preserved, so that the Word, which the Lord has entrusted to him for the salvation of souls, may not perish."[17]

Productivity amid Anxiety

Luther's letters from the Wartburg testify to his experience there, but they are just a tiny part of the writing that he did in those ten months.

---

15. "Table Talk for Winter 1542–3," in LW 54:439–40. Luther also recommended Melanchthon's Romans commentary and his own commentaries on Deuteronomy and Galatians.

16. "Letter to George Spalatin" (September 9, 1521), in LW 48:308; and "Letter to Nicholas von Amsdorf" (September 9, 1521), in LW 48:311–12.

17. "Letter to George Spalatin" (October 7, 1521), in LW 48:316.

The amount he wrote is impressive; the quality and significance is even more noteworthy. The narrow escape from Worms had again reminded Luther of his vulnerability. As in 1519 and 1520 after Leipzig, now again Luther raced from project to project, partly to add to his legacy, partly to deal creatively with his isolation.

It took some time for books and manuscripts to be sent from Wittenberg. Luther reported to Spalatin that he was "drunk with leisure" and hard at work on the Bible in Greek and Hebrew.[18] Even before supplies could reach him, Luther set out on writing projects that could be completed without his usual library sources. The first of these was a commentary on Psalm 68—an important liturgical text for the current season of the church year: the end of Easter, Ascension, and Pentecost.[19] Melanchthon was instructed to publish it if the presses were idle and to attach any dedication that he wished.[20]

He also wrote a treatise on confession, still a volatile theme with his Catholic opponents, and dedicated it to the German knight Francis von Sickingen, who had been a strong supporter at Worms.[21] He rushed through a commentary on Psalm 37 and dedicated it to the "poor little flock of Christ in Wittenberg," asking them not to worry about him and reminding them that he had come through three trials already—his appearance before Cajetan at Augsburg, his debate with Eck in Leipzig, and his appearance before Charles at Worms.[22]

The great task preoccupying him in the early weeks at the Wartburg was a reply to the Louvain theologian Jacobus Masson, who called himself by the Latin name Latomus. He was well-known as an enemy of the new learning and had attacked Erasmus two years

---

18. "Letter to George Spalatin" (May 14, 1521), in LW 48:225.
19. "Psalm 68" (1521), in LW 13:3–37. Despite the dramatic events that Luther has just experienced, the commentary makes little if any reference to these occurrences.
20. "Letter to Philip Melanchthon" (May 26, 1521), in LW 48:239.
21. "Letter to Francis von Sickingen" (June 1, 1521), in LW 48:246–47.
22. "Letter to the People of Wittenberg" (June 1521), in LW 48:248–50.

earlier. His book against Luther reached the Wartburg on May 26. Luther thought that the book was rather poor theologically but that the attack was important enough it needed a response, even if he had to work without the sources that would have been helpful.

What resulted was one of Luther's longest works to date, *Against Latomus*, a defense of the reality of sin, the bondage of the will, purgatory, indulgences, and other issues spanning 125 pages. In this treatise, Luther had the leisure to spell out in more detail than previously his understanding of the biblical basis for and implication of justification by faith. He dedicated this major work to his Wittenberg colleague Justus Jonas and, at the end of it, challenged Jonas, Carlstadt, and Amsdorf to take up the task of refuting this theologian more adequately than he was currently able to do. "I would like you to do something for the Word so that I could sometime have the leisure to help poor ordinary people."[23]

Luther knew the complex theology of *Against Latomus* was important, but he also understood that it was not in a form to inspire as many as his other works had. Luther's book generated surprisingly little response at the time of its publication. It was most helpful to Melanchthon, who was at that time preparing his *Loci* and made immediate use of Luther's arguments. But Luther would return to elaborate many of these themes in his refutation of Erasmus in the *Bondage of the Will* four years later at the end of 1525.[24]

As manuscripts arrived from Wittenberg, Luther could complete another project that was very dear to him. He had been writing a commentary on the Magnificat, Mary's song in Luke 1:46-55. He had almost completed it before leaving for Worms. He intended to dedicate it to Duke John Frederick, the young prince and presumed

---

23. *Against Latomus* (1521), in LW 32:260.
24. Martin Brecht, *Martin Luther*, vol. 2: *Shaping and Defining the Reformation, 1521–1532*, trans. James L. Schaaf (Minneapolis: Fortress Press, 1990), 7–9.

heir of Saxony who had so warmly supported him when troubles were mounting late in 1520. In some ways, his experience at Worms made him even more aware of the hidden ways of God, who in the words of the song puts down the mighty from their thrones and lifts up the lowly.

The resulting booklet was just the kind of thing that Luther was hoping to write, if others would take up the polemical tasks for a time. Bernard Lohse has called it "a pearl among [Luther's] interpretations of the Scriptures."[25] At the beginning, Luther contrasts the proud way that the world looks at everything, full of disdain for "the depths with their poverty, disgrace, squalor, misery and anguish." But God's way of seeing "looks into the depths with all their need and misery." This song of Mary teaches the Christian what a surprising source of power the Christian God is, and teaches a corresponding regard for the lowly and the humble.[26]

At the end, he spoke directly and perhaps rather bluntly to the future ruler concerning what he should have learned about his calling from the Magnificat:

> All these things were foreordained by God in order to terrify those in authority, to keep them in fear, and to admonish them of their peril. For great possessions, glory, power, and favor, as well as the flatterers no lord may be without, surround and lay siege to the heart of a prince, moving it to pride, to forgetfulness of God and neglect of the people and the common weal, to sensuality, blasphemy, arrogance, and idleness, in short, to every sort of vice and evil. Indeed there is no castle or city that is so heavily besieged and assaulted. Unless, therefore, one fortifies himself by means of such examples, and takes the fear of God for his defense and rampart, how can he endure?[27]

25. Bernard Lohse, *Martin Luther: An Introduction to His Life and Work* (Philadelphia: Fortress Press, 1986), 130.

26. "The Magnificat" (1521), in LW 21:300. For more on Luther's views of Mary in general, see Robert W. Jenson and Carl E. Braaten, eds., *Mary, Mother of God* (Grand Rapids, MI: Eerdmans, 1999).

27. LW 21:356–67.

Luther has often been portrayed as the uncritical tool of princes. This exhortation at the end of the treatise was his vow not to be a flatterer but to share the best that he knew, even if it forced him to deliver unwelcome news to authority.

In the fall, Duke John, Frederick's brother, visited the Wartburg and learned that Luther was there, but does not seem to have met with him. However, he passed a message along that he was struggling with the story of the ten lepers in Luke 17 and Jesus' command that they show themselves to the priest as having been healed. This was being interpreted as a defense of the traditional practices of penance, and Luther quickly wrote a sermon at the prince's request.

Such biblical interpretation excited Luther most in these months, but he kept being pulled away because of the conflicts of the day. All through the summer, they were debating celibacy in Wittenberg as some priests and even monks began to marry despite the vows they had taken. Luther had already questioned priestly celibacy in his *Appeal to the German Nobility* of 1520 but was less sympathetic to the complaints of monks who seemed to him to have taken their vows quite willingly. He followed the writings of Carlstadt and Melanchthon on this latest topic and was quite critical of the exegetical basis that they were using. Still, he did not criticize them in public because he knew the glee that their Catholic opponents would take at any sign that the Wittenbergers were divided. In any case, he told Spalatin, "They will not push a wife on me!"[28]

By the beginning of September, Luther had drafted "Theses on Vows." He hoped that these could strengthen the argument with which he was in basic sympathy. At this time, Albrecht of Mainz was dedicating his new cathedral in Halle, near Wittenberg, and announced a new indulgence available for purchase to visitors of

---

28. "Letter to George Spalatin" (August 6, 1521), in LW 48:290.

the building. Albrecht was also reported to have imprisoned several recently married priests, and this double outrage highly angered Luther. He had heard tales of Albrecht's own mistress kept in the Moritzburg Castle, and he was appalled by the reversion to indulgences and the hypocrisy of persecuting at a moral point where he was vulnerable himself. By November 1, Luther had completed a stinging treatment of the whole affair titled "Against the Idol of Halle."[29]

Spalatin and Melanchthon saw to it that this was never published in the form Luther wrote it; many of its arguments were instead incorporated into a later writing. What did eventually get sent was a letter from Luther to Albrecht. He chided him, saying, "Your electoral Grace should not think that Luther is dead," and threatening to reopen his public attacks on Albrecht himself.[30] Though there were many complicating factors involved, including Saxony's fear of trouble with Albrecht and Albrecht's fear of trouble with Luther, the cardinal backed down and wrote a very polite letter to Luther saying that he had already complied with the issues Luther was raising and that "I can do nothing of my own self, and confess that I stand in need of the grace of God."[31]

There were side skirmishes in this encounter, including a blistering letter to Albrecht's theological advisor Wolfgang Capito, a scholar friend of Erasmus from whom Luther expected more than he did from the prince-archbishop. Usually such polemics accomplish little, but in this case Capito was shaken enough by Luther's charges to visit him in 1522 in Wittenberg and soon thereafter to resign from

29. For this complicated history, see the preface to "Against the Spiritual Estate of the Pope and the Bishops, Falsely So-Called" (1522), in LW 39:241–45. This text includes one of Luther's full, early discussions on the right and wrong ways to be a bishop. See LW 39:269ff.
30. "Letter to Cardinal Albrecht of Mainz" (December 1, 1521), in LW 48:341.
31. A part of Albrecht's answer to Luther can be found in B. S. Kidd, ed., *Documents Illustrative of the Continental Reformation* (Oxford: Clarendon, 1967), 48.

Albrecht's service entirely. But the question of vows now needed fuller attention than the mere drafting of theses, and in three weeks in November, Luther wrote another of his most important works, *On Monastic Vows*.

He dedicated this work to his father, Hans Luther, and accompanied it with a letter to his father in which he acknowledged that Hans had been right to challenge his youthful decision to enter the monastery: "You had learned from numerous examples that this way of life turned out sadly for many. You were determined, therefore, to tie me down with an honorable and wealthy marriage. This fear of yours, this care, this indignation against me was for a time implacable."[32] Luther offers his critique of monasticism to his father as a peace offering, or at least a step in that direction. He admits that his parents were right to raise the question of his disobedience to them, but he also argues that from his bad decision God has brought something good—Luther's call to ministry and vocation on behalf of the gospel. Christ has "absolved me from the monastic vow and granted me such liberty" so that now Christ alone is "my immediate bishop, abbot, prior, lord, father and teacher."[33]

This treatise may well have been Luther's final step in his break with Rome.[34] It is not only a powerful critique of the whole institution of religious communities for men and women as the preferred way to serve God, but even more fundamentally it is a critique of any dual-track ethic with a lower road for laity and a higher road for clergy. Here again, his rhetorical power is employed in full force, and he argues that "Christian freedom is of divine right," given in Baptism, and is not something that can be surrendered.[35] His comprehensive critique comes in five parts, as he discusses how

32. "Letter to Hans Luther" (November 21, 1521), in LW 48:331, MLBTW3, 191–94.
33. LW 48:336, MLBTW3, 194.
34. At least, this is the judgment of Lohse, *Martin Luther: An Introduction*, 131.
35. "The Judgment of Martin Luther on Monastic Vows" (1521), in LW 44:297ff.

binding vows are against God's word, against faith, against Christian freedom, against the First Commandment, and even against reason and common sense. Love, not binding vows, must be the final word and highest criterion for Christians.[36]

The impact of this treatise in the next few years and even decades was stunning. All over northern Europe, men and women read his indictment of the failure of monasticism and began to leave their communities, taking up the new challenges of living as Christians in the structure of daily life: family, work, and civic responsibility. Luther did not rule out the possibility of set-apart religious life completely, but his critique was so powerful that it practically ended the vital witness of religious orders in the churches of the Reformation.

Preaching in Absentia: The Postils

The writings discussed above would make the time in the Wartburg one of the richest and most productive of Luther's life. But all of these were preliminary to the chief task that he discovered in his captivity. It was, after all, the word that had made everything possible so far. There had been clues from Augustine and German mysticism, encouragement from Staupitz and friends in Wittenberg. But the strength that Luther had discovered that gave him leverage against everything—from indulgences to Scholastic theology to the power of the papacy itself—was the word of God. He had taken his stand on it at Worms, refusing to submit to papal authority or even the decision of a general council. But how could that word be served and secured even beyond Luther's own lifetime?

One evident need was for a better German translation of the Bible. Luther was not the first to set his hand to this task. Eighteen

---

36. LW 44:393.

versions had already appeared by 1518. But they were either very rough or very wooden. Most were based on the Latin Bible of Saint Jerome rather than the original Greek and Hebrew. Luther was being encouraged by friends in Wittenberg to take up the task, as he had already shown skill in his German writings on the Bible. His Greek was excellent and his Hebrew was improving, but best of all was his fine ability to use the German language itself.

A translation alone would not do it. For the word to be powerfully available to ordinary people, those Luther was now calling the true priests of the church, there also needed to be preaching. Luther never thought the Bible was an easy book. He knew that Bible reading could calm the spirit or plunge one into deep despair. The word needed interpretation. So Luther planned to write an ambitious guide for preachers—model sermons and theological fodder for all the Epistles and all the Gospel lessons of the whole church year. These came to be known as postils: the Advent Postil, Christmas Postil, Lenten Postil, Summer Postil, and Festival Postil.[37]

He had already started one version of this task early in the year back in Wittenberg. He had written a series of comments on the Epistles and Gospels for the season of Advent—the first four Sundays of the Christian calendar. But these had been written in Latin, and he now came to see that if they were to foster and support preaching in German, they needed to be written in German.

For some weeks, no one in Wittenberg could find Luther's Latin Advent Postil manuscript. When it did not come, he began working on the Christmas section—eight sections for the Gospels for Christmas Eve through Epiphany and eight more for the Epistles.

37. Most churches today have a three-year set of lessons for the church year called a lectionary—with Old Testament readings, as well as Epistle and Gospel lessons. In Luther's time there was one set of readings used every year, and this did not (generally) include readings from the Old Testament. Luther did preach on those books as well, but not at the Sunday morning service.

This was work that he relished, the kind of project that he hoped to be free to carry out. He began work in June with interruptions along the way, but by November 19 he had finished the Christmas Postil, which was a book very dear to his heart. He asked that it not be printed by Gruenenberg in Wittenberg, who tended to do rather sloppy work, but by a better publisher who would take great care.[38] He asked Spalatin again and again that this project be pushed ahead of anything else that was awaiting publication.[39]

The Christmas Postil was dedicated to Count Albrecht of Mansfeld, one of the rulers of Luther's home territory. Albert and his brother had been faithful supporters of Luther since 1519, and he wanted to thank them both and encourage them in the ongoing task of protecting the gospel in the church. Luther knew that a dedication by an outlaw might backfire, so he made the best of the situation by comparing his low estate to the neglected and ignored gospel:

> In order that this preface conform in every respect to the gospel, therefore, the writer, too is a despised and damned person. By the grace of God I am under sentence of excommunication by the pope and in greatest disfavor; in addition his followers curse and hate me greatly. So I hope it should be all right for me to treat this despised, little, poor book of the gospel concerning the least and most despised child of God, and to forget about the high, big, and long books of the tiara-crowned king in Rome, even if it should be a bit above me, inasmuch as all universities, convents, and monasteries are tied to the tiara and disregard the youngest and littlest book, the gospel.[40]

The spirit of these sermons is very similar to that of the "Commentary on the Magnificat" that Luther had finished earlier in 1521. Luther

---

38. "Letter to George Spalatin" (August 15, 1521), in LW 48:292. Luther wrote: "What good does it do to work hard if such sloppiness and confusion causes other printers (who may reprint from this first edition) to make more mistakes that are worse? I do not want the Gospels and Epistles to be sinned against in this way; it is better to hide them than bring them out in such a form."
39. "Letter to George Spalatin" (July 31, 1521), in LW 48:276.
40. "Dedication to Count Mansfeld," in LW 52:5.

found in the Christmas stories a powerful occasion to speak of the tenderness and love of God, but also of God's surprising hidden ways. The birth of the Christ child is not the occasion for sentimentality for Luther, but the pledge that he is "a natural human being, in every respect exactly as we are. . . . The more we draw Christ down into nature and into the flesh, the more consolation accrues for us."[41] The message comes first not to the powerful and the rich, but to the poor and marginal, like shepherds "up and working during the night. They represent all the lowly ones who lead a poor, despised, unostentatious life on earth. . . . They are ready to receive the gospel."[42]

Luther always loved to preach about the Magi from the East who came seeking the Christ child. In the Christmas Postil, his remarks on the "Gospel for Epiphany" run to almost 130 pages—hardly a sermon that could actually be preached to any known audience. Luther finds the story of the Magi compelling as the clue to how even the powerful and the wise may find salvation if they put aside excessive trust in reason and their own judgment and follow the strange working of the gospel. The Magi lose their way when they turn from following the star to seeking information in Herod's court. That palace of the powerful has no information and no openness to the birth of this child. When they set out again and follow the star, they find their way to Bethlehem, not Jerusalem, for in this humble town the child is born. "This star will not fail you; without it you will never find the house which you hope to find."[43]

The Christmas Postil was published in March 1522 and the Advent Postil the following month. Luther valued these works highly and continued the series over the next years as his time allowed. Lutheran

41. "The Gospel for Christmas Eve" (1521), in LW 52:12.
42. LW 52:25.
43. "Gospel for Epiphany," in LW 52:276.

preachers used the postils for several centuries after Luther's time, but they have been largely neglected by theologians, even though Luther called the postil "the very best book I ever wrote."[44]

When the Christmas Postil was published, Luther attached to it one of his more remarkable smaller works, "A Brief Instruction on What to Look for and Expect in the Gospels." He says that two confusions have prevented people from obtaining the benefits that they should find in the Bible. The first is the tendency to speak of four Gospels when in fact there is only one gospel that comes in many forms. For Luther, Peter and Paul and Isaiah are just as much evangelists as Matthew, Mark, Luke, and John. The deep meaning of gospel is not a bare biography of Christ but the message of good news.[45] Indeed, sometimes the Epistles, or even readings from the Old Testament, may be more powerful forms of gospel than a passage from one of the four books called Gospels.

The second confusion is even more serious. Christians think that the Gospels are rulebooks and that Christ is a kind of second Moses who has come to tell and show Christians how to live. Of course, there is such material in the Gospels, Luther admits, but this is not their primary purpose. "The chief article and foundation of the gospel is that before you take Christ as an example, you accept and recognize him as gift, as a present that God has given you and that is your own. This means that when you see or hear of Christ doing or suffering something, you do not doubt that Christ himself, with his deeds and suffering, belongs to you."[46] The example will follow, but if you put

---

44. Cited in "Preface to Volume 52," in LW 52:ix. In the treatise "That These Words of Christ, 'This Is My Body' Still Hold Fast", Luther calls the "church postils" "a book" even though they were distributed separately as well as in compilation volumes. WA 23:278.

45. Robert W. Jenson, following Luther, defines the gospel as "The story about Jesus, told as a promise." Jenson, "A Theological Autobiography, to Date," in *Theologians in Their Own Words*, ed. Derek R. Nelson, Ted Peters and Joshua M. Moritz (Minneapolis: Fortress Press, 2013), 93.

46. "A Brief Instruction on What to Look for and Expect in the Gospels" (1521), in LW 35:119, MLBTW3, 72.

that consideration first, as the church of Luther's time was doing, you will never hear the good news in all its liberating power.

Translating the Bible

The postils and such short writings could help guide Christians in their approach to the Bible, but they still need Bibles to read. Luther began his translation of the New Testament after he returned from a brief visit to Wittenberg in December 1521 and finished the first draft in eleven weeks. He had been teaching this material for a decade and had Erasmus's splendid edition of the Greek New Testament to work with, but the difficulty of the assignment was quite surprising to him. Heiko Oberman observes that in this translation project Luther found "a task that was to demonstrate his shortcomings to him but that was to guarantee his fame for centuries to come."[47] And nearly four centuries later, the philosopher Friedrich Nietzsche, no friend of Luther's, could note, "In comparison with Luther's Bible, everything else in German is mere 'literature.'"[48]

Luther's friend John Lang was busy translating the Gospel of Matthew at the same time Luther was entering into his project. He expected to stay at the Wartburg until Easter to have time to finish the assignment. Lang should continue his own work, Luther wrote, because he hoped that "every town would have its interpreter." He could not imagine at this point what a standard resource his own version of the Bible would become.[49]

47. Heiko Oberman, *Luther: Man between God and the Devil*, trans. Eileen Walliser-Schwarzbart (New Haven: Yale University Press, 1989), 304.
48. Quoted in Heinrich Bornkamm, *Luther im Spiegel des deutschen Geistesgeschichte* (Heidelberg: Quelle & Meyer, 1955), 228.
49. "Letter to John Lang," in LW 48:356.

Image 18: The "Luther Room" in the Wartburg. Luther later called his time there using his ink pen to translate the New Testament "throwing ink at the devil," which later generations took literally.

As he worked, Luther began to develop various principles for translating. In later years, he often spoke of these in his Table Talk. You cannot simply follow the rules of grammar but need to ask those who have a better knowledge of the original language for their help. You can remember God is always speaking either law or gospel, in both of the testaments. This will sometimes help you find your way in an obscure passage. In the end, each book has its own message, and you must ask how all the individual parts fit with this. Luther translated very freely, but not recklessly, and in fact did not publish his translation until he had time to return to Wittenberg and go over the whole manuscript carefully with Melanchthon, taking advantage of his superior knowledge of Greek.[50]

The excitement of the translation project helped Luther pass his last two months in the Wartburg, but it also made him more eager to return to Wittenberg. He could complete a draft of the New Testament on his own, but finishing the entire Bible would take the insight of the whole Wittenberg faculty. He proposed to Amsdorf that if he needed to remain in hiding, perhaps he could live secretly in a room in Amsdorf's house and be part of a group translation project. Desire to work with others on the Bible translation was a contributing factor in his return to Wittenberg in March 1522. But in the meantime, a crisis was developing there that overshadowed even this important work.

Tumult in Wittenberg

Who would provide leadership in Wittenberg in Luther's absence? Luther wrote to the friends he trusted most—Melanchthon, Amsdorf, and Jonas—and spurred them to do what they could. But almost inevitably, the leadership fell to a more senior colleague, the dean of the faculty of theology, Andreas Bodenstein von Carlstadt (1486–1541). He had been with Luther at the Leipzig Debate, and though lacking some of the quickness and charm of his younger colleague, he had done well against their common opponent, John Eck. On many issues, he was slow to come to Luther's view of things, but when he changed his mind, it was often with great force. Sometimes he rushed past Luther in his eagerness to correct old ways.

Luther had suggested many changes in the life of the church, especially in *To the German Nobility* (1520), but none of the major ones had been enacted. Now, in his absence, there was a desire to move forward on changes in worship, especially saying Mass in the language of the people and offering both the bread and the cup to

50. See "Table Talk for Summer or Fall 1532," in LW 54:42–43; "Table Talk for May and June 1540," in LW 54:375–76; and "Table Talk for Winter 1542–3," in LW 54:445–46.

laity when Holy Communion was distributed. Private masses (at least the ones intended to shorten the deceased's time in purgatory) were being abandoned, priests were marrying, and members of religious orders were leaving their communities for life in the world.

For the most part, Carlstadt and Melanchthon worked together on these changes, or at least Melanchthon was kept informed of the discussion. Luther seems not to have communicated with Carlstadt directly, but on the whole he approved of the direction that things were going. He wrote to Philip on August 1 that he was glad they were in the process of restoring communion in both kinds to the people and that he was personally determined never to say another private mass.[51] At the beginning of September, nine masses were celebrated in Melanchthon's home, with students in attendance, at which the chalice was shared by all present. Those attending probably were in support of this change, so it did not create the kind of conflict with "traditionalists" that was sure to erupt if it had happened in a mass at the town church or castle church.[52]

But to both Spalatin and Amsdorf, Luther could write of his disappointment in the low level of argumentation that Carlstadt was providing, especially on the question of forsaking monastic vows. Luther held back from direct criticism, acknowledging that "occasion would thereby be given to our enemies to boast over our internal disagreements."[53] Luther's decision to write *On Monastic Vows* was partly personal but also partly to provide a better biblical and theological basis for the changes that were underway. In the fall of 1521, he was also writing "The Misuse of the Mass" (dedicated to his fellow Augustinians in Wittenberg) to be sure that his brothers had

---

51. "Letter to Philip Melanchthon" (August 1, 1521), in LW 48:281.
52. For this scene and a detailed account of developments in Wittenberg during Luther's absence, see Brecht, *Martin Luther*, 2:25–45.
53. "Letter to Nicholas von Amsdorf" (September 9, 1521), in LW 48:311. See also "Letter to George Spalatin" (August 15, 1521), in LW 48:293.

solid reasons to give when challenged on the changes that they were making.[54]

The Wittenberg situation was rapidly changing that autumn. In early October, the students threatened a monk of the Order of Saint Anthony who had come to town begging. On All Saints' Day, November 1, the town was filled with pilgrims to the All Saints' Foundation at the castle church. By November 12, thirteen monks had decided to leave the Augustinian monastery, and Luther was concerned about whether they knew what they were doing. He wrote to John Lang in Erfurt in mid-December: "I do not approve of that tumultuous exodus, for the monks could have parted from each other in a peaceful and friendly way." He advised Lang and Wenceslas Link, now the vicar-general, on how they should proceed at the coming chapter meeting that was to be held in Wittenberg. He told Link that those who wanted to leave should be free to do so, "but you and I will stay in the cowl." Luther also confided to Lang that he missed Staupitz and was troubled by rumors that Staupitz had allied himself with the conservative archbishop of Salzburg, Matthew Lang.[55]

In such a climate, Frederick the Wise had absolutely forbidden the publication of Luther's stormy indictment of Albrecht of Mainz, "Against the Idol of Halle." More tumult was ahead. On December 3, students disrupted Mass in the town church, and the next day they gathered in a threatening crowd outside the Franciscan monastery in Wittenberg. It was later claimed that visiting students from Erfurt had sparked these disturbances.[56]

54. "The Misuse of the Mass" (1521), in LW 36:127–230.
55. "Letter to John Lang" and "Letter to Wenceslas Link" (both December 18, 1521), in LW 48:356–59.
56. "Introduction to 'Sincere Admonition by Martin Luther to All Christians to Guard against Insurrection and Rebellion,'" in LW 45:55.

Just at that moment, Luther made a secret visit to Wittenberg. Frederick did not know of this visit, and Luther wanted to keep it a secret from him. How he was free to leave the Wartburg is not known, but sporting a beard and full head of hair, and wearing the clothing of a knight, he traveled with a servant. Some of his friends did not even recognize him when they first saw him. He spent several days at Melanchthon's lodging, also visiting with Amsdorf and friends Lucas Cranach and the goldsmith Christian During. This may be the occasion when Cranach made sketches for several of his portraits of Luther as "Knight George," Luther's code name. Luther felt restored by this time with his friends.

Despite the student uprisings that were going on at that very time, Luther took a generally good view of the situation in Wittenberg. He returned to the Wartburg in a few days, very confident that all was well. What did make him angry was Spalatin's delay in publishing several of the treatises that Luther had sent: "The Misuse of the Mass," "The Judgment of Martin Luther on Monastic Vows," and "Against the Idol of Halle." He wrote to Spalatin in great anger, and for a time their relationship was strained. "I came to Wittenberg and amid all the delight of being with my friends again, I found this drop of bitterness, namely, none of them has ever heard of or seen my little books and letters. Judge for yourself whether I should not consider my disappointment justified."[57] However, in time he came to agree that "Against the Idol of Halle" was not useful in its present form, and he gave it to Melanchthon to edit or save for another publication.[58]

57. "Letter to George Spalatin," (around December 5, 1521), in LW 48:351.
58. Brecht, *Martin Luther*, 2:29.

Image 19: Luther grew out his hair and beard
while hidden away incognito as "Knight
George" in the Wartburg Castle in Eisenach, a
possession of Frederick the Wise.

"The Misuse of the Mass" was promptly published and may have
added to the turmoil in Wittenberg when it appeared in January.
In it, Luther takes on the familiar targets of negligent bishops, the
Mass as sacrifice, and the papal system that violates all of the Ten
Commandments. Luther also for the first time attacked, in passing,
Frederick's All Saints' Foundation at the castle church, with its relics
and masses for the dead. Although Luther challenged the people of
Wittenberg to make changes peaceably and astonish others by their
increase in love, these few critical comments may have been part of
the reason for Spalatin's delay.[59]

59. "Misuse of the Mass," in LW 36:227–30.

A Peaceable War

Luther was back in the Wartburg by December 11. However reassured he may have been, he continued to have no love for disorderly or rebellious change, thinking it both against God's ways of working and likely to discredit the gospel. In response, he began writing one more treatise: "A Sincere Admonition by Martin Luther to All Christians to Guard against Insurrection and Rebellion." Within a few days, he was sending it to Spalatin with an exhortation to publish it as quickly as possible "to counteract those rough and foolish braggarts who boast of our name."[60]

The eighteen-page treatise is often slighted in favor of Luther's later writings on the necessity of obedience to political authority, but it provides some of the most fascinating clues to his thinking about how change will come and the proper role of ordinary Christians in those changes. He acknowledges at the beginning that there is currently great fear of rebellion and that in part he is glad for this because it may teach the church authorities a lesson—if they pay attention to this discontent. But he doubts that they are capable of such conversion and therefore expects them to be swept away not by human rebellion, but by the judgment of God for which Christians must wait.[61]

The rulers and the nobility can do something if they have the faith and the courage to take matters into their own hands, as Luther advised in *To the German Nobility*. But ordinary persons must stay calm, for the righting of wrongs is not an assignment given to them. Luther says quite plainly, "[Insurrection] never brings about

---

60. "Letter to George Spalatin" (around December 12, 1521), in LW 48:355. Either Luther wrote "Sincere Admonition" in a day or two (not impossible for him), or the letter should be dated a few days later.
61. "Sincere Admonition," in LW 45:57–61.

the desired improvement. For insurrection lacks discernment; it greatly harms the innocent more than the guilty."[62]

While ordinary people cannot take matters into their own hands, they may do what they can to press the nobility to carry out their rightful role. They may, as Luther himself has been doing, confess their sins, pray against the enemies of the gospel, and speak their minds. Even though, in Luther's view, forceful action to end injustice is impossible, vivid, lively, powerful speech is allowed and even mandated. Far from being discouraged that there is nothing to do, Christians who are leaning toward rebellion should instead consider the many actions legitimately open to them:

> Get busy now; spread the holy gospel, and help others to spread it; teach, speak, write, and preach that man-made laws are nothing; urge people not to enter the priesthood, the monastery, or the convent, and hinder them from so doing; encourage those who have already entered to leave; give no more money for bulls, candles, bells, tablets, and churches; rather tell them that a Christian life consists of faith and love. Let us do this for two years and see what will become of pope, bishops, cardinals, priests, monks, nuns, bells, towers, masses, vigils, cowls, tonsures, monastic rules, statutes, and all the swarming vermin of the papal regime; they will all vanish like smoke.[63]

This is neither resignation nor quietism; it is a call to massive but peaceful disruption of the corrupt church system.

Luther also takes aim at those who use his name as a cover for their rebellion—as many would do in years to come. When some have read as little as a page or two, understanding little or nothing, the urge to act is so strong that they "go at it slam bang" in a completely unevangelical way that uses force rather than persuasion. Luther is becoming increasingly aware of an issue that he will face shortly when he returns from Wittenberg: the problem of what he calls "the

62. LW 45:62–63.
63. LW 45:68.

weak"—those not yet ready for the changes that are coming. Here already, he is encouraging bold spirits to be patient with their sisters and brothers and to bring along into free compliance as many as they can.

This treatise is also famous as the first occasion when Luther protested calling his followers by his name:

> I ask that men make no reference to my name; let them call themselves Christians, not Lutherans. What is Luther? After all, the teaching is not mine. Nor was I crucified for anyone. St. Paul, in I Corinthians 3:27 would not allow the Christians to call themselves Pauline or Petrine, but Christian. How then should I—poor stinking maggot fodder that I am—come to have men call the children of Christ by my wretched name? Not so, my dear friends, let us abolish all party names and call ourselves Christians, after him whose teachings we hold.[64]

As Luther was advocating self-restraint, events were unfolding rapidly in Wittenberg. Carlstadt announced plans to celebrate the Lord's Supper in both kinds in the castle church on New Year's Day 1522. Frederick the Wise forbade this, and Carlstadt moved the plans up to Christmas Eve. A committee of professors who were to settle differences on changing worship could not agree.

At the Christmas Eve service, Carlstadt presided, wearing only ordinary clothing, using the German language, and sharing the cup with the congregation. It caused quite a sensation, and news immediately spread through Saxony and beyond. Protests were heard immediately from Duke George in the other part of Saxony. At the services on New Year's and Epiphany, more than a thousand persons communed each time—an amazing number for a small town like Wittenberg. In the meantime, Carlstadt announced his engagement to be married to a local girl, and he invited the elector to attend.[65]

---

64. LW 45:70–71.
65. For details see Brecht, *Martin Luther*, 2:38.

A few days after Christmas, three workingmen from Zwickau arrived in Wittenberg and presented themselves as agents of the Holy Spirit. These so-called Zwickau Prophets, clothier Nicholas Storch, weaver Thomas Dreschel, and former Wittenberg student Marcus Thomae or Stubner, had been influenced by the Zwickau pastor Thomas Müntzer. They had remarkable biblical knowledge but also claimed direct revelation from the Holy Spirit. Their call for an end to infant baptism led to their expulsion from Zwickau, and so they came to Wittenberg.

They met first with Melanchthon, who was quite taken aback by what they had to say. Was it possible that these humble folks were the harbingers of the outpouring of the Spirit that signaled the end of the world? Luther had taught him not to regard power and wisdom but to see that God often lifted up the lowly and humble. Even the tougher-minded Amsdorf was impressed with these visitors. On New Year's, Philip and Nicholas had to go to the court at Prettin to consult with Spalatin and the elector about what to do.

Frederick always said that he was no theologian, but he was not pleased with the account of these so-called prophets. He instructed that they be taught by the Wittenbergers and that there be no debate with them. So far as infant baptism was concerned, he doubted that they were wiser than Augustine on that subject. They discussed recalling Luther, but the time seemed dangerous both for the elector politically and for Luther's safety. The theologians went back to Wittenberg, where things became calmer for a time, but Melanchthon had a fresh realization of how strongly he missed Luther's leadership. Philip's inability to think clearly in this confused situation seemed to him a personal failure—even though others had taken the same view of the visitors.[66]

---

66. Ibid., 36–37.

Luther soon heard about the Christmas services, the Zwickau visitors, and Carlstadt's engagement. He wrote two long letters, one to Amsdorf and one to Melanchthon, on January 13. To Amsdorf, he spoke very positively about Carlstadt's wedding. He knew the woman in question and thought much good could come from this. He was still hoping to return to Wittenberg after Easter and work with his colleagues on translating the Old Testament. He rather quickly dismissed the Zwickau Prophets for their claim to "have conversations with God in his majesty." There was no such direct access to the God that Luther had come to know from the Bible, at least not in a way that could underwrite the unfolding Christian reform of the church.[67] Anyone certainly could receive revelations from God, but these must be tested against the witness of Scripture and in the presence of other people. The Zwickau Prophets, it seemed to Luther, trusted *only* their own experience, not the wisdom of the faithful. Therefore, they should not be believed.

With Melanchthon, he dealt with the visitors at greater length. He was surprised that Philip was so panicked by their claims. The Bible provides many tools for discerning true from false prophets. He wondered especially at the way in which they called attention to themselves and their apparent lack of suffering, or *Anfechtung*. Luther knew the medieval mystical literature very well and was skeptical of an experience of God that did not include "spiritual distress."[68] He was unmoved by their critique of infant baptism and began to assemble reasons defending it, preparation for several of his writings in the decade ahead. Finally, he told Melanchthon to prepare a room for him because he would be returning soon. In the meantime, he hoped to finish his translation of the New Testament.[69]

---

67. "Letter to Nicholas von Amsdorf" (January 13, 1522), in LW 48:363–64.
68. "Letter to Philip Melanchthon" (January 13, 1522), in LW 48:365–66.
69. LW 48:372. From these letters, Luther could seem to be making plans to live both with Amsdorf and with Melanchthon. The requests to prepare a room should be seen as affectionate.

Image 20: Spalatin worked at the court of the Electors
of Saxony. He frequently acted as a liaison to Luther,
who was also his good friend.

A few days later in writing to Spalatin, Luther seemed ready to
return to Wittenberg immediately. He says quite specifically that this
is not because of the Zwickau Prophets. He does not want to take
them seriously but does not want them jailed either. They have the
right to "use their mouths," to cite his advice to all in "A Sincere
Admonition," which was just now being published. Perhaps he had
heard of the great unrest of January 10, including the burning of
altars and images of saints in the Augustinian monastery. But in any
case, he now felt that the cause itself demanded that he leave the
Wartburg and appear in public again.[70]

In fact, Luther's plans were completely uncertain at this date. When he returned to Wittenberg,
he lived again, as before, in the Augustinian monastery, which after his marriage was given to
him as his private home.

70. "Letter to George Spalatin" (January 17, 1522), in LW 48:380–81.

Actually, it was not until more than a month later that Luther wrote directly to Frederick the Wise informing him of his decision to return. By this time, he had finished the New Testament translation that was such an important project for him. He had also heard much more about continuing disturbances in Wittenberg. He asked the elector to "have a little confidence in me" and teased him that after years of collecting relics he would now be receiving a real cross—in the form of all the troubles that are before him. But Luther wanted it to be clear that he was returning not at Frederick's request or with his permission, but by his own decision as a teacher and professor.[71]

In a return letter, Frederick tried to stop Luther's return, arguing that the time was wrong and that the danger was too great. But Luther in this instance refused to obey his prince, even though that was his ordinary counsel to all.[72] He now needed to see what he could do to help in Wittenberg with a situation that he had done so much to create and that was developing in dangerous ways. He reminded Frederick that he had stayed "in hiding for this year to please your Electoral Grace" but could no longer hide. As for providing Luther protection, the elector need not worry about that: "I have written this so Your Electoral Grace might know that I am going to Wittenberg under a far higher protection than the Elector's. I have no intention of asking Your Electoral Grace for protection. And if I thought that Your Electoral Grace could and would protect me, I should not go. The sword ought not and cannot help in a matter of this kind. God alone must do it—and with or without the solicitude and cooperation of men."[73] It was a testament to the faith that had seen Luther through what may have been the hardest and yet most productive year of his life.

71. "Letter to Elector Frederick" (February 22, 1522), in LW 48:387–88.
72. The letter from Frederick was likely written more to give him deniability than to express his actual views about Luther's return.
73. "Letter to Elector Frederick" (March 5, 1522), in LW 48:391.

Image 21: An edition of the New Testament from 1525. Luther's translation regularized much of the German language.

7

The Reformation in Wittenberg

1522–1524

The surge of energy that helped Luther get through ten months in the Wartburg Castle lasted through the first years of his return to Wittenberg. His return while under papal excommunication and the imperial ban was an act of great courage, but something that he also seems to have felt driven to do. He was rightly aware of the possibility of death throughout this period, as is evident in the first sermons that he preached on his return. Yet his health was basically very good for these next three years, and he seemed to thrive on sorting through the crises and challenges and responding to each—especially by continuing writing. His production of sermons and treatises in this period continues the remarkable pattern that he had sustained since the beginning of 1519.[1]

---

1. Martin Brecht argues that these years are so complex and so filled with Luther's writings that they defeat almost any potential biographer. See Martin Brecht, *Martin Luther*, vol. 2: *Shaping and Defining the Reformation, 1521–1532*, trans. James L. Schaaf (Minneapolis: Fortress Press, 1990), 58.

This was somewhat problematic because the Imperial Council of Regency in Nuremberg, acting in the emperor's absence, was always putting pressure on Frederick to see that Luther did not write anything else, lest he stir the people even more. Luther had to write a great many letters of explanation to the elector detailing his reasons for each new publication. Sometimes it was to respond to an enemy who had written first, such as King Henry VIII of England (although he was writing in response to an earlier version of Luther's writing). Sometimes he claimed simply to be interpreting the Scriptures and argued that no legislation could block God's word.

On the way back to Wittenberg, Luther had one last bit of fun with his disguise as Knight George. At the Black Bear Inn in Jena he met Johannes Kessler and another student who were making their way back to Wittenberg. The knight bought the students drinks and dinner, discussed the importance of studying biblical languages, and asked what people thought of Luther in their hometowns. The innkeeper told them the strange knight was Luther himself, but they could not believe this. A few days later in Wittenberg they met Luther again, now in his monk's cowl and without his beard.[2]

On his return, Luther wrote to Frederick one more time, providing a letter arranged with the lawyer Jerome Schurff which made it very clear he was defying the elector's orders by appearing in public. He cites his pastoral responsibilities for the Wittenberg congregation, the divisions and scandals caused by the changes introduced so abruptly, and the real dangers of rebellion. A postscript to a draft version that still exists tells the elector that if he is dissatisfied with this reasoning, he may provide his own draft that Luther will sign and that may be made public. Luther was in one sense defying Frederick and creating a host of new headaches for him; on the other

---

2. Brecht, *Martin Luther*, 2:42–43.

hand, his presence in Wittenberg was already reassuring Frederick's more cautious advisors.[3]

Calming the Storm

Luther's made his presence felt in Wittenberg through preaching, a task he made the central part of his work for the next three years. He did not resume his professorial duties until the summer of 1524, perhaps because he was under imperial ban or perhaps because he was so busy with the basics: preaching and Bible translation. He continued to have great confidence that only the startling liveliness of the word proclaimed could create the right conditions for changes that must be made. His critique of Carlstadt was largely that he had failed to build support through recurrent preaching for what he intended to do—instead simply forcing the issue with support from the town council.

Luther appeared in the pulpit of the town church on March 9, Invocavit Sunday (the first Sunday in Lent), and preached a series of sermons that lasted for eight days. [4] In these sermons, he discussed the recent changes in Wittenberg and offered his own critique of how things had been done. He admitted that he agreed with almost all of the changes that had been made, but he totally disapproved of the way they had been carried out. Love was the missing element—love for the traditionalists, love for the weaker brothers and sisters, love for those not yet convinced.

Luther also complains he had not been consulted about the changes made, though he was their regular preacher and his writings had stirred up so many of these issues. Yes, he was far away, but they could have written. So they went ahead, and in doing the right things

---

3. "Letter to the Elector Frederick" (March 7–8, 1522), in LW 48:398–99.
4. The name *Invocavit* comes from Ps. 91:15, "He will call on me and I will answer him," though "he will call" in Latin is actually *invocabit*.

in the wrong way they had potentially injured their cause. What had become of Christian freedom?

> Here one can see that you do not have the Spirit, even though you do have a deep knowledge of the Scriptures. Take note of these two things, "must" and "free." The "must" is that which necessity requires, and which must ever be unyielding, as, for instance, the faith, which I shall never permit anyone to take away from me, but must always keep in my heart and freely confess before everyone. But "free" is that in which I have choice, and may use or not, yet in such a way that it profit my brother and not me. Now do not make a "must" out of what is "free" as you have done, so that you may not be called to account for those who were led astray by your loveless exercise of liberty.[5]

Luther took up one issue after another—communion in both kinds, the role of images, private masses, the eating and avoiding of meat—and showed how he intended they move ahead: slowly and in an orderly, disciplined, and loving way.

The sermons were very effective in calming the situation, according to reports that have survived, especially letters written by Wittenberg students to their families. The town council rather quickly negated the ordinance of January 24 and gave Luther several presents honoring his return, including a new cowl. Of all the changes that Carlstadt had introduced, the only one sustained for the time being was the offering of both bread and wine to those laity who requested it, although communion in one kind continued to be an option for several years.[6]

Gabriel Zwilling, the other leader of the changes made in Luther's absence, quickly accepted the new arrangements and reconciled with Luther. In fact, Luther worked to secure various preaching positions for him in the years ahead. But relations with Carlstadt were much more difficult. He was held responsible for the mess, and Luther's

---

5. "Eight Sermons in Wittenberg" (March 9–16, 1522), in LW 51:74, MLBTW3, 291–92.
6. Brecht, *Martin Luther*, 2:64.

return was the beginning of ongoing trouble between them. Relations had never been particularly friendly, even at the time of the Leipzig Debate when they faced John Eck together. Carlstadt had also been named specifically in one of the papal bulls, and Frederick had sent him for a time after Worms to Denmark, but he returned to Wittenberg very soon.[7]

There were now several issues between Luther and his senior colleague. Luther felt that Carlstadt had no concept of Christian liberty but instead wanted to force his way by regulation. They also had different views of the binding character of the Mosaic or Old Testament law. Luther too was critical of images and the risk of idolatry that had surrounded their veneration. But he was willing to proceed cautiously to remove them or reduce their number. Luther had also become very suspicious of direct revelations of the Holy Spirit after the affair of the Zwickau Prophets. He wanted things settled by reference to the word because he refused to believe that the true Holy Spirit would work against the Spirit-inspired biblical books. In fact, Luther's later developed writings on the Holy Spirit are written in such a way that the Spirit and the word tied very tightly together: the Spirit is that which fixes the word in the believer's heart.

Carlstadt hoped for an opportunity to pursue his differences with Luther in a debate in writing, but the university senate would not allow this. They forbade the publication of Carlstadt's response to Luther in April 1522. By that time, Carlstadt was spending less and less time in Wittenberg, although still drawing his salary for his responsibilities there. Much of the time he lived on a farm in Worlitz.

7. Bernard Lohse, *Martin Luther's Theology* (Minneapolis: Fortress Press, 1999), 144–47. For more on Carlstadt, a good place to begin is Ronald Sider, *Andreas Bodenstein von Karlstadt: The Development of His Thought, 1517–1525* (Leiden: Brill, 1974); and, on theological matters, Amy Nelson Burnett, *Karlstadt and the Origins of the Eucharistic Controversy* (New York: Oxford University Press, 2011).

Occasionally he appeared in Wittenberg, making a fuss, for example, about the appropriateness of granting degrees in February 1523.[8]

The issues that had shaken Wittenberg were also problems throughout Electoral Saxony and beyond. The Invocavit sermons were published and circulated, but not by Luther himself. He intended to respond to changes in worship in a more systematic way. In letters from that spring to Nicholas Hausmann in Zwickau and to George Spalatin at the court, he describes the steps he had taken in Wittenberg and his plans for writing more generally about the gap between popular expectations for change and the continuing uncertainty of many official and ordinary Christians.[9] He urges Hausmann to calm Zwickau by proceeding in a way parallel to what he is doing in Wittenberg.

The treatise "Receiving Both Kinds in the Sacrament" was written partly in answer to the young prince John Frederick about whether to receive the sacrament in this way, but its scope is much larger than its title. It is a summary statement of Luther's whole plan for changes in worship and Christian life that will need several years to be carried out. Luther had made many suggestions in *Appeal to the German Nobility* (1520), but they were a catalog of possibilities rather than a clear plan. With the crisis in Wittenberg and other towns now a reality, he lays out a specific set of ten proposals:

1. Let most of the old practices continue for now.
2. Have priests stop using any liturgical language or prayer about sacrifice.
3. Emphasize in preaching: "This is my body . . . for you. This is my blood . . . for you."

---

8. "Table Talk for Fall 1532," in LW 54:54.
9. "Letter to Nicholas Hausmann" (March 17, 1522), in LW 48:400–402. See also "Letter to George Spalatin" (March 30, 1522), in LW 49:3–4.

4. Follow local usage—receive either one kind or both kinds as offered.

5. Stop celebrating private masses. Offer mass only when people want to commune.

6. Do not try to stop those priests who continue to offer private masses.

7. Private confession should be neither required nor abolished.

8. Permit images to remain, but preach about their proper use and understanding.

9. Priests are free to marry, and monks and nuns may leave their orders.

10. Feel free to eat meat on any day of the year, despite papal bans and threats.[10]

Finally, he added another round of advice for those who were claiming the name "Lutheran" or persecuting those who held it:

> You should never say, I am Lutheran, or a Papist. For neither of them died for you, or is your master. Christ alone died for you, he alone is your master, and you should confess yourself a Christian. But if you are convinced that Luther's teaching is in accord with the gospel and that the pope's is not, then you should not discard Luther so completely, lest with him you discard also his teaching, which you nevertheless recognized as Christ's teaching. You should rather say, Whether Luther is a rascal or a saint I do not care; his teaching is not his, but Christ's.[11]

The treatise was a great success. Luther used it for some time as a guide to answering questions that poured in. By May it was printed in Nuremberg and by June was even known in Switzerland. Luther had found a way to speak to the crisis in Wittenberg both locally through preaching and to his larger public through writing.[12]

10. "Receiving Both Kinds in the Sacrament" (1522), in LW 36:254–62.
11. LW 36:265.

Worship Matters

With the situation calmer in Wittenberg, Luther attended to the issues of piety and worship underlying the crisis. In a short time, people had turned from the papal church to follow the gospel without models or structures to help them know what doing so might mean. Some were throwing out everything traditional, which was appalling. But the problems with the Mass and patterns of devotion were too deep for simple surgery.

Luther was also working in several different arenas at the same time. He felt pressure to preach in other places, hoping that his presence and message there too might be calming. There were Catholic opponents to answer or ignore. Above all, there was the revision of the New Testament translation and the beginning of work on the Old Testament with the first five books of Moses. As a result, Luther's response to the need for new materials for piety and worship was spread over several years.

He turned first to the question of prayer and devotion as he had at the beginning of 1519. Anything he could do to help shape the actual faith of the people always took priority. By June, he had completed work on the *Personal Prayer Book*, which was aimed at laity seeking new evangelical patterns of devotion. He wove older materials together with new writing into one of his greatest successes ever. Prayer books for personal use had long been popular, and with advances in printing, a paperbound copy could be sold for only twenty pennies. There were many printings, two revisions that year, and greatly expanded subsequent editions. The original forty pages were expanded to over two hundred as Luther added some of his best

12. For a full analysis of the strategies and effects of printing, see Mark Edwards, *Printing, Propaganda and Martin Luther* (Berkeley: University of California Press, 1994).

devotional treatises from past years and fifty woodcuts of the major events of the Bible.[13]

The first edition opened with a preface from Luther that urged all to take up the habit of "this plain, ordinary Christian prayer."[14] The first parts contain catechetical material on the Ten Commandments to help with confession, on the Creed to help with faith, and on the Lord's Prayer to help with daily prayer. Luther then added an evangelical way to pray the Hail Mary in which no one prays to Mary, but "we recite what grace God has given her" and "wish that everyone may know and respect her."[15] Then follow eight psalms in German that cover the various occasions for prayer and several chapters from Titus (a sneak preview of the forthcoming New Testament translation) for help in living as a Christian.

Luther was also eager to free people from false burdens that the Roman Church had imposed, burdens that could be relieved simply by abandoning them. These "doctrines of men," or "uniform ceremonies instituted by human beings" as the Augsburg Confession would call them, included the requirements for fasting and for avoiding certain foods on certain prescribed days.[16] To strengthen the resolve of those who were now simply ignoring such church regulations, in May 1522 Luther wrote "Avoiding the Doctrines of Men," which consisted of his interpretation of ten Scripture passages that showed the freedom that Christians should feel from such requirements. Fasting or avoiding rich foods as an act of penance might be admirable as examples of personal devotion but should not be required of all Christians by the church.[17]

---

13. Introduction to "Personal Prayer Book" (1522), in LW 43:5–10.

14. LW 43:12–13.

15. LW 43:39–40.

16. Augsburg Confession, VII.3, in *The Book of Concord*, ed. Robert Kolb and Timothy J. Wengert (Minneapolis: Fortress Press, 2000), 42.

17. "Avoiding the Doctrines of Men" (1522), in LW 35:131–47.

He had wanted to dedicate the work to his host at the Wartburg, Hans von Berlepsch, and it undoubtedly originated in conversation between the warden and the monk while he was there. But Spalatin and the court decided that this was dangerous because it would give away Luther's hiding place, which might have to be used again. Instead, the treatise was dedicated, most appropriately, to the general reader. Luther says that he wrote it "for the comfort and saving of those poor consciences who are held captive . . . by man-made laws."[18]

There was urgency to produce materials for worship, but Luther first had to answer a question that concerned both supporters and opponents. What view should one take toward the sacrament of Holy Communion if the old understanding of sacrifice and transubstantiation were no longer held? People wondered whether there was any point in continuing the practice of adoration of the sacrament. This was an especially intense issue in Bohemia—the land of John Hus, whom many were now seeing as Luther's predecessor.

While Luther did not personally consider the question of adoration very important, he knew that these questions needed an answer from him. In early 1523, he wrote "The Adoration of the Blessed Sacrament" and argued that the key issue was to understand the promise of Christ in the Words of Institution. Meditation on this promise will lead to faith that Christ is present in the sacrament, even though reason's objections will have to give way. This is not a sacrifice but a free gift—all the more therefore it should be respected. "This sacrament does give life, grace, and blessedness, for it is a fountain of life and blessedness."[19]

This defense of the presence of Christ in the sacrament leads to Luther's answer regarding devotional practices toward it. Adoration

---

18. LW 35:127.
19. "Adoration of the Sacrament" (1523), in LW 36:289.

of the sacrament is understandable and praiseworthy, given the promise of Christ attached to it. However, such adoration is not biblically commanded. Believers are left with Christian freedom and may adore or not adore, but they may not fault each other for these behaviors. "Free, free it must be, according as one is disposed in his heart and has opportunity."[20]

This stress on freedom will be one key to Luther's developing understanding of worship. Not all things are free. The word may not be ignored because it is the source of everything. Nor can the Mass be performed as sacrifice, for that changes the emphasis from God's gift to the priestly action. But many matters about which Christians are prone to quarrel are in fact open questions. One ought to keep the weak in view and not act in a way that gives offense to others who might see in your casual attitude toward the sacrament an indifference to its deep promise and benefits.

By early 1523, Luther was ready to set down some of his own major principles for worship. In "Concerning the Order for Public Worship," which is one of Luther's shortest writings, he sketched out the new shape of Christian liturgy. Because private masses had been largely abandoned, churches were now usually closed every day but Sunday. Luther proposed that, instead of daily mass, there should be services of morning and evening prayer. His proposed times give us a clue about a world without effective artificial lighting for large buildings: the morning service should take place at four or five o'clock in the morning, and the evening service at five or six o'clock in the early evening.

These services would consist of familiar elements from monastic devotion—the reading of lessons and selected psalms. However, Luther's strongest insistence is that there should never be a gathering without the reading of the word, and never a reading without a

20. LW 36:295.

short sermon for the sake of interpretation. He suggested working through the Old Testament continuously in the morning and the New Testament in the evening, although there was—as always with Luther—room for local variation on matters at that level. Not everyone was expected to attend, but these services were to be aimed at clergy and students. There should also be singing by the whole assembly, but the number of psalms should be kept reasonable "for one must not overload souls or weary them, as was the case until now in monasteries and convents, where they burdened themselves like mules."[21] By March 23, 1523, these daily services were in place in the town church of Wittenberg.

On Sundays, the whole congregation should gather both in the morning for Mass and in the evening for sung Vespers. Preaching, of course, was expected at both services, and this should usually be from Sunday's Gospel in the morning and from the day's Epistle in the evening. The reception of communion would be available for those who sought it, but Luther did not want anyone coerced toward the sacrament. Chanting could continue, although the pastors needed to pay attention to some of the texts, especially for festivals and saints days, for "there is a horrible lot of filth in them."[22] Luther planned at this time for a radical simplification of the calendar, discontinuing most festivals of the saints. The Marian days—her Purification, Annunciation, Assumption, and Nativity—could be retained if they were interpreted in an evangelical way, but the days of the apostles might be best celebrated on the nearest Sunday.[23]

The most important thing was to give centrality to the preached word "instead of prattling and rattling that has been the rule up to now." Luther would come to more detailed questions later but

21. "Concerning the Order for Public Worship" (1523) in LW 53:12, MLBTW3, 308.
22. LW 53:13, MLBTW3, 309.
23. LW 53:14, MLBTW3, 309.

had confidence that "other matters will adjust themselves as the need arises." He ended with a reference to the Gospel story of Mary and Martha with Jesus. The church should attend to the one thing needful, "no matter how much care and trouble it may give to Martha."[24]

All this was helpful and influential advice, but Luther's friends wanted something more specific from him. What should the shape of that Sunday service be? Which elements should be retained and which must be eliminated? Luther was drafting an order for Sunday Mass but first completed something he found even more urgent—a German order for Baptism. He was very eager that the sponsors of an infant being baptized be able to follow the service, understand what was happening, answer the questions for the child, and join in the prayers.

Luther's "Order of Baptism" also appeared early in 1523. Here he followed the traditional rite carefully, with a slight modification of the order and a new prayer over the water—the so-called Flood Prayer that he had written himself. Recalling God's gracious actions in the flood and at the Red Sea, it calls on God to set apart and save the one being baptized that "he may be sundered from the number of unbelieving, preserved dry and secure in the holy ark of Christendom, serve thy name at all times fervent in spirit and joyful in hope, so that with all believers he may be made worthy to attain eternal life according to thy promise, through Jesus Christ our Lord. Amen."[25] Luther revised the order in 1526, but the original was widely used in a short time.

Wanting still more, Hausmann in Zwickau, among others, kept prodding Luther, and by the fall of 1523 he promised to send

24. LW 53:14; MLBTW3, 309.
25. "Order of Baptism" (1523), in LW 53:97. For more on Luther's developments in thinking about baptism, see Kirsi Stjerna, *No Greater Jewel* (Minneapolis: Augsburg Fortress, 2009).

something soon to his friend about the problem of Sunday morning. Luther had hoped that by this time private masses would have been abolished, or at least greatly reduced in number. For Luther, that step needed to come first, as private masses denied the gift character and communal emphasis of the Lord's Supper. But he was proceeding more cautiously than Carlstadt and others who were revising the Mass. Luther's liturgical conservatism—or conservationism—begins to show at this point. He tells Hausmann: "But I do not see why we should alter the rest of the ritual, together with the vestments, altars, and holy vessels, since they can be used in a godly way and since one cannot live in the church of God without ceremonies."[26]

"An Order for Mass and Communion for the Church in Wittenberg" was published in December 1523. The writing is dedicated to Hausmann, who had done so much to restore an orderly Reformation in Zwickau. Luther tells his readers that he thinks the time is now right and hearts have been prepared for the slight innovations he is here proposing. He asserts, "It has never been my intention to abolish the liturgical service of God completely, but rather to purify the one that is now in use from the wretched accretions which corrupt it."[27]

The structure he proposes for the precommunion portion preserves the shape and order of the Roman rite, but with simplification and greater flexibility.

Introit
Kyrie and Gloria in Excelsis (but the latter may be omitted)
Collect for the Day
Epistle

---

26. "Letter to Nicholas Hausmann" (end of October 1523), in LW 49:56.
27. "An Order for Mass and Communion for the Church at Wittenberg" (1523), in LW 53:20, MLBTW3, 312.

Gradual or Alleluia

Gospel (with or without candles, procession, and incense)

Nicene Creed (before or after the sermon)

Sermon (must be in the language of the people)[28]

The rite for Holy Communion retains historical prayers and responses (such as singing the Sanctus: "Holy, Holy, Holy") but with a very simple prayer at its heart that stresses Christ's Words of Institution—"This is my body," "This is my blood"—instead of the lengthy "canon of the mass" that was often in Luther's view the occasion for very damaging theology emphasizing our sacrifice or the priest's work rather than God's gift.

Luther would not compromise on certain basic principles—the need for preaching or the importance of avoiding the notion of sacrifice as our work, for example. But the overwhelming impression of his order is one of freedom and flexibility. It is the order for Wittenberg, and he does not insist that his followers use it precisely. Christians are children of freedom (specifically of the free woman, as Luther thinks of Paul's argument in Galatians 4), and they ought no more be bound to Luther than to the pope: "Further, even if different people make use of different rites, let no one judge or despise the other, but every man be fully persuaded in his own mind. . . . Let us feel and think the same, even though we may act differently."[29]

Perhaps there is another principle for Luther—avoiding undue length that will bore even a devout congregation. "In the church we do not want to quench the spirit of the faithful with tedium."[30]

Luther ends the order with a hope that German hymns will be written to be sung by the congregation. He predicts "poets are

28. LW 53:22–26, MLBTW3, 313–14.
29. LW 53:31, MLBTW3, 316.
30. LW 53:24, MLBTW3, 313.

wanting among us, or are not yet known, who could compose evangelical and spiritual songs."[31] He spent a great deal of time trying to get Spalatin to write some hymn texts but was apparently not successful.[32] Nevertheless, in 1523 and 1524 Luther and others were beginning to write the first hymns of what would be a very powerful Lutheran tradition.

Luther wrote his first hymn not with confidence in his poetic powers but in great sadness at the news of the first two people put to death for their support of his teachings. Augustinian monks Heinrich Voes and Johann Esch were burned at the stake in Brussels on July 1, 1523. In the Netherlands, the Edict of Worms was being strictly enforced, and those who preached in violation of it were imprisoned, with many put to death. These two men were the first of at least thirteen hundred men and women put to death under Charles V and his son Philip II in the Netherlands from 1523 to 1566.[33]

In response, Luther wrote a poem and set it to music—a tune that resembles a later and much more famous "A Mighty Fortress Is Our God."

> A new song here shall be begun
> The Lord God help our singing!
> Of what our God himself hath done,
> Praise, honor to him bringing.
> At Brussels in the Netherlands
> By two boys, martyrs youthful
> He showed the wonders of his hands,
> Whom he with favor truthful
> So richly hath adorned.[34]

---

31. LW 53:36, MLBTW3, 320.
32. "Letter to George Spalatin" (December 1523 and January 14, 1524), in LW 49:68–72.
33. "Netherlands," in *Oxford Encyclopedia of the Reformation*, ed. Hans J. Hillerbrand (New York: Oxford University Press, 1996), 3:136.
34. LW 53:214.

While this got a lot of attention as a broadsheet in 1523, it would not ordinarily be sung by a congregation today. Having started, Luther wrote an additional eight hymns by the end of 1524, including some still in use, such as "Dear Christians, Let Us Now Rejoice," "Out of the Depths I Cry to You," "Savior of the Nations Come" and "All Praise to Thee, O Jesus Christ." Those last two were adaptations of ancient hymns for Advent and Christmas, respectively. Others quickly took up Luther's challenge, including Elizabeth Cruciger, wife of Luther's Wittenberg colleague Casper Cruciger, who wrote an Epiphany hymn still in use: "The Only Son from Heaven."[35]

The first German hymnal was published within the year with thirty-seven hymns set for choirs by Luther's friend Johann Walther, the court musician in Torgau. Thirty-two of these were in German, and twenty four Luther himself composed. Luther contributed a preface to *The Wittenberg Hymnal*; in it he commended hymn singing as an especially God-pleasing activity and a way in which the gospel could be "noised and spread abroad." He defended the four-part settings as good for young people, who ought to be trained in music as an essential part of their education. This is one of Luther's strongest defenses of the arts, which had come under attack by many of the more radical reformers: "Nor am I of the opinion that the gospel should destroy and blight all the arts, as some of the pseudo-religious claim. But I would like to see all the arts, especially music, used in the service of Him who gave and made them."[36]

Lost and Found in Translation

If the carefully planned change in worship was Luther's most visible achievement in these post-Wartburg years, the publication of

---

35. For Luther's hymns, see LW 53. LW 53:11–14, 19–40, can be found in MLBTW3, 307–21. For additional information on the first German Hymnals see Brecht, *Martin Luther*, 2:129–35.
36. "Preface to the Wittenberg Hymnal," in LW 53: 316.

Luther's German New Testament was his proudest accomplishment. All through the spring and summer, Luther was working with Melanchthon on revisions. Spalatin was asked for help with the names of jewels in the book of Revelation, which Luther thought he might be able to learn about at the court.[37]

The New Testament was finally published about September 25, 1522, and sold for various prices depending on how elaborate the edition was. In November, it was being studied in Nuremberg. By December, it was being reprinted both in Wittenberg and in Basel. Cranach provided twenty-one illustrations for the book of Revelation, much influenced by the famous engravings of Albrecht Dürer. One of these showed the beast from Revelation 11 wearing the distinctive papal crown, or tiara, and this had to be changed in later editions.[38] Advance copies were sent to Spalatin, Elector Frederick, and to Dukes John and John Frederick in Weimar.[39] Luther provided marginal notes or glosses to help with the interpretation of difficult texts, as well as a preface to the New Testament as a whole and prefaces to individual books beginning with Acts. As in his earlier "Brief Instruction" attached to the Christmas Postil, Luther gives readers some general advice about interpretation. While there are four Gospels as stories of Jesus, gospel as the good news of the Christ is to be found not only in them but also in the writings of Saints Peter and Paul. The most important thing is not to regard Christ as a new Moses or lawgiver, for doing so misses the most important thrust of the New Testament, which is the story of what Christ has done for us and offers us freely.[40]

---

37. "Letter to George Spalatin" (March 30, 1522), in LW 49:4.
38. Brecht, *Martin Luther*, 2:53. The offending woodcut is shown on 54.
39. "Letter to George Spalatin" (about September 20, 1522), in LW 49:15.
40. "Preface to the New Testament" (1522—revised 1546), in LW 35:360, MLBTW3, 95.

In a closing comment that appeared in the first editions but not after 1537, Luther announces which he considers to be the most important biblical books, his so-called canon within the canon:

> John's Gospel and St. Paul's epistles, especially that to the Romans, and St. Peter's first epistle are the true kernel and marrow of all the books. They ought properly to be the foremost books, and it would be advisable for every Christian to read them first and most, and by daily reading to make them as much his own as his daily bread. For in them you do not find many works and miracles of Christ described, but you do find depicted in masterly fashion how faith in Christ overcomes sin, death, and hell, and gives life, righteousness and salvation.[41]

Luther has little use for the Epistle of James, which he calls "an epistle of straw" for its criticism of Paul and its stress on good works.[42] Luther actually separated Hebrews, James, Jude, and Revelation from the other books because he valued them less highly. He was especially critical of Revelation in his original preface, saying, "My spirit cannot accommodate itself to this book" with its confusing visions and lack of clear witness to Christ.[43] Perhaps Luther was simply being honest; many Christians have found the notion of a "canon within the canon" objectionable. But it does seem, practically speaking, unavoidable because equal weight cannot be given to every verse.

All through 1522, Luther was also working on the Old Testament, making such rapid progress that the first part—the five books of Moses, or Pentateuch—was published that December. In the middle of that month, Luther had asked Spalatin for help with the German names of biblical animals, as he was having trouble finishing passages containing lists of animals in Leviticus 11 and Deuteronomy 14.[44] This request was one of many that drew more and more people

---

41. LW 35:362, MLBTW3, 96. A little later in the document he adds Galatians and Ephesians to his list of most important books.
42. Of course, straw has important uses in its own way.
43. "Preface to Revelation" (1522), in LW 35:399.
44. "Letter to George Spalatin" (December 12, 1522), in LW 49:19–20.

into the translation process for the Old Testament, which lasted until 1532, though revisions continued until Luther's death. Eventually, when they came to the difficult passages in the prophets, they had weekly translation seminars in Wittenberg. Luther was uniquely able to convene such a circle and draw out the best gifts of his colleagues. He had always understood that he could not go this road alone; now he was seeing more concretely how to collaborate.

In a preface to the first part of the Old Testament written early in 1523, Luther distanced himself from those who "have little regard for the Old Testament."[45] He reminded Christians that it was not just for the Jewish people but was to be diligently read by followers of Christ. Luther was convinced that the two testaments work together; the first points forward to Christ as the second points back to him. Luther took his own advice seriously and did some of his most outstanding preaching and lecturing for the rest of his career on the Old Testament—especially Genesis, Deuteronomy, Isaiah, and the Minor Prophets, and of course also the beloved Psalms to which he was always returning.[46]

Hundreds of Sermons and Lectures

Luther intended to lead the Reformation in Wittenberg and from Wittenberg with the word of God, or rather to let the word of God flow freely in the church and be satisfied with the pace and kind of Reformation it made possible. But his own activity was focused in these three years not only on Bible translation but also on preaching, and eventually on resuming his work as professor of Bible.

---

45. "Preface to the Old Testament" (1523, revised 1545), in LW 35:235, MLBTW3, 97. The document is actually a preface to the books of Moses, which form the first part of Luther's Old Testament translation.
46. This is true despite the fact that his liturgical reforms, discussed above, did not extend to mandating the reading of Old Testament lessons during Sunday worship services, though sometimes these were read.

He was regularly in the pulpit of the town church in these years, and occasionally preached elsewhere. We have sixty-four sermons from 1522, forty from 1523, and sixty-three from 1524, most from Sunday mornings and festivals. Luther also preached on 1 Peter, 2 Peter, and Jude from May 1522 until early 1523, and then he began a series of sixty-two sermons on Genesis that lasted until the fall of 1524.

Luther considered 1 Peter one of the most valuable books of the New Testament, and preaching on it gave him an opportunity to discuss many of his favorite themes. This was especially evident in the second chapter, where he found some of his most convincing biblical support for the concept of the priesthood of all the baptized. "It would please me very much if this word 'priest' were used as commonly as the term 'Christians' is applied to us. . . . Therefore note this well, in order that you may know how to differentiate between those whom God calls priests and those who call themselves priests. For it must be our aim to restore the little word 'priests' to the common use which the little word 'Christians' enjoys."[47] Luther clearly sees the work of declaring "the wonderful deeds of Him who called you out of darkness into His marvelous light" as the task of the whole Christian community.[48]

Although Luther did not resume his formal professorial duties until the summer of 1524, early in 1523 he began lecturing on Deuteronomy in the Augustinian monastery to a small group that included Bugenhagen and a few students. He had just recently published his translation of the book and worked on its interpretation in 1523 and 1524. The revised lectures that were published were dedicated to the friendly bishop of Samland in Prussia, Sir George von Polenz.[49]

---

47. "Sermons on I Peter" (1523), in LW 30:63.
48. LW 30:64.
49. "Lectures on Deuteronomy" (1524–1525), in LW 9:3.

It might be thought that Deuteronomy—a reinterpretation of the law—would not be congenial material for Luther, but he found the book very exciting. For him, the law and the gospel must always be distinguished; the gospel is the Christian's great hope, but this does not mean that the law is to be ignored. Nor should Christians neglect Moses, from whom there is so much to learn about obedience and disobedience to God. Luther is amazed, for example, that God does not accept Moses' request to enter the Promised Land. Yet, here is the occasion to learn from one of God's greatest servants what it means, in Paul's words, that "we do not know how to pray as we ought" (Rom. 8:26). Moses must be content with God's answer and not insist on his own way.

An unusual feature of the commentary is the brief allegory that Luther added to the end of each chapter. He had largely abandoned this mode of interpretation, which he found so fanciful and far from the plain sense of the text. But he believed that some level of allegory was inevitable and wanted to show how it could be done more modestly and correctly than it had been done by earlier interpreters.[50]

Luther's busyness and absence from teaching created great problems for Wittenberg. In March 1524, Luther wrote to Frederick the Wise to ask that Melanchthon be allowed to lecture on the Bible, in addition to teaching Greek. Because his original appointment had been in classics, Philip was apparently reluctant to make a change without permission. The elector often ignored Luther, especially if spending money was any part of his request, but in this case he promptly agreed that Melanchthon should lecture on the Bible, and he increased his salary by one hundred gulden a year.[51]

50. LW 9:42–43.
51. "Letter to Frederick the Wise" (March 23, 1524), in LW 49:75–76.

Casting a Wider Net

Though Luther concentrated on the problems of Wittenberg in these years, he was sometimes drawn away to preach. As early as the end of April 1522, he was urged to visit towns in Electoral Saxony to provide the same calming effect he had brought to Wittenberg and to preach about the possibilities for orderly change. So he preached to crowds in Borna, Altenburg, Zwickau, and Torgau and was generally well received. Again in mid-October, he spent some days in Weimar at the court of Duke John, and also preached in Erfurt at that time. The sermons from this tour show Luther spelling out the basics of the Christian faith—the love of God and the love of one's neighbor: "Christ came down from heaven to make himself known to us. He stepped down into our mire and became a man. But we do not know him, nor do we accept him, who came to help us out of every need and fear. But he who accepts Christ, acknowledges and loves him, he fulfills all things and all his works are good; he does good to his neighbor; he suffers all things for God's sake."[52]

Even when he was at home, he was always being drawn into the wider fortunes of the Reformation because people generally looked to him as its leader. He advised the Christians in Leisnig on many matters confronting them, including their right to choose their own pastor rather than having one imposed by the abbot of the nearby Cistercian monastery. In a treatise with the wonderfully long title "That a Christian Assembly or Congregation Has the Right to Judge All Teaching and to Call, Appoint, and Dismiss Teachers, Established and Proven by Scripture," Luther told the people of Leisnig that, by their neglect and incompetence, the bishops had forfeited their traditional right to appoint pastors. And even if they were bishops who "wanted to have the gospel and wanted to institute decent

52. "Sermon in Weimar" (October 19, 1522), in LW 51:109.

preachers," they still should not do this without the consultation or consent of the local community.[53]

He wrote to the Christians in Prague advising them to stop collaborating with Rome, which refused to ordain their pastors for fear that they would offer communion in both kinds, the old Hussite demand. Prague had been sending these potential clergy to Venice, where they paid a fee, promised not to do the forbidden, and went directly home to do it. In "Concerning the Ministry" (1523), Luther urged them to elect their own bishops as the apostles had done. He did not persuade the Bohemians to take this courageous step, but the continuing refusal of bishops to ordain any Lutheran candidates meant that his followers would eventually have to forge a solution.[54]

Luther was also called on to deal with the complex consequences of so many men and women leaving religious communities. During Easter 1523, twelve nuns escaped from a convent near Grimma in Ducal Saxony, where Duke George had forbidden anyone to forsake religious vows. They had been inspired by Luther's writings critical of the religious life and on the Tuesday after Easter were brought to Wittenberg, where it was suddenly Luther's challenge to deal with them. There was no provision for being a single woman in the sixteenth century, and since only three were able to return to their families, homes in Wittenberg had to be found for the other nine. There was hope that marriages could eventually be arranged for all of them.

One distinguished member of this company was Magdalena, the sister of Johann von Staupitz, Luther's old mentor. Another was Katherine von Bora, who perhaps because she was from a noble family was placed in one of the most distinguished homes in the

53. "That a Christian Assembly or Congregation Has the Right to Judge All Teaching and to Call, Appoint, and Dismiss Teachers, Established and Proven by Scripture" (1523), in LW 39:311–12.
54. "Concerning the Ministry" (1523), in LW 40:39–40.

town, that of the painter Lucas Cranach and his wife Barbara, two of Luther's friends. In a letter to John Oecolampadius in Basel that June, Luther complained a bit: "The nuns and monks who have left [their orders] steal many hours from me, so that I serve everyone's needs—to say nothing of the mixed multitude of people who claim my services in many ways."[55]

But Luther did feel some responsibility to help people experiencing the consequences of actions that his writings had inspired. When he learned of the sufferings of one nun in his home territory of the County of Mansfeld, a young noblewoman named Florentina, he was incensed and wrote a preface to introduce her own account of being forced into a religious vocation by her family (her aunt was the abbess) and not being allowed to leave. She was punished when she wrote to Luther, but eventually escaped and wrote her defense. Luther also interceded for her with the counts of Mansfeld, his childhood rulers, and for several others who needed support.[56]

By late 1523 in Wittenberg, the problem of monks leaving their orders became a practical one when Luther and his prior were the only two residents left in the huge Augustinian monastery. They could not pay the taxes that were owed to the town, and their use of the building did not make any sense. Luther put the matter before Frederick the Wise directly: "Further, Most Gracious Lord, I am now living alone in this monastery with the Prior. . . . I have delayed this Prior more than a year to serve me; I cannot and do not wish to prolong his stay here any further, since his conscience requires him change his [way of] life. In addition, I cannot endure the daily moaning of the people whom I must admonish to pay the rents. Therefore we are inclined to relinquish and hand over the monastery

55. "Letter to John Oecolampadius" (June 20, 1523), in LW 49:45. For more about the twelve nuns, see Brecht, *Martin Luther*, 2:100.
56. "How God Rescued an Honorable Nun," in LW 43:85–96.

with all its property to Your Electoral Grace, as the last heir."[57] Frederick did not like to think about unpaid taxes and monks leaving for the sake of conscience to get married, so he did nothing about Luther's request.[58]

Allies Lost: Müntzer, Carlstadt, and Erasmus

One of the great problems Luther faced in these years was dealing with his former follower Thomas Müntzer and his former colleague Andreas Carlstadt. Müntzer was an early ally of Luther, and Luther helped him obtain a pastorate in Zwickau. There Müntzer's radical intensity brought him trouble with the authorities, and the town council dismissed him in April 1521. He had influenced many people, including the Zwickau Prophets, but for the next few years had difficulty finding a position. By Easter 1523, he had obtained a rural pastorate in Allstedt, near Weimar, despite the objections of Duke John. From that base, he built a strong local following and also wrote several pamphlets attacking Luther and the Wittenberg version of the Reformation. By the summer of 1524, he was forced to leave Allstedt and fled to Muhlhausen, where he wrote his sharpest attack on Luther, with the catchy title "The Highly Necessary Defense and Answer against the Soft-Living Flesh of Wittenberg, Which in Miserable and Perverted Fashion Has Soiled Poor Christendom." This was printed in Nuremberg in December 1524 on the eve of the great social upheavals of 1525.[59]

Carlstadt and Luther came back into lively contact in August 1524 when Luther was urged to go on a preaching tour through the Saale River valley, where religious and political dissent was very intense.

---

57. "Letter to Frederick the Wise" (mid-November 1523), in LW 49:58.
58. For Frederick's opposition to clerical marriage, see Brecht, *Martin Luther*, 2:92.
59. Müntzer's complex career through 1524 and the difficulties of interpreting him fairly are splendidly summarized in Brecht, *Martin Luther*, 2:146–57.

Carlstadt was serving at the time as pastor in Orlamunde. An attempt in April 1524 to get him to resume responsibilities at Wittenberg had ended in failure, and over the summer there had been contacts between Carlstadt and Müntzer, although they differed sharply on whether to resort to violence, which Carlstadt, despite his fervor, completely opposed. When Luther preached in Jena on August 22, Carlstadt was in the audience, not very successfully disguised.[60]

Later that day, they had a long and heated conversation at the Black Bear Inn, where Luther had earlier had his delightful contact with the two Wittenberg students. (In that case, at least Luther's disguise was more successful.) Carlstadt wanted to be sure Luther understood that he differed from Müntzer on the question of violence, even though they had many points of agreement on the sacraments. Luther suggested that they air their differences in writing, in effect challenging Carlstadt to a literary duel. Through the latter part of 1524, Luther was working on a major response to the questions raised by the Zwickau Prophets, Müntzer, and Carlstadt: "Against the Heavenly Prophets in the Matter of Images and Sacraments." The first part was published at the end of 1524, and the second part at the beginning of 1525.[61] By this time Luther's temper was rising, and he was feeling a little under siege. He also had another significant problem that would spill over into 1525. The great Erasmus had given up his neutrality and in his treatise of August 1524, "On the Freedom of the Will," had attacked the heart of Luther's theology.[62]

---

60. For Carlstadt and Luther in this period, see Brecht, *Martin Luther*, 2:157–64.
61. "Against the Heavenly Prophets in the Matter of Images and Sacraments" (1525), in LW 40:5–223. The significance of this work will be discussed in chapters 8 and 9.
62. Luther writes to Hausmann in Zwickau near the end of 1524, indicating that he will respond to Erasmus but must first deal with Carlstadt, who "has poured out his poison, as he promised me to do when he accepted the gulden from me." "Letter to Nicholas Hausmann" (November 17, 1524), in LW 49:88. Most of Erasmus's text can be found in Gordon Rupp, ed., *Luther and Erasmus: Free Will and Salvation* (Philadelphia: Westminster, 1969), 35–101.

Thinking about Politics

Religious and social problems were so closely connected at the time of the Reformation that it was impossible to address the changes needed in the church without stumbling into the widespread desire to address long-standing social discontents. The religious changes unleashed hopes for social change and sometimes inadvertently made things worse. The collapse of monasteries and convents eliminated some of the best institutions for tending to the education of the young and caring for the sick and the poor. Luther was very busy with such issues in 1522 through 1524.

Luther had written his warning against insurrection from the Wartburg at the beginning of 1522, but by the end of that year he had to take up the question of obedience to temporal power again. The dangers of an uprising continued, but at the same time many of the loyal Catholic princes were banding together, burning Luther's books and punishing those who owned them. Did Christians have to submit to princes who were taking such steps against the gospel?

Luther addressed these questions, as well as the role and responsibilities of the Christian prince, in two of his October sermons in Weimar in the presence of Dukes John and John Frederick. Duke John encouraged Luther to write again and more extensively on this topic, and the resulting pamphlet, dedicated to Duke John, was one of Luther's most important writings on politics: "Temporal Authority: To What Extent It Should Be Obeyed." It was completed by Christmas 1522 and appeared the next spring, leading Luther's opponents like Duke George to complain about it immediately.[63]

Luther realized that he was fighting on more than one front. In the first part of the treatise, he argues for the divine origin of temporal

---

63. Introduction to "Temporal Authority: To What Extent It Should Be Obeyed" (1523), in LW 45:77–80.

authority and against the Roman notion that its power was derived from the church. But in the second part, he sets out the limits to that authority, which cannot compel Christians to act against faith and conscience. He gives the contemporary example of princes in Ducal Saxony, Bavaria, and Brandenburg who are ordering that all copies of Luther's German translation of the New Testament be surrendered. "This should be the response of their subjects: They should not turn in a single page, not even a letter, on pain of losing their salvation. Whoever does so is delivering Christ up into the hand of Herod, for these tyrants act as murderers of Christ just like Herod. If their homes are ordered searched and books and property taken by force, they should suffer it to be done. Outrage is not to be resisted but endured; yet we should not sanction it, or lift a finger to conform or obey."[64]

The third part of the treatise is especially interesting. Here Luther discusses the duties and responsibilities of the prince who wishes to rule as a Christian. Luther's advice stands in interesting contrast to the harshly realistic advice that Machiavelli gave to the rulers of Florence in his treatise *The Prince* a decade later. The four great challenges of the Christian prince are to be truly devoted to his subjects, to beware the snares of "the high and mighty and of his counselors," to deal justly with evildoers, and to subject himself to God and God's will. Luther adds, with his own realism, that if the prince does all this, he can expect not praise but resistance—he can expect to bear a cross.[65]

Luther's stress on the subject's ordinary duty of obedience and his deep aversion to rebellion have led many to understand Luther's two-kingdom theology as giving a totally free hand to the princes. Luther had much experience of evil rulers in his time and was not naive about the corruption power brings. But this early and foundational treatise shows that there are limits. Luther had earlier written to

64. "Temporal Authority," in LW 45:112, MLBTW3, 446.
65. LW 45:118–26, MLBTW3, 453–54.

Frederick the Wise: "Human authority is not always to be obeyed, that is, when it undertakes something against the commandments of God; yet it should never be despised but always honored."[66]

He maintained this complex position throughout these years. That meant, on the one hand, criticizing manifestations of spiritual privilege and pretensions to be above secular rule, as when the canons in Stettin refused to pay taxes because they were clergy. Luther said this did not excuse them. "For it is un-Christian, even unnatural, to derive benefit and protection from the community and not also to share in the common burden and expense, to let other people work but to harvest the fruit of their labors."[67] At the same time, Luther regularly interrupted the work of his princes by appealing for justice on behalf of those he felt had not been treated fairly, as in the case of a poor fisherman who came too close to the reserved waters of the elector and was fined six hundred pieces of silver—a punishment Luther considered far too severe and one that would "deprive him of his living."[68]

In this period, Luther was much concerned with questions regarding marriage, both the question of the church's regulation of marriage in general and the continuing question of whether those who had taken vows of celibacy could marry. Luther had published a widely read "Sermon on Marriage" in 1519, but found it necessary to return to the subject in the latter half of 1522. He was not enthusiastic about getting involved, and he opened the new treatise with this admission: "How I dread preaching on the estate of marriage! I am

---

66. Cited in Lohse, *Martin Luther's Theology*, 150.
67. "Letter to the Council of the City of Stettin" (January 11, 1523), in LW 49:27. Luther follows long precedent in conceiving wrongful gain of money, such as through usury, as "unnatural" along sexual, reproductive lines. Just as certain kinds of sexual activity lead to reproduction, so too should just economic activities lead to the multiplication of money.
68. "Letter to George Spalatin" (June 7, 1522), in LW 49:9.

reluctant to do it because I am afraid if I once get really involved in the subject it will make a lot of work for me and for others."[69]

Thinking about Marriage

Luther plunged in, simplifying the list of persons forbidden to marry, outlining the circumstances under which divorce was possible, and giving another account of the divine institution and goal for married life. While Luther is generally opposed to overregulation by the church and can be quite pastorally sensitive to difficult cases, he could hardly be called permissive. In the case of adultery, he supports Wittenberg's town council punishment of flogging and expulsion from the community.[70]

In 1523, Luther was involved in attempts to persuade both celibate persons and not-yet-married persons to marry. After some contact with Albrecht the Grand Master of the Order of Teutonic Knights, he urged this noble monk (a cousin of Luther's long-term opponent Albrecht of Mainz) to abandon his vows, turn Prussia into a secular state, and rule it as a prince rather than an ecclesiastical ruler. In 1525, Albrecht took Luther's advice, and Prussia rapidly became a Lutheran stronghold.[71]

That same summer, Luther wrote a commentary on 1 Corinthians 7, in which Paul treats marriage questions, and dedicated it to Hans Löser, the marshal of Saxony, who was not in orders but was deciding about marriage. Luther took on Paul's advice about whether to marry or to burn and refuted the traditional Roman interpretation that the apostle supported celibacy as the preferred path. Chastity is "the rare

---

69. "The Estate of Marriage" (1522), in LW 45:17.

70. "Letter to the City Council of Zerbst" (October 8, 1524), in LW 49:86. Later in life, Luther came to favor beheading for adulterers.

71. "An Exhortation to the Knights of the Teutonic Order That They Lay Aside False Chastity and Assume the True Chastity of Wedlock" (1523), in LW 45:133–58.

gift," but God has created and still creates human beings with a clear intention that man and woman marry.[72]

> And what matter if the whole world were to complain about the state of matrimony? We see right before our eyes that God daily creates not only men but also women and maintains their lives; and yet it is certain that he does not create any women for the purpose of fornication. But since God's work and Word stare us in the face, declaring that women must be used either for marriage or fornication, these heathenish pretenders should shut their blasphemous mouths and leave God's Word and work uncriticized and unhampered; unless perhaps they would like to teach us according to their own famed sagacity and contrary to God that all women should be strangled or banished. This would make a fine fool of God.[73]

The next year Luther performed the marriage of Löser and Ursula von Portzig—a woman who was frequently curious to know when Luther himself was going to get married.

In the spring of 1524, Luther was forced to write about marriage again, this time regarding a complex set of questions about parental consent. Luther did not believe that children should marry without the consent of their parents. He was completely opposed to parents forbidding children to marry, and he was very skeptical about parents forcing a child to marry against her or his will. The title of the treatise itself suggests the mutuality that Luther stressed: "That Parents Should Neither Compel nor Hinder the Marriage of Their Children and That Children Should Not Become Engaged without Their Parents' Consent."[74]

---

72. "Commentary on I Corinthians 7" (1523), in LW 28:55.
73. LW 28:6.
74. "That Parents Should Neither Compel nor Hinder the Marriage of Their Children and That Children Should Not Become Engaged without Their Parents' Consent" (1524), in LW 45:381–93.

Money and Schools

The question of caring for the poor has always haunted Christians, and Luther struggled with this problem in Wittenberg and when the town of Leisnig appealed to him for practical advice on this matter, as they had on worship. Luther visited Leisnig twice in 1522 and 1523. Working with local officials, he developed the concept of the common chest to meet the needs of the local poor. It was to receive revenues from monasteries that closed as well as part of the town's annual taxes. Instead of begging, those in need could appeal every Sunday to a group of trustees who represented the nobility, the town council, the town citizens, and the rural peasants. Careful accounts were to be kept, and three times a year at a meeting of the parish a report was to be given on the administration of these funds.[75] The chest containing the money had four locks on it, so the one petitioning for aid would have to persuade at least four key holders to be sympathetic to their need.

There were many practical problems, including the continuing hold of the nearby Cistercian Abbot over the affairs of the parish. Matters remained unresolved until the Saxony Visitation of 1529. Luther published the "Fraternal Agreement on the Common Chest of the Entire Assembly at Leisnig" with his own preface; Leisnig's plan was influential in local communities that had accepted the Reformation—they now had to wrestle with such issues.[76]

Luther also wrote again on issues of economics in 1524. James Strauss, a preacher in Eisenach, stirred up a great deal of discussion in the Electoral Court by his preaching and writing against the practice of charging interest for lending money. In October 1523,

75. "Fraternal Agreement on the Common Chest of the Entire Assembly at Leisnig" (1523), in LW 45:161–94.
76. On this and related matters, see the analysis of Samuel Torvend, *Luther and the Hungry Poor* (Minneapolis: Fortress Press, 2008).

Chancellor Gregory Brück appealed to Luther for a judgment on the issues Strauss had raised, which seemed to have biblical support in Deuteronomy 15.

Luther replied that Strauss was basically right but that, since the world was not completely Christian, the practice would probably continue or at least not disappear immediately. Strauss, like Carlstadt, seemed to want quick, literal (and probably selective) implementation of Old Testament law. Luther was alarmed by Strauss's teaching that people who had borrowed money at interest need not repay it. But the situation was too complicated to address by letter.[77] In the latter half of 1524, Luther published an attack on corrupt business practices and attached to it a revised version of his 1520 "Longer Sermon on Usury."[78] Luther hoped that the Diet of Nuremberg of 1524 would take up some of these long-standing questions of general welfare, but this did not happen. His sermons in these years often touched on the need for Christians to deal honestly with their neighbors in the conduct of daily business.

Of all the pending social issues, that of education was closest to Luther's heart. He was defensive about humanist critiques that the Reformation was hostile to learning and led to lowered educational standards. In March 1523, he wrote to the Erfurt scholar and poet Eobanus Hessus reassuring him of his continuing regard for education, not only in the Bible but also in humanistic studies.

> Do not worry that we Germans are becoming more barbarous than we ever have been, or that our theology causes a decline of learning. . . . I myself am convinced that without the knowledge of the [humanistic] studies, pure theology can by no means exist. . . . I realize that there has never been a great revelation of God's Word unless God has first prepared the way by the rise and the flourishing of language and learning, as though these were forerunners, a sort of [John] the Baptist.

77. "Letter to Gregory Bruck" (October 18, 1523), in LW 49:52–55.
78. "Trade and Usury" (1524), in LW 49:245–310.

Certainly I do not intend that young people should give up poetry and rhetoric. I certainly wish that there would be a tremendous number of poets and orators, since I realize that through these studies, as through nothing else, people are wonderfully equipped for grasping the sacred truths, as well as for handling them skillfully and successfully.[79]

For this reassurance to amount to anything, new schools had to take the place of the monastery and convent schools that had previously done much of the teaching. In February 1524, he published "To the Councilmen of All Cities in Germany That They Establish and Maintain Christian Schools," one of his more important and influential writings from any period. The broad reference to "all cities in Germany" is perhaps an echo of the bold *Appeal to the German Nobility* of 1520, but here Luther challenges members of town councils with the need for education.[80]

He begins by acknowledging the current crisis and how the end of the monasteries has made things worse. Still, people have been set free from many expenses formerly required for "indulgences, masses, vigils, endowments, bequests, anniversaries, mendicant friars, brotherhoods, pilgrimages, and similar nonsense." Some of that money ought now go for education.[81]

Of course, some would argue that the matter should simply be left to parents. But Luther knew that many parents were incompetent to arrange such education for their children or indifferent to the opportunity. It was a community opportunity and community responsibility to see that schools were provided for the children.[82]

Luther knows this audience, the kinds of people who are on these town councils, sympathetic for the most part to the Reformation but

79. "Letter to Eobanus Hessus" (March 29, 1523), in LW 49:34.
80. "To the Councilmen of All Cities in Germany That They Establish and Maintain Christian Schools" (1524), in LW 45:347–78, MLBTW3, 456–74.
81. LW 45:351, MLBTW3, 458.
82. LW 45:354–55, MLBTW3, 460.

very frugal. He taunts them about the ways they will cut corners if they establish a school: they will not bother with Latin, Greek, and Hebrew because, they will say, "We could just as well use German for teaching the Bible and God's word, which is enough for our salvation."

> I reply: Alas, I am only too well aware that we Germans must always be and remain brutes and stupid beasts, as the neighboring nations call us, epithets which we richly deserve. But I wonder why we never ask: "What is the use of silks, wine, spices, and other strange foreign wares, when we ourselves have in Germany wine, grain, wood, flax, and stone not only in quantities sufficient for our needs, but also of the best and choicest quality for our glory and ornament?" Languages and the arts, which can do us no harm, but are actually a greater ornament, profit, glory, and benefit, both for the understanding of Holy Scripture and the conduct of temporal government—these we despise. . . . Are not we Germans justly dubbed fools and beasts?[83]

Precisely what kind and level of education was Luther recommending? Both boys and girls should be sent to school. They should be treated kindly and not subjected to the impossibly harsh treatment Luther remembered from his own school days. The young need some pleasure and enjoyment, so the teaching of music and singing should be mixed with languages, history, and mathematics. That is what Luther would want for his children if he were a father.[84] Books—not only Bibles and religious books, but also those covering language, arts, and all useful forms of learning—will also be needed for a good education, and these ought to be available in a library in any considerable town.[85]

Luther's energy is amazing in these years, not only for preaching and translating, but also for the practical problems of worship and

---

83. LW 45:357–58, MLBTW3, 462.
84. LW 45:369–70, MLBTW3, 469.
85. LW 45:373–74, MLBTW3, 471–72.

community life. When advocating education, he tapped into one of his own deepest passions: appreciation for what he had been able to learn and frustration at the obstacles he encountered along the way that were still holding many back. His ideas were as timely as Melanchthon's plans for university reform, and in the next few years, ambitious schools were established in Eisenach, Magdeburg, Nordhausen, Halberstadt, Gotha, Danzig, Nuremberg, and Luther's birthplace of Eisleben. He took part in the launching of that school at the invitation of Count Albrecht of Mansfeld and traveled there April 16, 1525, with Melanchthon and John Agricola, who was also from Eisleben. It must have been a very satisfying homecoming.[86]

Resistance to Perceived Heresy

While Luther was pouring himself into all these projects to support the gospel, his opponents were also busily at work trying to stop the spread of the Reformation, and even turn it back, if possible. Much depended on the leadership that the emperor and pope would provide. But in these years, Charles was away from Germany, and the papacy underwent several changes. Leo X had died December 1, 1521. There was great support for—but also intense opposition to—Leo's nephew and private secretary Cardinal Giulio de' Medici being named as his successor. The election in January turned to a surprising compromise choice, Cardinal Adrian of Tortosa, who was originally from the Netherlands and had been the emperor's tutor when he was a boy. The deciding voice for this candidate was Cardinal Cajetan—Luther's examiner at Augsburg in 1518.[87]

The election of a non-Italian pope shocked Rome and all of Italy (there would not be another non-Italian until John Paul II in 1978). The election of a close advisor of the emperor (he had been his

86. Brecht, *Martin Luther*, 2:141.
87. Ludwig Pastor, *The History of the Popes*, vol. 9 (London: Routledge, 1950), 23.

regent in Spain since 1516) was devastating news for the king of France. Francis I had great fear of a combined effort by the pope and Charles V against him, and in time his fears were justified. But even the cardinals who had voted for Adrian VI, as he called himself, were speechless when he arrived in Rome and told them of the high moral standards expected from them. He insisted on little ceremony at his coronation, which was a good decision because Leo had left the papacy bankrupt and the city of Rome was suffering from the plague.[88]

Adrian's papacy only lasted about a year and a half until his death on September 14, 1523; during that brief period he suffered great opposition and hostility in Rome. But his new leadership was the cause of high hopes in Germany among many of the loyal Roman Catholics. They hoped he would be able to make needed changes in the church in a way that undercut Luther's appeal and solved the Luther problem without turmoil or revolution. Eck arrived in Rome in January 1523 and gave Adrian a briefing on the current situation in Germany. The grievances of the German people had to be addressed, and the credibility of the church had to be improved.

Eck's recommendations fit well with the report that Adrian had sent to the Diet of Nuremberg. His representative Francesco Chieregati read it on January 3, 1523: Luther was to blame for the troubles in Germany, and it was shameful that even some among the princes were supporting this heretic. The Edict of Worms must be enforced against Luther immediately. But Adrian did not stop there. Taking an approach very different from that of Leo X, he went on to catalog the wrongs in the church with disarming candor:

> We all, prelates and clergy, have gone astray from the right way, and for long there is none that has done good; no, not one. To God, therefore, we must give all the glory and humble ourselves before Him; each one

88. Ibid., 68–69.

of us must consider how he has fallen and be more ready to judge himself than to be judged by God in the day of his wrath. Therefore, in our name, give promises that we shall use all diligence to reform before all things the Roman Curia, whence, perhaps, all these evils have had their origin; thus healing will begin at the source of the sickness.[89]

Luther was completely dismissive of the new pope as a tool of the emperor and no improvement over the previous one. Still, it is quite intriguing to think what might have happened had Adrian VI lived and found a way to pursue his reforms in Rome itself. He was no friend of Luther, and it is true that his papacy "represented the dream of every king-emperor since the eleventh century—an Imperial client on Peter's throne."[90] But even if he were a stooge of Charles V, Adrian might have addressed the internal problems of the Roman Church, something that did not begin in any serious way until the election of Paul III in 1534. When Adrian died, the church was then ready for Leo's nephew Giulio de' Medici, who ruled as Pope Clement VII from 1523 until his death in 1534. From this pope the Curia had nothing to fear.

During his brief reign, Adrian put pressure on his countryman Erasmus to stop his covert support for Luther. Erasmus had written to congratulate Adrian on his election and to assure the new pope of his orthodoxy. Adrian replied in a letter on December 1, 1522, in which he invited the scholar to engage in a literary war with Luther. That might really prove his orthodoxy and bring back into the church some who had been led astray. Adrian invited Erasmus to work on this project in Rome, where he would be given every resource and could enjoy the society of pious and learned men.[91] Since Adrian was finding life in Rome anything but pious and learned, it is not

---

89. Ibid., 135.
90. Thomas A. Brady, *German Histories in the Age of Reformations, 1400–1650* (Cambridge: Cambridge University Press, 2009), 208.
91. Ibid., 144–46.

surprising that Erasmus rejected this part of the invitation, claiming that his health was too frail to make such a journey. But it may be that Erasmus's attack on Luther in the summer of 1524 had its origin in this prodding from the Dutch pope.

In 1524, Clement VII sent the distinguished Cardinal Campeggio to Nuremberg to work with the diet on enforcing the Edict of Worms. He was not very successful. The German estates said that the edict could not be enforced until the abuses and problems in the church had been corrected. Then they would deal with Luther. If a general council were impossible, then they would convene a German national council to deal with the life of the church in Germany. This German gathering was to Campeggio's mind even worse than a general council, which he also opposed. In the end, Charles V and Clement VII together forbade the gathering of the German national council that had been called for Speyer in November 1524.[92]

Luther Fires Back

As an attempt to enforce one aspect of the Edict of Worms, Frederick periodically put pressure on Luther not to publish his work.[93] Luther felt that he could easily justify his biblical translations, commentaries, worship materials, and practical advice as nonpolemical, but his opponents hardly agreed. In their view, he was not to publish at all. Strong polemical writings were harder to get through the Electoral Court, but Luther's reply to King Henry VIII's attack on him is one stinging example that made it through. He wrote "Against Henry, King of England" in the summer of 1522 as soon as he received the German and Latin versions of Henry's *Defense of the Seven Sacraments*.[94]

---

92. Ludwig Pastor, *The History of the Popes*, vol. 10 (London: Routledge, 1950), 10:113–16.
93. "Letter to the Elector Frederick" (May 29, 1523), in LW 49:35–42.

Despite his appreciation for the elector's protection, Luther did not hold back from attacking Frederick's own favorite treasure—the All Saints' Foundation, which administered the relics and carried out the endowed masses in the castle church in Wittenberg. Luther had pled with Frederick to abolish the whole enterprise even before his return from the Wartburg. Again and again in 1523 and 1524, Luther put pressure on the canons of the foundation to abolish private masses and to give communion in both kinds. Even when they seemed willing, the elector refused to allow any changes.

Luther was troubled to find this stubborn clinging to old ways in Wittenberg itself, and late in 1524 he wrote vehemently against the worship at the castle church in "The Abomination of the Secret Mass."[95] Finally, Luther got what he wanted through the combined appeal of "the Burgomaster, ten members of the council, the rector of the university, and Bugenhagen" as the pastor of the town church. They insisted on a change in worship that Frederick did not support but did not oppose. For Christmas 1524, a new evangelical order of worship was begun at the castle church. Luther had won this long battle against his most determined local Roman opponents.[96]

But for all this concerted opposition, the Lutheran movement enjoyed much growth in 1522 to 1524. The burning of Luther's books called fresh attention to them. Luther could report to his friend Wenceslas Link late in 1522 that Hamburg and Friesland, far to the northwest in Germany, were requesting that evangelical ministers be sent to them.[97] There was great interest in the gospel to the northeast—in Prussia and even as far away as Riga in what is now Latvia. Luther wrote to the Christians in Riga in early 1524,

94. Brecht, *Martin Luther*, 2:85. "Against Henry, King of England" is another serious omission from the American edition of *Luther's Works*.
95. "The Abomination of the Secret Mass," in LW 36:311–28.
96. See Brecht, *Martin Luther*, 2:129.
97. "Letter to Wenceslas Link" (December 19, 1522), in LW 49:22.

praising them for their interest in the gospel and urging them to start Christian schools to sustain this interest.[98] In September 1524, Luther wrote to his Augustinian brother Henry of Zutphen in Bremen that the gospel was being accepted in Magdeburg, Hamburg, Hesse, the Palatinate, Strasbourg, Augsburg, and especially Nuremberg.[99]

Nuremberg was the great prize for the Reformation movement from these years. It was one of the most important cities of Germany, the seat of the Imperial Council of Regency during Charles V's absence. It was a town with high literacy, effective preachers such as Andreas Osiander, and civic leaders interested in reform. At this time, it was also the home of Germany's greatest artist, Albrecht Dürer. In 1524, the city council arranged for a disputation on the currently debated religious issues; as a result, Nuremberg became the first city in Germany that was officially Lutheran.

That Luther found the energy to accomplish all that he did in these three years remains astonishing. He was still in considerable danger, especially from the emperor and the estates. But the crisis in Wittenberg drew him back, and the various theological and practical challenges seemed to draw him out in new and surprising ways. The writings of this period cannot compare with the groundbreaking theological insight of those written 1519 and 1520, but it was not clear until he engaged in these tasks that Luther would also have such great skills as a preacher, a translator, and a practical reformer.

In contrast to the time in the Wartburg, Luther relished the company of his friends and colleagues in Wittenberg—especially Melanchthon, Amsdorf, Jonas, and now John Bugenhagen, who came into Luther's life in this period as one of his most important coworkers. Bugenhagen was two years younger than Luther and

---

98. "Exposition of Psalm 127, for the Christians at Riga in Livonia" (1524), in LW 45:317–37.
99. Brecht, *Martin Luther*, 2:345.

came from Pomerania, located to the northeast, so that he was often called Dr. Pommer or Pomeranius. He had studied at Greifswald and been a rector of a school. He came to Wittenberg in 1521, partly drawn to Luther's teachings but initially quite shocked by the radicalness of *The Babylonian Captivity*. He became close to Melanchthon in Luther's absence and quickly established himself as one of the best biblical lecturers in a town full of talent.[100]

Bugenhagen and Luther quickly became friends when Luther returned from the Wartburg, and by that September Luther was writing to Spalatin at the court full of anxiety that they would lose him to the University of Erfurt.[101] In 1523, Bugenhagen became pastor of the town church in Wittenberg, a position he filled so well that Luther was soon calling him the bishop of Wittenberg.[102]

Bugenhagen became one of Luther's close friends, but he also served effectively as his pastor. Luther confessed to him privately for the rest of his life, and he remarked that Bugenhagen was one of three—along with his wife Katie and his colleague Philip Melanchthon—who could minister to his discouragement. In a Table Talk from 1531, Luther paid this tribute: "Right here at this table, when the rest of you were in Jena, Pomeranius sometimes consoled me when I was sad by saying, 'No doubt God is thinking: What more can I do with this man? I have given him so many excellent gifts, and yet he despairs of my grace!' These words were a great comfort to me. As a voice from heaven they struck me in my heart, although I think Pomeranius did not realize at the time what he had said and that it was so well said."[103]

100. Bugenhagen is still neglected in English-language publications, despite his clear significance as the third Reformer of Wittenberg—with Luther and Melanchthon. A sympathetic portrait can be found in David Steinmetz, *Reformers in the Wings* (Philadelphia: Fortress Press, 1971), 82–90.
101. "Letter to George Spalatin" (September 20, 1522), in LW 49:15.
102. See Brecht, *Martin Luther*, 2:71–72, for this and for the complicated negotiations with the All Saints' Foundation by which Bugenhagen eventually came to hold this position.
103. "Table Talk for November 30, 1531," in LW 54:15–16.

Friends at a distance were also important to Luther in this period. He wrote often and once sent a dog to Wenceslas Link.[104] He frequently quarreled with the elector through Spalatin, and yet when the electoral chaplain was ready to resign in 1524, Luther talked him out of it.[105] He said in that same Table Talk in which he paid tribute to Bugenhagen's support that "those who are troubled with melancholy ought to be very careful not to be alone." Both Luther and Melanchthon suffered from such deep pangs from time to time, but Luther talked openly about this so that others who also struggled would seek help and not remain isolated.[106]

Luther did not simply ask for help from others but also appears to have given it generously. He wrote many letters of advice and encouragement in this period, especially toward individuals and communities who were suffering because of their support for the gospel. One priest asked Luther to pray for him. Luther replied: "You also ask for my prayer; I will be glad to do whatever is in my power. But I am myself a sinner in need of various things. I, rather than someone else, need help through the prayers of others."[107] Luther could both ask and give in these very busy years.

During this period, Luther's estranged relationship with his old mentor Johann von Staupitz pained him. Luther wrote to him occasionally: in June 1522 and in September 1523. Luther could not believe that Staupitz had become a Benedictine abbot, that he was supporting the pope, that he was away from Luther and all his other friends at a time when they so needed his counsel. Yet there is also

---

104. "Letter to Wenceslas Link" (December 19, 1522), in LW 49:21. Evidently, he had been promising to do this for a long time, though it is not known why.
105. "Letter to George Spalatin" (November 20, 1524), in LW 49:91–94.
106. "Table Talk for November 30, 1531," in LW 54:16.
107. "Letter to Henning Teppen" (November 21, 1522), in LW 49:16. Many other examples are found in LW 43, *Devotional Writings* 2. See, for example, 51ff., 61ff., 77ff., and 103ff.

growing recognition in these letters that Staupitz is gone and is not coming back.[108]

A last letter from Staupitz to Luther was written April 1, 1524. In it, Staupitz explains that he can neither support the Reformation that is developing nor oppose his old friends. He pledges continuing deep affection for Luther and longs for them to have one hour together of private conversation. He continues to have high regard for Wittenberg and what is being accomplished, and he is sending them a student who is bringing the letter.[109] Its warm and gentle style shows not only his continuing regard for Luther but also much about the tone of their relationship:

> My love for you is most constant, passing the love of women, always unbroken. Spare me if, on account of the slowness of my mind, I do not grasp all of your ideas and so keep silent about them. It seems to me that you condemn mere externals which profit nothing to faith and righteousness, but are indifferent, and, when done in the faith of our Lord Jesus Christ, do not burden the conscience at all. Why, therefore, should simple hearts be disturbed, and why should the monastic garb be a stench in your nostrils, when many wear it in the holy faith of Christ? Alas, abuses creep into all things human, and there are few who measure all things by faith, but there are some, nevertheless, who do, and the substance of a thing is not to be condemned on account of some accidental evil which is found in it. You abrogate all vows at once, for the sake of a very few, or, perhaps only one. Therefore I pray you, dearest friend, to remember the little ones, and not disturb fearful consciences. Please do not condemn what is indifferent and can exist along with sincere faith. Cry out and never cease against what is really repugnant to faith. We owe you much, Martin, for having led us from the husks of swine back to the pastures of life and the words of salvation.[110]

---

108. See LW 49:10–13 and 49:48–50.

109. Brecht, *Martin Luther*, 2:96–97.

110. Preserved Smith and Charles M. Jacobs, eds., *Luther's Correspondence and Other Contemporary Letters*, 2 vols. (Philadelphia: Lutheran Publication Society, 1918), 2:226–27.

He closed by calling himself Luther's "precursor in the evangelical doctrine," one who still hates "the Babylonian captivity."

Staupitz died in Salzburg in December 1524, and he was buried in Saint Peter's Abbey. It was the first of two great losses for Luther, as Elector Frederick would die the next spring. But Luther was going his own way. On October 9, 1524, Luther stopped wearing his monk's cowl and began appearing in Wittenberg in the ordinary dress of a professor.[111]

---

111. "Table Talk for March 18, 1539," in LW 54:337–39. This gives a date of 1523, but Brecht argues for 1524 and has good evidence for doing so. See Brecht, *Martin Luther*, 2:95.

8

Becoming Martin Luther

The Decisive Year 1525

Luther had been carried through the first years of the decade by repeated surges of energy. One came after Worms, when he survived what was probably the most dangerous situation he ever experienced. Though unhappy and lonely during his ten months of captivity in the Wartburg Castle, he knew that his work was unfinished and found meaning in writing, especially in his Advent and Christmas Postils and in his translation of the New Testament into German. The crisis in Wittenberg provided the occasion for his return to public life in the relatively safe setting of Electoral Saxony. The years of 1522 to 1524 were filled with another burst of creative activity on many fronts, from changing the liturgy to reforming society.

By the beginning of 1525, Luther was aware of two mounting threats to the progress of the gospel. The first was increasing fragmentation among those who had opposed the Roman Church and some of its policies. He had been attacked sharply in the second half of 1524 from Erasmus on one side and from Carlstadt and Müntzer on the other. The latter attacks were signs of another danger to this movement: rising social tension might overwhelm Luther's preference for deliberate changes negotiated with sympathetic rulers and replace that approach with direct action against both religious and social abuses.

These years were also a time of personal transition for Luther. Staupitz was dead by the end of 1524, and Frederick the Wise was old and ailing. Most of his friends had married, and living almost alone in the large Augustinian monastery, he confronted a milder version of the loneliness that he had experience in the Wartburg. Yet it was hard for him to think of beginning a new life when he was not sure that he would survive. Division and social chaos could create circumstances in which public opinion would no longer protect him, allowing the emperor to enforce the Edict of Worms by seizing Luther and sending him to Rome. He was deeply moved by the martyrdom of his supporters and allies in Brussels, Vienna, Budapest, and northern Germany in 1523 and 1524. He knew that he could be the next one put to death.

By the end of the eventful year, the social revolution would have run its tragic course, and Luther's own attempts to mediate would have been a colossal and discrediting failure. Luther would have responded to his opponents—especially Carlstadt and Erasmus—so vigorously that any prospect of patching together the antipapal forces would be practically lost. And Luther himself would have married and begun to explore the path he had commended to so many others—serving God not in a set-apart religious life but in the ordinary structures of family and work. Frederick and Müntzer would be dead, and Luther would have become *Luther*—on the far side of mentors and advisors cautioning him to "hold back" for strategic purposes.

Prophets False and True

Luther had been lecturing since mid-1524 on the Minor Prophets—biblical books that were part of his current work of Old Testament translation. But the prophets interested Luther in other ways, especially because he found in their testimony a pattern that illuminated his own current experience. In treating Amos at the end of 1524 and beginning of 1525, Luther forecast troubles that were sure to come soon: "Whenever some great upheaval threatens, whenever some great evil threatens, He sends his prophets or ministers of the Word to announce His Word, to foretell the ills which are coming, and after preaching the Word, to turn at least a few hearts and call them to repentance. No doubt, since we have the Word of God so very clearly, we ought to be waiting for a great upheaval. But only the Lord knows what will happen in the future and when it will happen."[1] Luther strongly identified with Amos's humble origins as a shepherd and the challenge such a man faced speaking to the wise and powerful, just as Luther considered himself called to speak "the Gospel of Christ against so powerful a kingdom as that of the pope."[2]

But Luther was in competition with other prophets, others who claimed to be bringing the right word from the Lord. At the beginning of 1525, Luther was completing one of his longest works of this period, "Against the Heavenly Prophets in the Matter of Images and Sacraments," a two-part reply to Carlstadt and other critics.[3] Luther felt compelled to take on his old colleague, whose influence was spreading and who now attacked not only images in the churches but also the practice of infant baptism and the

1. "Lectures on Amos" (1524–1525), in LW 18:127.
2. LW 18:129–30.
3. "Against the Heavenly Prophets in the Matter of Images and Sacraments" (Part 1: 1524, Part 2: 1525), in LW 40:75–223.

understanding of Christ's presence in the Lord's Supper. Carlstadt had written a series of pamphlets taking up Luther's challenge, and in them he denounced Luther as no better than the pope because of his hesitancy to make the changes that Carlstadt considered biblically warranted.

By writing this defense of the correct use of images (that is, religious art), Luther had become more determined of his position, though of course he continued to acknowledge that idolatrous veneration can be a problem. But he wanted to have more artwork rightly understood rather than destroyed, as Carlstadt and his followers were doing.[4] He reflects how good it would be to have wall paintings of creation, Noah and the ark, and other biblical stories.[5] He challenges Carlstadt, saying that he will end up with Müntzer, defying all authority by teaching the mob to go into churches and destroy the images there because of a supposed requirement in the law of Moses.[6]

Carlstadt may consider Luther too papal in retaining certain ceremonies, but Luther is coming to think that Carlstadt and the pope actually have much in common. Both of them want these decisions to be a matter of law, whereas Luther is trying to protect Christian freedom. Luther and his followers have found a middle course and will hold to it:

> We however take the middle course and say: There is to be neither commanding nor forbidding, neither to the right nor the left. We are neither papistic nor Karlstadtian, but free and Christian, in that we elevate or do not elevate the sacrament, how, where, when, and as long as it pleases us, as God has given us the liberty to do. Just as we are free to remain outside of marriage or to enter into marriage, to eat meat or not,

---

4. The conflict between Carlstadt and Luther over images is well-covered in Carlos Eire, *War against the Idols: Reformation of Worship from Erasmus to Calvin* (Cambridge: Cambridge University Press, 1986), 54–73.
5. LW 40:99.
6. LW 40:104–5.

to wear the chasuble or not, to have the cowl and tonsure or not. In this respect we are lords and will put up with no commandment, teaching, or prohibition.[7]

In addition, Luther's followers were not convinced that one could restore all the precise conditions of worship in the New Testament. Carlstadt says the elevation of the cup is forbidden, but how does he know this? Will he use red wine or white, barley or wheat bread?[8] Luther challenges those considering following Carlstadt to consider what they are embracing. He asks especially for Carlstadt's articulation of the main points of the gospel. Luther has not read that in any of his pamphlets, so preoccupied are they with details of worship. "For in no place do they teach how we are to become free from our sins, obtain a good conscience, and win a peaceful and joyful heart. That is what really counts."[9]

Melanchthon was appalled by the sharpness of this attack on their former colleague and neighbor, but Luther was discovering for the first time how Catholic he himself was in his approach to worship and the sacraments.[10] Such strong words would ordinarily have marked the end of any relationship between Luther and Carlstadt, but their next encounter, after Luther's wedding, was one of many surprises ahead in this strange year.

In March 1525, Luther was busy telling the story of one of the early Reformation martyrs—his friend and fellow Augustinian Henry of Zutphen. Luther had been deeply troubled by reports of his death at the hands of an angry mob in the village of Dithmarschen on December 10, 1524. Henry had been a colleague of Luther's in the

7. LW 40:130. A chasuble is a garment worn over a robe by the one presiding at communion. A tonsure is a ring-shaped haircut worn by some monks.
8. LW 40:133.
9. LW 40:222–23.
10. Martin Brecht, *Martin Luther*, vol. 2: *Shaping and Defining the Reformation, 1521–1532*, trans. James L. Schaaf (Minneapolis: Fortress Press, 1990), 169–70.

order and an effective pastor and preacher in Bremen. Luther used his own memories and the accounts that were sent to him to write "The Burning of Brother Henry," which was published in March 1525. He proclaimed that "in our day the pattern of true Christian life has reappeared, terrible in the world's eyes, since it means suffering and persecution, but precious and priceless in God's sight."[11]

Luther continued to be occupied with liturgical and sacramental matters, writing to Theobald Billicanus in Nördlingen to affirm the validity of the sacrament even if the presider were "an ungodly man."[12] This was ancient Catholic teaching from Augustine, and Luther did not challenge it because it affirmed that the power and effectiveness of the sacrament was in the word of promise rather than in the sanctity of the minister or faith of the recipient.

To his good friend Hausmann in Zwickau he sent a new text, "Exhortation to the Communicants," which addressed the difficult question of who might rightly take the sacrament. Luther called for faith from each participant "that Christ has suffered death for all his sins." The faith might be weak or wavering, and the Lord's Supper was especially for the weak and struggling, but open scoffers and "those who cling . . . to greed, hatred, anger, envy, profiteering, unchastity, and the like" ought to be barred. Yet each person must finally judge for herself or himself.[13]

At this time, Luther also published "The Abomination of the Secret Mass." This is an expanded version of a sermon from November 1524 when Luther had been campaigning to end the traditional masses at All Saints' Church (the castle church) in Wittenberg. But in the published version, Luther went through the liturgy of the Mass and commented on every word and every action traditionally used by

---

11. "Burning of Brother Henry" (1525), in LW 32:265–66.
12. "Letter to Theobald Billicanus" (March 5, 1525), in LW 49:100–101.
13. "Exhortation to the Communicants" (1525), in LW 53:104–5.

the priest. He was trying to show how the institution of Christ was overwhelmed by prayers and actions that called attention to what the priest was doing or what God requires rather than to the free gift that is the heart of the sacrament.[14]

Luther suspended his biblical work for a few weeks, but he did send a brief writing to the Livonia on the question of worship, especially regarding orderly change. The local preacher Melchior Hoffman claimed Luther's authority for radical and rapid change, but Luther again asserted his preference for a balance of freedom and order, achieving what consensus might be possible within the community "in a friendly way." He reminds them of Paul's teaching: "For even though from the viewpoint of faith, the external orders are free and can without scruples be changed by anyone at any time, yet from the viewpoint of love, you are not free to use this liberty, but bound to consider the edification of the common people as St. Paul says . . . 'Knowledge puffs up, but love builds up'" (1 Cor. 8:1).[15]

Ever-Shifting Politics

On February 24, the political situation in Europe changed dramatically when Charles V, long absent from Germany, defeated the French king Francis I in the Battle of Pavia in northern Italy. This left no power in Europe able to stand against the emperor and was a terrible blow to Pope Clement VII, who feared domination by Charles, who now controlled both northern and southern Italy. Clement foolishly became part of an alliance against the emperor, a move that would lead eventually to a war between the Catholic emperor and the pope, and to Charles's troops occupying and sacking Rome itself on May 5, 1527.

14. "Abomination of the Secret Mass" (1525), in LW 36:309–28.
15. "A Christian Exhortation to the Livonians Concerning Public Worship and Concord" (1525), in LW 53:47.

The implications of Charles's victory were not clear in northern Germany for some months. But an exciting political development from the same period was the embracing of the Reformation by Landgrave Philip of Hesse. Luther had met this energetic young prince at Worms, and Philip had expressed interest Luther's teachings for some time. In May 1524, when Melanchthon was returning to Wittenberg from a visit to his family in the town of Bretten, the young prince Philip and some of his knights met him and made him spend the night with them while they questioned him about the new teachings. When he returned to Wittenberg, Philip Melanchthon wrote a "Summary of Doctrine" for Philip of Hesse.[16]

There was talk of an alliance between Electoral Saxony and Hesse to counter the alliance of Catholic princes that had been assembled at Regensburg the year before. In March, Philip of Hesse met with Duke John and with Melanchthon to discuss possibilities. Luther was happy for the protection of princes, but he was also dubious about taking action to make things turn out "right," for he continued to teach that the fortune of the gospel was in God's hands alone and that the Reformation could only come by God's action. Frederick the Wise was ailing by this time and turning more and more of the administration of Saxony over to his brother and heir.

Frederick, long ill, finally succumbed and died May 5, 1525, in his castle at Löbau. Just before he died, he wrote to his brother John that an impending rebellion by the peasants might well be the judgment of God on the princes and the sign of a great shift in sovereignty in the world.[17] The dying elector did not rally his troops, but instead took care of matters like providing for his sons by his longtime mistress, Anna Weller. They had never married, perhaps because of

16. Philip Melanchthon, "Summary of Doctrine" (1524), in *Melanchthon: Selected Writings*, ed. E. E. Flack and Lowell J Satre, trans. Charles L. Hill (Minneapolis: Augsburg, 1962), 92ff.
17. Heiko Oberman, *Luther: Man between God and the Devil*, trans. Eileen Walliser-Schwarzbart (New Haven: Yale University Press, 1989), 18.

unequal social status, but Frederick saw that these boys would receive one of his many castles and one thousand gulden per year for the rest of their lives.[18]

A week later, Frederick was buried in the castle church in Wittenberg. Frederick had received communion in both kinds from his chaplain Spalatin on his deathbed, a final sign of his support for the Reformation. Luther preached the funeral sermon; there was nothing ambiguous about that, as it had clearly been the elector's choice that the Reformer would play this role.[19] There was no requiem mass, in a church that was built for the saying of masses, but rather there was preaching on two days, stressing confidence in the resurrection as the only hope, even at the death of a prince.[20]

Luther had lost a very significant force in his life with the death of Frederick. It is not too dramatic to say that Frederick saved Luther's life several times—by refusing to send him to Rome, by his presence and authority at Worms, by hiding him in the Wartburg, and by working to delay the enforcement of the Edict of Worms in Germany. In later years, Luther reflected with appreciation not only on Frederick's support for him, but also on the excellence of his rule in Saxony: "It's a great gift to have a good and wise prince, such as Elector Frederick, who was truly the father of his country. He governed excellently. He could fill barns and haylofts, and had large trenches dug in the fields to store provisions. Every year he spent twelve thousand florins on building. . . . Still the elector had enough money, for he was his own tax collector . . . and required exact accounts of his officials and servants."[21]

18. Ibid., 286.
19. Ibid., 20.
20. Brecht, *Martin Luther*, 2:183–84.
21. "Table Talk for Spring, 1533," in LW 54:194–95. Luther could count nine castles built by this prince. In an earlier reflection at the death of Frederick's brother John, Luther said that Frederick's great quality was prudence and John's was clemency. "Table Talk for August 18, 1532," in LW 54:164.

It is astonishing to think that the two men never met face-to-face, except at Worms. Not long before, Luther had reflected on how strange this was in "Against the Heavenly Prophets" where he reported "I have in my whole life never spoken one word with this prince, nor heard him speak, nor have I ever seen his face, except once in Worms before the emperor (April 18, 1521) when I was being examined for the second time."[22]

It was to be quite different with the new elector, Duke John of Saxony, who would be the ruler until his death in 1532. Luther already knew him well and was used to face-to-face contact with him and with his son and heir, Duke John Frederick. To mark the death of Frederick, Luther wrote a commentary on Psalm 26 the next week, not filled with reminiscences of the ruler but full of hints about the harshness of the times they were living through. "The devil does not rest or take a holiday," says Luther at the beginning of his exposition.[23] Reports were coming in about the great slaughter of peasants in Thuringia and Württemberg, and Luther's harsh pamphlet appeared to egg the rulers on to greater violence just when the threat was over and the peasants were suffering terribly.

Luther complained in his Psalm exposition about the proud, who assault the faithful in all times and places. He speaks of the arrogance of his students who know it all: "What do we have to be so puffed up and proud about? We have many students here who are so full of knowledge after they have been in Wittenberg half a year that they suppose they are more learned than I am. When they go out into the country to other people, their knowledge breaks out like a cloudburst. It seems to weigh a hundred pounds, but if you put it on a scale, it would only weigh an eighth of an ounce."[24] While

---

22. "Against the Heavenly Prophets" (1525), in LW 40:102.
23. "Psalm 26" (1525), in LW 12:183.
24. LW 12:189.

Luther is speaking of students, he seems to have a wider range of humanity in mind, from arrogant and violent peasants to princes who use their legitimate role of maintaining order as an excuse to unleash wholesale plunder and killing. In any case, on May 15 Luther took the strong step of ordaining one of his own students, George Rörer. It is unlikely that a bishop could be found in those days who would have done this for a Wittenberg graduate.[25]

The Peasants' War

Luther had traveled through Mansfeld two months earlier, and it was here that his awareness of what was happening with the peasants was heightened. He was actually traveling to his birthplace, Eisleben, with his colleagues Melanchthon and Agricola (also from Eisleben) to be part of organizing a Christian school there. It delighted Luther to see the counts of Mansfeld acting in response to his call for the establishment of schools, and thus a measure of steady social improvement seemed on its way. But Luther encountered plans for social change in Mansfeld that worked *against* the authorities, not with them.

A few dozen members of various peasants' groups had met to draft twelve articles making demands for justice against the Swabian League, in which several imperial estates and cities promised mutual defense and enforcement of taxes and laws.[26] The twelve articles called for relief from unfair taxes, hunting and fishing rights, more control over local churches, and so on. These were widely discussed and publicized; in the first two months after their publication in March 1525, they were reprinted an astounding twenty-five thousand times.[27]

25. See LW 12:ix.
26. For the text of "The Twelve Articles," see LW 46:8–16.

The peasants had some reason to suppose that Luther would be supportive. He had referred to himself as a son of peasants, and his theology was associated with "freedom." Of course, Luther did not equate this with the freedom not to pay one's taxes. Still, he had shown himself time and again to be interested in improving the spiritual and material lives of rank-and-file Germans. All sides clamored for him to take a public position. Luther read the "Twelve Articles" of the peasants in the early spring of 1525. He noticed several positive things, including the acknowledgment of the legitimacy of secular authority, the request to be able to elect their own pastors (which he had advocated since 1523), and a generally moderate tone. Some accompanying documents also suggested the dispute be resolved through mediation (rather than open revolt), and Luther was named as one of the persons who could be part of such negotiations. He had good reason to insert himself into the controversy, especially as so many of the articles echoed issues that he had raised in the past eight years in one writing or another.[28]

His initial response was called "Admonition to Peace: A Reply to the Twelve Articles of the Peasants."[29] It was a stinging indictment of both sides, an attempt to mediate, and a strong warning against violence, but its publication was delayed and thus came far too late in the uprising, well after violence had broken out across the German lands. If read independently of later developments, it is not hard to see Luther's efforts at balance and fairness—even given his deep abhorrence of revolt and insurrection. The first section, although brief, is a stinging critique of the role of the princes and lords,

---

27. Peter Blickle, *The Revolution of 1525: The German Peasants' War from a New Perspective*, trans. Thomas A. Brady and H. Erik Midelfort (Baltimore: Johns Hopkins University Press, 1985), 18.

28. Helpful relevant documents are collected in Tom Scott and Bob Scribner, *The German Peasants War: A History in Documents* (Amherst, MA: Humanity Books, 1991).

29. "Admonition to Peace: A Reply to the Twelve Articles of the Peasants in Swabia" (1525), in LW 46:5–43.

especially the ecclesiastical princes: "We have no one on earth to thank for this disastrous rebellion except you princes and lords, and especially you blind bishops and mad priests and monks, whose hearts are hardened even to the present day. You do not cease to rant and rave against the holy gospel, even though you know that it is true and that you cannot refute it. In addition, as temporal rulers you do nothing but cheat and rob the people so that you may lead a life of luxury and extravagance. The poor common people cannot bear it any longer."[30] Luther counsels them "to give way a little" so that they may "prevent the spark that will kindle all Germany and start a fire that no one can extinguish."[31] While there are no direct citations from the Minor Prophets on whom Luther had been lecturing for the past year, something of that prophetic tone shapes this first part of the treatise.

But Luther is also very harsh toward the peasants in the second part of his booklet. Many of their demands may well be just by natural law, but they have claimed to be a Christian association and at the same time have taken matters into their own hands, using force to press their case. This is an impossible contradiction in Luther's view and shows that they are not acting from a Christian basis. Do they not know that the Christ himself teaches that "all who take the sword will perish by the sword"?[32]

To put the matter another way, their resort to force has set them as judges of their own case. If this were to be sustained, it would be the end of all government, no matter how earnestly they acknowledge the legitimacy of such rule. Luther appeals to their reason and experience:

Can you not think it through, dear friends? If your enterprise were

---

30. LW 46:19.
31. LW 46:21–22.
32. LW 46:24–25. The Scripture citation is Matt. 26:52.

right, then any man might become judge over another. Then authority, government, law and order would disappear from the world; there would be nothing but murder and bloodshed. As soon as anyone saw that someone was wronging him, he would begin to judge and punish him. Now if that is unjust and intolerable when done by an individual, we cannot allow a mob or crowd to do it. . . . What would you yourselves do if disorder broke out in your ranks and one man set himself against another and took vengeance on him? Would you put up with that? Would you not say that he must let others, whom you appointed, do the judging?[33]

Luther goes on to comment on many of the articles' specific demands, without a great deal of sympathy for the way they have been argued, even if there is some case for justice contained in them.

In a final section, Luther warns both rulers and peasants that they are fighting on heathen rather than Christian terms. Both sides are so stubborn that unless they repent, enormous destruction and great damage to Germany will result. Both must repent of their approaches to date and instead "choose certain counts and lords from among the nobility and certain councilmen from the cities and ask them to arbitrate and settle this dispute amicably. You lords, stop being so stubborn! You will finally have to stop being such oppressive tyrants—whether you want to or not. Give these poor people room in which to live and air to breathe. You peasants, let yourselves be instructed and give up the excessive demands of some of your articles."[34] Luther's suggestions were quite defensible, and consistent with his own previous teachings. However, they came at a late stage of the conflict, and there was even more delay before "Admonition to Peace" was actually published.

At the heart of Luther's reaction to the uprising of the peasants were two factors: his opposition to resorting to violence and his deep

33. LW 46:27.
34. LW 46:42.

aversion to the theology of Thomas Müntzer. He had already dealt with the question of rebellion in two earlier writings: "A Sincere Admonition to Guard against Insurrection and Rebellion," written from the Wartburg in early 1522, and his more systematic "Temporal Authority: To What Extent It Should Be Obeyed," written in 1523. By the summer of 1524, he was so concerned about Müntzer's advocacy of rebellion that he wrote and published a warning to his rulers: "Letter to the Princes of Saxony Concerning the Rebellious Spirit."[35] Luther equates Müntzer with Satan and says that he has now "made himself a nest in Allstedt, thinking he can fight against us while enjoying our peace, protection, and security."[36]

Luther urged the princes not to wait too long to confront the menace, and to listen to Müntzer's message and look at the behavior that follows from it. Luther did not believe that the princes should interfere with Müntzer's preaching; instead, they should investigate what he is teaching about obedience and rebellion. On the basis of this warning, Müntzer and the Allstedt town council were summoned to Weimar to give an account of themselves to the dukes. Müntzer did not wait for a decision but fled from the territory of Electoral Saxony to Muhlhausen, where he came to have control over that city, and from there he played a leading role in the Peasants' War in Thuringia, though other regions had different instigators.

It was also from Muhlhausen that Müntzer wrote his most stinging attack on Luther, "Against the Mindless Soft-Living Flesh in Wittenberg."[37] He says that Luther, whom he calls "Dr. Liar," writes

35. "Letter to the Princes of Saxony Concerning the Rebellious Spirit" (1524), in LW 40:47–59.
36. LW 40:50.
37. Thomas Müntzer, "Vindication and Refutation" (1524), in *The Collected Works of Thomas Müntzer*, ed. Peter Matheson (Edinburgh: T&T Clark, 1994), 324–50. It is difficult to summarize this sustained cry of rage against Luther and the princes. The editor writes: "The flaws of the 'Vindication' are manifest: *ad personam* polemic, the wild accusations, the simplistic, dualistic categories. One wonders who would have read it, if it had not been suppressed!" See 326.

what the princes want for money: "he is indulgent about their faults in order to eat his fill of their wealth and honors and especially of the fine-sounding titles at their disposal."[38] It ends with what might be considered a prophecy or curse: "O Doctor Liar, you wily fox. With your lies you have saddened the heart of the just man. . . . For you have strengthened the power of the godless evildoers, so that they could continue on in their old way. Therefore your fate will be that of a fox that has been hunted down; the people will go free and God alone will be their Lord."[39]

Such writings actually made many literate folks sympathetic to Luther, but these people were not the chief players in the uprisings of this year. Luther also remained suspicious of Carlstadt, but on issues of obedience to authority they were actually very close. Carlstadt was at this time in Rothenberg on the Tauber, and when the uprising reached that region, he strongly urged the peasants to avoid violence. That he took such a stance was crucial in Carlstadt's temporary reconciliation with Luther a few months later.[40]

As the revolt spread from southern Germany into the region of Thuringia in the spring of 1525, Luther was pressed to confront the issues again. He had already written to his friend Lazarus Spengler, a Nuremberg town official, on how to deal with radical preachers. Luther was always cautious about secular authorities intervening in the content of preaching, no matter how heretical they might judge it to be. However, those same officials had a duty to uphold order, and if these preachers would not "acknowledge and obey the secular government," then "they have forfeited their rights to property and person."[41] This was important, principled advice, but hard to apply in a very unsettled situation.

---

38. Ibid., 333. In German, *Lügner*, which means "liar," sounds like "Luther."
39. Ibid., 350.
40. Bernard Lohse, *Martin Luther's Theology* (Minneapolis: Fortress Press, 1999), 157–58.
41. "Letter to Lazarus Spengler" (February 4, 1525), in LW 49:99.

Luther's attempts to preach in a calming way, as he had done in 1522, were also quite unsuccessful. He was heckled and interrupted during his sermon in Nordhausen in April. On May 1 in Wallhausen near Eisleben, he preached on the text "Beware of False Prophets" (Matt. 7:15-23).[42] He stressed that Jesus ended the Sermon on the Mount with a warning against false prophets, and so even now the people must test those who came among them to see their true spirit, and what fruits came of it. The genuine messenger from God does not seek to be served but to serve, and one key test is whether they seek their own self-interest (as Luther thought the peasants were doing) or whether they offer practical help to others.[43] These careful reflections were no match for the excitement of Müntzer's preaching, and on several occasions Luther was greeted with hostility and even with threats.[44] On May 4, he wrote an urgent letter to his friend and family connection John Ruhel, an advisor to the counts of Mansfeld, pressing that Ruhel urge these rulers to do all they could to oppose and stop the peasants because of the great risk they now represented to all legitimate authority. Luther felt they would eventually come to Wittenberg and kill him. "But I would rather lose my neck a hundred times than approve of and justify the peasants' actions."[45]

Such events, coupled with displeasure at the continued threats and uprisings from the peasants, led Luther to write in early May a far stronger book, *Against the Robbing and Murdering Hordes of Peasants*. One of the most shocking publications Luther ever wrote, it appealed to the rulers to use force to stop the uprising.[46] Luther amplified the advice he had sent through Ruhel to the counts of Mansfeld

42. This Sermon is not available in the American edition of Luther's Works but can be found in J. N. Lenker, ed., *Sermons of Martin Luther* (Minneapolis: Lutherans in All Lands, 1904), 246ff.

43. Ibid., 260.

44. Brecht, *Martin Luther*, 2:178–79.

45. "Letter to John Ruhel" (May 4, 1525), in LW 49:111.

46. "Against the Robbing and Murdering Hordes of Peasants" (1525), in LW 46:47–55.

in this generalized appeal to the authorities to restore order. Even rulers who did not support the gospel had Luther's blessing in taking whatever measures necessary to stop the peasants. Luther, who knew that he had a history of intemperate expression, urged these rulers on: "rebellion brings with it a land filled with murder and bloodshed; it makes widows and orphans, and turns everything upside down, like the worst disaster. Therefore let everyone who can, smite, slay, and stab, secretly or openly, remembering that nothing can be more poisonous, hurtful, or devilish than a rebel. It is just as when one must kill a mad dog; if you do not strike him, he will strike you, and the whole land with you."[47] Luther also promised a blessed death to any who die in this just cause.

By late April, more than three hundred thousand armed peasants were in the field, and contemporary observers agree that there was much pillaging and general violence, especially toward monasteries and convents.[48] This was not a particularly organized or centralized affair, however. Thomas Müntzer was the acknowledged leader of many of them. Princes like Philip of Hesse and Duke George of Saxony—ordinarily religious opponents—took common harsh action to suppress the peasants. They joined forces against Müntzer and his eight thousand men at the Battle of Frankenhausen in northern Thuringia on May 15. It was a one-sided slaughter of the peasants; around five thousand were killed. The princes' side had, at the most, four men killed in this "battle." Müntzer fled the battlefield and the next day was caught in bed in Frankenhausen, pretending not to know there had been a battle. He was tortured and executed two days later.[49] His head was cut off and hung on a pike. Afterward, taxes imposed on peasants actually increased so that the princes could

47. LW 46:50.
48. See Holborn, *The Reformation*, 173.
49. Ibid., 174.

pay off their war debts. More were slaughtered throughout Germany. Spalatin wrote in horror, "Of hangings and beheadings there is no end."[50]

By the end of May, the situation was quiet throughout Germany, except in some places in the Alps. But in the final stage of the battle, just as the tide had turned and the princes seemed most at fault in their slaughter of the peasants, Luther's harsh condemnation of the peasants appeared. Luther had intended to direct his attack against only *some* of the peasants. After learning of the pillaging of monasteries, castles, and abbeys, Luther published two works together as one pamphlet: one was the "Admonition to Peace and Reply to the Peasants in Swabia," and the other had the crucially worded title "Also, against the Murdering and Robbing Hordes of the *Other* Peasants."[51] In Luther's mind, he was distinguishing between the peasants who had reasonable protests against injustice and those who simply rebelled violently. But when the book was published in Leipzig, Mainz, Nuremberg, and elsewhere, the word *other* was omitted. In addition, the book appeared in the public's hands just after the awful battles, making Luther look even crueler.

Historians estimate that as many as one hundred thousand people were killed in the uprising, the vast majority of them peasants.[52] The loss was not only of life, but also, for many, of hope for social and even religious change. Historian Hajo Holborn contends that 1525 represents a great shift in public opinion in Germany: "Here ended the days when it had seemed that the Protestant Reformation would be embraced by all classes of the German nation and would give to the subjected groups some sense of participation in the great

50. Quoted in Ernst Belford Bax, *The Peasants' War in Germany, 1525–1526* (New York: Russell and Russell, 1968), 353.
51. Emphasis added. For this line of reasoning I am indebted to David M. Whitford, *Luther: A Guide for the Perplexed* (London: Continuum, 2011), 142–45.
52. Blickle, *Uprising of 1525*, 165; and Holborn, *Reformation*, 174.

issues of public life. These groups now fell back into apathy or rather superficial conformity. Bitter jibes at religion were heard, and even stronger thrusts were taken at Luther as the pseudo-prophet who could twist the Scriptures to suit his own ends even more than the old princes could."[53]

What drove Luther to such unguarded expression? No doubt his experiences in Thuringia brought him close to the attitudes of the revolt, while others filled him with stories. He resented the failure of his mediation, even though it was too late. He had a fear of mob violence that was understandable, especially given the way that it had been used against his supporters. One only has to read his "The Burning of Brother Henry" from March 1525 to see a horrific account of how a mob could be manipulated into a terrible and unjust action.[54] Luther could find no biblical basis for this kind of revolution, nor did he know of any revolution that had ended well for those who had been wronged and fought back.

Luther was not, as he always admitted in calmer times, an expert in matters political. His hysteria could be contrasted with Frederick's calm deathbed sense that God's will would be done by either the success or the failure of this war. Perhaps such detailed matters should be left to princes, which was Luther's normal advice. Moreover, his timing was terrible; he now seemed cruel and vindictive when everyone could see that the tide had turned. Most of the princes of Luther's day did not need any special encouragement to "smite, slay and stab."

---

53. Holborn, *Reformation*, 176–77.
54. "The Burning of Brother Henry," in LW 32:283–86. For example: "The crowd in general spent the whole night guzzling. At eight in the morning a council was held in the market place to decide what was to be done. The drunken peasants shouted, 'Go ahead, burn him! To the fire with him! Today we shall gain favor with God and man. The longer we let him live the more people he will pervert with his heresy. What is the use of a long deliberation? He has to die anyway.' Then the good Henry was condemned to the stake without even a hearing" (285).

Image 22: Thousands of farmers died during the Peasants' War, both in battle and afterward. Here a man tied to a stake is burned and suffocated by smoke.

But this captures only part of the situation. There is ample evidence that Luther thought the world was ending in these upheavals. He had written to Ruhel of his intention to go home to Wittenberg and prepare for his own death. But even more telling is the very ending of *Against the Robbing and Murdering Hordes*: "To this let every pious Christian say, 'Amen.' For this prayer is right and good, and pleases God; this I know. If anyone thinks this too harsh, let him remember that rebellion is intolerable and that the destruction of the world is to be expected every hour."[55] Lohse agrees that for Luther the Peasants'

War had apocalyptic meaning: "the devil was attempting to extend his rule." The only recourse was for the authorities to act, even if that meant supporting an old enemy of the gospel like Duke George.[56]

Luther quickly realized that he had misjudged the situation and written in a way that discredited himself. Even princes found the harshness of his language appalling for a theologian and pastor. By the end of May, he was writing to Amsdorf, the friend to whom he could always speak in the most open and unguarded way. He bristled at the accusation that he was now called "a toady to the Sovereigns" and told Amsdorf to warn his preachers not to curry favor with the peasants and their sympathizers even now, but to support the princes even if "all the peasants should be killed."[57]

This same belligerent defense of his course of action is characteristic of Luther's third writing on the uprising. In July, his friends finally persuaded him that he needed to say something more in defense of his own role, and he published a letter to Casper Müller, a chancellor of the counts of Mansfeld, with the title "An Open Letter on the Harsh Book against the Peasants." It contains little that is new except Luther's own sense of the rightness of his cause and a startling judgment that those who now sympathize with the peasants after the fact are rebels themselves. He does denounce the harshness of some princes after peasants were defeated, but nothing in the treatise could have helped Luther's case with those critical of his one-sidedness and especially of the violence of his language.[58] Years later in his Table Talk, he was still saying, perhaps even weirdly boasting: "I, Martin Luther, slew all the peasants in the uprising, for I ordered that they be put to death; their blood is on my neck."[59] Luther did write to his old

---

55. LW 46:55.
56. Lohse, *Martin Luther's Theology*, 159.
57. "Letter to Nicholas von Amsdorf" (May 30, 1525), in LW 49:113–14.
58. "An Open Letter on the Harsh Book against the Peasants," in LW 46:63–85.
59. "Table Talk for January 1533," in LW 54:180–81.

enemy Albrecht of Mainz to intercede for a certain Asmus Gunthel of Eisleben, who allegedly had not been part of the violence but was caught eating and drinking with the rebels after they had finished.[60]

The rebellion could have been a great opportunity for Charles V to advance his issues in Germany, but he was deeply involved in matters in Italy and very little affected by the events of the war.[61] Rome was preoccupied with Charles's recent victory and the threat to the Papal States, and, as was often the case in these years, it lacked accurate information about what was happening in Germany. Clement VII wrote to Philip of Hesse congratulating him on a great victory without realizing he had embraced the Reformation some months before. They also rejoiced in Rome at a rumor that Luther had been captured, which turned out to be false.[62] Despite Luther's fears, the peasants never reached Wittenberg, and Luther's day of judgment in the Peasants' War came not at sword point, but in the court of public opinion.

Luther Marries

On June 13, a month after the burial of Frederick, Luther married Katherine von Bora in Wittenberg. His friends, especially Melanchthon, had doubts about his timing, with Germany deeply sobered by so much death in the recent uprising. But perhaps even more interesting is the event's proximity to Frederick's death. He was until the end very conservative on some issues, especially on the marriage of priests. Perhaps Luther felt a freer hand to proceed with this towering but controlling figure out of the way.

60. "Letter to Albrecht Mainz," in *Luther: Letters of Spiritual Counsel*, ed. Theodore Tappert (Philadelphia: Westminster, 1955), 174–75.
61. Karl Brandi, *The Emperor Charles V* (London: Jonathan Cape, 1939), 193.
62. Ludwig Pastor, *The History of the Popes*, vol. 10 (London: Routledge, 1950), 119–20.

Image 23: In 1525 Martin Luther married former nun and noblewoman Katharine von Bora.

In February, Luther had preached one of his many sermons on Matt. 11:25-30, a favorite not only because it stressed Christ's invitation, "Come unto me," but because it contrasted God's way of hiding things from the wise with God's way of revealing them to infants. Luther seemed to be exhorting both the Wittenberg congregation and himself to hear the comfort and promise in this Gospel: "[The yoke of Christ] is called gentle, sweet, and easy because he himself helps us carry it, and when it grows too heavy for us he shoulders the burden along with us. The world looks upon it as heavy and intolerable, but it is not, for then one has a good companion and, as the saying goes: With a good companion the singing is good. Two can carry a burden easily, though one alone may not carry it well."[63]

63. "Sermon for St. Matthias' Day" (February 5, 1525), in LW 51:132.

With the sermon ending on such a theme, it is hard not to guess that Luther had marriage on his mind.

While in Mansfeld the next month for discussions about the new school, Luther visited his parents and discussed with them the possibility of his getting married. The idea was well developed in his mind by this time. Spalatin was considering getting married, and as Luther left Wittenberg he wrote to his friend, hinting at what was coming:

> Incidentally . . . I do not want you to wonder that a famous lover like me does not marry. It is rather strange that I who so often write about matrimony, and get mixed up with women, have not yet turned into a woman, to say nothing of having married one. . . . But you are a sluggish lover who does not dare to become the husband of even one woman. Watch out that I, who have no thought of marriage at all, do not some day overtake you too eager suitors—just as God usually does those things which are least expected.[64]

His parents were very happy and enthusiastic about the prospect and came to Wittenberg for the marriage feast in late June. It is probably for that reason that we have the memorable Cranach portraits of Luther's parents—an amazing thing that such ordinary people should have been painted. There were plenty of paintings of ordinary people in the early sixteenth century, but they are always anonymous—part of a crowd scene at the crucifixion or the last judgment. Discussing the matter with his parents allowed Luther to think of his marriage as an act of obedience, perhaps as a way to make up for becoming a monk against their will. It was also a further way to encourage Albrecht of Mainz to marry to "set an example."[65]

---

64. "Letter to George Spalatin" (April 16, 1525), in LW 49:104–5. In this letter Luther also jokes (mysteriously, from our vantage point) that he has lost several wives already, perhaps referring to the many runaway nuns for whom he was working to arrange marriages.
65. *D. Martin Luthers Werke: Briefwechsel*, 18 vols. (Weimar: Hermann Bohlaus Nachfolger, 1930-85), 3:482. Hereafter WABR.

His marriage to a former nun could not help but enrage both his staunch opponents and many who were neither Lutheran nor Roman Catholic at this point, but hoping that the options would clarify in time. They had admired Luther's slow and steady pace of reform, his patience with "the weak" (which was von Staupitz's last advice to him), and his opposition to violence. But in this case, Luther himself seemed rash and impatient, even though he was almost the last of his circle to marry. People questioned his timing—with the slaughter of the peasants so recent—his choice of a former nun, and in some cases the choice of this particular woman, Katherine von Bora.

She had come to Wittenberg in 1523 with the dozen nuns who escaped the Nimbschen convent in Grimma (near Leipzig) in the wagon of Leonard Koppe. She was from a noble but impoverished family; after her mother died, the family put her in a convent school at age five and had her committed to the religious life at Nimbschen where she took her vows at age sixteen in 1515. Her aunt Magdalena was a member of the same community. Katherine could not have had much to say about this decision, but it meant that her family would not have to find a dowry for her, a considerable problem given her need to marry someone of comparable social rank.[66]

When she and the other nuns came to Wittenberg, she was assigned to live in the home of the painter Lucas Cranach the Elder and his wife Barbara. It seems likely that the von Bora name made it appropriate that she live with prominent people, and by ending up with the Cranachs, she probably came to know Martin Luther, who was a frequent guest in their home.

There were various attempts to find a husband for this young woman, who was twenty-four when she arrived in Wittenberg. From the Cranach portraits, she seems to have been reasonably

---

66. A brief account of her life can be found in Timothy F. Lull, *My Conversations with Martin Luther* (Minneapolis: Augsburg, 1999), ch. 6.

attractive, lively, and with significant education, including some knowledge of Latin. A student from Nuremberg, Jerome Baumgartner, was interested, but when he went home to discuss it, his family was opposed, and that was the end of that possibility. Baumgartner keeps showing up as a minor character on the edge of the Luther story, and Luther sent him greetings in later years from "his old flame." The Danish king Christian II admired her and gave her a ring, but on his visits to his uncle, Frederick the Wise, in Wittenberg, he was looking for political support rather than a wife.[67]

Katherine eventually expressed her unwillingness to marry anyone but Dr. Amsdorf or Dr. Luther. She said this to Amsdorf, who was working with her on the possibility of marrying an elderly doctor, so it may have been polite to include him. However, Amsdorf seems to have been a confirmed bachelor by this time, and Luther may well have bristled at her boldness.[68] It was said that he did not like her because she was too pushy. But other possibilities had slipped away, and Luther seemed to conclude that they should marry within a few weeks. The conversation with Amsdorf took place in March 1525, and by May 4 Luther was writing to John Ruhel, "If I can manage it, before I die I will still marry my Katie to spite the devil, should I hear that the peasants continue. I trust they will not steal my courage and joy."[69]

Marriage in the sixteenth century took place in two parts: first, a betrothal before a few witnesses, and then a church procession and wedding feast when convenient for out-of-town guests. Martin and Katherine were married on a Tuesday, June 13, in a small ceremony conducted by Bugenhagen and witnessed by Jonas, the Cranachs,

---

67. A splendid summary of the whole history of the relationship and eventual marriage is in Brecht, *Martin Luther*, 2:195–201.

68. Amsdorf's status as a bachelor helped make him a logical candidate to be the first bishop ordained as an evangelical in 1542.

69. "Letter to John Ruhel" (May 4, 1525), in LW 49: 111.

and John Apel, a local jurist who had already married a nun. Copulation took place at that time and had to be witnessed (in the newlywed Luthers' case, from an observation deck above the bed) so that it was clear the marriage was consummated. Jonas was one of those witnesses and found it a hard task, but in a few days was praying that God "grant the excellent honest man . . . all the happiness."[70]

The absence of Melanchthon is striking and has not been completely explained. What is clear today is that he did not approve of this wedding at all. We do not know what he may have said to Luther, but he poured his heart out in a letter to his friend Camerarius a few days later on June 16.

> Greetings. Since dissimilar reports concerning the marriage of Luther will reach you, I have thought it well to give you my opinion of him. On June 13, Luther unexpectedly and without informing in advance any of his friends of what he was doing, married Bora, but in the evening, after having invited to a supper none but Pomeranius and Lucas the painter, and Apel, he [Luther] observed the customary marriage rites. You might be amazed that at this unfortunate time, when good and excellent men everywhere are in distress, he not only does not sympathize with them, but, as it seems, rather waxes wanton and diminishes his reputation, just when Germany has especially need of his judgment and authority.
>
> These things have occurred, I think, somewhat in this way: The man is certainly pliable; and the nuns have used their arts against him most successfully; thus probably society with the nuns has softened or even inflamed this noble and high-spirited man. In this way he seems to have fallen into this untimely change of life. The rumor, however, that he had previously dishonored her is manifestly a lie. Now that the deed is done, we must not take it too hard, nor reproach him; for I think, indeed, that he was compelled by nature to marry. The mode of life, too, while, indeed, humble, is, nevertheless holy and more pleasing to God than celibacy.[71]

---

70. Jonas wept as he stood by the bridal bed. The whole report can be found in Oberman, *Luther*, 282.

Melanchthon is clearly talking himself and his friend into making the best of it. There had long been tensions between the two great figures of Wittenberg about tone and style, and Melanchthon concludes by mentioning one way in which marriage might actually improve his friend: "I have hopes that this state of life may sober him down, so that he will discard the low buffoonery which we have often censured." The conservative jurist Jerome Schurff was also displeased by the wedding and predicted—quite correctly—that Luther's opponents would write jubilantly and sarcastically about the marriage of a monk and a nun.[72]

In those same days, Luther, both exuberant and astonished at the step he had taken, was writing to friends urging them to attend the wedding feast on June 27. The letter to Spalatin of June 21 is a rather simple appeal for this old friend, now at a distance, to attend if at all possible and to use his influence at court to see if some venison could be provided. The town of Wittenberg had donated twenty gulden and a barrel of beer as a marriage gift.[73]

Writing on the same day to Amsdorf, who was living in Magdeburg, Luther confides a great deal more—giving various reasons why "the rumor is true that I was suddenly married to Katherine." He says that he did this to "silence evil mouths" and in the hope that he might still obey his father's wish for progeny. But there theological considerations too: "I also wanted to confirm what I have taught by practicing it, for I find so many timid people in spite of such great light from the gospel. God has willed and brought about this step. For I feel neither passionate love nor burning for my spouse, but I cherish her."[74] He hopes that Amsdorf can be present

---

71. Philip Melanchthon, "Letter to Joachim Camerarius" (June 16, 1525), in *Luther's Correspondence and Other Contemporary Letters*, ed. Preserved Smith and Charles M. Jacobs (Philadelphia: Lutheran Publication Society, 1918), 2:325.

72. Oberman, *Luther*, 282.

73. "Letter to George Spalatin" (June 21, 1525), in LW 49:115–16.

at the banquet the following Tuesday and is clearly excited that his parents will be there. Another guest was Leonard Koppe, who had driven the escape wagon for the twelve nuns.

Luther had not been receiving any regular salary, but soon it was arranged that he should have two hundred gulden a year—the same as Melanchthon—and in coming years this salary was raised to three hundred and then to four hundred gulden. Duke John also sent one hundred gulden as a wedding present that was quickly spent to equip their home.

Luther had a slowly dawning sense of being married and came in time to love his wife more deeply than he had at the beginning. In a letter in mid-August, he was still saying that he had taken this step to spite his enemies: "I have now testified to the gospel not only by word, but also by a deed: I have married a nun to spite the triumphant enemies who yell: 'Hurrah, hurrah!' I have done this so that it does not seem that I am yielding. Even though I am old and foolish, I shall, if I can, still do other things which will pain them, and thus confess the Word."[75] But in the Table Talk in later years, he reflected in a different way on the changes that had come in his first year of marriage:

> Man has strange thoughts the first year of marriage. When sitting at the table he thinks, "Before I was alone; now there are two." Or in bed, when he wakes up, he sees a pair of pigtails lying beside him which he hadn't seen there before. On the other hand, wives bring to their husbands, no matter how busy they may be, a multitude of trivial matters. So my Katy used to sit next to me at first while I was studying hard and would spin and ask, "Doctor, is the grandmaster the margrave's brother?"[76]

---

74. "Letter to Nicholas von Amsdorf" (June 21, 1525), in LW 49:117.

75. "Letter to John Briessmann" (August 15, 1525), in LW 49:123.

76. "Table Talk for June, 1532," in LW 54:191. Luther says at another place that some of his worst bouts of anxiety or temptation came "when I was in bed at my Katy's side." LW 54:90.

The former nun and long-term monk both had much adjusting to do.

An astonishing development took place only a few days after the wedding feast. The Carlstadt family arrived in Wittenberg. They were desperate for a place to stay and without any prospects, so Martin and Katie took them into their new home for eight weeks. There was plenty of room, of course, but it was stunning that one who had fallen out so deeply with Luther would turn to him for shelter and help.

Luther did much more than take them in. He wrote to the elector to arrange a place for Carlstadt to live. This took some negotiation because there was general fear that Carlstadt was and would always be a troublemaker. But eventually they were permitted to move to Seegrehna, where the former professor took up farming. In March 1526, a delegation from Wittenberg journeyed there for the baptism of Andreas Carlstadt the Younger, whose baptism had been overlooked in the turmoil of recent years. Jonas, Melanchthon, and Katherine Luther were the sponsors, and Luther himself participated in the ceremony.

Unfolding Consequences

The second half of the year had fewer great events, but the consequences of all that had happened slowly unfolded. In midsummer, Spalatin left the new elector's service and on August 6 became chief pastor in Altenburg—an important town that was the location of one of the major castles of the ruling family. Spalatin continued to be an important advisor to John and later to John Frederick, and often accompanied them to conferences, such as the Diet of Augsburg in 1530, to offer both theological and political advice.

His friendship with Luther remained strong, but they had less contact than when Spalatin was the go-between for Luther and Frederick the Wise. Luther deeply regretted being unable to attend Spalatin's wedding in November. Luther seemed to fear for his own safety, perhaps because of fresh tension with Duke George or even with Elector John's courtier. In any case, he said he was "restrained by the tears of my Katie" and stayed home to finish his reply to Erasmus.[77]

The success of the Catholic princes in the Peasants' War had emboldened them to form a Catholic League in mid-August consisting of Albrecht of Mainz, the margrave of Brandenburg, and Duke George of Saxony. Understandably, Elector John as a new ruler was concerned about these powerful princes who surrounded his territory, and he also sought allies. Cooperation with Philip of Hesse to the west was already established, and now there was the possibility of a new alliance with the territory of Brandenburg-Ansbach-Kulmbach to the south. Margrave Casimir at this point was embracing the Reformation in his territory, and the documents that had been developed were submitted to Luther and his colleagues. Luther, Jonas, Bugenhagen, and Melanchthon replied that they strongly approved of the practical positions these documents outlined.

But Luther had other occasions to negotiate with Elector John in the second half of 1525. Luther benefited from his long friendship with Spalatin, who helped make his case and provided direct access to the prince. In the fall, there was especially deep concern about the finances of the university. Luther had written earlier and apparently irritated the duke. Now he wrote several letters of appeal that turned out to be quite successful. Melanchthon's salary was doubled.

---

77. "Letter to George Spalatin" (November 11, 1525), in Tappert, *Luther's Letters of Spiritual Counsel*, 322–23.

Bugenhagen and several others received needed raises. There were funds for improvement in the teaching of rhetoric and, most importantly, a transfer of the revenues from the All Saints' Foundation to the government, from which regular payments were sent to the university. Spalatin helped with all these arrangements, despite his move to Altenburg. Luther and Duke John also began discussing the need for a visitation to all the parishes in Electoral Saxony to survey conditions and create new financial arrangements for pastoral salaries and for the care of elderly clergy.[78]

Luther's own academic and pastoral work centered on the Old Testament in these months. He had been lecturing on the Minor Prophets since March 24 but paused after the completion of Micah in early April to involve himself with the Peasants' War and to get married. He began again in mid-summer to lecture on Nahum. During the course of the year he completed Habakkuk, Zephaniah, and Haggai, and he was completing Zechariah by the end of the year.[79]

He was also in the middle of a long series of seventy-seven weekday sermons on Exodus that stretched from October 1524 to February 1527. In August, he preached the very important "How Christians Should Regard Moses," which contains some of the richest material on Luther's developed view of the authority of the Old Testament for Christians.[80] The distinction between law and gospel means that the law of Moses cannot be binding in detail for Christians. This was the mistake of the "fanatics," as he called both Carlstadt and Müntzer. It led them astray not only in their opposition to images but also in their developing a form of Christianity in which law took the place of Christian freedom.

---

78. Brecht, *Martin Luther*, 2:239–42. Luther's letters include "Letter to Elector John" (October 31, 1525) and "Letter to Elector John" (November 30, 1525), in LW 49:130–39.
79. See the helpful summary of dates in "Introduction to Volume 18," in LW 18:xi.
80. "How Christians Should Regard Moses" (1525), in LW 35:155–74, MLBTW3, 107–15.

Luther insists that he wants "to keep Moses and not sweep him under the rug." There are three things in Moses of abiding value. The first is the example of how he ruled and governed Israel. Many things from this law could be adopted today, and we are "free to follow him in ruling as he ruled."[81] Second, Moses has many "promises and pledges of God about Christ." Luther continues to read the Old Testament christologically, so he finds not only law (as demand) but also gospel (as promise).[82] Third, Moses' books contain fine examples relevant still to Christians: "In the third place we read Moses for the beautiful examples of faith, of love, and of the cross, as shown in the fathers, Adam, Abel, Noah, Abraham, Isaac, Jacob, Moses and all the rest. From them we should learn to trust in God and love him. In turn there are also examples of the godless, how God does not pardon the unfaith of the unbelieving; how he can punish Cain, Ishmael, Esau, the whole world in the flood, Sodom and Gomorrah, etc."[83] Luther would develop this third use of Moses especially powerfully in his *Lectures on Genesis* (1535–1545).

Luther was still busy with preaching, worshipping, and defending his views of the sacraments in the second half of 1525. In September, he finally published the Lenten section of his postil, following the Advent and Christmas sections that had been completed at the Wartburg in 1521. The lessons for this season, especially those for Holy Week, gave Luther a great opportunity to show how preachers should treat the Lord's Supper and stress the promise of Christ's presence.

On October 29, Wittenberg experienced the first full celebration of Luther's German Mass, and it was definitively introduced on Christmas Day. It had taken four years since Carlstadt's abrupt

81. LW 35:166, MLBTW3, 110.
82. LW 35:168–69, MLBTW3, 111.
83. LW 35:173, MLBTW3, 114.

changes at Christmas 1521 for Luther to work out all the details of the revised rite—both in words and in music. In his preface, he tries to explain the balance of freedom and order that he has been seeking:

> In the first place, I would kindly and for God's sake request all those who see this order or service or desire to follow it: Do not make it a rigid law to bind or entangle anyone's conscience, but use it in Christian liberty as long, when, where, and how you find it to be practical and useful. For this is being published not as though we meant to lord it over anyone else, or to legislate for him, but because of the widespread demand for German masses and services and the general dissatisfaction of offense that has been caused by the great variety of new masses, for everyone makes his own order of service. Some have the best intentions, but others have no more than an itch to produce something novel so they might shine before men as leading lights, rather than being ordinary teachers.[84]

The German Mass did not mean, for Luther, abandoning services that used a great deal of Latin. He still preferred those for people who could understand the language, and he says that he wishes they could have masses "on successive Sundays in all four languages: German, Latin, Greek and Hebrew." He feared the loss that would come if people knew only their local language (which he says was happening in Bohemia) and could not communicate with others.[85] He also sensed that there would be little progress in people's understanding of worship until a good catechism is produced—a foreshadowing of one important thrust of Luther's work over the next four years.[86]

On ritual matters, Luther was open to abandoning some traditional aspects such as vestments and candles, although there need not be uniformity in those matters. But he did think that altars should be moved and that the priest should stand facing the people, "as Christ doubtlessly did at the Last Supper."[87] He very much wanted to retain

84. "The German Mass and Order of Service" (1526), in LW 53:61.
85. LW 53:63.
86. LW 53:64ff.

the sung Mass, but hoped that the whole congregation could sing the various sections, such as the Kyrie. In many cases, new German hymns could be used, such as "Isaiah 'twas the Prophet," which could serve as a form of the Sanctus. The elevation should not be abolished, but people should be taught that Christ is rightly apprehended "only by faith, for we cannot see how Christ gives his body and blood for us."[88]

Luther had begun the year with a passionate defense of the real presence of Christ in the Supper, and he was ending it with a liturgy that hoped to protect the mystery and yet invite people to faith. At the very end of the year, he was discussing these matters with Caspar von Schwenckfeld, who was visiting Wittenberg at that time and would eventually become Luther's final opponent on the understanding of the Supper.[89] He could feel a genuine sense of being back to work after the troubles of the spring and summer. The greatest proof was that, by the end of 1525, Luther was finally able to publish his massive response to Erasmus's attack on Luther in *The Freedom of the Will*, which Erasmus had published in mid-1524.

Battle with Erasmus

The feud between Luther and Erasmus had been building since the beginning of Luther's public career eight years earlier. Erasmus initially was receptive, even supportive, of Luther. He hinted in a 1518 preface that Luther was right to prefer doing good works to paying for indulgences. And when the faculty of theology at Louvain published their sharp condemnation of Luther in 1520, Erasmus, a member of that faculty, refused to sign it. But his misgivings about Luther were growing. As Erasmus read more of Luther, he came

87. LW 53:69.
88. LW 53:82.
89. See LW 49:149n3.

to think that, at the heart of things, Luther was a Christian, but the form of Christianity he was advocating had dangerous moral implications.[90] He was angry when he learned his publisher had published editions of Luther's Latin writings. He disliked Luther's focus on hairsplitting accuracies in doctrine. For him, Christianity was about loving one's neighbor, devoting oneself to learning, and using that learning to better the world. He resented academic theologians like Luther "not because they taught false doctrines but because they taught too many doctrines."[91]

Image 24: Erasmus, the greatest scholar in Europe, was thought to be sympathetic to the Reformation, but never joined the movement.

90. An essay that led up to *The Freedom of the Will* was a dialogue between the good "Aulus" and the barbarous "Barbatus," which were code names for Erasmus and Luther, respectively. Aulus is surprised that, on nearly all matters, Barbatus is not just orthodox but downright insightful.
91. James Kittelson, *Luther the Reformer* (Minneapolis: Augsburg, 1986), 204.

The first step in true religion, as Erasmus thought of it, is to "reject evil."[92] When he finally attacked Luther in print, he reasoned that because humans seem to choose all the time from among better and worse moral options, and even between good and evil, then of course they must have free will. The Bible was less than clear on this matter, since passages supporting and opposing freedom could be found. For Erasmus, this meant that a theologian must not make "assertions" and that the matter probably could not be resolved. But since better religion (that is, more love toward neighbor) would result from teaching that humans had free will and must choose the good, then Erasmus was going with free will. When he read Luther's Heidelberg Disputation thesis that "Free will, after the fall, even when doing what it is able to do, commits a mortal sin," he shuddered to think of the practical effects of not exhorting people to avoid sin.[93]

Luther's response is called "On Bound Choice" and is one of his fiercest rejoinders.[94] If religion required humans to reject evil and then ask God for mercy, Luther thought we were doomed. Why would you require a sick person to stop being sick for long enough to go to the doctor's office for healing? The whole point of the gospel was that *God* took the initiative. God sought human sinners out and loved them. In characterizing this debate, which was more like two people talking past each other than a real debate, Roland Bainton wrote, "Erasmus the moralist said 'Let God be Good.' And Luther the theologian said, 'Let God be God.'"[95]

92. "De Immensa Dei Misericordia," in *Collected Works of Erasmus*, vol. 70: *Pastoralia and Spiritualia* (Toronto: University of Toronto Press, 1998), 136.
93. LW 31:40, MLBTW3, 15.
94. LW 33:5–295 (the introduction, part 6, and conclusion can be found in MLBTW3, 138–70). Calling it "The Bondage of the Will" is an unfortunate translation that misses the fact that it is not a faculty of human willing that is bound. Rather, Luther is emphasizing that the choices that the will makes are limited.
95. Roland Bainton, *Erasmus of Christendom* (New York: Scribners, 1969), 190.

Erasmus gave the example of a toddler learning to walk. If a father holds a child's hand while the child struggles to stay on his feet, of course the most important role is played by the father. Yet the child is doing *something*, is he not? In a similar way, God may play a larger role in salvation than the human does. But the human does something, and does it "freely." Erasmus writes, "By free choice we mean a power of the human will by which a man can apply himself to the things which lead to eternal salvation or turn away from them."[96] To Luther, this sounded more or less like what Pelagius had taught in the early church, and Augustine had labored mightily to refute this heresy. It might be nice to believe what Erasmus was saying; it would be convenient to have a God who saw our fumbling steps and counted them as worth much more than they actually were. But was this not another version of the old "Do your best, and God will do the rest" theology of Biel? Was not the thrust of the gospel the notion that God came to sinners, not vice versa? In making this point, Luther went to rhetorical extremes. Earlier, Luther had spoken of God hidden "in" revelation, such that we could be surprised by discerning God's action in a situation we had not predicted. But against Erasmus, Luther wrote that God might also be hidden "behind" or "outside" of revelation, which reserved a measure of mystery and sovereignty for God but also terrified the soul.

Such statements about the hidden or, better, *hiding* God were designed partly to provoke Erasmus and partly to highlight the majesty of God. If God truly were free to be God in any way imaginable, it was even more amazing to think that God chose sinners, lowly Israel, a humiliated Jesus, the corrupt church, and many other sites of revelation to show the eyes of faith how God promised to be. Luther the pastor was concerned to assuage consciences

96. Erasmus, "On Free Choice," in *Luther and Erasmus*, ed. Gordon Rupp and Philip Watson (Philadelphia: Westminster, 1969), 47.

tormented about the promises of God. It was wrong of Erasmus, from the comfortable position of detached observer, to be unwilling to make any "assertions" on a difficult-to-interpret set of biblical passages. With words sure to hurt Erasmus enormously, he wrote, "What more ungodly assertion could anyone make than that he wished for the liberty of asserting *nothing* in such cases?"[97]

Luther did not think, as many suppose he did, that humans were robots preprogrammed in every way by God or the devil. Humans have free will and use it all the time in deciding what to wear, whom to marry, and even how to behave in moral situations. The difference between Erasmus and Luther was that Luther thought that none of this matters for the question of salvation. Erasmus had confused the kind of freedom that humans have, which has been profoundly limited by sin, with the kind that God has, which is not. A human choosing to join herself to God without first God bestowing on her the gift of faith would be like a teenager choosing to drive a car without first being given the keys.

It was repugnant to common sense to say that God could do whatever God wanted to do, including be triune, save sinners, harden Pharaoh's heart, be present in communion, and so on. It was not rational, and Erasmus was an eminently reasonable man. Luther admitted, "This repugnant thought has caused many distinguished people of all times to go to pieces. And who would not find it repugnant? More than once it hurled me down to the deepest abyss of despair and made me wish I had never been born—until I learned how salutary this despair is, and how close to grace."[98] What a thought—that despair is close to grace: the one who has nearly drowned knows better what it is to be saved. And, anyway, Luther

---

97. LW 33:22.
98. This translation, much better than the one from LW 33:190, is from Steven D. Paulson, *Lutheran Theology* (London: T&T Clark, 2011), 83.

and Erasmus both were toying with an abyss: Erasmus's was the abyss of uncertainty; Luther's the abyss of powerlessness. The gospel spoke better to the second than to the first, Luther bellowed.

9

The Birth of Lutheranism

1526–1531

That the Luther story continues very far past 1522 at all depends on facts and events that are as much political as they are theological. Luther was able to continue work as a theologian and professor of Bible almost entirely because he had the protection of a powerful house in Electoral Saxony and its skillful and accurately named leader Frederick the Wise. Therefore, when Frederick died in 1525, Luther had reason to be nervous.

Preoccupation with Politics: An Overview of the Period

Luther's punching match with Erasmus could be conducted from the privacy of their respective studies. Meanwhile, very public tempers raged, involving not the interpretation of Bible passages but rather threats of violence among princes and kings. The Battle of Pavia in February 1525 saw Charles V destroy the French king Francis I. The French had controlled Lombardy, in northern Italy, since 1521.

Charles's decisive victory, despite being outgunned, made him appear even stronger to the evangelical princes in Germany.

Pressure mounted for the Edict of Worms to be enforced; though Luther's teaching was officially condemned by that document, Charles had thus far not succeeded in having Luther punished or killed. Elsewhere, the edict had provided a basis for executions, as in the case of Caspar Tauber of Vienna and a bookseller in Buda. Both were burned at the stake in 1524.

Friends of the reformers seemed few and far between. Relations with Henry VIII of England, already bad, were made worse in these years. Luther had gotten false information from Christian II of Denmark that Henry was leaning toward the evangelical side, so Luther sent Henry a fawning letter apologizing for his earlier counterattack. The response came across as terribly naive and silly, and Henry gladly published Luther's private letter along with some ridicule of it. Henry also took this opportunity to charge Luther with starting the Peasants' War, destroying ethics by preaching justification by faith, and violating his monastic vows by marrying. Luther tried to respond again, but the essay was a failure.[1] Henry would be of no help to Luther's cause.

The history of the Holy Roman Empire's various princes is complicated but essential to understand Luther's story.[2] In 1524 at Regensburg, in southern Germany, Catholic princes united in an alliance to resist the Reformation. The Dessau League, led by Luther's nemesis Duke George of Saxony and Duke Joachim of Brandenburg, followed suit. Evangelical princes wanted to respond in kind. Albrecht of Magdeburg asked Luther for his counsel, and Luther said

---

1. WA 23:17–37. See Martin Brecht, *Martin Luther*, vol. 2: *Shaping and Defining the Reformation, 1521–1532*, trans. James L. Schaaf (Minneapolis: Fortress Press, 1990), 345–49, for the full story.
2. Of the very many treatments of this vital history, by far the best is the magnificent account in Thomas A. Brady, *German Histories in the Age of Reformations* (Cambridge: Cambridge University Press, 2009).

that an alliance against the government (that is, against Charles V) was rebellion and could not be permitted. God was to be trusted, not one's own army. But general defensive alliances were of course fine. Such arrangements were made by the evangelicals. Electoral Saxony joined together in a variety of ways in these years with Hesse, leading to the formation of the Torgau League in 1526. This later evolved into the Schmalkadic League, which incorporated more princes and a much larger army.

That same year, a potential resolution had seemed possible, as an imperial diet was called. At the last moment, Charles V became unable to attend, but the meeting was held anyway, at Speyer, near Heidelberg. Instructed to negotiate for peace, the emperor's brother Ferdinand I temporarily suspended the enforcement of the Edict of Worms. He reasoned that a council of the church, rather than the civil authorities, should decide on the religious question and that princes should act "in such a way as they would answer to God and Emperor." The greatest historian of these years calls this statement "the era's most pregnant act of political weaseling."[3] This bought the evangelicals some badly needed time to get organized. Having powerful Philip of Hesse on the side of Electoral Saxony buoyed many spirits in Wittenberg. Philip had made his position on Roman Catholic laws and practices known at the diet by barbecuing beefsteaks on the first Friday of the assembly.

Three years later, the diet convened again at Speyer, but this time it was more decisive. Charles V, again not in attendance, had sent a letter instructing his brother to seek conciliation. The instructions did not arrive in time, however, and Ferdinand declared that Roman Catholicism must be practiced in all the emperor's lands. Disobedience would be punished with execution. The evangelical

---

3. Brady, *German Histories*, 215.

princes in attendance, about fourteen in number, officially registered their protest, and the movement got itself a new name. Officially, the protest stated that the princes would follow no religious practice that "violated the word of God or their own consciences." Around this time, flags and shields in the princes' armies more frequently bore the letters VDMA, for the motto *verbum domini manet in aeternum*: "the Word of the Lord remains forever."

We have left out an important part of this story, however, for the dominant fear at Speyer was less the Reformation than the very real threat of Ottoman invasion. The Turks (as their enemies called them) took once-Christian Constantinople in 1453 and gradually swept north and west up the Danube. Their great leader Suleiman the Magnificent captured Belgrade in 1520, Rhodes in 1521, and much of Hungary by 1526. Europe was terrified. In October 1529 at the gates of Vienna, that grand symbol of old Catholic culture, finally Suleiman was turned back. Yet no one knew how long this temporary victory would last, when the Turks would attack again, or how Europe—fragmented, squabbling, preoccupied Europe—would fare in the next round. For Charles, these two threats were nearly of a kind; he was a committed Roman Catholic, yes, but he was also utterly committed to his Hapsburg family's imperial dreams. Fragmentation for religious reasons was as bad for a would-be emperor as attack from foreign armies.[4]

4. Heiko Oberman, *Luther: Man between God and the Devil*, trans. Eileen Walliser-Schwarzbart (New Haven: Yale University Press, 1989), 13–49, devotes an entire chapter to the political context here in seeing the Reformation as "A German Event."

Image 25: Many times during the Reformation
Charles V was unable to turn his attention to
Germany because he feared the Ottoman Sultan
Suleiman's armies to the east.

Luther's involvement with the Turkish question had a long
backstory. In his Ninety-Five Theses, Luther had actually suggested
that resisting the Turk was resisting God, who was using the menace
of the Turk to show divine judgment against a corrupt, pretend
church.[5] This was typical overstatement, of course, but Luther had
been held responsible by his opponents for Turkish victories. When
Luther did address the issue more systematically, he did so not to
bellow back at his critics but with pastoral concern for those with
troubled consciences who wanted to know his considered opinion.

His response appeared in early 1529 in a book called *On War against
the Turk*.[6] He finds the idea of a "holy war" or crusade waged under

5. LW 31:91–92.

the sponsorship of the church to be utterly wrong. Never should the church usurp the temporal authority in such a way. His main point is to show how war can be fought with a clear conscience. Only two men may fight the Turk: the emperor, who by virtue of his office is compelled to defend his subjects who have been attacked, and the Christian. The Christian should examine his conscience, repent, and live according to the gospel. If he does this, God will have no need to use the Turk as an instrument of judgment, and then the Turk could not win the war.[7] Such a view seems odd to the modern mind until one considers how seriously Luther took God as the author of all history. His position is rather like the prophet Isaiah's view of Israel's history. Luther was, after all, lecturing in Wittenberg on the prophets.

The imperial politics of the period came to a head in 1530. Dissatisfied with the results of Speyer, Charles V summoned the princes who had protested to come to Augsburg in April. It was not clear whether they would be given a chance to be heard. Charles was fresh from more victories and was still keeping Pope Clement VII under house arrest. (Sensing the irony of this, Luther quipped, "Christ reigns in such a way that the Emperor who persecutes Luther for the Pope is forced to destroy the Pope for Luther.")[8] Now he was on his way back to Germany to settle "the Luther matter." He had a right to be confident—he was nearly at the height of his powers. And Charles was always confident. You would expect as much from a man who commissioned over two hundred portraits of himself during his lifetime.

We will pick up the story of this period from Luther's perspective later in the chapter, but for now let this much be said. The

6. LW 46:157–205.
7. LW 32:170–71.
8. LW 49:169.

evangelicals were allowed to present their views. Melanchthon drew up a confession of faith—the Augsburg Confession, often called by its Latin name *Augustana*—which was publicly read on June 25, 1530. It was immediately denounced by the emperor's officials, who issued a *Confutation*. It seemed that peaceful resolution was not possible. The evangelicals went home with more worries of war than ever. Before the year was over they had formed a group, called the Schmalkaldic League, after the city where a pact of mutual defense was made.

War did come, but not for fifteen years. Previously, Luther kept saying he would not accept protection if that meant armed resistance. He wrote to Elector John, "If it gets to the point that our overlord, that is, the emperor, wants to attack us, [then] each one has to defend his own faith for himself, and has to believe or not believe in the face of his own risk."[9] In short, Luther would rather die than kill, and he prayed that the princes of the German-speaking lands would agree.

But after Augsburg, Luther was much more concerned, and he issued a "Warning to the Dear German People."[10] Here, for the first time, Luther approved of armed resistance against the emperor. He has therefore been accused of flip-flopping on this issue. That criticism misses a crucial point, however. He wrote, "If war breaks out—which God forbid—I will not reprove those who defend themselves against the murderous and bloodthirsty papists, nor let anyone else rebuke them as being seditious, but I will accept their action."[11] Armed resistance against the emperor at this point was not rebellion because the evangelicals had consistently sought peace, the emperor was the aggressor, and the evangelical position had not and could not be condemned without a general council. Obedience to God normally meant obedience to temporal authority. But if

9. LW 49:250.
10. LW 47:5–57.
11. LW 47:19.

obedience to God meant armed resistance—even against an emperor—Luther consistently permitted it, citing Acts 5:29.[12]

Martin Luther, Family Man

To deal constantly with knotty political issues will wear on anyone, even someone skilled at politics, the "art of the possible," which Luther was not. But the stresses of these years were much abated by Luther's supportive and challenging home life. As there were ever more problems in Luther's public life, there were increasingly many people in the Luther home.

Luther had to withstand harsh criticisms for marrying when he did, and not just from Melanchthon. It was humiliating to some of his friends, such as Jerome Schurff, who thought that Luther's opponents would now appear right to dismiss the Reformation simply as a frustrated monk's desire to marry. Erasmus—himself born out of wedlock to a priest—and others had cheerily spread the rumor that Luther had impregnated Katie before their betrothal. Luther's enemy Cochlaeus indignantly claimed that Luther had, after all, been conceived when the devil raped his mother in an outhouse.[13] Such attacks did not much subside during the early years of Luther's marriage, yet he and Katie seem to have ignored them with heads held high.

Luther wrote to his friend Gabriel Zwilling, then pastor in nearby Torgau, in January 1526 because he had a special order. As a bachelor, he had been willing to sleep on the ground, as he had in

---

12. On this and related political matters, see the useful essay by David M. Whitford, "Luther's Political Encounters" in *The Cambridge Companion to Martin Luther*, ed. Donald McKim (Cambridge: Cambridge University Press, 2003), 179–91.

13. Cochlaeus's one-sided "biography" of Luther, which argues that the Reformation was caused by the Augustinians' jealousy of the Domincans (such as Tetzel) is paired with Melanchthon's equally one-sided work in praise of Luther in Ralph Keen et al., eds., *Luther's Lives: Two Contemporary Accounts of Martin Luther* (New York: Palgrave, 2002).

the monastery. But now that he was married, he needed a mattress. Zwilling had one made and sent to Luther. The mattress evidently was suitable; Katherine was soon expecting a baby.

A prevalent superstition ran through Saxony in those days that the product of an unholy union would be a two-headed monster. When their first child was born to Katherine, and it was a one-headed, healthy baby boy, Luther expressed his deep relief.[14] The proud father fawned in other ways, as well. When the boy, christened Hans after Johannes Bugenhagen, first successfully filled his diaper, Luther was beside himself with joy. He lightheartedly described the boy as "vorax ac bibax"—a voracious glutton and drinker.[15]

It is almost always a mistake to separate Luther the man from Luther the theologian, for in such family scenes we glimpse Luther's insight into vocation, or calling, and his understanding of the doctrine of creation more generally. When discussing the Apostles' Creed and what it meant to call God "creator," Luther wrote in his catechism two years later, "I believe that God has created me together with all that exists. God has given me and still preserves my body and soul: eyes, ears and all limbs and senses; reason and all mental faculties."[16] Gone was any medieval ideal of fleeing the body to free the soul. Within God-intended limits, flesh was good, sex to be enjoyed, family life to be honored, food to be relished, and the physical stuff of life to be appreciated as the gift from God that it was.

The word *vocation* had earlier been reserved exclusively for ordained clergy and cloistered monastics. They were the ones called by God to live a holy life, for they engaged in continual prayer and frequent self-abasement. In extreme forms of this theology, ordinary believers relied on the merits of those with vocations for their own

14. For more on this, see Brecht, *Martin Luther*, 2:203–4 and Oberman, *Luther*, 278.
15. WABR 4:210.
16. *Small Catechism*, in Robert Kolb and Timothy J. Wengert, eds., *The Book of Concord* (Minneapolis: Fortress Press, 2000), 354.

reward in heaven. Luther found this unbiblical, and his rhetoric shocked some but delighted most. He thought that a mother nursing the child or a father changing a diaper, a baker at his oven or a carpenter in his shop was doing something as God-pleasing as a monk.[17] "God, with all his angels and creatures, is smiling—not because that father is washing diapers, but because he is doing so in Christian faith."[18]

There were soon even more diapers in the Luther household. Daughter Elizabeth was born in December 1527, but she died during an outbreak of the plague in August 1528. Of her death Luther wrote, "So much has grief for her overcome me. Never before would I have believed that a father's heart could have such tender feelings for his child."[19] The next year a third child, Magdalena, was born, followed by sons Martin and Paul in 1531 and 1533 and daughter Margaret in 1534. Katharine suffered a miscarriage in 1539. As we shall see, when Magdalena—the apple of Luther's eye—died of illness at the tender age of thirteen, Luther was inconsolable. It was perhaps his darkest personal hour. The source of his joy in these years was thus also the site of great grief.

Not long after the Luthers' marriage, the elector generously offered the couple the former Augustinian cloister to have as their personal house, thereby setting a very high standard for wedding presents. The number of persons living in the Luther home varied but was usually at least twenty. In addition to the six children the Luthers themselves had borne, there were also Katie's aunt Lena, the six children of Luther's dead sister, and some children of another sister.

17. For example, Luther thought, "If you are a manual laborer, you find that the Bible has been put into your workshop, into your hand, into your heart. It teaches and preaches how you should treat your neighbor. . . . Indeed, there is no shortage of preaching. You have as many preachers as you have transactions, goods, tools, and other equipment in your house and home." LW 21:237.
18. "The Estate of Marriage" (1522), in LW 45:40.
19. LW 49:203.

Students frequently boarded at the Luther home (then a widespread practice) and sometimes paid rent. Imagining the workload of laundry, cooking, cleaning, and bookkeeping such an arrangement would require is enough to make anyone tired, which Katie often was.

Enormous credit must be given to Katherine Luther for the small delights and grand successes of domestic life. No aspect of material life seemed beyond her reach, and she capably participated in the mental life of the university town as well. Gardening, trading, raising pigs, and brewing beer were among her many responsibilities. Her beer was highly regarded, and not just by her husband. Displeased with the swill in Dessau, he once wrote his wife, "I said to myself what good wine and beer I have at home, and also what a pretty lady (or should I say lord). You would do well to ship the whole wine cellar and a bottle of your beer to me here, as soon as you are able."[20] Luther's most common verb for describing his feelings for his wife was "esteem." His letters to her from his many times on the road are peppered with playful nicknames. Luther called her "the Empress," "Dr. Luther," "Lord Katie," and even "Queen of the Pig Market" in honor of her able swineherding. Luther had not been very attentive to domestic needs before marriage, once neglecting to change the straw in the bed for so long that it rotted from sweat. Katie gradually took over the management of the house and got things in splendid shape.

She did so despite the fact that income was a very real problem for the Luther family. Luther himself had a long-standing commitment not to charge tuition for his lectures nor to benefit financially from his publications. Eventually he was given a salary, first of one hundred gulden per year, then two hundred, from the elector's chest. But he was never particularly good with money. He happily posted collateral

20. LW 50:81.

for others who wanted a loan. He was not so happy when a loan default meant he had to pawn three nice drinking cups he had received as a gift. In 1527, faced with the fact that preaching and teaching might not pay the bills, the clumsy-handed Luther went so far as to order a lathe.[21] He wrote tongue-in-cheek to his friend Link to complain that the lathe was faulty; it did not turn itself while Luther's famulus (part-time house servant) Wolfgang Seberger snored away the day while sitting in front of it.[22]

He mended his own pants rather than pay a tailor, and he fancied himself an able gardener. The family benefited from frequent benefactions, such as free paint, wine from the castle cellar, cuts of cloth, and sometimes fish, tallow for candles, and firewood. Observers at Leipzig five years earlier had described Luther as "gaunt," whose "bones could be counted below the skin." But increasingly frequent portraits undertaken by the Cranachs show a healthier, filled-out man of middle age. Such creature comforts were not distractions to be shunned, as Luther the monk had been taught. Rather, Luther's earthy theology of creation saw healthy, though not indulgent, physical life to be both blessing and command. "Even if Satan and his members rage, I shall laugh at them and in the meantime I will turn my attention to the gardens, that is, to the blessings of the Creator, and enjoy them to his praise."[23]

His friend Agricola once mentioned in passing to Luther that he liked a pewter bowl that he had seen in a shop. Luther later received such a bowl from Nicholas Hausmann, and Luther wanted to forward it to Agricola. But Katie intervened and hid the bowl from Luther, conspiring with Bugenhagen and Jonas to keep its location hidden. Luther figured he would get the upper hand eventually, writing in

21. LW 49:169.
22. WABR 4:203.
23. LW 49:158; see also WA 49:434.

a postscript to Agricola, "Now look, just as I wanted to give the letter to the carrier and as I searched for the little dish, my Katie, this stealthy woman, has hidden it. I would have searched for it, but I am prevented from doing this. Just wait until the dish is freed by Katie's confinement to childbed; then I will steal it and carry it off."[24] Such is life among loving friends. Katie did something similar when Albrecht of Mainz, Luther's great opponent on the matter of indulgences, sent the Luthers twenty gulden as a wedding present in 1526. Martin refused to accept the gift, but Katie secretly put the money to good use.

Luther had less contact in these years with his friend Spalatin, who had married and taken a position in a church in Altenburg. This disappointed Luther, for he had come to rely on the political insights of this influential man. Other friends sustained him, however. Wenceslas Link and Lazarus Spengler, both of whom lived in Nuremberg, sent Luther seeds and tools for his garden and those of his friends. In his letters, Luther thanks them but sadly reports that the seeds seemed to be growing well in everyone's garden except his own.[25]

Relations with his colleague Agricola soon became strained for two theological reasons, both having to do with the concept of obligation. First, Agricola opposed the imposition of church orders in the Saxon lands. When Luther had returned to Wittenberg from the Wartburg Castle and preached his Invocavit sermons, had he not insisted on the freedom of conscience? Had he not brought about reform simply by setting an example and preaching the gospel? Agricola therefore thought that using the government to enforce evangelical practices in the region was coercive. A second sore spot was the relation of law and faith. Agricola had come to think that the Wittenbergers had

24. LW 49:151.
25. LW 49:167.

reverted too far back toward the Catholic position on the binding nature of the law. He taught that faith did not necessarily lead to good works and that simple folk should not be encouraged to do them. Luther's break with Agricola would come later; for the time being Luther urged his friend to keep his views private until greater clarity could be achieved. Agricola was a favorite court preacher of the electors and would be a delegate to the important Diet of Augsburg. In 1537, he returned to Wittenberg as a professor, and in the next chapter we shall pick up the ending of this sad story.

It was not only his children and friends who were on the family man's mind in these years. While in Coburg Castle in 1530, Luther had a dream in which he lost an extremely large tooth. Popular superstition connected such a vision with the imminent death of a loved one.[26] Luther's father died two days later, and when word of his death reached Luther, he was inconsolable. He had written his father a marvelous letter earlier in the year in which he invited his parents to live out their days in Wittenberg. It was tenderhearted, pastoral, and theologically rich; "trust the promise of God" sounds the loudest note in the letter. It also does much to discredit the caricature of Luther as a moping son with unresolved "father issues" who had problems with authority. After Hans died, Luther took his Psalter and went to be alone. He reportedly cried so intensely he could not function the following day.[27]

A year later, his mother died. To her, too, Luther had written a heartfelt letter.[28] Using John 16 and 1 Corinthians 15 as a starting point, Luther emphasizes the finality and certainty of Christ's victory over death, a victory promised to the faithful again and again in word and sacrament. He encourages his mother to affirm her faith in the

26. For more on this, see Oberman, *Luther*, 310–11.
27. His own reaction is tenderly recounted in LW 49:318–19.
28. LW 50:17–21.

face of the coming darkness and adds his prayers that she will have the strength to do so.

In seeing him cope with these periods of loss, we glimpse Luther's theology in full. The purpose of pastoral care is not to minimize pain, nor should one gloss over it or explain it away. Its reality is never to be denied. Luther would have no time for those who coo, "Oh, it's really not so bad." Instead, the purpose of the pastor is to contextualize the pain, to remind those who feel loss of the promises of God and to stand with the griever in solidarity and compassion. Letters to the Jonas family when their baby son died, and to the Link family upon the death of their young daughter, show his approach time and again. To comfort means to strengthen; Luther saw this as his task as preacher, theologian, pastor, and friend—all of which are, in Luther's mind, somewhat synonymous. He thus confirmed later what he had written in 1520: "No believer ever lives alone or dies alone, but is defended and carried by the communion of saints."[29]

Practical Leadership

In addition to being a spiritual counselor, Luther was frequently called in these years to offer practical leadership. He gave input regarding the daily considerations of church life and worship, social issues, and the continued implementation of the Reformation.

One great achievement was the completion and distribution of the German Mass. Luther had been working on this for several years. His *Formula Missae*, which was a reworking of traditional Catholic worship, removing what he considered medieval accretions, had been used since 1523. There he emphasized a balance of word and sacrament: preaching the gospel was the twin center along with receiving Holy Communion—itself understood not as the work of a

29. WABR 2:152.

priest but as the gift of a promising God. Eucharistic prayers evoking sacrificial language were shortened or removed. It was in Latin, except for the sermon.

But the German Mass of 1526 gained far more traction. It was entirely sung, except for the sermon, and was all in German, often with familiar words and tunes. It was very widely used, though Luther insisted that uniformity was not to be demanded in matters of worship.[30] When reformers in Nuremberg asked for his advice on worship matters, he repeated basic evangelical principles and suggested they apply them in Christian freedom.[31]

Rather than have music provided solely by chanting monks or a professional choir, most of the singing now came from worshippers themselves in the form of hymns, sung prayers, and other songs. For the Sanctus (Holy, Holy, Holy), postcommunion canticle, and other portions of the service, Luther offered favorite German hymns, many of which he eventually wrote himself. The Epistle was sung in a fairly minor key, and the Gospel lesson in a pleasant one. Such a move presupposed and furthered Luther's theology of grace. Because the Words of Institution ("In the night in which he was betrayed . . .") are "the gospel in a nutshell," they were chanted to the same tune as the Gospel lesson.[32] The pastor faced the congregation during communion and stood behind the altar, which had been moved away from the wall. The host was elevated after the Words of Institution, but no "Sanctus bell" was rung, as it was associated with the rejected doctrine of transubstantiation.[33] Confession of sin was not part of the worship service, but Luther strongly endorsed the practice of private

30. When the Saxon nobleman Hans von Minckwitz wrote his own version of the Mass in Sonnewalde, Luther affirmed his right to do so. This would have been unthinkable in other parts of the Reformation, such as Strasbourg and Zurich. See WABR 3:384.
31. LW 49:204–10.
32. LW 36:56 and LW 35:106, for example; MLBTW3, 222.
33. LW 53:69.

confession and wrote a short order for confession as well as an essay: "How One Should Teach Common Folk to Shrive Themselves."[34]

What Luther had in mind for worship was actually three forms. He thought that continuing the Mass in Latin was a good idea. It would help teach people (especially students) Latin and would help them worship in other lands when they traveled. Then, there should be regional worship services, adapted to accommodate local customs (such as architecture), needs, and language. He also wished for worship to happen more frequently in homes, where people might gather "to pray, to read, to baptize, to receive the sacrament, and to do other Christian works," and "one could also solicit benevolent gifts to be willingly given and distributed to the poor."[35]

Concern for the poor and afflicted was one of Luther's most cherished commitments. In 1527, when the former Franciscan monastery in Wittenberg stood empty, Luther intervened and requested that the elector convert it to a hospital for the poor and sick.[36] There were frightfully many afflicted folk that year, for in July a terrible plague swept through Wittenberg. Nearly all who could flee did so; however, Luther and Bugenhagen stayed behind, even though the elector and others encouraged Luther to escape. He felt duty bound by his office as a pastor to care for the sick. He explained why in a long letter, later published as the essay "Whether One May Flee from a Deadly Plague." The answer to the title's question is, briefly, yes, but those who lived with special and public responsibilities to others needed to remain, including pastors, mayors, police, doctors, and neighbors of those who were sick with no one else to care for them.[37]

34. LW 53:116–18 and LW 53:119–21.
35. LW 53:63–64.
36. LW 49:169–71.
37. LW 43:113–38, MLBTW3, 475–87.

Bugenhagen's pregnant sister Hanna was among the thousands who died. A postmortem caesarian section did not save her baby. Luther was desperately sad about this, not least because his own wife was suffering a difficult pregnancy. In grief, Luther wrote to Jonas, "May my Christ, whom I have purely taught and confessed, be my rock and fortress."[38] That little word *fortress* often evokes a supposed militaristic, triumphalist, hypermasculine note in Luther's theology. In this very month, he wrote his familiar hymn "A Mighty Fortress Is Our God."[39] Yet singers who know that the pain of loss, of childbirth, stillbirth, and disease were decisively on Luther's mind may find his lyrics refreshingly unfamiliar, after all. It was no cataclysm of empires but love for a dead mother and child that led him to sing,

> God's Word forever shall abide, No thanks to foes, who fear it;
> For God, our Lord, fights by our side with weapons of the Spirit.
> Were they to take our house, goods, honor, child or spouse,
> Though life be wrenched away, they cannot win the day.
> The Kingdom's ours forever!

Luther weighed in on other social issues, too. On family life, Luther wrote a new "Order for Marriage" in 1529 and the book *Marriage Matters* the next year. Canon law, which had regulated such issues before, was now rejected by Protestant princes. Luther repeatedly states that he should not be thought of as a lawmaker but as a pastor strengthening the consciences of authorities who must govern. He considered such issues as kinship, disparity of religion, previous marriage, ordination, and impotence when making his judgments.[40]

He also took up the question of pacifism raised by concerned former solider Assa von Kram. Luther's response, called "Whether Soldiers, Too, Can Be Saved," again makes use again the concept of

---

38. LW 49:173.
39. LW 53:283–86.
40. LW 46:262–320.

vocation.[41] The best way to understand vocation is as the concrete form life takes when one follows God's law in daily life. There were three "estates" where this happened: the household (including the economy and therefore occupations), the church, and the temporal authority. Because the temporal authority had the responsibility to wage war in defense of the innocent, those appointed by their office to do that work acted justly. Luther counsels sternly against the abuse of the office, likely in response to the gross excesses of the Peasants' War.

Lack of order tends to be bad for the vulnerable. An unregulated economy will be a boon for some, but disastrous for the weak. For this reason, and for no other reason, God provides the estate of the temporal authority. Luther thus saw enormous responsibilities on the shoulders of the princes, where they themselves might be tempted to see merely perks of an office. When Electoral Saxony decided to investigate the state of parish life throughout the land, Luther was deeply involved. This project, called the "Visitation," started in 1528. All who participated were deeply disappointed by what they found. Moral life was unspeakably corrupt, virtually no one knew the basics of the faith, and many ministers were perfectly content with such low standards. Luther himself opined, "Dear God, what misery I beheld! The ordinary person, especially in the villages, knows absolutely nothing about the Christian faith, and unfortunately many pastors are completely unskilled and incompetent teachers. Yet supposedly they all bear the name Christian. . . . As a result they live like simple cattle or irrational pigs, and, despite the fact that gospel has returned, have mastered the fine art of misusing all their freedom."[42]

Luther's response was to write two catechisms, a short one for daily use by all people and a larger one for use by those who teach the

41. LW 46:93–137.
42. "Preface to the Small Catechism," in Kolb and Wengert, *Book of Concord*, 347–48.

faith. Luther said he read from his own catechisms every day, and many millions of people since have memorized the Small Catechism. They give basic instruction in essential parts of Christian faith and life, focusing on the Lord's Prayer, Apostles' Creed, Ten Commandments, and sacraments. One of the startling features of the catechisms is how much attention this preacher of grace focuses on the goodness of the law. Over half of the Large Catechism is devoted to the Ten Commandments.

The catechisms were soon used all over the Reformation lands, which were themselves expanding. The important imperial city of Lübeck had been teeter-tottering between evangelical and Roman since 1522. In 1530, Bugenhagen went there to oversee the institution of a Reformation church ordinance, aided by writings of Luther. In a letter to the council of the city, Luther encouraged them and their pastors to be primarily about the preaching of the gospel; liturgical, sacramental, and other reforms could be instated in due course.[43] Luther learned of some positive developments in England and reported rumors of evangelical preaching in Spain.[44] Plagues, political intrigue, and personal depression notwithstanding, Luther was ever resilient, ending his letter with the words "Christ, who has begun this work, will bring it to completion." This was a common theme for Luther—active as he was, he thought that the word was doing the real work. He said from the pulpit, "And while I slept or drank Wittenberg beer with my friends Philip and Amsdorf, the Word so greatly weakened the papacy that no prince or emperor ever inflicted such losses upon it. I did nothing; the Word did everything."[45]

43. LW 49:262–64.
44. LW 49:265–66.
45. LW 51:77, MLBTW3, 294.

Biblical Work in This Period

The years 1526 through 1531 saw a flurry of interpretive work on the Bible. Luther lectured regularly and published much of what he lectured. He also wrote many occasional essays and commentaries on biblical books. The largest pieces from this time are his interpretation of Isaiah and commentaries on Deuteronomy and Zechariah.[46]

Luther understood the Bible to be about *God*, not about the mental states of the authors of its books. And there is only one God, who is Father, Son, and Holy Spirit. The fact that Isaiah was not thinking consciously about Jesus when he prophesied hundreds of years before Christ's birth would not have troubled Luther in the slightest. He read the whole Bible with the promise of the gospel in Christ in mind. Others had said that the Old Testament was now of no worth to Christians. But in keeping with the Renaissance tradition of "back to the sources," Luther took Moses seriously as a source of the faith.[47] He treated the first eleven chapters of Deuteronomy as an extended interpretation of the First Commandment. This is what it meant to "have one God."

The key to the book, for Luther, came in Deut. 18:15: "The Lord your God will raise up for you a prophet like me from among your own people; you shall heed such a prophet." The new prophet was Christ, whose gospel was to be heeded. The law as Moses understood it no longer mediated divine favor to God's people. It convicted one of sin—what Luther would call the "theological use" of the law—by showing what God expected. Thus, Luther concluded that "nothing greater can be taught and transmitted, so far as laws are concerned, than the Law of Moses. For all things reach their climax in him, except that the great Law was to give way to the even greater

---

46. His interpretation of Isaiah is found in LW 16–17. His commentary on Deuteronomy is found in LW 9. And all 350 pages of LW 20 are dedicated to Zechariah.

47. For more on this theme, see Brecht, *Martin Luther*, 2:244–46.

Gospel."[48] Nevertheless, Luther continued to extol the great virtues of the law to generate justice in the political world and to improve the lives of people in communities. The prince, as symbol for this "civic use" of the law, ought to have a loaf of bread emblazoned on his insignia to remind him and all citizens of the law's purpose of generating justice.[49]

Between 1528 and 1530, Luther lectured very often on Isaiah—one of his favorite books—because he was busy translating the Old Testament and it was thus very much on his mind. The extraordinarily busy professor also joked to his friend Link in Nuremberg that he needed to do so in order to avoid being idle.[50] His interpretation began historically. He noted that a different book began at chapter 40, and called the first thirty-nine chapters the first book of Isaiah and the remainder of the text the second book of Isaiah. He took Isaiah's oracles of judgment against Judah seriously in their original, historical setting and cautiously appropriated them to speak to his own time. But Luther's central point in this expansive work is to drive home the "for me" dimension of the gospel in Isaiah. Words mean nothing unless they are appropriated; promises mean nothing unless they are directed to someone. He thinks Isaiah 53, with its depiction of a "suffering servant," prefigures Christ, and he urges readers to understand these as words of promise, directed to the believer who receives them in faith. He also criticizes theologies that do not seek to comfort and strengthen believers in this way.

Luther tended to emphasize the "literal" meaning in his interpretation of Scripture but thought that the other "spiritual" senses had their place, too. The problem with allegory was that one could make a passage mean almost anything one wanted. In

48. LW 9:311.
49. Large Catechism, in Kolb and Wengert, *Book of Concord*, 450.
50. LW 49:165.

fact, playing with the different senses made interpretation into a kind of "game."[51] Rather than be cast afloat on such a sea, Luther thought, better to anchor the meaning of a text to its literal sense; an anchored ship can still move about freely on the surface to the best nearby water.[52] So when Isaiah speaks of "Jerusalem being saved," it is permissible to interpret Jerusalem allegorically as "the believer's conscience" because the literal sense and allegorical sense cohere. In fact, Luther understood there to be a surplus of meaning in the Bible, one that could never be exhausted and whose conflicts must be mediated in faith and community. "Every Scripture passage is of infinite understanding. Therefore, no matter how much you understand, do not be proud, do not fight against another, do not withstand, because they are testimonies, and perhaps he will see what you do not see, and what is to him statute or utterance is still testimony to you. Therefore it is always a matter of making progress in the understanding of Scripture."[53]

Luther did not always take his own good advice about caution in allegorical readings. Zechariah, for instance, is an evocative book full of visions and images. When judgment is warned, Luther finds it accompanied by grace and mercy. But he too readily identifies those who are judged in Zechariah with his own present enemies, and he puts himself and his followers on the side of the righteous. With a rhetorical flourish, Luther would comment on Zech. 14:5 ("Together they shall be like mighty men in battle, trampling the foe in the mud of the streets") that Müntzer, the pope, and the Sacramentarians were the mud in the streets, though Luther derisively called them "poop in the streets" instead.[54]

---

51. LW 26:440–41, 27:311–13.
52. For example, see his criticisms of Jerome and Origen and their "allegorical clan" in LW 16:327.
53. LW 11:433.
54. LW 20:302–3.

Luther lectured weekly on Ecclesiastes for four months in late 1526. His perspective on that perplexing book is a unique one. One of the book's main themes is nothingness, or "vanity." Much of the late medieval commentary that Luther had learned treated this from the monastic viewpoint; the physical world was "nothing" and to be fled from. Thus, they read the book as a mandate to pursue a more purely "spiritual" life. But Luther read this book with christological assumptions. He conceived of Solomon's sermon as a kind of elaborate "hypothetical" description of what the world would be without Christ—that is, "under the sun," a phrase that appears many times in Ecclesiastes.[55]

All human strivings and attempts at making meaning will be frustrated in efforts directed at self-security. It is folly to rely on ourselves and on our own strength alone. He writes, "By a sort of continuing induction from particulars, Solomon concludes that the efforts and endeavors of men are vain and useless, so that he draws a universal conclusion from particulars and shows that the efforts of all men are vain. He denies (9:11) that bread is to the wise or the race to the swift or the battle to the strong. In fact, the wiser or holier or busier someone claims to be, the less he accomplishes, and his wisdom, his righteousness, and his work are useless."[56] This is good news for those who are not wise, wealthy, righteous, or swift. Luther thus sees the gospel of God's justifying work all over the Old Testament. His lectures on Jonah, Habakkuk, Hosea, and Micah from these years bear this same imprint.

In interpreting Ecclesiastes, Luther broke from medieval patterns, largely for the good. But he continued other medieval practices, such as refusing to see the sexual love language in the Song of Songs as erotic. Bernard of Clairvaux—whose influence on Luther was

---

55. See LW 15:12.
56. LW 15:7.

significant and has been underappreciated—and many other medieval writers had seen the book as an allegory for the love that Christ had for the church, his bride. All the sex was thus quickly whisked away. Luther saw the book as an allegory, too, but one for the *political* world! It might have pleased the elector to know that politics would be successful when "married" to God, but few others have been convinced, and, when the book was published years later, Luther himself allowed that he might well be wrong.[57] It is hard to blame him for reading the book in this way, as war-torn and pained as Europe seemed to be in those days. Perhaps in a vein of wishful thinking, Luther wrote, "Song of Solomon rightly belongs with Ecclesiastes, since it is an encomium of the political order, which in Solomon's day flourished in sublime peace."[58] It is an underwhelming argument, indeed, but then again, peace in Europe would certainly have been nice.

The Sacraments, Again

In some ways, Luther was a radical. In other ways, he was very much a conservative. His views on sacraments were an example of the latter. Luther understood the church in Rome to have strayed far from the apostolic witness on the sacraments, and thus he sought to restore and conserve what he thought was proper clarity—but also *mystery*—regarding them. Soon he was debating this issue on many fronts. In *The Babylonian Captivity of the Church* of 1520, Luther criticized the doctrine of transubstantiation, which taught that the form of the elements of communion stayed the same (it looked and tasted like bread and wine before and after the Mass) but their substance changed from bread and wine to body and blood.

57. LW 15:264.
58. LW 15:195

This was an application of Aristotle's principles of physics. Luther did not teach, as many have concluded, that therefore Christ was not really present in the bread and wine. In fact, Luther absolutely thought that Christ was present "in, with, and under" the forms of bread and wine. The relevant issue for Luther was, rather, the interpretation of the Bible. When Paul writes, "The bread which we break, is it not the communion of the body of Christ?" (1 Cor. 10:16, KJV), he seems to teach that there is bread broken at communion. Not "something that merely looks like bread," but rather *bread*. If one was forced to use the categories of Aristotle, then one might speak of "consubstantiation" because both bread and the body of Christ are present for the faithful. But why try to force Christians to believe one particular way of explaining the presence, as the Fourth Lateran Council did with transubstantiation? Better to say that the bread is there, and Christ is there, and to approach the altar rail in wonder. The church has the responsibility to teach rightly and ought to use reason to assist the faith. But it must not let reason trump faith. In this vein, Luther is glad to quip, "The Philosopher was smart, but the Holy Spirit knows even more than Aristotle."[59]

Few future debates about the presence of Christ in the Eucharist would come on the Roman front, however. Luther said, "I would rather drink sheer blood with the Pope than mere wine with the Fanatics."[60] By "fanatics" he meant those he curiously called the *Schwärmerei*, or the "enthusiasts." Luther's newer opponents on sacraments would be Carlstadt, Schwenckfeld, and Zwingli.

Luther's colleague Carlstadt further alienated himself from the rest of the Wittenbergers by diverging from the Reformer on several matters, Holy Communion chief among them. As we saw earlier, Luther had challenged Carlstadt to a theological duel in the Black

---

59. WA 6:511.
60. WA 26:462. The translation in LW 37:317 badly misrepresents the sense Luther is giving here.

Bear Inn in Jena, and tossed him the traditional golden coin to seal the deal. Carlstadt responded by penning dozens of treatises explaining his divergences from Luther. He kept making the central point that when Jesus said "this is my body" at the Last Supper, he was not referring to bread. He was instead referring to his physical body, which was about to be crucified. The Words of Institution therefore predict the passion and should call to mind the cross for those who hear the words in later memorials.

HVLRICVS ZVINGLIVS,

Image 26: Zwingli lost his life on the battlefield, after standing his ground against the Wittenberg reformers at Marburg.

Carlstadt fled Wittenberg in disgrace and went to Strasbourg as a fugitive, then later to Basel. He influenced other pastors in his sacramental views, notably the great Zurich reformer Ulrich Zwingli and his partner in Basel, John Oecolampadius. Zwingli ended up taking a slightly different approach to the doctrine, however. Zwingli thought that the word *is* in the phrase "this is my body" did not imply that the bread of communion should be equated with the body of Christ. Instead, it meant *signified*. Those who receive communion are symbolically brought into the presence of Christ who is in heaven, having ascended to the right hand of God.

Some have thought that Zwingli was merely trying to be "rational." On this account, he was trying to purge the church's theology of its superstitious accretions and develop a doctrine of communion that was less earthy, physical, and "magical."[61] This is only partially true. A deeper explanation has to do with the fact that he was in the large city of Zurich. The Reformation in cities, as opposed to smaller towns like Wittenberg, tended to criticize the sacramental, priest-focused orientation of medieval religion in favor of a spiritual community of more or less equal true believers. Therefore, Zwingli's objections to the doctrine of the real presence show that he cared less about what was happening to bread and wine on the table, and more about what was happening in his heart when he received it. One did not need some superior "priest" to preside over that.

Capito and Bucer, the reformers in Strasbourg, wrote to Zwingli and Luther to ask what they thought about the relationship of John 6:63 ("It is the Spirit that gives life; the flesh is useless") to Holy Communion. Years before, Luther had published his considered opinion on the matter: "The Lord says nothing about the sacrament in this passage. Rather, he is talking about faith in . . . Christ."[62] Zwingli disagreed strongly; based in Zurich, he was very influential throughout Switzerland, and his views were widely shared in its cities.

---

61. Indeed, the medieval doctrine of the Eucharist became associated with "magic"; "hoc est corpus meum" ("this is my body," in Latin) is the origin of the phrase "hocus pocus."
62. WA 6:80.

Philip of Hesse knew he would need a united front to face off against Charles V. Naturally, he needed Luther, Zwingli, and the rest to come to some accord. To do this, he convened a gathering at Marburg. All the major parties attended, and all went home unhappy. Those present included Luther and the Wittenbergers, Zwingli of Zurich, Oecolampadius of Basel, Bucer and Hedio of Strasbourg, and Brenz of Württemberg. Luther and Zwingli, especially, could not see eye to eye. At one point, Luther secretly scribbled on the table in chalk the words "this is my body" and covered the writing with a tablecloth. Later in the debate, when called on to provide a scriptural warrant for the real presence, Luther dramatically tore back the cloth and let the words speak for themselves. Passions ran high throughout the discussions. Noting again that the finite could not bear the infinite, Zwingli cited John 6:63 and told Luther, "You'll break your neck on that one." Luther snarled back, "Necks don't break so easily here in Hesse as they do in Switzerland."

In the end, Luther penned fourteen articles indicating the general consensus among those present. Only a fifteenth, on the real presence, lacked consent. Because perfect theological agreement did not exist, a military alliance could not happen. Philip of Hesse, among many others, was crushed, and prospects for the Reformation suddenly looked bleaker.[63]

On the matter of laity receiving both bread and wine, there was much broader consensus. In Halle, there was a pastor named George Winkler who was sympathetic with Luther's theology. He began the practice of giving both bread and wine to parishioners. Because of this, he was summoned to Mainz to answer to Archbishop Albrecht in 1527. It is not known what happened at their meeting, but on Winkler's way home to Halle he was murdered. Many, including

---

63. For a brief but full account of the nuanced theological positions, see Bernhard Lohse, *Martin Luther's Theology*, trans. Roy A. Harrisville (Minneapolis: Fortress Press, 1999), 169–77.

Luther, suspected Albrecht of complicity, but few said so publicly. Luther wrote to Winkler's congregation a letter of consolation, which was widely reprinted. It was both withering polemic and pastoral encouragement. To Luther's mind, Christ had plainly and graciously commanded his followers to receive both wine and bread at communion; to make a law forbidding that practice in direct contradiction to this divine law was unconscionable. Luther also shared his theology of the cross with those at Halle. To possess the holy cross was to come together in the midst of suffering, to undergo harm at the hands of a fallen world, and to turn ever again to the one who knew that best, Christ.[64]

The Winkler episode, as mysterious as it is, and the failure of the Marburg Colloquy highlight how high the stakes were in controversies with sacraments at the center. Luther targets the Silesian pastor Caspar Schwenkfeld and his followers, who taught that Christ is consumed spiritually at communion by those who ascend to heaven,[65] and he also criticizes various "Anabaptist" groups that emphasized the need for a profession of faith by a candidate for Baptism. Because his thoughts on Baptism changed relatively often, Luther frequently clarified them, though always with the understanding that he was in keeping with what the church had always taught on the matter.

A Second Wartburg: Luther Anxious at Coburg Castle

"We go with our prince. Meanwhile, continue to love the preached word. May God preserve us." Luther ended a sermon with these words to the Wittenbergers on April 3, 1530, as a very select few

---

64. LW 43:139–65.
65. Luther's treatises "The Sacrament of the Body and Blood of Christ—Against the Fanatics" (1526), in LW 36:331–62, and "That These Words of Christ, 'This Is My Body' Still Stand Fast against the Fanatics" (1527), in LW 37:37–150, contain much of this material.

of them prepared to travel to Augsburg for the diet.[66] The elector, Luther, Melanchthon, and Jonas went to Torgau later that day, meeting the others who would travel with them: the trustworthy Spalatin to serve as advisor and the uncompromising Agricola to be his preacher. They went as far as Coburg, the southernmost castle in Electoral Saxony. Luther could go no further toward Augsburg, for he was still under the death sentence. The elector had asked the town council of Nuremberg to allow Luther to stay there and thus be closer to the action. But they declined, wanting to stay out of trouble; in their response they sheepishly said, however, that they were "entirely supportive" of Luther.

The day before Easter, Luther preached a sermon to the group. The text was the passion narratives, and Luther spoke about suffering. In a fallen world plagued by sin and death, evils will come, and all simply *must* follow Christ's example in suffering them. "None should dictate or choose his own cross and suffering, but rather, when it comes, patiently bear and suffer it."[67] Strength to do so came from faith, for "we should not only believe in the crucified Christ, but also be crucified with him."[68] Here as elsewhere when writing on suffering, Luther emphasizes the "exchange" motif. In the mystery of faith, the benefits of grace were conferred on the believer, and the pains of the believer were borne by Christ. To enter ever again into this exchange simply *is* the life of faith, dramatized in the church's Easter worship.[69] Luther called this "the possession of the sacred cross." The next day, the elector led the way to Augsburg.

---

66. WA 32:28.
67. LW 51:199.
68. LW 51:198. These thoughts are amplified in another short piece written about the same time, "That a Christian Should Bear His Cross with Patience," found in LW 43:183–87.
69. See also sermons from this time period where the exchange motif is prominent in LW 51:285 and LW 51:316.

Luther would suffer himself in a variety of ways during those lonely days left behind at the Coburg with his nephew Cyriac Kaufmann and helper Veit Dietrich. He would have preferred to return to Wittenberg. As we have seen, Luther was an intensely social person whose successes depend enormously on conversation partners and collaborators. He loved his solitude too, yes, but only episodically. To be alone in the wilderness was awful. Luther imagined the processions and speeches at the diet, filled with pomp and ceremony. Yet he joked that he had his own. A jackdaw is an especially loud kind of crow, and there were hordes of them at Coburg. He signed some of his letters "from the Kingdom of the Birds." Speaking of the "diet" of the squawking birds, Luther wrote, "Here you might see magnanimous kings, dukes, and other noblemen of the kingdom. . . . They also show contempt for the foolish luxury of gold and silk," preferring instead a simple black plumage. Just like the emperor, princes, and theologians, they too make speeches and process about the court, and "they have unanimously decided to make war throughout this whole year [first] on the barley, the raw as well as the malted."[70]

It pained Luther to be so far out of the loop of the diet's actions. Luther wrote angrily to Melanchthon to protest the lack of letters coming from Augsburg. He displays his sharp wit in challenging Melanchthon to a silence contest. "I see that you all have decided to torment us with silence. Consequently, so that we don't pine away unavenged, we announce to you by means of this letter that from now on we shall compete with you in the matter of silence. Should you perhaps despise this, let me add that I praise the Wittenbergers who, although they are extremely busy, write three times before you idle people write once. . . . I stop my pen here, not to make you even more silent by my writing."[71]

70. LW 49:295.

In June 1529, Melanchthon had already penned the basic outlines of evangelical theology—or, as he would have said, what the church had always believed. He had some help in the matter from Luther and probably Justas Jonas. These outlines were used as the basis for the Marburg Colloquy with Zwingli (though Luther himself ended up writing most of the final articles at Marburg) and were presented at Schwabach (near Nuremberg) in October. These Schwabach Articles were then amplified as the Torgau Articles, which were themselves the basis for the Augsburg Confession.

The Torgau Articles were shared with Elector John at Torgau as the Wittenberg delegation headed toward the diet. They began with their understanding of the triune God, the second person of which had become human and had personally united his human and divine natures. Original sin was truly sin, not just a sickness, a point made against Zwingli. The office of ministry and the sacraments of Baptism and Holy Communion (in both kinds) were given by God to mediate faith, which alone justified the sinner. To differentiate themselves from the radical reformers, Melanchthon and Luther stated that the order of civil government was also a gift of God to safeguard freedom; they also endorsed voluntary private confession and absolution.[72]

News finally came from Augsburg to Luther that the Torgau Articles had been found insufficient, and thus Melanchthon had been given the task of composing a fuller statement of faith. This was going to take a while, so Luther coped with anxiety by putting himself to work.

On the mountain at his transfiguration, Jesus asked Philip, James, and John to build three booths: one for himself, one for Moses,

---

71. LW 49:321.
72. For this outline we are indebted to Brecht, *Martin Luther*, 2:327–32. On the fate of private confession and absolution, see Ronald Rittgers, *The Reformation of the Keys* (Cambridge, MA: Harvard University Press, 2004).

and one for Elijah. At Coburg, itself perched high on a hill, Luther quipped that he needed to build three literary "booths": one to the prophets, one to the Psalms, and one to Aesop.[73] He wanted to turn again to his translation of the prophets, begun in his lectures in earlier years. And he quickly dictated to Dietrich a brief commentary on Psalms 1–25. He also painted on a wall of his room some words from Psalm 118: "I shall not die, but live, and proclaim the works of the Lord." Luther had been moved by these words, which had been set to music and sent to him by his friend, the composer Ludwig Senfl. You are never alone if you have music, Luther thought.

Aesop was also a friend, though he was merely "secular." Luther had a love for the old fables, many of which were translated already into German but in editions that included many coarse stories unfit for young ears. Luther thought Aesop's stories were a wonderful way to teach the young the tricky ways of a fallen world. A dog carrying a bone sees its reflection in the water and barks at it, losing its bone to the river. Firmly realistic stories like these curb naïveté and teach children to live peaceably in a hostile, dangerous world.

Many more writings poured from Luther's pen in the Coburg, including a plea for the education of the young. His essay "Sermon on Keeping Children in School" urged families to appreciate the goodness of education. This effort ran against the materialistic tide that equated a child's worth with his or her immediate earning potential. "Gelehrte sind verkehrte" went a common German rhyme: "the learned are perverted." Not so, Luther said. The church, the government, and even business needed people who could reason well and communicate with grace and force. This sermon, published in August, was the needed follow-up to his 1524 appeal "To the Councilmen of All Cities in Germany That They Establish and

73. LW 49:288.

Maintain Christian Schools," which had been one of the earliest calls in history for universal public education.[74]

Exhortation to All Clergy Assembled at Augsburg was Luther's attempt to be present at the diet even in his absence.[75] The book was an instant hit until it was summarily forbidden at Augsburg and was unusual in its lack of polemic. Luther tried to summarize his critique of the princes and bishops (not the emperor or pope) and point out the benefits of modest reforms. On the principle that "the enemy of my enemy is my friend," Luther also vigorously asserted that he was the ally of the princes because he, too, was the enemy of the anarchist "enthusiasts and fanatics." Luther even conceded that the bishops might for the time being retain their considerable political power and vast holdings if they would permit the evangelicals to go about their work preaching. A "pretend" church had been growing up along the apostolic one for centuries, and Luther was beginning to understand that he would have to negotiate with pretense to nurture the apostolic faith. After listing more than one hundred common practices of this "pretend church," Luther said, "This is the sum of what I think: If these things had been kept as playthings for children and students . . . if these "customs" had been allowed to remain just that . . . then many of these things could be tolerated. But for us old fools to go about in bishop's miters and fine vestments, and take it seriously—so seriously, in fact, that it becomes an article of faith, so that whoever does not adore this child's play thereby sins: to say this is wicked!"[76] Traditional practices might well be fine and even fun, but they had to be understood as optional—as matters of freedom.

Replacing laws with freedom is risky. Luther noticed during the visitation that removing the requirement to attend Holy

74. LW 45:339–78, MLBTW3, 456–74.
75. WA 30/II:237–356.
76. WA 30/II:353.

Communion in favor of letting people freely choose meant that people freely chose not to come. In another book he wrote at the Coburg, *Admonition concerning Christ's Supper*, he said that Christ himself had mandated receiving the sacrament, which alone should be enough. But there was grace, too. In receiving the sacrament, the Christian thanks God and thus "makes him God," meaning that the Christian "makes the one, true God the one who is in fact God of the believer." Humans are idol factories, but coming to worship, receiving the sacrament, and giving thanks to God can curb this tendency. The Swiss, upon reading the book, were especially impressed, noting that Luther seemed to be taking more seriously the "remembrance" dimension of communion. Luther wrote, "The ornaments and glitter of all churches . . . are as refuse compared with this glorious remembrance of Christ. A single expression of this divine worship rings clearer, sounds better, chimes further than all drums, trumpets, organs, and bells . . . even if they were all in one place and would all simultaneously ring out with all their might."[77] And, what is more, Holy Communion is a key to social ethics. Being fed at the altar can and must equip and spur those who commune to feed and care for their neighbor. This is human service after the worship service.[78]

Luther wrote even more during this incredibly productive six-month period. At the end of June, Luther had finished his lengthy commentary on Psalm 118, called the "Beautiful *Confitemini*." He also wrote an essay in which he reflected on his experience translating the Bible.[79] It contains Luther's defense that the purpose of translating is to capture the sense that the author was trying to convey, not merely to mechanically replace words in one language with their

---

77. LW 38:108, translation altered.
78. Especially useful on this front is Samuel Torvend, *Luther and the Hungry Poor: Gathered Fragments* (Minneapolis: Fortress Press, 2008).
79. LW 35:181–202.

corresponding ones in another. For instance, when Gabriel greets Mary in Luke 1:28 the Latin version of the Bible, called the Vulgate, read, "Ave gratia plena," or "Hail, full of grace." Luther thought that "Hail" was far too formal and could not have been what Luke meant when describing this encounter. Since the Ave Maria was such an important prayer for Rome, there had been protest. But Luther defends himself by insisting that the purpose of translation is to recapture the "sense" of a text for a new audience. "Up to now that has simply been translated according to the literal Latin. Tell me whether that is also good German! When does a German speak like that, "You are full of grace"? What German understands what that is, to be "full of grace"? He would have to think of a keg "full of" beer or purse "full of" money. Therefore I have translated it, "Thou gracious one," so that a German can at least think his way through to what the angel meant by this greeting."[80]

While waiting with anxiety in the Coburg, Luther was immensely productive on theological matters, publishing an incredible array of work. Yet he was attentive to private matters as well, showing care and concern for his family back in Wittenberg, deciding on his own private seal, and writing his will. Worrying that his son Hans might be acting up, Luther wrote a tender letter:

> My beloved son: I am pleased to learn that you are doing well in your studies, and that you are praying diligently. Continue to do so, my son.
>
> I know of a pretty garden where there are many children. They pick fine apples, pears, cherries, and plums; they sing, jump, and are merry. They also have nice ponies with golden reins and silver saddles. I asked the owner of the garden whose children they were. He replied: "These are the children who like to pray, study, and be good." Then I said: "Dear sir, I also have a son, whose name is Hänschen Luther. Might he not also be permitted to enter the garden, so that he too could eat such fine apples and pears, and ride on these pretty ponies, and play

with these children?" Then the man answered: "If he too likes to pray, study, and be good, he too may enter the garden. And when they are all together there, they will also get whistles, drums, lutes, and all kinds of other stringed instruments; and they will also dance, and shoot with little crossbows." So I said to the man: "Dear sir, I shall hurry away and write about all this to my little Hänschen.

Therefore, dear son Hänschen, do study and pray diligently."[81]

Luther now had his own personal seal. He chose an image that summed up what he had experienced, learned, and taught. A black cross is placed in a red heart—the heart keeps its natural color—to call to mind the centrality of suffering to the life of faith. The heart is placed in a white rose, a symbol of the comfort of faith. A gold ring and blue sky encircle the rose, heart, and cross, symbols for an eternal union with God.

Image 27: Luther chose this white rose as his personal symbol.

81. LW 49:324, translation slightly altered.

The elector, who would soon buy Luther a ring that bore this seal, returned to collect his theologian in October. The group made their way home to Wittenberg. These five years had ranged from the near demise of the Reformation in the Peasants' War to one of its signature moments with the reading of the Augsburg Confession. Yet nothing was won or lost, no certainty established. When Luther arrived home, he found his family in good health. But he was plagued by ringing in his ears, fainting spells, poorer vision, a sore throat, and many toothaches. The Reformation—as well as middle age—was taking its toll. Though it infuriated his printers in Wittenberg, eager to profit from his work, Luther needed to rest.

10

Being Martin Luther

1532–1539

Luther and John of Saxony returned to Wittenberg, uneasy about the political fortunes of this movement spun out of control. Shortly thereafter, Halley's Comet streaked across the sky. Every side in the Reformation dispute took it as a sign of disastrous things to come for their opponents. Not surprisingly, each side was wrong, as the real story was much more subtle.

The Death of John of Saxony and Accession of John Frederick

Almost any army with the prospect of facing mighty Charles V would be an underdog. This is even true of the expansive Schmalkaldic League, which was the evangelical princes' answer to the recess (declaration of decisions) imposed by the Diet of Augsburg. After the Augsburg Confession was read and its *Confutation* published by the emperor's theologians, the majority of Roman Catholic

303

princes signed the recess, which stated that all the ceremonies and practices of the medieval church must be maintained.[1] Evangelical princes gathered in the Thüringian town of Schmalkald to strategize resistance. They were able to make some solid political gains because Charles V knew he would need the Saxons to fight the Ottomans. Everyone knew that, actually: for decades, a common saying in Austria chided, "The Turk is the Lutherans' Luck."[2]

It might have been due to luck, religious sentiment, or political gain, but several others joined the league; the regions of Anhalt, Pomerania, and Württemberg, as well as the free imperial cities of Augsburg, Kempten, and Frankfurt had joined Electoral Saxony, Hesse, and the others.[3] To join the Schmalkald League, one had only to agree to the Augsburg Confession and pledge to defend the others in the event of an imperial attack. Several Roman Catholic French-speaking areas even joined for a time. However, no good generals did, and that fact would be decisive.

Archbishop Albrecht proposed terms of peace: the Augsburg Confession could be peaceably believed and even taught as truth until a free general church council met to decide things. This sounded good to everyone but Luther, who saw the agreement as purely political and thus abhorrent. He urged trust in God, not in contracts. He was first ignored and then later persuaded to follow the tide. Temporary peace was achieved at Schweinfurt in 1532, adjacent to the diet at Regensburg.[4]

Elector John was nicknamed the Steadfast because of his unflinching support of the evangelical cause. Such support in

1. Ruth Kastner, *Quellen zur Reformation 1517–1555* (Darmstadt: Wissenschaftliche Buchgesellschaft, 1994), 507.
2. See Mark U. Edwards, *Luther's Last Battles: Politics and Polemics, 1531–46* (Minneapolis: Fortress Press, 1983), 108–9.
3. Free imperial cities are subject only to the emperor, not to a duke, prince, or bishop.
4. For the whole story here, see Martin Brecht, *Martin Luther*, vol. 2: *Shaping and Defining the Reformation, 1521–1532*, trans. James L. Schaaf (Minneapolis: Fortress Press, 1990), 421–27.

tumultuous times came at great cost to his psychological and physical well-being. He had difficulty breathing after Augsburg, a gangrenous toe was amputated in 1532, and he suffered a stroke and died in August of that year. Luther had been his pastor at the end, and he preached, teary-eyed, the funeral sermon for this much loved prince. John's son, Frederick's nephew, became elector. He hoped to embody the strengths of both his predecessors and even bore both their names: the new elector of Saxony was John Frederick.

This man had been raised as Luther's spiritual son (he was twenty years younger) and thus always tended to encourage Luther, no matter what the context. This would have negative effects later, as Luther lost an important "check" against his temper. In addition, in future years, as a result of his fame and John Frederick's goading, Luther would make pronouncements on all kinds of public issues, many of which Luther understood pitifully poorly. John Frederick was a generally capable ruler, but with an important fault. In Luther's words, "If I drank as much as the elector, I'd drown. If the elector drank as much as I do, he'd die of thirst."[5]

Luther knew much more about drinking and the Old Testament than he did about politics. Nevertheless, In 1534 Luther wrote a lengthy commentary on Psalm 101.[6] This was his *Fürstenspiegel*, a mirror for the prince. It is less well-known than Machiavelli's *The Prince* (first published publicly just two years earlier) but contains comparable material, mostly spiritual advice for how to think about governing. Luther saw ruling as, on the one hand, discerning whether mercy or justice was required in a given situation (Ps. 101:1 reads, "I will sing of mercy and of justice") and, on the other hand, growing in knowledge of the deeper meaning of both justice and

---

5. D. Martin Luthers Werke: Tischreden, 6 vols (Weimar: Hermann Bohlaus Nachfolger, 1912-21), 4:14. Hereafter WA Tr.

6. LW 13:143–224. Luther also wrote one for Elector John in 1530, this one a commentary on Psalm 82.

mercy. Justice is not the same as punishment, and mercy is not the same as laxity. He took the opportunity to jab at the elector's vice, too: "Every land must have its own devil—Italy hers, France hers. Our German devil would be a good wineskin and would bear the name Guzzle, because he is so thirsty and parched that he cannot be cooled even by all this great guzzling of wine and beer."[7]

Nonetheless, the two enjoyed a good relationship, one often mediated by the chancellor Gregory Brück, who was a kind of second Spalatin. Luther frequently interceded on behalf of one or another Saxon, pleading for mercy or aid so frequently that Luther was informed that John Frederick would not have time to read all his requests. The new elector promptly made Luther dean of the faculty at Wittenberg in 1535. The university was still young and on uneasy footing, but John Frederick showed his commitment by transferring funds to support it.

It is hard to overestimate how central to the Reformation Europe's universities were. Quite unfairly, many believed that the more educated one became, the less time one had for the "superstitious" accretions of the medieval church. There are many examples of this, but one is particularly telling. A Swabian mother of the Roman Catholic faith sent her son, a student of Luther's, a small wax lamb to keep him safe. Her son's reply was, "Dear Mother, I am grateful to you for sending the little wax *Agnus Dei* to protect me, but honestly it won't do me any good. God's word teaches me to trust only in Jesus Christ. I'm sending it back. I pray to God you won't believe any more in sacred salt and holy water and all this devil's tomfoolery. Read Dr. Luther's New Testament, on sale in Leipzig. Love to our family."[8]

Melanchthon made sure that the Augsburg Confession officially became the norm for the Wittenberg theology faculty in 1533

7. LW 13:216.
8. Quoted in Bainton, *Here I Stand,* 239.

because it was "the true and reliable conviction of the catholic church of God."[9] He also reintroduced the quarterly and festive "disputations" wherein a nervous graduate student would be publicly grilled by a professor, sometimes Luther.[10] As dean, Luther was only occasionally active in university politics. In a move that showed his commitments, in 1541 he insisted the university hire a full professor of music (in the theology faculty, not the arts; music was for and from God). Osiander and Rheticus, Luther's colleagues on the faculty, did much to promote the new astronomy of Copernicus, though Luther was lukewarm and uninvolved in most of the discussions. He was very involved in the constant squabbling between the theology and law faculties, most of which centered on the applicability of the Roman canon law and the distribution of scholarships.

Luther was forced daily to preside over practical churchly matters. Most of them he found to be distractions, but because there were few others willing or able to lead, Luther did what he could. Consider three examples. Luther was asked to approve the appointment of Simon Haferitz as pastor in Kamenz in 1532. Luther responded, "I do not intend to be a new pope, appoint all pastors, fill all pulpits, etc."[11] Yet he also felt that he should offer his opinion when asked. Because Haferitz had earlier been a supporter of Müntzer, Luther could not recommend him. On matters of discipline, Luther preferred to have superintendents of the visitation, rather than the courts, handle things. Melanchthon wanted the accused rapist Johann Gülden pardoned. Luther did not. John Frederick sided against Melanchthon and executed the disgraced pastor of Weida in 1535.[12] Luther was

9. Quoted in Martin Brecht, *Martin Luther*, vol. 3: *The Preservation of the Church, 1532–1546*, trans. James L. Schaaf (Minneapolis: Fortress Press, 1993), 115.
10. An analysis of some of these key disputations from later in Luther's life is Paul Hinlicky, et al., *The Substance of the Faith: Luther's Doctrinal Theology for Today* (Minneapolis: Fortress Press, 2008).
11. Quoted in Brecht, *Martin Luther*, 3:7.
12. WABR 7:191–93.

very close with a former Augustinian monk named Michael Stifel who was pastor in Lochau. Luther presided at the marriage of Stifel to his predecessor's widow but watched in dismay as Stifel, a noted mathematician, used numerology to predict a coming doomsday for October 19, 1533. The world did not end that day, as it turned out. Stifel was removed as pastor for inciting such a disturbance, but Luther offered mercy. Stifel "fell prey to a tiny temptation, but it will not hurt him."[13] The Luther family took in the dispossessed man until he could get back on his feet.

Deciding which pastors went where brought up another practical question: what should the evangelicals do about ordination? For a long time, this had been a job for bishops. But no bishops were won to the evangelical cause. Luther had counseled the Bohemians in 1523 to elect their own. This would be better than their sham ordinations, wherein a candidate would go to Italy, denounce Hus to praise the pope, receive ordination from a bishop, return to Bohemia, and renounce the pope to praise Hus. In Saxony, things would be different. In 1535, John Frederick, likely after consulting with Luther, instructed candidates for ordination that they should go to Wittenberg to be examined by the theology faculty and be ordained there. The castle church was the site for this. Luther wrote a brief rite (not a liturgy for a sacrament), "Ordination of Ministers of the Word," shortly thereafter.[14] He argued that the power to ordain comes from God and is mediated through the church.

---

13. WABR 6:544–46.
14. LW 53:122–26.

Image 28: Philip Melanchthon wrote the most
important document of the Reformation, the
Augsburg Confession, in 1530.

In these confusing times, when the identification of the church with
any particular institution was up in the air, one could know the
church by its "marks," or identifying practices. There were at least
seven of them. The institution that ordains, namely the church, is
the gathered people where (1) the word of God is preached, (2)
Holy Baptism and (3) Holy Communion are administered according
to the word, (4) the forgiveness of sins is declared, (5) ministry is
instituted with care, (6) God is worshiped publicly, and, always a
surprise to modern ears, (7) there is suffering or, as Luther put it,
"holy possession of the sacred cross."[15] Where those signs could be
discerned, that was the real church. Luther saw that in Wittenberg
and thus approved of the first ordination there in October 1535.

15. "On the Councils and the Church" (1539), LW 41:9–178, MLBTW3, 263–83 (Part III).

He described what was happening not as consecrating a priest but as bestowing an office. There would be over eight hundred more ordinations in the ten years before he died.[16]

Continuing Work on Bible, Preaching, and Practical Theology

For personal renewal, for professional interest, and from political necessity, Luther constantly turned to the Bible. During these years, he lectured on Psalms and Galatians (in 1531 and 1532), publishing a much larger commentary on Galatians in 1535 than the one he produced in 1519. He noted, after rereading the first one, how one-sided it had been because of the need to counter works righteousness. The published lectures span nearly two full volumes.[17] In brief, however, the central insight is this: "Faith justifies, because it takes hold of and possesses this treasure, the present Christ."[18] That is to say, in faith itself, Christ is really present to the believer. The word does this. In calling to mind the words of an old friend, that friend might in some small way be "present" to us. But in an infinitely greater way, in hearing the word, Christ comes to the believer in the mystery of faith. This is called "justification by faith." On that basis, Luther could say, "Therefore Christian faith is not an idle quality or an empty husk in the heart. It is a sure trust and firm acceptance in the heart. It takes hold of Christ."[19]

Luther adopted the traditional "two natures" Christology of the church fathers, confirmed at the Council of Chalcedon in 451. Yet he ranges quite freely within the bounds of that teaching, considering that Christ may save sinners according to a "joyful exchange,"[20] that

---

16. Cited in Brecht, *Martin Luther*, 3:125.
17. LW 26–27.
18. LW 26:130.
19. LW 26:129.
20. "By this fortunate exchange with us He took upon Himself our sinful person and granted us His innocent and victorious Person. Clothed and dressed in this, we are freed from the curse of the Law, because Christ Himself voluntarily became a curse for us." LW 26:284. Luther's notion

a kind of penal substitution may take place,[21] or that the believer "puts Christ on" like a cloak.[22] Later Lutheranism insisted that grace was only "imputed"—that is to say, God the judge decides not to convict someone who was and remains guilty of sin—which is a sharp narrowing of Luther's own expansive views. Even when joined with Christ in faith, the believer remains partly tied to the world of sin. Christians who count themselves "saved" yet still feel the sting of sin have found this notion—that the Christian is *simul justus et peccator*, "at once saved and sinner"—to be a welcome interpretation of their experience.[23] Luther thought of the book of Galatians as the clearest example of the gospel. In a phrase that praises both of the terms compared, he called it "My Katie von Bora."[24]

In addition to his lecturing, Luther, as dean of the faculty, had to examine candidates for advanced degrees. This required mastery of a great breadth of learning, including the technicalities of medieval Scholastic theology. These examinations usually had Luther draft a set of theses that the candidate was required to defend against Luther's attacks. Several of these, including "Theses Concerning Faith and Law" (1535), "The Disputation concerning Man" (1536), "The Disputation concerning Justification" (1536), and "The Licentiate Examination of Heinrich Schmedenstede" (1542), have been translated.[25] Here we see a restatement of basic evangelical theology (such as the seriousness of sin) but also an appreciation of the

---

of the "exchange" owes much to his appreciation of German *Minnesang*. In this tradition, a first stanza sang of the love of a man for a woman, the second of the love of a woman for a man, and the third stanza, the most erotic and suggestive of all, of their "exchange."

21. E.g., LW 26:177.
22. E.g., LW 27:279.
23. LW 26:232, and also 26:235 and 27:231.
24. While thousands have praised Luther's exegesis through the centuries, it is important to note the problematic way Luther viewed a supposed "legalism" in biblical Judaism. For instances of his one-sidedness, see LW 26:237, 243–44, 304–5, 340, 399; 27:147, 323–24, as well as J. Louis Martyn, *Galatians* (New York: Doubleday, 1997), 35.
25. LW 34:107–323, MLBTW3, 39–42 and 504–5.

continued goodness of humans, their reason, and their strong capacities. Luther also seems to make progress in understanding the relation of faith and works. Faith justifies and works do not, but there might be other, inferior kinds of faith that would not justify. This helps Luther in his continuing debate with the book of James and its statement that "faith by itself, if it has no works, is dead."

Luther's view toward reason is explained well in another of these examinations, a "Disputation on John 1:14" ("the word was made flesh and dwelled among us"). Here he argues against the idea that philosophy had to be subservient to theology. Philosophy would never be able to account for the miracle of the incarnation, wherein the word overwhelms the flesh and yet honors it. In this case, theology would be the only explanation. But philosophy still had its utterly vital role to play in explaining the order of nature.[26] Philosophy and theology had been locked in a mutually suffocating embrace, Luther thought. If each could let the other go, both would thrive. Luther made a similar point about the study of history in his "Preface to Galeatius Capella's *History*."[27] The discipline of history should be done as objectively as possible in service to the truth, never bowing to the demands of the powerful.

What is fascinating to note about Luther is how, in the very same day, he could write sophisticated, technical commentary on very difficult points in academic theology (such as the Galatians commentary) and also down-to-earth, useful practical theology for the laity. Perhaps no finer example of this second kind of work can be found than the book he wrote because his barber asked him how he should pray. Luther's book, called *A Simple Way to Pray*, was widely reprinted and became a favorite writing.[28] Luther's advice was

---

26. LW 38:237–77.
27. LW 34:271–78. Luther wrote many prefaces to historical works in this period. Many of them can be found in WA 50.
28. LW 43:189–211.

practical. Take your Psalter, go to a quiet place or a church, say a portion of the catechism, and read a psalm with this basic teaching about God on one's mind. Always read the Bible from the perspective of the gospel and consider what the gospel means *for you*, at *this time*. Christians must keep their minds on prayer as attentively as a barber watches his razor blade. And Luther suggested a fourfold way of approaching one's meditation on the word: see it as instruction, thanksgiving, confession, and petition, "thereby fashioning a garland of four strands."[29] In seeing the Seventh Commandment, for instance, as "instruction," one contemplates why God would teach us not to steal. Then one gives thanks for this law, which protects us from theft and inspires us to look after our neighbor. Noting our shortcomings in doing so, we confess them. And finally we pray for strength to grow in love of God and others.

Luther's barber, a man named Peter Beksendorf, took some of Luther's advice to heart, but not all of it. His daughter married a rival barber, and Luther was godfather of their first child. One day in 1535 at a festive meal, the son-in-law bragged to Peter that his army days had given him the ability never to be wounded in a fight. Picking up a carving knife to test the claim, a drunken Peter proved him tragically wrong. Melanchthon and Luther helped reduce the subsequent murder charge to manslaughter, and Beksendorf was banished instead of executed. Other criminals were less fortunate, though Luther rendered what mercy he could. The arsonist Valentine Teuchel was condemned to be burned at the stake for torching thirty Wittenberg houses. As his pastor and counselor, Luther urged the man to pray with repentance so that punishment would harm his body, not his soul.[30]

29. LW 43:200.
30. WA 48:708–9.

It is hard to know how to approach Luther as a man of prayer because this was an utterly private part of his life. Unlike his table at mealtime or his extensive correspondence, both of which became public as a result of his fame, his prayers remain his alone. Only a few of them, such as the morning and evening prayers he recommended in his catechisms, are known. He told a friend, "Tomorrow I have to work from early until late. I have so much to do I shall have to spend three hours in the morning in prayer."[31]

A woman once wrote him asking for advice on prayer, and Luther's response is tellingly personal. When he prays at night, he told her, he says something like, "My dear God, now I lie down and turn your affairs back to you; may you do better with them than I. . . . When I awake, I will gladly try again."[32] Morning and evening prayers framed the day and thus allowed one's experiences to be placed in their proper context as they related to God. Luther's *Personal Prayer Book* of 1522 tried to give laypersons help by supplying fixed forms for thinking but also encouraging freedom in making use of those forms.[33] For example, if one wanted to pray on one of the commandments, Luther gave pithy examples of what breaking or keeping the commandment meant. As was usual for Luther, ethics were here understood not primarily as refraining from doing certain things. One should not think of the godly life simply as *not* swearing, *not* dancing, *not* trusting in witchcraft, but rather one should see it as growing in faith in God and making that faith active in the love of others.

Luther was invited to preach after a grand hunting party hosted by the princes of Anhalt and Brandenburg shortly after they had

---

31. The source for this quotation is Veit Dietrich, not a written attestation of Luther's own hand. See Timothy J. Wengert, *The Pastoral Luther* (Grand Rapids, MI: Eerdmans, 2009), 186.
32. WABR 6:468–69.
33. LW 43:5–47.

adopted the Reformation. Luther's lengthy "Sermon on the Sum of the Christian Life" nicely illustrates this ethic.[34] The sum of life is that "love issues from a pure heart, good conscience and sincere faith."[35] The essence of the law is good and calls for selfless love. But the law brings one to God's judgment seat, whereas the gospel brings one to God's mercy seat. Princes responsible both for justice and mercy would understand the distinction. Law and gospel must both be taught, and the two must not be confused.

Always careful to avoid a new legalism, Luther preached about freedom when addressing the pressing issue of drunkenness and gluttony.[36] Too many, especially children, were drunk too often in Wittenberg. But rather than emphasize only God's commandments against drunkenness, Luther held up the possibilities for happiness, justice, and above all *faith* if this vice were curbed. After all, "when a man is drunk his reason is buried; his tongue and all his members are incapable of praying."[37]

The Psalms were never far from Luther's mind. A particular favorite was Psalm 147. He dedicated a lengthy commentary on it to his friend Hans Löser. Löser invited Luther and others on a hunting trip. Luther never warmed to hunting (he called it the "sweet-sour sport"), and while others filled their bags with animals, "I did some spiritual hunting on my own as I sat in the carriage; I bagged Psalm 147, *Lauda Jerusalem* . . . and this was my happiest hunt and grandest game. Now that I have brought it home and carved it . . . I am sending Your Honor the whole thing, and yet I am keeping all of it for myself. This kind of game can be shared among friends in such a wonderful way that everyone gets all of it while no one comes short."[38] Luther is frequently pictured as the solitary worker, the lone

34. LW 51:257–88.
35. LW 51:260.
36. "Sermon against Drunkenness and Gluttony" (1539), in LW 51:289–300.
37. LW 51:295.

protester singing out, "Here I stand!" What this view misses is that countless people, such as Löser, his barber Peter Beksendorf, and even Seberger his handyman, supported Luther, challenged his views, and pushed him to develop his thought further and in new contexts.

A particularly poignant example of Luther as collaborator is the appearance, in full, of the entire German Bible. Begun in the Wartburg Castle a dozen years before, the translation was finally finished by Luther and his friends in 1534. Luther conferred with rabbis for help in understanding the precise meanings of plants and animals named in the Old Testament. At least fifteen people, especially Melanchthon, Cruciger, Jonas, and Bugenhagen, were substantially responsible for contributing to the project. They continually revised their work in light of new discoveries and advances in learning. Before Luther died, there would be an astonishing ninety-one printings of the Bible in Wittenberg alone. This is in addition to several hundred outside Saxony. A half-million copies were in circulation by the time of his death in 1546; there were about two and a half million German-speaking households, and most people could not read. In addition to the theological consequences of this revolutionary reality, there were also the many linguistic consequences. "Germany," always a collection of independent regions, came to seem a bit more unified, with the conventions of language and turns of phrase now written down and daily read.[39] Many who are unsympathetic to Luther's theology have nonetheless been moved by his translation, including the Jewish painter Marc Chagall, who memorably illustrated an anniversary edition.

Luther's translations frequently coincided with his lectures. The second-to-last biblical passages on which Luther lectured were

38. LW 14:110.
39. See Eric W. Gritsch, "Luther as Bible Translator," in *Cambridge Companion to Martin Luther*, ed. Donald K. McKim (Cambridge: Cambridge University Press, 2003), 62–72.

Psalms 90 and 130 in 1535. This is because, for a full ten years, from 1535 to 1545, Luther lectured exclusively on the book of Genesis. Summarizing this massive output is impossible. Luther normally lectured for about three hours a day, usually starting at about six or seven in the morning, and thus ten years of lectures, even when edited down for concision, is a monumental undertaking.[40] Behind Abraham, Jacob, and Joseph, hidden in the words of the psalmists, Luther saw the promise of God to save those with faith to believe. Death, God's enemy, would be defeated. *Anfechtungen*—the afflictions, temptations, and struggles of this world—would be everywhere. But the Christian joined to Christ in faith could and would have strength for the challenge.

The Larger Lutheran Movement

Luther wrote "against" Anabaptism in 1528 while admitting that he did not know what he was supposed to be against.[41] That group, whose name means "rebaptizers," after their key practice of baptizing again as adults those baptized as children, had so many differences among its many factions that it was hard to nail down what they stood for. By 1532, Anabaptists were on Luther's doorstep, teaching in and around Eisenach. He harshly denounced them, calling them "Infiltrating and Clandestine Preachers."[42] "I have been told how these infiltrators worm their way to harvesters and preach to them in the field during their work, as well as to the solitary workers at charcoal kilns or in the woods. Everywhere they sow their seed and spread their poison, turning the people from their parish churches.

---

40. LW 1–8. See the prefaces to these volumes as well as Jaroslav Pelikan's companion volume to the whole series for an orientation to this resource. Pelikan, *Luther the Expositor* (St. Louis: Concordia, 1959). Luther did lecture very briefly on two chapters of Isaiah in 1543 and 1544, but he did not publish the lectures.
41. "Concerning Rebaptism," in LW 40:227–63, MLBTW3, 240–61.
42. LW 40:381–94.

There you see the true print and touch of the devil, how he shuns the light and works in the dark."[43]

Image 29: Luther in the late 1530s has filled out, and cast aside his monk's garb for an academic robe and hat.

Luther lived before pluralism; he could not conceive of there being more than one "church" in a given area. There cannot be two electors of Saxony, nor two mayors of Wittenberg. He could therefore see such activity only as subverting God-given authority. In his criticism, Luther lambasts the Anabaptists, asking, "Why do you come so furtively . . . and crouch as in a corner?"[44] Well, the answer to that was simple—Anabaptists had been persecuted all over Europe! Many had been chased from their towns, and many others executed, often by the cruelly ironic means of drowning. In Luther's view, they

43. LW 40:384.
44. LW 40:385.

had taken the notion of a "priesthood of all" and claimed an "office" they did not have. To be a preacher, one needed to have both a call to ministry and a public attestation of that call. These people had neither. What would keep them accountable? Why would they not just preach whatever they happened to think up next? Their ideal was to purge the church of any unbelievers, which is why they wanted adult baptism by those who professed to believe. But Luther thought that keeping sinners out of the church was a ridiculous idea. In fact, the church could only be populated by sinful people, there being no other kind. Ministry was to be done in public for the public, not in secret by and to a chosen few.

Therefore, Luther objected on a different front to the continued practice of private masses.[45] Luther emphasized the communal nature of the sacrament of Holy Communion. The Last Supper was Christ's promise of new life, a gift given to believers, assuring them of forgiveness by joining the believer to the real flesh and blood of Christ. Sinful humans could offer nothing to God that would be of any lasting worth; they could only extend an open hand to receive. The language of "sacrifice" was only appropriate to use of one's heart and words in response to the gift of communion. It follows, then, that the practice of a single priest, mumbling words to himself in a corner of a church all alone, will lead people to misunderstand the purpose of the sacrament. Holy Communion is done for the benefit of those who are present. If those who participate are strengthened in their faith, they will share that faith with those who are absent. Therefore, the "private mass" ought to be abolished. It was, as he saw it, a "terrible innovation" of a pretend church.[46]

The timing of his book on the private mass, which appeared in 1533, is telling. Luther consistently objected to the practice but

---

45. "The Private Mass and the Consecration of Priests," (1533), in LW 38:141–214.
46. LW 38:163.

seemed willing to listen to the Roman Catholic response to evangelical objections. If private masses were understood in a different light and, most of all, reframed as examples of something one might do from Christian freedom, they might be tolerable. But after the 1530 Diet of Augsburg, Luther became steadily less hopeful that such a dialogue would happen. Luther wanted to hold onto what he saw as the core of the western Catholic Church's teaching, removing only practices that had developed which were fundamentally incompatible with the gospel.

The unfolding story of the Reformation, with its many factions and splinter groups, is the story of how difficult it would be to determine such things. Reforms did take hold permanently in other countries. Olavus and Laurentius Petri (known also by their more approachable names Olaf and Lawrence Petersson) were Swedish brothers who took the preaching of justification by faith to Sweden. In King Gustav Vasa they found a sympathetic ear, and the Reformation was established in Sweden by 1531. Denmark, too, made the Augsburg Confession its official teaching in 1536 under Christian III. The Finn Michael Agricola, who studied with Luther in Wittenberg, led the way in the Baltic, translating the New Testament into Finnish in 1537. These groups, which did eventually bear the name "Lutheran" (much to Luther's dismay), were in reality far from unified; they mostly had in common a perceived shared enemy: a papacy too embroiled in politics. Henry VIII cast his lot with an established Church of England in 1534. Still other groups, notably those influenced by John Calvin, took hold in Geneva, the Netherlands, Scotland, and a few areas of Germany. Luther was aware of many of these developments and was both glad to hear of them, but deeply regretful of the resulting disunity. He also viewed such developments in the light of his expectation that the world was groaning in its last days.

A brief glimpse of hope for evangelical unity appeared in the signing of the Wittenberg Concord. Still stung by the disappointment of the Marburg Colloquy, where Luther and Zwingli traded barbs in disunity, the relentless optimist Martin Bucer had been working for seven years to bring the sides together. He was able to convene a meeting in Wittenberg where Luther and Melanchthon, wary as they were, discussed a different way of coming at the sacramental controversy. Christ's union of two natures—divine and human—might provide a way of looking at how the body and blood joined with bread and wine in Holy Communion. Those who communed without faith still received the real body and blood but did so to their condemnation, not forgiveness. The result of these discussions was the Wittenberg Concord of 1536, signed by Luther, Melanchthon, Bucer, Capito, and their close associates. But Bucer later disavowed the truce. Luther kept attacking Zwingli (calling him a "Nestorian" after the heretic Nestorius who did not think Christ's human and divine natures were joined) and other Swiss thinkers. The concord got no traction with Zwingli's successor Bullinger, who invented a new word when he got the document from Bucer: *bucerisare*, or "to Bucer," loosely translated as "to waffle."[47] The Swiss would not sign it; to insist that those who were unworthy still received Christ's body in communion made it sound like the presence of Christ was "objective" in a way they could not affirm.

In a way, the Wittenberg Concord was a compromise because the Lutherans did not insist that their former opponents renege on their interpretation of John 6:63. And yet some of the exact wording of this compromise ended up being included in the later *Formula of Concord* (1577), which is often thought to be a document that emphasizes

47. This was in a letter to Ambrosius Blaurer, in *Briefwechsel der Brüder Ambrosius und Thomas Blaurer*, ed. Traugott Schiess (Freiburg: Fehsenfeld, 1908), 308.

the distinctiveness of Lutheran positions over against Protestants who were more radically counter to Roman Catholic doctrines.

Through all of these negotiations, we consistently see a defining characteristic of Luther, though it is hard to say exactly what that characteristic is. He was notoriously closed off to the idea of compromise. And he constantly shrugged off the task of making strategic decisions aimed at advancing any kind of "cause." In his own mind, he was not the leader of a movement. He was a professor of Bible, and he rendered judgment on emerging matters when asked. He had a sharper eye and more energy for pointing out abuses than he did of deciding new directions.

For instance, once when discussing his faith as it related to his many opponents, he said: "For I cannot pray without also cursing. If I were to say 'Hallowed be thy name' I must also say 'Cursed, damned and shamed be the Papists' name and those who slander your name.' If I say 'Thy kingdom come' I must also say 'The Papacy must be cursed, damned and destroyed along with all the kingdoms on earth that oppose your kingdom.' . . . Truly everyone who believes with me in Christ prays this way daily."[48]

Is this stubbornness? Is it self-righteousness? Is it the self-assuredness of conviction? It is all these and more. If Luther thought he was right, then opponents were wrong. One should not hold positions one did not think were the correct ones. Luther could accept paradox where teaching was unclear, but when Christ had clearly taught something, then it was the only truth, and all rival claims were fiendish.

And yet Luther's belligerence in defense of his positions was never unreasoned. His distinguished biographer Roland Bainton explained his twofold attraction to Luther. "The first, naturally, that Luther would defy Church and State in the name of reason and conscience.

48. WA 30/III:470.

The other, that after taking his stand he was willing to reconsider. In a moment calling for decision [Worms], he took a firm stand and then undertook to convince himself all over again."[49] Luther was distressed throughout his life by the question "Are you alone wise?" Back in 1520 in his treatise "The Misuse of the Mass," Luther confessed, "How often did my heart punish and reproach me with its single strongest argument: Are you the only wise man? Can it be that all the others are in error and have erred for so long a time? What if you are mistaken? Finally, Christ with his clear, unmistakable Word strengthened and confirmed me, so that my heart resists the arguments of the papists, as a stony shore resists the waves, and laughs at their threats and storms!"[50] Certainty for Luther was never simply a matter of thinking long and hard enough about various positions.[51] It was not a calculated decision one makes after weighing the options. Rather, it was an all-consuming, self-rending leap into the arms of Christ. It was a matter of dying to the truth. Certainty does not come to the *mind* in the way that a scientist defends a hypothesis. Certainty comes to the *conscience*, like the utter self-surrender involved when a mother realizes she must protect her child. To ask Luther to give even an inch on a teaching he connected strongly to the gospel would, in short, ask him to betray his conscience. And this would undo him.

Near Death and Recovery

For much of Luther's adult life, he was a sick man. Consider the list of various illnesses that Luther had. He suffered for many years from tinnitus (ringing in the ears) and frequently had dizzy spells and fainting. Once he fainted in a pulpit and fell from it. He had

49. Roland Bainton, *Here I Stand* (Nashville: Abingdon, 1978), xiii.
50. LW 36:134, translation slightly altered.
51. On this issue, see the important recent study by Susan Schreiner, *Are You Alone Wise? The Search for Certainty in the Early Modern Era* (Oxford: Oxford University Press, 2010).

uremia, a kind of kidney failure. He had also gout, which is pain in one's joints caused by the buildup of uric acid. It pained his large toe so much that he once threatened to cut it off. During 1532, in a lengthy sermon series on 1 Corinthians 15 (which deals with death and resurrection), Luther was so sick he could not continue. In fact, he said, "Christ grant that this year I may enter heaven."[52] Luther praised his medicines coming from the *Dreckapotheke* (excrement pharmacy), including slurries of swine feces for reducing blood flow and horse dung for better breathing. Perhaps not surprisingly, they seem not to have helped much.

His health became the worst it had been in 1537. It reached crisis levels in February. This time the problem was kidney stones. He passed a large one on February 8, which caused much bleeding. Ten days later Luther became unable to urinate. The court's physician unfortunately prescribed massive amounts of water. When this only made things worse, he tried a mixture of garlic and raw manure. In excruciating pain, Luther expected—and hoped for—death. Finally, relief struck. Riding home from Schmalkald to Wittenberg, the sharp jostling of his carriage broke the stone loose. Over a gallon of urine poured forth uncontrolled.[53] Shocked by his survival, he exclaimed that night, "Luther lives!"

Luther was in Schmalkald because he was preparing for a possible church council. The temporary peace in Europe and toleration of the Augsburg Confession would last only until the "religious question" could be determined decisively. The evangelicals made it clear they would only attend a general church council, or consider it to be legitimate, under certain circumstances. Since the pope was one of the disputants in the case, it was out of the question that he would preside at it. Charles V asked Clement VII to call one already in 1532,

---

52. Quoted in Brecht, *Martin Luther*, 3:22.
53. LW 50:167.

but the pope declined. In response, Luther penned a satire, "written" by the Holy Spirit, who expressed his sadness at the stubbornness of the pope. The Holy Trinity all signed the letter, which was delivered by Archangel Gabriel. Even in disappointment and sickness, Luther could laugh.[54]

Clement died in 1534, and his successor, Paul III, moved forward with plans for a council. He planned one for Mantua, to be held in 1537. To prepare for it, the evangelical princes met in Schmalkald and asked Luther to come. He was to write a summary of their teaching. The Augsburg Confession had been condemned, so it would be difficult to use it verbatim. It was conciliatory in tone, written by the gentle Melanchthon. But Luther's Schmalkald Articles thundered. He could not contain his invective against the papacy and all that it stood for. Melanchthon, also at Schmalkald, penned a supplementary (and much softer) "Treatise on the Power and Primacy of the Pope," which was adopted by the princes present. Luther's articles were not, but they later were included in the *Book of Concord*, a collection of writings taken by the evangelicals to be binding doctrine. When not railing against abuses, Luther's writings in the Schmalkald Articles show his evolving theology. An important article on "the gospel," for instance, adds a way that God acts in the world: not just through preaching, sacraments, and confession and absolution, but also through "the mutual conversation and consolation of brothers and sisters."

The council at Mantua was a nonstarter. Financial difficulties in the city made it hard to meet. Paul III moved the proceedings to nearby Vicenza, but few bishops came. Luther, as it turns out, would have been willing to come. Paul III had sent a messenger named Vergerio to Wittenberg in 1535 to sound out possibilities for Luther's

---

54. "Convocation of a Free, Christian Council," in WA 38:280–89.

attendance at a council. Luther was pleased to learn of the next day's visit of Vergerio. He went to his barber and was bathed, trimmed, and shaved (usually he reserved this treatment for the day before important sermons). In a weird scene, he put on his finest fox fur–lined robe, the delicate stockings of a nobleman, and a gold pendant so gaudily huge his barber protested. He filled his fingers with rings borrowed from friends. He made Bugenhagen ride with him to the city gates in a carriage to meet Vergerio, a distance of only a few blocks. Obviously, Luther wanted to convey the impression of youth, worldliness, and vigor.

Luther and Vergerio debated back and forth all day, sometimes cheerily and other times more sharply. Luther surprised the Italian by advocating two fast days per week, but only if declared by the emperor, not the pope. Luther was polite but would not use the official titles for the pope or his ambassador. He mostly spoke German, leaving Vergerio doubting that this peasant miner's son had written the Latin works that bore his name, and he defended the ordinations that were taking place in Wittenberg without a bishop. Luther fumbled on the most important point, however. When asked about the council, he quipped, "You are wretched men led astray by your godless teachings, and you are the ones who need a council."[55] This put the German princes in an awkward position they resented, for they had no intention of attending a council under the wrong circumstances. The council was finally held at Trent from 1545 to 1563, and the evangelicals, with brief and minor exceptions, did not attend.

In one last theological writing considered in this chapter, Luther described what made a good theologian. A large edition of his German writings was about to appear in 1539, and Luther looked

55. WATR 5:634, quoted in James Kittelson, *Luther the Reformer* (Minneapolis: Augsburg, 1986), 265.

back on his career to compose a preface. A theologian must do three things, he said, signified by the three words *oratio*, *meditatio*, and *tentatio*. Prayer is the first, diligent and close meditation on the word of God is the second, and the struggle of faith in everyday life the third. An excerpt from this writing is the favorite of many readers new to Luther. He concludes with a vivid caution:

> If, however, you feel you have made it, flattering yourself with your own little books, teaching, or writing, because you have done it beautifully and preached excellently; . . . if you perhaps look for praise, and would sulk or quit what you are doing if you did not get it—if you are of that stripe, dear friend, then take yourself by the ears, and if you do this in the right way you will find a beautiful pair of big, long, shaggy donkey ears. Then do not spare any expense! Decorate them with golden bells, so that people will be able to hear you wherever you go, point their fingers at you, and say, "See, See! There goes that clever beast, who can write such exquisite books and preach so remarkably well." That very moment you will be blessed and blessed beyond measure in the kingdom of heaven.[56]

Glimpses of Daily Life in Wittenberg

Humility as a theologian was not actually Luther's strong suit. He did better on this score at home. Like many husbands bailed out by their wives in gift-buying situations, Luther wrote home from Torgau, "I am unable to find anything to buy for the children in this town even though there is now a fair here. If I am unable to bring anything special along, please have something ready for me!"[57] Luther took an active role in raising his children, but, like his culture around him, he thought of this primarily as the work of mothers.

Luther's view of women has been the focus of much attention over the years. In the main, he held the same views as others in the sixteenth century. He thought that women were weaker, more prone

56. LW 34:288, MLBTW3, 42.
57. LW 50:50.

to emotional outburst, and less reasoned. When he wept over the loss of his first daughter, he complained that God had given him an "almost womanish" heart. He opposed the ordination of women in his 1539 "On the Councils and the Church," including them with incompetent persons and children as unfit for office, though it must be said that women's ordination was never actually considered in that time.[58] His denunciation of monastic vows cut off the one avenue of full-time religious work available to women (though this was good news for women sent to convents more or less against their will). Luther deserves more blame than others for continued subjugation of women, however, because the incredible popularity of his writings gave his conventionally sexist views a wide audience.

However, in the ways in which Luther departed from his culture—which ought to signal something deeper about his thought than the defaults of his context—Luther often viewed women more favorably than one might expect. His many writings on marriage consistently took seriously the claims of women. And his defense of marriage as a noble Christian institution was generally good news for women, who in the later Middle Ages often struggled to find men willing to marry. His strong endorsement of a healthy sexuality extended to women and men, loudly condemning earlier views that "marriages fill the earth, virginity fills heaven."[59] He went against the norms of German law and made his wife the executor of his will, as we shall see in the next chapter. He strongly encouraged Argula von Grumbach, a noblewoman in Bavaria who wrote and published Reformation pamphlets, including a letter to the faculty of the University of Ingolstadt who had arrested a student for Lutheran

---

58. LW 41:154, MLBTW3, 372.
59. LW 33:84. This comment originates with St. Jerome in 384 CE but was widely repeated in the medieval church.

views. Women ordinarily would never do such a thing, yet Luther did not think twice about urging her on.[60]

Image 30: This medal depicts Argula von Grumbach, a noblewoman whose defense of Protestant doctrine Luther strongly encouraged.

Reading his Table Talk provides more glimpses into domestic life at the Luther house, but it can be exhausting: given how many hours he spent thinking and writing about God and the life of faith, one might expect him to want some time off. Luther was in the habit of discussing various psalms as evening devotions. One evening in 1536, after saying grace at his dinner table, Luther expounded Psalm 23.

60. WABR 3:247.

His student George Rörer, who transcribed many of Luther's lectures and sermons, wrote down Luther's commentary and published it later that year.[61] The text runs over thirty pages, making one wonder how cold the food was when it was finally served.

Music was an ever-present delight for the Luther family. We have mentioned in earlier chapters Luther's contributions to hymn writing and liturgy. But music was also for the home. Luther relaxed by playing the lute, a kind of guitar. Once, as Luther sat with his family, listening to students sing motets, he exclaimed, "If our Lord God has given us such noble gifts in the outhouse of this life, what will there be in that life eternal where everything will be perfect and delightful?"[62] He wrote a lengthy poem in praise of music to be included as a preface for hymnals. Part of it reads as follows:

Of the joys of the Designer
There is none that could be finer
Than the one that comes in singing
Sweetest voices clearly ringing.

Song permits no wicked mood;
Harmony makes our souls renewed.
Gone be anger, hate and envy
When the heart makes music friendly.[63]

Guests at the Luthers' home noted that his appetite for singing was insatiable.

As it is for many families, Christmas was an especially favorite time for the Luthers. A hymn Luther wrote is still popular, tying the meaning of Christmas not to family celebrations but to the incarnation and the gospel: "From Heav'n above to Earth I come / To bring Good News to everyone; / Glad tidings of great joy I bring

61. LW 12:145–79.
62. Quoted in Martin Marty, *Martin Luther: A Life* (New York: Penguin, 2004), 115.
63. WA 35:484, freely translated.

/ To all the world, and gladly sing." Legends that Luther was the first to decorate a Christmas tree, that he wrote the lyrics to "Away in a Manger," or that he instituted gift giving as a holiday practice are mistaken. Perhaps they were believed because they were believable, given his love for the season. And he did encourage charity especially strongly at Christmas. In one Christmas sermon in Wittenberg, he chided the self-righteous who imagined themselves at the manger: "You think to yourselves, 'If only I had been there! How quick I would have been to help the Baby!' . . . You say that because you know how great Christ is. But if you would have been there at that time, you would have done no better than the people of Bethlehem. Why don't you do it now? You have Christ in your neighbor. You ought to serve him, for what you do to your neighbor in need you do to the Lord Christ himself."[64]

64. Quoted in Roland Bainton, *The Martin Luther Christmas Book* (Minneapolis: Augsburg, 1997), 31.

11

Darkness with Shafts of Light

1540–1545

Winston Churchill is reported to have said, "You have enemies? Good. That means you've stood up for something some time in your life." By that measure, Luther must have stood up for many things. By 1540, Luther found himself hated (and beloved by others) even more intensely than in his polarizing younger years. He did not find this surprising, and in fact he almost welcomed it. There are complex reasons for this. First, Luther thought of himself as locked in a struggle between good and evil in the world. He thought the devil operated in daily life by persecuting the gospel and the church that preached it. In history, this had happened originally at the hands of the Roman Empire, then by various heretical groups, and finally, worst of all, from within. In fact, the devil had so corrupted the church from the inside that the antichrist himself sat upon the throne of the bishop of Rome. He was genuinely shocked and horrified in 1518 when he heard Eck, a Catholic theologian, defend at Leipzig the sale of indulgences as truly Christian.[1] In his later years he became more convinced, not differently so, that evil forces were violently at work in the church in Rome and against the church elsewhere.

Early in his career, Luther connected the gross underside of physical pains and realities—such as disease, defecation, and death—with wicked powers. "Sin, death, and the devil" were three sides of the same reality. There is no lack of coarse citations in his writing, including his dismissal of papal "decrees and decretals" with the vulgar Latin joke "excrees and excretals." After about 1539, Luther rarely wrote in refined Latin prose, signaling that he was less eager to reach an academic audience. Instead, he wrote in German and tended to assume that his readers would be less interested in subtle argument. Add to this the colossal physical infirmities of his own, the bitter disappointment over the divisions in Christianity, the pains of deep personal loss, and a sense of profound disempowerment. Combining all these facts with Luther's gift for provocative language, one might expect Luther in his last years to be even more graphic and abusive in his rhetoric. This is, sadly, exactly what we see.

Yet this picture of an irascible, hateful Luther is only part of the story. There was deep darkness in his last five years, yes. But there were also shafts of bright light. There were challenges, both personal and professional, but Luther found sources of resilience to meet them. What we see in Luther's last years is not a different man than we have seen before, but rather a more pronounced version of him. Always willing, as in previous decades, to attack the haughtily comfortable or those he thought to be in error, old man Luther attacked even more ferociously. Always ready in younger years to comfort those who suffered, old man Luther consoled even more tenderly.

---

1. "It horrified me to hear this, not from a Jew, nor a Turk, nor a Bohemian heretic, but from a Catholic theologian." WA 1:298. This is from Luther's "Asterisks," his reply to the charges of Eck's "Obelisks."

Institutional Realities

During these last years, it became increasingly apparent that, quite against Luther's earlier wishes, reformation would happen *against* the church of Rome, not within it. The resulting institutional realities—in both political and church life—gradually emerged.

The most important political fact to know about these years of Luther's life is a strange one: Philip of Hesse was in love. Philip was devoted to the evangelical cause, and his army was one of the strongest in Europe. His support for the Reformation was vital. At the age of eighteen, he had married a girl named Christina, daughter of Duke George of Saxony. This was largely a political arrangement. Less than a month later, he complained that he had no feelings for her. She stank, she was cold-hearted, and she was an alcoholic, Philip later declared to Luther, and he said he would not touch her. This cannot be the whole picture of the marriage, as they did have ten children together, including three after Philip had taken a second wife.

Philip was tormented, he said: his body by syphilis and his conscience by many extramarital affairs. These related facts led him to receive Holy Communion only very rarely. In 1539, he met young Margaret von der Saale and wished to marry her. Her mother would not permit her to be his mistress—she would have to be his wife. Bigamy was prohibited by church law, however, and the punishment was death. Understandably nervous, Philip asked Luther for advice.

Image 31: Philip was the sledge hammer of the Schmalkadic League. His powerful army protected the Reformation in its early years.

He confessed to adultery, blamed it on his loveless marriage, and with more than a little manipulation stated that he could fight harder for the evangelical cause if his conscience were clearer. After all, he said, how could he punish vice in his realm if he were guilty of it himself? His letter to Luther ended with the statement that he had more or less decided that he would marry Margaret and what he really wanted was Luther's blessing on the marriage. Ordinarily, the person to ask for this was the pope, for he could pardon sins, or perhaps the emperor, who pardoned crimes. Philip's siding with the evangelicals eliminated these possibilities. Changing sides just to get a divorce would be bad all the way around.

Four options seemed available to Luther: self-denial, divorce, concubinage, and bigamy. The first seemed totally unrealistic, Christ allowed the second only for adultery, and Mrs. Von der Saale forbade the third. Because wife Christina claimed to be indifferent to there being a second Mrs. Philip, Luther reasoned that, of all the bad options, bigamy was the least bad. The Old Testament had its share of patriarchs with multiple wives, after all, as Philip had eagerly pointed out. He approved Philip's bigamy in the context of confession so that it could be kept a secret. Philip, unbidden, sent Luther a barrel of wine as a thank-you present.[2] This infuriated everyone once the news was leaked, which of course it quickly was. Luther defensively and weakly rationalized that a confessor sometimes had to counsel exceptions to the rule to protect the integrity of the rule, in this case marriage.

Luther was humiliated and felt betrayed. These feelings intensified when he learned in later months that Philip was not satisfied with two sexual partners, continuing with repeated affairs while carrying his venereal disease. Luther wrote that if he had known the whole story, "not even an angel would have gotten me to give such advice."[3] Luther saw his role in the mess as a pastor assuaging a conscience. It fell to Melanchthon to draft the official legal paperwork and to witness the second marriage. Overcome with guilt and loathing, Melanchthon fell gravely ill, very nearly dying in 1540. Philip of Hesse was lost for the Schmalkald League because, in exchange for overlooking his bigamy, Charles V forced Philip to abstain from religious politics. This was the only kind of abstinence Philip could handle.

2. WABR 9:117–18.

3. Quoted in Eric Gritsch, *Martin—God's Court Jester* (Philadelphia: Fortress Press, 1983) 81.

This whole situation left deep effects on the Reformation, discrediting Luther, Melanchthon, Landgrave Philip, and virtually everyone else involved. In fighting against perceived clerical abuses, the Lutherans thought they had the moral high ground. No such claims were possible after blatantly permitting bigamy. Luther's error was not a theological one; in fact, given the circumstances, almost any theological response other than Luther's would have been worse. His mistake lay in misjudging Landgrave Philip. When confronted with the whole truth, Luther immediately admitted his errors, though this did not diminish the negative political consequences. And he never would reveal exactly what he had told the landgrave, for the confessional was sacred. Better to say "Martin Luther was made a fool by giving in" than to break the seal of the confessional.[4] Personal conscience was more important than politics, anyway.

A further disappointment for the movement came when a series of theological discussions failed to make real progress between the major factions. Wittenberg and Nuremberg came to greater unity, but efforts to come closer with Rome went nowhere at Hagenau in June 1540, nor at Worms in January 1541. The emperor was present at a diet at Regensburg in April 1541, where theological matters were again discussed. There were faint hopes that some reconciliation might be possible in lieu of a general council, which still seemed not to be forthcoming. Some progress was initially made, including on understandings of sin and grace, but in the end nothing came of the months of discussions and politicking at Regensburg. Many mistakenly think that the Reformation was simply a dispute about grace, faith, and works. What Regensburg shows is that the Reformation was really a crisis of *authority*. Justifying grace was the spark that set off the theological debates of the Reformation, but,

4. WABR 9:149.

in the end, the real issue was the question of *how* such questions should best be determined, as had been the case with many doctrinal struggles of previous centuries.

Perhaps aware of the practical benefits of maintaining nearby Anhalt on the evangelical side, Luther agreed to be the godfather of Prince John of Anhalt's son, Bernard. Luther preached in John's church in Dessau at three services, including the baptismal service, in April 1540. In fact, Luther continued to preach about fifty to one hundred times per year during the last decade of his life. Luther's gift to the boy, gratefully accepted by his parents, was the promise to pray for baby Bernard and his mother. His baptismal sermon, as much of his preaching in these last years, stands again on the bedrock of Luther's theology: the glorious, blessed exchange wherein Christ takes our sins and grief and gives us blessing and new life.[5] Once again the foes are named: those people who "what they think is this: Even though I am a sinner, there is no need to worry, I can take care of the matter; I will do this or that to the praise of God and he will accept it."[6]

In addition to the papacy, Luther was now including Islam in the Ottoman Empire in his list of "works-righteous" religions. In 1542, he penned a new hymn, the first stanza of which was, "Lord, keep us in thy Word and work, / Restrain the murderous Pope and Turk, / Who fain would tear from off thy throne / Christ Jesus, thy beloved Son."[7] That year he also wrote, at the request of the elector, "An Appeal for Prayer against the Turk." He had done something similar in 1529 when Vienna was under Ottoman siege. This time the tone is less optimistic, and his criticisms of the people much stronger. Many would suffer, there is no doubt, but God's judgment is just, and all

---

5. LW 51:316.
6. LW 51:317.
7. WA 35: 467–68, common translation. Catherine Winkworth's sanitized translation replaces the line about pope and Turk with "Curb those who by deceit or sword."

have need of repentance. The Christian soldier is not less guilty than the Muslim one, Luther says, counseling that they confess their sins, hold tightly to the creeds and Lord's Prayer, and fulfill the duties of their office without delighting in violence.[8]

One last institutional transition came in 1541. The bishop of Naumburg died, leaving open a position within Saxony that had been very opposed to the Reformation. The cathedral priests secretly elected a bishop loyal to Rome, but the congregation preferred an evangelical. Elector John Frederick would have to approve any candidate, so it would almost certainly be a Lutheran. In the end, Nicholas von Amsdorf, Luther's longtime coworker and confidant, was chosen. Besides his eminent competence, one consideration may have been Amsdorf's status as a confirmed bachelor; at least with Amsdorf, the Roman Catholics in the diocese would not have to suffer the sight of a bishop with children and wife in tow.

Luther presided at the ordination service in the cathedral in January 1542. He intended, with the other Wittenbergers, that this be an example for how other such services might happen, publishing the book *Example of How a Christian Bishop Is to Be Consecrated* in March.[9] The book opens by stating that less pomp, and more piety, ought to characterize the service. Luther writes, with more than a little sarcasm, "We poor heretics have once again committed a great sin against the hellish unchristian church of the most hellish father the pope, in ordaining and consecrating a bishop in the Naumburg foundation without any chrism oil, and also without any butter, lard, fat, coal-tar, grease, incense, or charcoal."[10] At first reticent and uncomfortable in this role, Amsdorf communicated frequently with Luther, asking that he not be referred to as a bishop or prince. He

---

8. LW 43:215–41.
9. WA 53:219–60.
10. WA 53:231; Martin Brecht, *Martin Luther*, vol. 3: *The Preservation of the Church, 1532–1546* (Minneapolis: Fortress Press, 1993), 304, translation altered.

still thought of a bishop as a holy person, whereas Luther thought of the bishop as a sinful person filling a holy office to the best of his abilities. The Naumburg model did not catch on in Germany. The reformation of the Saxon diocese in Merseburg went better because the bishop's churchly authority and governing responsibilities were divided there. How best to organize the institution of the church and how best to conceive of the office of bishop have remained live questions for five hundred years in Lutheran circles.

The Continuing Pain of Loss

Death, threats, and reminders of death surrounded Luther in his last years. In January and February 1540, Katie became gravely ill. Little is known about the disease, but Luther and others feared for her life. Rather suddenly in March, she recovered. Luther later remarked, "Our Lord God always gives more than we ask for. If we ask properly for a piece of bread he gives us a whole acre. I prayed God to let my Katie live, and he gives her a good year in addition."[11] Reflecting later that same year on his own experience of being near death in 1537, Luther remarked,

> Being certain that I was about to die I said farewell to everybody, called Bugenhagen . . . and asked him to absolve me of my sins. I requested my dear Elector to keep me in his cemetery in Gotha, but he said, "Doctor, I don't want to have you here; you ought to go back home." Thus with a peaceful mind and without any struggle at all I would have fallen asleep in Christ. But Christ wished me to live on. So also my Katie, when we had all given up hope for her life, would have died willingly, happily, and with complete peace, and she said nothing at all but, "In thee, O Lord, do I seek refuge; let me never be put to shame" [Ps. 31:1]. She repeated this more than a thousand times.[12]

The Psalms were a source of resilience for husband and wife alike.

11. LW 54:370.
12. LW 54:374.

In 1541, Bugenhagen wrote a brief commentary on Psalm 29. He showed it to Luther, seeking his opinion. Noticing that one of Bugenhagen's comments referenced "little children," Luther suggested adding some words of consolation for mothers who had lost babies during pregnancy. Bugenhagen declined the editorial suggestion but asked Luther to write something on the matter himself. Luther happily agreed, and his appendix long outlived Bugenhagen's book.[13] For Luther the pastor, the issue was that miscarriages and stillbirths prevented the consolations of Baptism. He counsels grieving women not to interpret the death as God's judgment against them. And, further, mothers who worry about the soul of the unbaptized infant can find comfort in remembering that it was out of love that God instituted Baptism in the first place and that God receives the earnest prayers of longing hearts with favor.

Luther remained active in raising his children. Many letters testify to gifts purchased for the children and Katie by the well-traveled father. Firstborn Hans was enrolled in the university at the ripe age of seven and "graduated" at thirteen in 1539. This was probably done merely as a way to honor Luther. Boys should be raised more strictly than girls, he thought, and there was great pressure on the boys to imitate their powerful father. Luther hoped that one would be a scholar, one a peasant, and one a soldier; they turned out to be (all joking aside) a lawyer, a minister, and a doctor. Luther played with his sons less often than with his daughters but was extremely consistent and generous in his role.

Tragedy struck the family in 1542. Magdalena, a healthy girl of thirteen, suddenly became ill. Both parents were especially fond of "Lenchen," perhaps because her birth had helped them cope with the earlier loss of infant Elizabeth. Father Luther consoled the dying girl, asking if she was willing to go to her father in heaven. She calmly

13. LW 43:247–50.

affirmed her faith, then died in Luther's arms.[14] Katie wept for days, and Luther was virtually undone. As he had done when his father died, Luther grabbed his Psalter and ran to pray alone. As she was placed in her casket, Luther cried out, "Go ahead—close it! She will rise again at the last day!" Luther composed a poem for the young girl's epitaph.

> I, Lena, Luther's beloved girl
> Sleep among the saints of the world
> And lie here at peace and rest,
> For now I am our God's own guest.
>
> A child of death I was, 'tis true
> From mortal seed my mother bore me through;
> Now I live and am rich with God.
> And so I thank Christ's death and blood.[15]

These years saw the deaths of many other familiar names, including Luther's comrade Spalatin in 1545 and his longtime foes Carlstadt in 1541, Aleander in 1542, Eck in 1543, and Albrecht of Mainz in 1545. With his own death on his mind, Luther prepared a will. The norm in Saxony at this time would be to leave the inheritance to one's sons and to make a provision that something be set aside for one's widow and perhaps some others through a guardian. Bucking this convention, Luther left everything to Katie, even making her the executor of the will. This showed enormous trust in his spouse. In its preamble, Luther wrote, "A mother will be the best provider for her own children."[16]

14. LW 54:430.
15. WA Tr 5:196.
16. LW 34:296, MLBTW3, 505.

Image 32: The death of his daughter
Magdalena in 1542 nearly crippled
Luther.

An accounting done just before his death showed that the Luthers had several plots of land, domestic animals, household goods, and the Black Cloister. It was worth about 1,030 gulden. There would have been much less, actually, if Luther had his way. He had a nearly compulsive habit of giving money to the poor. Always willing to take in foreign travelers as well as expected visitors, the Luthers usually had between five and twenty-five guests staying in their home, in addition to the twenty or so who lived there. Sometimes the guests swindled him. One woman knocked on the door claiming to be a nun, though she was actually a thief from Franconia. The Luthers housed and fed her, and even paid her to watch their children, until discovering that she stole, lied, and was now pregnant. One might be manipulated, yes, but still one *must* help the poor in whatever ways one can, Luther thought.[17]

Ill health continued to afflict Luther in his old age. His physical and emotional pain in these last years was so intense he frequently prayed that he be allowed to die. Many of these illnesses were mentioned in the previous chapter, including uremia, gout, ringing in the ears, fainting spells, and kidney and bladder stones. In his last five years, that list would be expanded to include a painful perforated eardrum (which festered pus for weeks), severe diarrhea and vomiting, an abscess on his throat, and an acute inner-ear infection. He went blind in his right eye from a cataract in 1542. He had dysentery in 1539, rheumatism in 1540, and occasionally crippling angina pectoris episodically from 1540 until his death. The combination of ringing in his ears, infections, and poor balance points to a diagnosis of Meniere's disease. A particularly ridiculous medieval treatment made matters worse for his ulcerous leg. At the suggestion of his doctor, Luther used a sharp stone constantly to keep open a slice in his shin. This was thought to provide relief from many ailments but in reality just helped keep his leg painfully infected for three years. Later medical advice persuaded Luther to switch strategies and take up sneezing powder instead.[18]

Despite this pall of death that shrouds Luther's last years, there were also many wells of support and moments of delight and satisfaction. Music filled the house, especially after dinner, when Luther would frequently direct the chorus of eaters in singing four- or six-part harmony. As in the past, when dealing with his deep afflictions, or *Anfechtungen*, Luther reminded himself, "I am baptized!"[19] A circle of friends buoyed his spirits, kindled his intellect, and occasionally

---

17. WA Tr 5, no. 6165.
18. A helpful summary of Luther's physical sicknesses and corresponding productivity by year can be found in Gritsch, *God's Court Jester*, 155–58.
19. WATR 6:217.

succeeded in defusing his rage. At table he said, "I'd sooner seek out John my swineherd than be alone" when facing depression. More out of delight than arrogance Luther could say, "I've had help from people who didn't have as much theology in their whole body as I do in one finger."[20] A final source of resilience was the deep sense of obligation Luther felt when asked by others to write a book, treatise, or preface on some matter. Despite old age and infirmity, Luther nearly always said yes to this.[21] But in these last years, sadly, he wrote a book or two too many.

Luther and the Jews

We come now to the most chilling and gruesome—and perhaps also the most confusing—element of Luther's life and work: his vicious attack on Jews and Judaism in his very last years. Entire books have been written simply to catalog and categorize the other books that have been written on this subject.[22] In order not to get lost, it will be easiest to proceed chronologically through Luther's writings on the Jews. This gives the impression, however, that Luther at some point in time fundamentally changed his mind on Judaism, which he did not. So, following the short history, we will examine the difficulty of interpreting that history.

Luther wrote a treatise in 1523 called *That Jesus Christ Was Born a Jew*.[23] His purpose was to defend against criticisms that alleged he did not believe in the virgin birth. Here he discusses the lineage of Jesus and takes the opportunity to advocate for friendlier treatment of Jews, insisting that Christians examine their own complicity in

---

20. Quoted in Martin Marty, *Martin Luther: A Life* (New York: Penguin, 2004), 181.
21. See WABR 10:614 for an example of Luther's willingness to work despite not having the energy to do so.
22. For example, Johannes Brosseder, *Luthers Stellung zu den Juden im Spiegel seiner Interpreten* (Munich: Heuber, 1972).
23. LW 45:199–229.

not living out the gospel. Perhaps if they were treated better, more Jews might be open to converting to Christianity. Denouncing both oppression of Jews and the sorry state of theology, Luther concluded, "If I had been a Jew and had seen such dolts and blockheads govern and teach the Christian faith, I would sooner have become a hog than a Christian."[24] Another early writing, the published sermon "How Christians Should Regard Moses," showed Luther's admiration for Moses and the law he shared with Israel. He said this in part to counter some fringe groups in the Reformation who wanted to dispense with the Old Testament.[25]

After this time, however, beginning perhaps around the mid-1530s, Luther's references to Jews tend to grow much more negative, and his praise more muted. No one knows why this happened, and searches for a silver bullet to explain it turn up nothing.

Since 1432, Jews had not been permitted to reside permanently in Saxony. But then in 1536, for reasons that remain unclear, Elector John Frederick forbade them from even conducting business in or traveling through Saxony. Josel of Rosheim (near Strasbourg) was a rabbi who functioned as a mediator on behalf of Jews all over Germany and Poland at this time. He wrote a letter to Luther, asking to meet with him so that Luther could recommend him to the elector. Josel wished to broker some kind of deal with the Saxon princes, as he had earlier done in other lands. In a mostly friendly letter, Luther refused, saying, "For the sake of the crucified Jew, whom no one will take from me, I gladly wanted to do my best for you Jews, except that you abused my favor and hardened your hearts."[26] Josel came to Wittenberg anyway. He could not meet with Luther but did

24. LW 45:200.
25. LW 35:155–74, MLBTW3, 107–115.
26. WABR 8:91, quoted in Brecht, Martin Luther, 3:337.

meet with the elector, who mitigated his stance a tiny bit: Jews were permitted to travel through Saxony but still could not live or conduct business there.

In part, this reflects widespread oppression and hatred of Jews generally in the sixteenth century, as in so many previous centuries. Migrant life was the tragic necessity for Jews all over Europe; with no homeland to call their own, Jews lived at the mercy of capricious rulers. They suffered from a great many stereotypes, especially the belief that they were greedy. Luther preached against usury (the practice of lending money at high interest) all his life. He thought it was an "unnatural" way to make money. Because moneylending was one of the relatively few occupations open to Jews, many did so. Officially, it was against the law for Christians, but many hypocritically engaged in the activity while condemning Jews who did it legally.

Hatred of Jews was not limited to the lower classes. On the contrary, many of the leading intellectuals of the day, including Erasmus and Eck on the Roman side and Zwingli and Luther on the evangelical side, espoused such views. In 1541, John Eck, Luther's longtime opponent on the faculty of Ingolstadt, wrote "Refutation of a Jew-book," which addressed a strange murder case. In Freiburg in 1503, a man had confessed to killing his son, who had obviously bled to death. The man claimed he wanted to sell the blood to the Jews, who were thought to pay for such things. Then he changed his story and said Jews killed the boy. There were many phony claims and much conflicting testimony over the years, and the man was executed. Eck, writing with the reasoned voice of an esteemed scholar, dedicated his book to proving that yes, Jews did routinely kill Christian children for their vicious rituals; they did in fact desecrate the bread of communion, poison wells, ruin crops, and hex animals. His rejection of Judaism was total and is all the more chilling for its fake objectivity. Luther's friend and colleague Andreas Osiander of nearby Nuremberg forcefully combated these claims. Though both Eck and Osiander were former students of the eminent Hebrew scholar Johannes Reuchlin, only Osiander continued his mentor's fondness for and protection of Judaism.[27]

The normally rational, cool-headed Erasmus, too, was a ferocious hater of Judaism. The well-traveled humanist refused to visit Spain because it was "crawling with Jews," and he praised France for not allowing Jews to "infect" their culture. He stated, "If it is Christian to detest Jews, on this count we are good Christians, and to spare."[28] Zwingli, too, saw the Jews as a terrible threat to civil order, and the early Anabaptist preacher Balthasar Hubmaier was a notorious hater of Jews and Judaism.[29]

Most of these prejudices rested on misinformation, gossip, legend, and myth. They also derived from New Testament descriptions of Jews as more concerned with scruples than with faith and thus had little to do with real Judaism in the sixteenth century. Relations with Jews were also made harder because medieval Europe conceived of itself as a seamless whole, united under the banner of Christendom, even if divided politically. Jews therefore did not fit into the mental picture. Contemporary criticisms of Judaism were not at all limited to theological objections, either. One sixteenth-century pamphlet goes on for many pages describing in detail Jews' overuse of garlic in cooking and the unpleasant sounds their dancing makes.

---

27. Admittedly, there is some element of personal and ideological clashing here: Osiander the evangelical would have opposed nearly anything Eck the Dominican would have supported, and vice versa.

28. See James D. Tracy, *Erasmus of the Low Countries* (Berkeley: University of California Press, 1999), 100–101.

29. On Zwingli, see Heiko Oberman, *The Roots of Antisemitism* (Philadelphia: Fortress Press, 1984), 140. On Hubmaier, see Hartmut Lehmann and R. Po-Chia Hsia, eds., *In and Out of the Ghetto: Jewish-Gentile Relations in Early Modern Germany* (Cambridge: Cambridge University Press, 1995), 163–64.

It is quite difficult to say what Luther actually knew about the lives of real Jews in Europe at the time. He knew a lot about technical scriptural interpretation by the rabbis. But that does not mean he understood everyday Jewish culture in the least. In 1539, he read a book, really more of a screed, by a Jewish convert to Christianity named Anton Margaritha. The treatise, called *The Whole Jewish Faith*, includes accusations frequently made by Christians against Jews, such as their wish to rebel in violence against their Christian rulers (supposedly praying three times daily for the destruction of the Holy Roman Empire), their eager blasphemy against Mary and Jesus, and their tendencies to greed. It calls them hypocrites for being attentive to detail in rituals but claims they lack real piety. Most of the attacks on Jewish practices contained in his later writings Luther more or less repeats from Margaritha. An experienced historian, Luther should have known better than to trust pure fiction as reliable truth.[30]

Luther's vehemence came to a head in 1543 when he published the lengthy book *On the Jews and Their Lies*.[31] It is best known for the cruel practical and political recommendations it makes in the third part of the book. But most of the work is devoted to withering theological criticism of the way Jewish rabbis understood the Hebrew Scriptures. He says that he does not wish to convert the Jews, which he now deems impossible. Instead, he wants to attack them. He identifies several claims allegedly made by Jews that he finds abhorrent: (1) that their physical descent from Abraham ennobles them; (2) that they gratefully pray every day that they are humans, not animals, Jews, not gentiles, men, not women; (3) that their

---

30. Among the many activities at the Diet of Augsburg in 1530 was a debate between Josel of Rosheim and Anton Margaritha on the matter of Judaism. Josel trounced his opponent, and Charles V kicked Margaritha out of the empire. The debate took place on June 25, in fact, the very same day as the public reading of the Augsburg Confession. What if Luther had been there to see this refutation of his libelous source for Judaism?

31. LW 47:137–292.

circumcision joins them with God; (4) that they possessed and kept the law of Moses; and (5) that they were given the land of Canaan.

Luther ferociously and cruelly attacks each claim. On the first: were not gentiles also descended from Noah through his son Japheth just as Jews were through his son Shem? And had not God damned all flesh anyway, irrespective of lineage, when circumcision was instituted in Genesis 17? On the second: women were beloved human beings created in the image of God. To be thankful not to be one dishonored both women and God. On the third: Abraham had circumcised Ishmael and his slaves; are not their descendants just as blessed, then, as the Jews? On the fourth: Israel had received the law and thus become the bride of God, but their wickedness and disobedience made them "a defiled bride, yes, an incorrigible whore and an evil slut with whom God ever had to wrangle, scuffle, and fight."[32] On the fifth: God gave the land of Canaan to Israel but punished them by taking it away through their defeats to Babylon, Assyria, and Rome. All these attacks came dressed in breathtakingly aggressive and vulgar language.

The tract went on and on. Luther then "defended" Christianity against alleged Jewish slanders, such as that Mary conceived Jesus while menstruating and that Jesus used numerology to do magic by the power of "the ineffable name" (*Shem Hamphoras*).[33] He concludes the book with a rhetorical flourish endorsing great cruelty, making recommendations about what to do with this perceived threat to the Christian faith. He says that Jewish synagogues and schools should be burned or buried. Rabbis should not be permitted to teach. Their books should be burned and their homes destroyed. Once their wealth had been confiscated, Jews should be banished.

---

32. LW 47:166.
33. This refers to YHWH, the proper name for God which is not spoken aloud by observant Jews. Luther also wrote a fuller discussion of this allegation, along with another blistering rant against Judaism in 1543. WA 53:579–648.

Four hundred years later, Nazi propagandists made much use of this material. It is difficult not to read these passages with horror in light of the unspeakable suffering of Jews in the Holocaust. This perspective makes Luther's own characterization of these recommendations even stranger: he called it "sharp mercy." Such measures were needed because "we must practice a sharp mercy to see whether we might save at least a few from the glowing flames."[34] In contrast, the "soft mercy" he endorsed earlier in the 1520s coddled the Jews in their errors, giving them time, in his view, to grow worse and worse.[35]

Fortunately, Luther's recommendations for "harsh mercy" were basically ignored from the time they were published until the Nazis dragged them out of the dustbin to try to add some religious respectability to their hatred. Elector John Frederick briefly reneged on some concessions he had made regarding Jews in Saxony, and a neighboring count made it more difficult for Jews to travel through Neumark. For the most part, the later works were hardly even read. *That Jesus Christ Was Born a Jew*, the affirming writing of 1523, was published in many cities in thirteen subsequent editions, ten in German and three in Latin, so that it could appeal to an even broader audience. By contrast, *On the Jews and Their Lies* was printed just three times, only in German, and only in Wittenberg.[36]

The interpreter of Luther seeking an explanation for such vile hatred necessarily comes up empty-handed. This far removed from the events, it is impossible to know exactly how to account for such virulence. In some ways, these writings bear the imprint of a raving lunatic, but they also contain vast learning and insight. Explanations arguing that Luther simply changed his mind on Jews because he

---

34. LW 47:268.
35. LW 47:272.
36. For a fuller history of this, see Mark U. Edwards, *Luther's Last Battles: Politics and Polemics, 1531–46* (Minneapolis: Fortress Press, 1983), 135–36.

was mad they did not convert to Christianity neglect the fact that Luther consistently thought of Judaism as essentially blasphemous, just as he and virtually all his contemporaries would have thought of every other religion.

Some of his rage may have had a personal basis. Three rabbis came once to visit Luther to protest his way of reading passages from the Old Testament as pointing to the Messiah. He debated them vigorously in his home. From 1535 to 45 Luther was lecturing on Genesis, and he was thus very aware of how his interpretations differed from those of the rabbis. He saw promises of God to be trusted where, in his opinion, rabbis tended to find rules to be followed. He thought he won the argument on the grounds of interpretation and was livid when, at the end, they fell back on the authority of their tradition rather than continuing to debate from Scripture.[37] In this way, Luther connected Judaism with Roman Catholicism, which he thought guilty of doing the same thing. Luther did write these visitors a letter of introduction that would grant them safe passage home "for the sake of Christ." Because it contained this reference, they did not use the letter.[38]

It is not as though *On the Jews and Their Lies* was somehow the only way Luther could speak about Judaism. His treatise "On the Last Words of David" was also published in 1543, and yet it contains no attacks on Judaism at all.[39] Instead, it fills out his understanding of how the Old Testament points forward to Christ. In doing so, he stands much in keeping with his theological contemporaries. And unlike many theologians before and since, Luther never made the image of Jews as "killers of Christ" the center of his attack. In fact, in 1544, the year after his hateful polemic, he rewrote a hymn that

37. WA 53:461–62; LW 47:192.
38. WATR 4:619–20.
39. LW 15:265–352.

insisted just the opposite, that the Jews bore no blame for the crucifixion. The final stanza of Luther's "O, You Poor Judas, What Did You Do" reads,

> T'was our great sin and misdeeds gross
> Nailed Jesus, God's true Son, to the cross.
> Thus you, poor Judas, we dare not blame,
> Nor the band of Jews; ours is the shame."[40]

Luther's enmity toward Jews was not basically racial in nature. "Race" was not really a category of thinking at this time, but "blood" was, and Luther does not use this designation to criticize Jewish people as a whole. Explanations arguing that Luther was simply anti-Semitic (essentially a racial claim, as opposed to the theological claim that he was anti-Jewish) neglect the fact that he warmly welcomed former Jews, such as Bernard Gipher, into his life.[41] Bernard was a rabbi from Göppingen, near Stuttgart, who was baptized in 1519. His son was baptized in 1523 with Luther present. Bernard occasionally taught Hebrew at the university in Wittenberg, and the Luther family often helped take care of his children and helped him financially for many years.[42] Luther forcefully denounces any who say that Jewish converts to Christianity are suspect and should be treated as second-class Christians. In that sense, Luther goes against the norms of his context.

Luther also rejected the category of "blood" being used to exclude marriages between Christians and Jews. He was heavily critical of

---

40. WA 35:576–77, quoted in Brecht, *Martin Luther*, 3:349.
41. The most helpful way to understand this comes from Gavin Langmuir, *History, Religion and Anti-Semitism* (Berkeley: University of California Press, 1990). Anti-Semitism is anachronistic before the nineteenth century when "race" became more developed as a concept. Langmuir argues that "irrational" speech characterizes nationalistic or racist anti-Semitism, and "non-rational" speech characterizes theological anti-Judaism.
42. Luther wrote a letter to Bernard in 1523 that clearly shows this view. WABR 3:101–2. See this letter collected with many other relevant documents in the useful book edited by Brooks Schramm and Kirsi Stjerna: *Martin Luther, the Bible and the Jewish People: A Reader* (Minneapolis: Fortress Press, 2012), 84–86.

Roman Catholic medieval law that forbade such unions. In 1522, he had written,

> Just as I may eat, drink, sleep, walk, ride with, buy from, speak to, and deal with a heathen, Jew, Turk, or heretic, so I may also marry and continue in wedlock with him. Pay no attention to the precepts of those fools who forbid it. You will find plenty of Christians—and indeed the greater part of them—who are worse in their secret unbelief than any Jew, heathen, Turk, or heretic. A heathen is just as much a man or a woman—God's good creation—as St. Peter, St. Paul, and St. Lucy, not to speak of a slack and spurious Christian.[43]

There is no evidence that he ever changed his mind on this point, which makes understanding the virulence of the later attacks even harder to comprehend.

The best explanation for the viciousness of Luther's late anti-Jewish polemics is a combination of many factors. None is solely responsible, and some may be more important than others. But these are the factors. First, Luther had been lecturing on Genesis for eight full years before he published *On the Jews and Their Lies*. He was a theologian to the core. Thus, his objections have primarily to do with the way rabbis had read the Scriptures. Luther put his rhetorical gifts to the task of trying to discredit their message by discrediting the messengers. The attack on Judaism may not be solely a theological matter, but theology is surely a large part of the story. Second, there is Luther's temper. By his own admission, anger was his special vice. It did have its place—he once said, "Anger refreshes all my blood, sharpens the mind, and drives off temptations"—but his intemperance often ran out of control.[44] An old man ready to die, whose friends and superiors no longer restrained him as they had in the past, is more likely to devolve into invective. And the self-critical element

---

43. LW 45:25.
44. WA Tr 2:455. "Temptations" here translates "*tentationes*," the Latin equivalent of *Anfechtungen*.

that characterizes much of Luther's earlier writings is gone by 1543. This may have something to do with the fact that Luther's pastor Bugenhagen, to whom he often confessed his sins, was absent during this time. Third, there is his decrepit physical and mental state, already discussed above. Fourth, there is his apocalyptic worldview. Luther viewed his time as the last days in the struggle between God and the devil, and all those who resisted the gospel fought on the devil's side. Fifth, there is a sense of growing disempowerment and disappointment. For Luther, the Scriptures were clear. The Old Testament pointed to Christ. The rabbis knew this, he thought, and deliberately tried to mislead their people from believing it.[45] Sixth, there is Luther's near-total ignorance of actual Jewish life.

No single factor can explain the content or tone of his anti-Jewish writings. Luther wrote in his catechisms that essentially all sins are acts against the First Commandment: failures to fear, love, and trust God above all else. He sought to protect God's "honor" from what he could only interpret as insults from Jews who did not accept Christ. He forgot that God's honor is best left to God to defend. In his last month, Luther raged that the counts of Mansfeld had not done enough to purge Jews from their midst. This of course violates his own counsel that the church should never try to rule directly. Luther's great sins against Judaism violate even his own considered principles.

---

45. See here especially LW 47:176.

Image 33: In 1305 a "Jewish Sow" was carved on the town church in Wittenberg. A rabbi is depicted looking into its anus, as other Jews suckle at its teats. The equation of Jews and swine was common in medieval Germany.

The Oldest Enemy

Luther's pen found other targets in these last years, including, not surprisingly, the papacy and rival princes. Not all the polemics were vulgar. A disputation from 1539, for example, refutes the legitimacy of the papacy based on Luther's understanding of the three "estates," or hierarchies, God has ordered: the family, the temporal authority, and the church.[46] Most, however, displayed invective and coarse

46. WA 39/II:34–91.

language. Luther's consistent tactic was to frame his opponents as vigorous opponents of the gospel and thus in cahoots with the oldest enemy, the devil himself.

"Against Hanswurst" was Luther's contribution to a mudslinging match between John Frederick of Saxony and his Roman Catholic enemy Duke Henry of Brunswick.[47] Henry was a strong supporter of Charles V in northern Germany and remained loyal to the papacy. They argued back and forth in print about a variety of political issues that stemmed from their opposition on theological matters. Henry hated Luther and at one point claimed, in a long book called *Rejoinder*, that Luther impudently referred to his elector as "Hanswurst" ("Hans" is short for Johannes, as in John Frederick).[48] Hanswurst was a popular fictional carnival figure usually pictured as a clown wearing a sausage (wurst) necklace. Luther felt compelled to defend himself against this charge and took the opportunity to shovel some abuse of his own. His response was incredibly vulgar, which was weirdly fitting because it reflected the tone of the earlier salvos in this war of words.

Luther did not think the untrained duke had much business writing books about theological matters. In fact, he wrote, "You should not write a book before you have heard an old sow fart; and then you should open your jaws with awe, saying, 'Thank you, lovely nightingale, that is just the text for me!'"[49] Luther charged Henry with adultery, arson, cowardice, theft of church property, and murder. It was the same thing in Luther's mind to attack Henry or to attack the devil, since they were doing the same work. Of Henry's writing, Luther laughed,

---

47. LW 41:181–256.
48. For the background of these disputes, and especially the lengthy and colorful titles, see Edwards, *Luther's Last Battles*, 143–55.
49. LW 41:250.

Speaking for myself, I am very glad that such books are written against me, for it makes me tingle with pleasure from head to toe when I see that through me, poor wretched man that I am, God the Lord maddens and exasperates both the hellish and worldly princes, so that in their spite they would burst and tear themselves to pieces—while I sit under the shade of faith and the Lord's Prayer, laughing at the devils and their crew as they blubber and struggle in their great fury.[50]

Then he switches targets to holler at the devil.

Indeed, since you and your Harry [that is, Duke Henry] are such gross blockheads that you think such lewd and stupid gossip will harm me or bring you honor, you are the real Hanswursts. . . . Some people probably suppose that you regard my gracious lord as Hanswurst because by the grace of God (whose enemy you are) he is strong, plump, and somewhat round. But think what you will, so go crap in your pants, hang it around your neck, then make a jelly of it and gobble it like the gross sows and asses you are![51]

He attacks the devil and Duke Henry with vigor for pages and pages, and defends his Elector John Frederick with equally coarse verbiage: the elector drank too much, yes, but you, Henry, gulp down devils like Judas at the Last Supper. It is almost baffling to see both how foul the language of "Against Hanswurst" can be and also how subtle Luther's arguments are. He differentiates between the ancient church (the one he understood himself to be continuing) and the false new church that had sprung up in the Middle Ages and was now being ruined by the papacy. He notes and interprets key Reformation events of his autobiography. The many dimensions of these writings make them impossible to categorize. The pamphlet war between Henry and John Frederick lasted through the year and then through 1542. Showing surprising restraint, Luther stayed out of it.[52] Increasingly, the rival princes used literary forms such as

50. LW 41:185.
51. LW 41:187, translation altered.

satires, poems, and even graffiti to win the war of public opinion. Such creative—and abusive—use of the new medium of printing would have been unthinkable just a generation earlier.

Luther did not stop writing polemics, however. Many more came from his pen, notably "Against the Thirty-Two Articles of the Louvain Theologists" and "Against the Papacy in Rome," both published in 1545.[53] The first of these was a response to that faculty, which had issued several theological positions it claimed all Christians were required to be believe. Not to be outdone, Luther wrote more than twice as many against them.

The polemic against the papacy shows Luther's declining abilities. It rambles, and while it is filled with foul language, it does not come to a coherent sharpness. There is some argument in it, however. He claimed that the Council of Constance in 1415 affirmed the superiority of a council over the pope; thus, the pope should not get to decide the rules for the council called to settle the disputed matters about grace and the gospel. The papacy had been trying to undo this for a century. Playing games with the emperor, the popes, who did not wish a council to meet, set terms for having a council with which no one could reasonably comply. The pope also claimed to be the only one able to crown a German emperor and claimed superiority over all Christendom. Luther pointed out that Greece, India, and Persia had gotten along without him all along, and others could do the same. The pope was the enemy of God, the tool of the devil, the very antichrist. Breathtakingly vulgar, Luther refers to Pope Paul III as "Her Sodomitical Hellishness Paula III" and "The Virgin Paula" to make fun of clerical celibacy. Evidently, in Luther's mind, one could

---

52. When Henry was imprisoned by Philip of Hesse and Elector John Frederick for, among other things, paying arsonists to destroy Saxon houses, Luther wrote an open letter (probably at the request of the Elector) insisting that he not be released. "To the Saxon Princes," in LW 43:259–88.

53. LW 34:341–61. LW 41:259–376.

be simultaneously a virgin and a sodomite. Building to a flourish, Luther rails,

> The pope is not and cannot be the head of the Christian church. Instead, he is the head of the accursed church of all the worst scoundrels on earth, a vicar of the devil, an enemy of God, an adversary of Christ, a destroyer of Christ's churches; a teacher of lies, blasphemies, and idolatries; an arch church-thief and church robber of the keys and all the goods of both the church and the temporal lords; a murderer of kings and inciter to all kinds of bloodshed; a brothel-keeper over all brothel-keepers and all vermin, even that which cannot be named; an Antichrist, a man of sin and a genuine werewolf.[54]

Perhaps fearing that the point he was making was too subtle, Luther also commissioned a series of a dozen images that showed the graphic claims he made. These depicted peasants defecating into the papal crown, the pope being birthed from the anus of the devil, and so on. Evidently, Cranach the artist took his instructions too far, and Luther censored at least one engraving because it dishonored women.

As disappointed as he was in 1545, Luther felt that great gains had been made in the cause of the gospel, and he was ready to defend them at any cost. Included in his defense was a vigorous offense that was, in many cases, truly offensive. But these polemics cannot be explained as a product only of Luther's own theology and personality. The coarse tenor of the arguments was partially set by other people, as in the case of Hanswurst. In some cases, these polemics came at the demand of Luther's superiors. And, in part, they are the product of a man riddled with sickness and thoroughly fatigued. This does not excuse, but at least helps to explain, these shocking last treatises.

---

54. LW 41:358, translation slightly altered.

Last Achievements

Luther remained busy and enormously productive in his last years, and not just by slinging mud. He looked back over his achievements and took some pride in what had been accomplished and some disappointment in what had failed. He is particularly conscious, in these reflective moments, of what has happened in the lives of ordinary Christians of the sort whose pastor he was and for whom the medieval church was more a burden than a source of joy. Many theologians do not notice such people, let alone care for them and write for them. His friends were consistently surprised that he rebuked those who disrespected common folk.[55] So when he takes on his old opponents on sacramental matters one last time, he does so because he himself takes such genuine comfort from Holy Communion. He wishes the same for others. And he thinks Zwingli, Oecolampadius, and now Schwenckfeld get it wrong in ways that damage Christian conscience. His "Brief Confession concerning the Holy Sacrament" once again defended the view that Christ's body and blood are truly, bodily present in the bread and wine of communion.[56] He reviews his understanding of the others' positions. They try to dance around the fact that Christ promises at the Last Supper to be present in the bread of communion. Of course, Luther wanted to be right about this matter, but his main interest is pastoral. The consciences of Christians, even small children, need to be able to trust that God keeps promises. He refutes Schwenckfeld on these grounds: "However, this is his opinion: One shouldn't worship the creature because it is written, 'You shall worship the Lord your God and him only shall you serve.' Then he thinks, 'Christ is a creature and therefore I shouldn't worship Christ as a human being.' But

55. For example, Wolfgang Capito, in James Kittelson, *Wolfgang Capito from Humanist to Reformer* (Leiden: Brill, 1975), 83–84.
56. LW 38:281–319.

children recite without being offended, 'I believe in Jesus Christ, his only Son, our Lord, who was conceived by the Holy Spirit,' etc. So the fool makes two Christs: one who hangs on the cross, and another who ascends to his Father."[57]

Luther spent more time in his study and less time at the university, but he did finally bring to completion his massive ten-year lecture series on the book of Genesis in 1545. He had not wanted to publish the lectures but was persuaded by his former student and scribe George Rörer to do so, beginning in 1543. Throughout the lectures, Luther tended to stick to the "literal" sense of the text, moving to the "spiritual" senses such as allegory only when it seemed most appropriate. The published lectures maintain their spoken style, peppered with earthy German allusions and expressions. He ties his interpretation closely to his context: the natural bond between Adam and Eve speaks against forced clerical celibacy; institutions, such as families and the church, had been given by God from the beginning to order human life; the devil (which Luther identified with the serpent) was behind temptations not to trust the promise of the word but rather to rely on and "justify" oneself by blaming God for sin.

Here we sense a major principle of his mature biblical interpretation: take the word at face value, approach it with reverence expecting it to speak to your own situation, and remain open to new insights that challenge your assumptions and conclusions. As one might expect with the transcript of ten years' worth of lectures, there are discrepancies. For example, in discussing relationships between men and women, Luther can say,

> Although Eve was a most extraordinary creature—similar to Adam as far as the image of God is concerned, that is, in justice, wisdom and happiness—she was nevertheless a woman. For as the sun is more excellent than the moon (although the moon, too, is a very excellent

57. LW 54:469.

body), so the woman, although she was a most beautiful work of God, nevertheless was not the equal of the male in glory and prestige. . . . This sex may not be excluded from any glory of the human creature, although it is inferior to the male sex.[58]

But he also asserts more or less the opposite of this position when he writes, "She was in no respect inferior to Adam, whether you count the qualities of the body or those of the mind."[59] Explaining such inconsistencies has kept Luther scholars and students busy for centuries. And Luther seemed sometimes a bit too sure that the literal sense of the text straightforwardly meant what he thought it meant. He relied heavily, perhaps too heavily, on Augustine's way of reading Genesis but still came to many new insights that have stood the test of time, though many have been rightly discarded.[60]

The Reformation brought about not only the first ordination of an evangelical bishop—Amsdorf in Naumburg—but also the first dedication of a church constructed explicitly as an evangelical building. Luther was asked to preach the dedication sermon at this church in Torgau in October 1544. He used the opportunity to articulate again principles of worship. Ceremonies and traditions can be very good, and the church should make use of them. But they must remain matters of freedom and subject to the word.[61] To add to the worship life of the churches, Luther continued to write hymns and verse. In the last few years of his life, Luther published dozens of new hymns, and arranged and edited many more. Speaking of stale

58. LW 1:68–69.
59. LW 1:115.
60. For one that he got right, Luther is one of the first to point out that "image of God" and "likeness of God" in Genesis were just different ways of saying the same thing, and most modern biblical scholars agree. On the other hand, Luther seems to have shared Augustine's incredibly rosy (and speculative!) view of humanity in the Garden of Eden. He thought that, were it not for the Fall, babies would have come out walking just like baby chickens do, that they would have needed less time to nurse, that women would have been able to have more of them, and so on.
61. LW 51:337.

chanting, he complained, "Why is it that we have so many fine poems and so many beautiful songs of the flesh, but of the spirit we have such cold, worthless things?"[62] In response, Luther set many of these hymns to the tunes of beer-drinking songs—not because they were born in taverns but because they were good tunes. Luther composed an especially daring polyphonic motet based on his favorite text from Psalm 118, "I shall not die but live, and declare the works of the Lord."[63] He was encouraged and helped in this by his friend the composer Ludwig Senfl. Even at sixty-two and about to die, Luther tried his hand at something new.

In 1545, when a large collection of his Latin writings was published, he looked back on his life. One never knows how seriously to take a man's memory of things that happened decades earlier, especially with such an immensely chaotic life between the events and their recollection. Yet the picture he paints of his life in the preface to this collection is worth repeating, even if it must be interpreted with caution.[64] He tells of the harm he saw done by the sale of indulgences in 1517 and recounts the story of his actions against them. Then he becomes more personal, telling of a great transition in his thinking that he underwent at that time. What seemed instantaneous thirty years later was probably more gradual. Yet, either way, his mind was changed about a fundamental way of understanding God.

> I hated that word "righteousness of God," which, according to the use and custom of all the teachers, I had been taught to understand philosophically regarding the formal or active righteousness, as they called it, with which God is righteous and punishes the unrighteous sinner. . . . Though I lived as a monk without reproach, I felt that I was a sinner before God with an extremely disturbed conscience. I could not

62. WATR 5, no. 5603, quoted in Brecht, *Martin Luther*, 3:284.
63. LW 53:337ff.
64. LW 34:325–39, MLBTW3, 496–97.

believe that he was placated by my satisfaction. I did not love, yes, I hated the righteous God who punishes sinners. . . . Thus I raged with a fierce and troubled conscience. . . . At last, by the mercy of God, meditating day and night, I gave heed to the context of the words, namely, "In it the righteousness of God is revealed, as it is written, 'He who through faith is righteous shall live.'" There I began to understand that the righteousness of God is that by which the righteous lives by a gift of God, namely by faith. And this is the meaning: the righteousness of God is revealed by the gospel, namely, the passive righteousness with which merciful God justifies us by faith, as it is written, "He who through faith is righteous shall live." Here I felt that I was altogether born again and had entered paradise itself through open gates.[65]

Though it is not autobiographical, his very last sermon in Wittenberg sums up much of his life's thinking about theology: even when saved, humans remain sinful; they should turn to Christ for healing and strength; they must remember the waters of Baptism; and they need to stick together in faith. Preached in January 1546, a month before he died, Luther explained,

After baptism there still remains much of the old Adam. For, as we have often said, it is true that sin is forgiven in baptism, but we are not yet altogether clean, as is shown in the parable of the Samaritan, who carried the man wounded by robbers to an inn. He did not take care of him in such a way that he healed him at once, but rather bound up his wounds and poured on oil. . . . Adam fell among the robbers and implanted sin in us all. If Christ, the Samaritan, had not come, we should all have had to die. He it is who binds our wounds, carries us into the church and is now healing us. So we are now under the Physician's care. The sin, it is true, is wholly forgiven, but it has not been wholly purged. . . . The Holy Spirit must cleanse the wounds daily. Therefore this life is a hospital; the sin has really been forgiven, but it has not yet been healed.[66]

---

65. LW 34:337, MLBTW3, 497.
66. LW 51:373. It is characteristic of the later Luther that this tenderness and insight are paired with brutal criticisms of the Wittenbergers to whom he is preaching.

12

Death and Vindication

1545–1555

When Luther saw that his sickness was very serious and was bringing him close to death, he asked that his body should be placed on an altar and be worshiped as a god. . . . Therefore, as soon as his body was laid in the grave, at once a terrible uproar and noise were heard, as if the devil and hell had collapsed. . . . But the following night at the very place where the body of Martin Luther had been buried, everyone alike heard an uproar greater than the first. . . . When it became day, they went to open the grave where the impious body of Martin Luther had been laid. When this grave was opened, they saw clearly that there was neither body, flesh, bone, nor any clothes. But it was full of such a sulfurous smell that it made all sick who stood round about.[1]

At least that is what some people thought. A short pamphlet from which this quotation is drawn reached Philip of Hesse's hands in March 1545, a year *before* Luther's death. He thought it was humorous, so he had it translated and sent to Luther. Luther had the farce published along with a note from his hand indicating that

---

1. "An Italian Lie concerning Martin Luther's Death," in LW 34:365–66.

he was very interested to learn of his death and these strange circumstances. We glimpse here Luther's knack for using the press to his advantage; the Italian who wrote the pamphlet wanted to shock the common folk into hating Luther, but Luther's clever response actually won him the upper hand. He had earlier said, "The art of printing is the highest and ultimate gift whereby God advances the cause of his gospel."[2]

And it was never just the printed word that Luther put to use, but also the image. In 1529, his handsome book for home devotions sold thousands of copies, in large part a result of its illustrations. Of it he had written, "I thought it good to add to the *Personal Prayer Book* the old *Book of the Passion*, above all for the sake of children and simple folk, who use pictures and images better to recall divine stories than mere words or doctrine."[3] By the time he neared his own death, he had fully grasped the power of the image and the printed word to reach the far corners of the world.

The Quarrel of the Counts

Luther was asked to return to the county of Mansfeld, the place of his birth, to mediate a dispute between its rulers. Its counts—three brothers—were constantly fighting, partly because they had so little to fight over. According to one legend, Mansfeld got its name from being so small that it was the size of a field around whose perimeter a man could ride in a day. All the counts were eager to tax the mines and smelters in the area but unwilling to share their revenues with each other or for the common good.

Though he was not especially known for his ability to broker a political deal, Luther agreed to do what he could to settle the dispute.

---

2. Quoted in Lewis Spitz, *The Protestant Reformation* (New York: Harper and Row, 1985), 89.

3. LW 43:43, translation altered. On this issue see Robert W. Scribner, *For the Sake of Simple Folk* (Cambridge: Cambridge University Press, 1981).

Some of his extended family had their livelihoods at stake, and Luther felt sentimentally tied to this place of his humble origins. His last sermon in Wittenberg had spoken of life as a hospital, and Luther dragged his weary and sick self into a wagon with his three sons and his colleague Justas Jonas. He preached at many churches along the way, notably in Halle and in the church where he was baptized in Eisleben, his birthplace.

He was in relatively high spirits. In letters home from the journey, Luther joked to Katie that he had not been "tempted" by sights of pretty women along the way.[4] When the party could not cross the Saale River because ice on it had broken and the river overflowed its banks, Luther joked, "A huge female Anabaptist met us with waves of water and great floating pieces of ice; she threatened to baptize us again."[5] This happened on January 25, 1546, the commemoration of the conversion (or "turning around") of the apostle Paul. Luther joked too about being turned around by the river.

But there was much not to laugh at on the trip or during the negotiations. Luther wrote Philip Melanchthon several letters, frequently asking for his prayers and describing various ailments, including a severe bout with angina pectoris and a cold wind that "turned my brain to ice." He blames Satan for a fire that broke out in the room where he had been staying, and Jewish passersby in Eisleben for his dizzy spells. In his room in Eisleben, while on the toilet (an unusually eventful place in Luther's life), he reported that "a stone almost fell on my head and nearly squashed me as in a mouse trap."[6] In another letter to Katie, he tried to persuade her not to worry so much about him. "I have a caretaker who is better than you; he lies in the cradle and rests on a virgin's bosom, and yet he sits on the right

4. LW 50:291.
5. LW 50:286.
6. LW 50:304.

369

hand of God. Therefore be at peace."[7] For Christ to be "at the right hand of God" always meant for Luther that God had thrust his right arm *into* the world to be present in faith for strength and consolation; this is why he criticized some Reformed theologians for imagining it to be a kind of fixed chair that tethered Christ to heaven.

The negotiations themselves, when they finally began on January 28, 1546, were also problematic. Luther's lifelong hatred of lawyers came out as he expressed disgust with the quibbling lawyers with whom he was working, calling them "plagues of the human race," with too many "ambiguities, sophistries, and chicaneries."[8] He thought they were overly concerned with the interests of their employers, caring little for the common good. "They fool themselves with their little bits of knowledge of the law, while in my opinion they all together have not the slightest idea of the usage of the law. Like hired pettifoggers they behave without any honor; they care nothing about peace, the commonweal, or religion."[9] Humans were selfish enough without the help of lawyers convincing them to press their own interests further.

Eventually, Luther and his colleagues were able to help reach a resolution. The counts arranged financial matters among themselves and pledged to pay for a school for girls and boys with remaining funds. Following custom, Luther preached a sermon as the negotiations concluded with a worship service. The text was Matthew 11, where Jesus prays, "I thank you, Father, Lord of heaven and earth, because you have hidden these things from the wise and the intelligent and have revealed them to infants." Luther warned against trusting false wisdom and insisted on sticking to the word.

7. LW 50:302.
8. LW 50:297.
9. LW 50:294.

Before he could finish, Luther complained of weakness and had to lie down.

Death

He had been staying at the house of Eisleben's town clerk, John Albrecht. On February 17, he rested there, and grew short of breath and suffered chest pains. He was able to eat dinner with his friends, where the discussion turned to the question (a macabre one, in retrospect) of whether dead friends would recognize one another after the resurrection; Luther was of the opinion that they would. After dinner, Luther retired to his room, and he would not come out again alive.

Various people attended to him, including his companion Jonas and Count Albrecht and his wife Anna. The primitive state of medicine in this age is shown by two measures taken to "help" Luther as he contracted death sweats. Not surprisingly, neither the ground "unicorn powder" given to him just before he died, nor a humiliating enema administered to his corpse just after his death, did any good.

In sixteenth century Germany, a major figure was expected to die in a ceremonial way. It was not uncommon for people to think far ahead of time how they might want to die, what they might say or do when their time came. This is called the *ars moriendi*—the art of dying.[10] Perhaps with this in mind, Luther had penned some final words, found on a slip of paper in his pocket after he died. It shows him reflecting on his life and also reflects his liberal arts education and his priorities. It read as follows:

Nobody can understand Vergil in his *Bucolics* and *Georgics* [poems about shepherding and farming] unless he has first been a shepherd

10. Luther was actually quite critical of many books that proposed to teach Christians how to die. His thoughts and an array of views from others on this matter can be found in Austra Reinis, *Reforming the Art of Dying* (Aldershot: Ashgate, 2006).

or a farmer for five years. Nobody understands Cicero in his letters unless he has been engaged in public affairs of some consequence for twenty years. Let nobody suppose that he has tasted the Holy Scriptures sufficiently unless he has ruled over the churches with the prophets for a hundred years. Therefore there is something wonderful, first, about John the Baptist; second, about Christ; third, about the apostles. "Lay not your hand on this divine Aeneid, but bow in reverence before its footprints!"[11]

Then the famous lines, in German and Latin, "Wir sind Pettler, Hoc est verum." "We are beggars. That is true."

Lifelong commitments were also shown in his last spoken words. Over the course of several hours, spanning from late evening until early morning on February 18, he frequently repeated Bible verses. John 3:16 came frequently from him, as well as Ps. 31:5, "Into your hand I commit my spirit; you have redeemed me, O Lord, faithful God." Finally, losing strength, he whispered a few times the words of Simeon in Luke 2:29, "Lord, let your servant depart in peace. Amen." Sensing that the end was very near and knowing that the circumstances of Luther's death would be closely studied by his followers and enemies, Jonas asked Luther a final question. "Reverend Father, are you ready to die trusting in your Lord Jesus Christ and to confess the doctrine which you have taught in his name?" "Yes!" was Luther's loud response. Then he died.[12]

Requests to bury his body in Eisleben were quickly denied, and his body was prepared for the trip back to Wittenberg. Perhaps in the spirit of whistling in the graveyard, Luther had earlier joked, "If I get back home to Wittenberg I'll lie down in a coffin and give the maggots a fat doctor to eat."[13] There was first a brief funeral

11. LW 54:476, translation altered.
12. There were multiple accounts of Luther's death. For a summary of diverging views, see Michael B. Lukens, "Luther's Death and the Secret Catholic Report," *Journal of Theological Studies* 41 (1990): 545–53.
13. WA Tr 6.302, no. 6975.

in Saint Andrew's Church in Eisleben, with Jonas preaching. Along the procession back to Wittenberg, the crowd following the wagon grew so large by Halle that people could hardly walk on the side streets and in the town square.

When the news of Luther's death reached Wittenberg, Melanchthon quoted Elisha's words after Elijah ascended, "Dead is the charioteer of Israel, who has led the church in these last times."[14] A large funeral took place in the castle church on February 22. Luther's casket was buried in the floor, just next to the pulpit where he preached hundreds of sermons. Bugenhagen preached, full of emotion, about the clarity of Luther's understanding of Scripture and his resilience in teaching. Melanchthon then gave an address in Latin on behalf of the university. This eulogy was full of praise for Luther's approachability in pastoral concerns and his brilliance as a teacher. But he also was honest about Luther's brashness and violence. He quoted Erasmus, saying, "On account of the sickness of our times, God has given us a harsh physician."[15]

Wittenbergers and the Schmalkaldic War

About a month after Luther died, the long-feared war between Emperor Charles V and the Schmalkaldic League broke out. The Saxon princes had a strong army (fewer soldiers but more cannon than the emperor) and many allies. Philip of Hesse, in exchange for having his bigamy pardoned, had promised not to fight the emperor in any war except this one. The sides were therefore quite evenly matched. The outcome would have been hard to predict. One fact changed all that, however. Duke Moritz of Saxony, Lutheran and cousin to Elector John Frederick, switched sides and fought for the

14. Quoted in Martin Brecht, *Martin Luther*, vol. 3: *The Preservation of the Church, 1532–1546* (Minneapolis: Fortress Press, 1993), 378. The scripture passage is from 2 Kgs. 2:12.
15. Brecht, *Martin Luther*, 3:380.

emperor. This earned him the position of new elector of Saxony but also the nickname "Judas of Meissen." He had followed Heinrich IV as successor to the Roman Catholic Duke George, Luther's longtime enemy. Moritz was happy to make Ducal Saxony Lutheran, and he conveniently expropriated many church properties and money. The war was decided at the battle of Mühlberg in April 1547. John Frederick and Landgrave Philip (who ended up fighting after all) were thrown into prison. Emperor Charles marched through his newly reconquered lands, stopping in Wittenberg itself on May 19, 1547. He was brought into the castle church and shown Luther's grave. When asked whether he wished to exhume the remains to burn and dishonor them, Charles sneered, "I do not make war on dead men."[16]

Because of the war, Katie had to flee to Magdeburg and later to Brunswick. She was able to return after a time but then left again because of an outbreak of the plague. Life was extremely difficult for her after her husband's death. She faced opposition from some Saxon clerks in her financial affairs and was stricken with long grief for her husband. In Torgau in the fall of 1552, she was thrown off a horse cart in an accident and fell into a ditch filled with cold water. She never recovered from her injuries, and she died and was buried in Torgau around Christmas of that year. Catching a knack for dying well from her husband, her last words were "I will stick to Christ as a burr to a top coat."[17] Her four surviving children went on to live productive lives, especially Paul, who became physician to the elector and experimenter in alchemy. The last direct descendant of Luther died in 1789; the family continued through Luther's brother James.

After the loss at Mühlberg, John Frederick was charged with heresy but refused any religious concessions. He was imprisoned until 1552.

---

16. Quoted in Spitz, *Protestant Reformation*, 121.
17. Quoted in Kirsi Stjerna, *Women in the Reformation* (Oxford: Wiley-Blackwell, 2008), 67.

The occasion for his release was that the turncoat Moritz of Saxony turned his coat again and fought against the emperor. Upon his release, the landless ex-elector was allowed to live in Weimar, a small city near Erfurt. While there, he persuaded his old court painters, the Cranachs, to paint a magnificent altarpiece in memory of Luther's life and work. The work depicts Christ twice—once trampling on death and the devil, and a second time hanging on the cross. John the Baptist, Lucas Cranach, and Luther stand at the foot of the cross, with Luther pointing to a Bible. Blood pours from Christ's wounded side and lands squarely on the forehead of the layman Cranach; no intercession of Mary, saints, or priests is needed for that Protestant. The Weimar work is a rather more adventurous effort than the well-known Wittenberg altarpiece the Cranachs were able to finish just before the Schmalkaldic War overturned the city. The lower panel in the earlier work has a scene with Christ crucified in the middle, with the Wittenberg crowd looking on from the left. Luther is shown in a pulpit at the right, his hand pointing to Christ.

Image 35: The altarpiece begun by Cranach in Weimar was one of his last works, and was finished by his son in 1555.

The Interim

Life in Saxony in the wake of the victory of Charles V was complicated, to say the least. To oversimplify a very complex story,

Charles V produced a genuine compromise on the religious questions facing his empire. This was a very surprising position for him to take. The 1548 document, *Augsburg Interim*, allowed for provisions until a general council of the church could make its statements. The document allowed Lutheran lands in the empire to remain "Lutheran" for a time, but the only changes permitted to the medieval church were clergy marriage and laity receiving the cup at Holy Communion. In Catholic lands, not even these changes were permitted. Lutherans were forced to readopt the medieval practice of seven sacraments, the sacrifice of the Mass, and most other medieval rites. In some ways, Charles could be a visionary (for example, he is credited with being the first to suggest a canal be built across Panama), but, as often happens to people who try to effect compromise, Charles was attacked vigorously from both sides.[18]

Catholic princes were aghast that Lutheranism was viewed as an alternate form of the Christian faith to be tolerated, rather than merely a heresy to be extinguished. Further, the fact that Charles V would even issue the document seemed to aggrandize the power of the emperor, which they were hoping to diminish. Protestant princes, on the other hand, thought the measures were drastic and at any rate impossible to enact. Philip Melanchthon viewed the *Augsburg Interim* as basically a bad idea that might be the best the Protestants could achieve, given the magnitude of the destruction of the Schmalkaldic War. He tried to win more concessions with the *Leipzig Interim*, but that document did not get very far either. He thought that much of what Charles V tried to enforce could be considered *adiaphora*, or "middle things." They did not touch the essence of the Christian faith, but rather its edges. So long as justification by grace through faith could be preached, along with

18. Lesley A. DuTemple, *The Panama Canal* (Minneapolis: Lerner, 2003), 88.

core doctrines such as the Trinity and the primacy of Scripture, Protestants could live with the rest of the medieval dross for the time being until the precious metal of the church could be refined and purified.

Image 36: Charles V is shown enthroned above all those he has conquered: Pope Clement VII, Suleiman the Magnificent, Philip of Hesse, Elector John Frederick, King Francis I and the Duke of Cleves.

This won Melanchthon a number of enemies, who accused him of punting on Luther's main teaching. For instance, Melanchthon suggested that Lutherans could affirm that a human's will participates in salvation, even though the act of willing does not effect it. God does not drag humans like a "block of wood" through the process.[19] The fractures that emerged in the bedrock of German Lutheran

19. Of the very many texts that have been written to condemn or defend Melanchthon on this point, a balanced treatment can be found in Gregory Graybill, *Evangelical Free Will: Philip Melanchthon's Doctrinal Journey on the Origins of Faith* (New York: Oxford University Press, 2010).

theology would be settled, somewhat, after stability returned a quarter century later with the *Book of Concord*. Lutheranism in other lands, unaffected by the political situation of 1550s Germany, remained cool to the *Formula of Concord*, leaving pride of place among Lutheran documents to the Augsburg Confession. What Luther would have thought about all this is anyone's guess, and many different sides have sought to draft his influence to support their vision. Eventually, the Peace of Augsburg (1555), later basically affirmed at Westphalia (1648), allowed for divergent religions in the land, and Charles's dream of an empire united under princes of the same faith was over.

A Last Look Back: Why Luther Was Wrong about Wittenberg

This book began with a look at Luther facing a crisis: the crisis of his disappointment with the course of the Reformation in his own Wittenberg. He clearly wanted things to have gone much better there than they seemed in 1545. An old man expecting eternity, he had no time for utopians. Yet he also knew that one must not expect too little from people. In his view, that was the problem with the medieval church: it did not demand too much from Christians, but too little. His theology focused more on God taking the initiative in grace and less on the Christian's actions and merit. So why had things not turned out better for the movement, given the enormous investment so many brave and competent souls had poured into it? Especially in the movement's center, Wittenberg?

Historian Steven Ozment puts the basic problem well. He writes,

> The great shortcoming of the Reformation was its naïve expectation that the majority of people were capable of radical religious enlightenment and moral transformation. . . . Such expectation directly contradicted some of its fondest convictions and the original teaching of its founder. Having begun in protest against allegedly unnatural and

379

unscriptural proscriptions of the medieval church and urged freedom in the place of coercion, the reformers brought a strange new burden to bear on the consciences of their followers when they instructed them to resolve the awesome problems of sin, death, and the devil by simple faith in the Bible and ethical service to their neighbors. The brave new man of Protestant faith, "subject to none [yet] subject to all" in Luther's famous formulation, was expected to bear his finitude and sinfulness with anxiety resolved, secure in the knowledge of a gratuitous salvation, and fearful of neither man, God, or the devil. But how many were capable of such self-understanding?[20]

Luther expected so much to happen so quickly because he thought there was so much more of the gospel around than had been before. But where were its fruits? Just before his death, as he reacted with anger against the shortcomings of his home, he must have been aware of the burdens Reformation Christianity imposed on its followers. A person of his intellectual abilities, with supportive colleagues and extensive training, had the luxury of disassembling the problematic medieval church and piecing together a new version of the ancient faith. Yet could others, with fewer resources, be expected to catch up so quickly?

So in 1545, as Luther's heart grew cold about Wittenberg and all that the small city represented to him, the achievements and failures of his years there weighed heavily on his mind. Morals were low; morale was lower. And yet Luther found the means to work through this crisis as well. Because he was unusually silent about his thoughts, we cannot piece together his sources of resilience. As this book has argued, however, the likeliest place to turn is not Luther's psychology, but his theology. His doctrine of sin led him to low *expectations* for communities. In this respect, he was the furthest thing from naive. And yet his doctrine of grace led him to high *hopes* for what God might do through such imperfect people.[21] These were the

20. Steven Ozment, *The Age of Reform, 1250–1550* (New Haven: Yale University Press, 1980), 437.

binoculars through which Luther saw the world, and resolving the two lenses into one image was difficult. Or, to alter the metaphor slightly, perhaps just before his death Luther's view of the world came through a kaleidoscope, which, when just a quarter turn off, shows a mess. With a slight adjustment, beauty comes through again. As a reformer, Luther was a man without a plan. As a theologian, Luther trusted in God's plan, no matter the detours and apparent dead-ends.

A thesis of this book has been that the best way to understand Luther is by grasping his resilience. Luther's genius comes from the fact that, rather than seeing crises that came upon him as interruptions distracting him from his real calling, he saw these crises—imprisonment, facing death, the loss of Magdalena, and so on—as opportunities. Luther used those very setbacks as occasions for revising his work. Each of these very negative experiences motivated him to a high level of achievement, especially given that he feared he had little time left to work. In each case, these staggering interruptions were the inspiration for some of his most remarkable work rather than a distraction from brilliant work already underway.

One of the editors of the American edition of Luther's Works, Jaroslav Pelikan, wrote a bestselling book about Jesus called *Jesus through the Centuries*.[22] Each chapter takes its name from a title ascribed to Jesus that seems somehow an emblem for a century's worth of thinking about Jesus. The chapter on medieval mysticism calls him "The Bridegroom of the Soul," and the chapter on the Enlightenment is called "The Teacher of Common Sense." None of the titles exhausts or perfectly exemplifies the complex whole, yet each in its own way tells the truth. Among figures of more recent

---

21. One place to find a brief examination of Luther's doctrines of sin and grace is Derek R. Nelson, *Sin: A Guide for the Perplexed* (London: T&T Clark, 2011), 14–16.

22. Jaroslav Pelikan, *Jesus through the Centuries: His Place in the History of Culture* (New Haven: Yale University Press, 1999).

history, Luther alone seems ripe for this kind of analysis, as titles of all sorts have been ascribed to him.[23]

Liberator. In 1934, a Baptist minister from Atlanta, Georgia, named Michael King went with ten colleagues on a trip to the Holy Land and then to Germany. He was deeply inspired by what he learned about Martin Luther and his efforts to confront a corrupt and failing system. When he returned to the segregated American South, he changed his name to Martin Luther King and did the same for his five-year-old son, now called Martin Luther King Jr. To them, Luther meant freedom of conscience and the darinig courage to return to one's ideals. This evokes Luther's early experiment in renaming himself *Eleutheria*, Greek for "freedom." At about the same time that Martin Luther King Jr. got his new name, the Nazi propaganda machine was gathering steam, and the Nazis were happy to uncover Luther's late tracts against Judaism in the name of their xenophobia and hatred. To them, Luther meant German heroism and a supposed "purity" of thought and culture with precious little room for dissent and difference. Among the many slogans available to be co-opted from Luther, "freedom" was certainly not one of them. Luther's writings can thus cast him either as a hero to the depleted masses or as the thumb under which the masses might be held down.

Bible scholar. Luther's translation of the Bible into German was momentous. His insistence that theology take Scripture as its ultimate source and then subject its own claims to the scrutiny of biblical interpretation brought the Bible to the fore in a way it had not been in a millennium. Luther held fast to Scripture, insisting that its clearest parts were clear enough and that its murkier parts should be studied more deeply. Ironically, the freedom with which he tried to differentiate what was clear and central from what was peripheral

23. For early titles ascribed to Luther, see Robert Kolb, *Martin Luther as Prophet, Teacher and Hero: Images of the Reformer, 1520–1620* (Grand Rapids, MI: Baker, 1999).

led directly to historical criticism in the eighteenth and nineteenth centuries. This called into question any easy correlation of biblical narrative with historic events and quickly led to an erosion in trust in the Bible and then to a reactionary, defensive fundamentalism that cast aside the scholarly care of professors like Luther.

Prophet. Biblical prophets did one or both of two things. They criticized the social order of their day, and they did so with a special sense of the future toward which God was calling God's people. In both senses, Luther can be called a prophet, but that title must be qualified in different ways. He was certainly eager to criticize the corruption of the church in his day and has therefore been justly celebrated as a rebel and progressive.[24] Yet his social conservatism did not extend to a denunciation of the civil authority as such. Their blockheaded actions, yes. But not their right to govern in a hierarchy that Luther thought God had ordained. And so this same Luther who is quick to prophesy against authority deferred to it just as often. He was prophetic in raising the status of marriage, and in that way the status of women, but he also reflected the conservatism of his age on that matter, as on many others. Liberals and conservatives alike have found themselves and support for their agendas in Luther's writings.

Pastor. The one title Luther has been given on which there can be virtually no equivocation, one that does not have two sides, has no "yes, but," is *pastor.* On the most momentous day in a turbulent life—the day of his examination at the Diet of Worms—Luther rose early so that he could hear the confession of several people with heavy hearts. His emphasis on "certainty" was not certainty of a detached, scientific sort but of an existential, pastoral type. He did not want to be right about doctrine for the sake of being right but for being

24. For example, the cover of Alister McGrath, *Christianity's Dangerous Idea: The Protestant Revolution—A History from the Sixteenth Century to the Twenty-First* (New York: Harper, 2007), shows Luther in a way that evokes communist revolutionary Che Guevara.

helpful to troubled consciences. His concern for preaching, both his own and that of others, trumped everything else in his theology. Many have understandably been disappointed that Luther spent an incredible amount of time writing his postils (model sermons for others) rather than spending that time in other ways, but here we see Luther's priority and self-understanding.[25] The word *pastor* literally means "shepherd," and Luther was like a German Shepherd in more ways than one.

In Place of an Ending

Luther's final sermon was preached in his birthplace of Eisleben on February 14 or 15, 1546, a few days before he died. He preached on the comforting words of Jesus, "Come to me, all you that are weary and are carrying heavy burdens, and I will give you rest" (Matt. 11:25–30). Luther is filled with wonder at the ways of God that reveal truth to the simple and hide wisdom from those the world considers wise. A strong line runs from the *Heidelberg Disputation* (1518) to this sermon almost thirty years later.

But there are two tensions at the end. One is that Luther is disappointed in the response of the people—his people—to the free availability of the gospel. "In past times we would have run to the ends of the world if we had known of a place where we could have heard God speak. But now that we hear this every day in sermons, indeed, now that all books are full of it, we do not see this happening."[26] Also, Luther's opponents weigh heavily on him so that his usually clear preaching is here clouded by so much attention to the pope and his supporters, to "wiseacres."

25. The world still lacks a first-rate book in English on Luther's understanding of himself and his work as pastor. In German, the best is Gerhard Ebeling, *Luthers Seelsorge: Theologie in der Vielfalt der Lebenssituationen an seinen Briefen dargestellt* (Tübingen: Mohr Siebeck, 1997).
26. LW 51:390.

Finally, as he concludes—or really in place of a conclusion, because he fell ill and had to sit down—he comes to some clarity and is able to focus on the good news. "The wise of this world are rejected, that we may learn not to think ourselves wise . . . indeed, to shut our eyes altogether, and cling only to Christ's Word and come to him, as he so lovingly invites us to do, and say: Thou alone art my beloved Lord and Master, I am thy disciple."[27]

And so he is left alone with Christ but must now pass the task on to others. His very last words of preaching were these: "This and much more might be said concerning this Gospel, but I am too weak and we shall let it go at that."[28]

What Luther last said from his pulpit is true also of his life, and therefore of this book: much more could be said, and we shall let it go at that.

27. LW 51:392.
28. LW 51:392.

The Forty-Six Players in the Lutheran Reformation

A Brief Guide

Adrian VI (or Hadrian VI, 1459–1523). Adrian Floriszoon reigned as pope in 1522 and 1523. He was the tutor to Charles V when the future emperor was a child.

Agricola, Johannes (1491–1566). Friend of Luther's and fellow reformer in Wittenberg (also called Johannes Bauer). He later broke with Luther and developed an "antinomian" theology.

Albrecht of Brandenburg (1490–1545). Bishop of Madgeburg from 1513, archbishop of Mainz and elector from 1514. His attempts to solidify power by being named bishop of multiple places were funded by John Tetzel's selling of indulgences.

Albrecht III of Mansfeld (1486–1560). Count of Mansfeld, near Saxony, and sympathetic political figure to Luther's changes.

Aleander, Jerome (1480–1542). Papal delegate who tried to force Luther to recant his views on the reform of the church.

von Amsdorf, Nicholas (1483–1565). Pastor and later first bishop consecrated in the Reformation. A confirmed bachelor, he was the other man Katie Luther said she would marry if Martin would not marry her.

Brück, Gregor (1484–1557). Chancellor to the electors of Saxony from 1525 and intermediary for Luther on many political issues.

Bucer, Martin (1491–1551). Statesman and informal mediator between many Reformation factions. Centered in Strasbourg, a town on the border between French and German lands, Bucer had personal relationships with Luther, Calvin, and Zwingli.

Bugenhagen, Johannes (1485–1558). Pastor of the Reformation, leader of the town church in Wittenberg, and Luther's confidant. Also known as "Pommern," as he was from the region of Pomerania.

Cajetan, Thomas (Jacobus de Vio, 1469–1534). Cardinal from 1517, scholar of Thomas Aquinas's theology. Cajetan "examined" Luther at Augsburg in 1518 while dressed in fabulous clothes that revealed to Luther the opulence of the Italian church in contrast to its German counterpart.

Carlstadt, Andreas Bodenstein von (ca. 1480–1541). Formerly Luther's professor, Carlstadt became friends with Luther as colleagues on the Wittenberg faculty. Carlstadt "radicalized" certain of Luther's teachings in very extreme ways. For instance, he believed many church traditions like ordaining ministers and wearing clergy vestments, should be discarded. Luther and Carlstadt later had a falling out.

Charles V (1500–1558). Duke of Burgundy and king of Castile from 1507, king of Spain (1516–56), king of Germany and emperor of the Holy Roman Empire (1519–1556).

Clement VII (Giulio de' Medici, 1478–1534). Frequent opponent of Charles the V, he served as pope from 1523 to 1534.

Cranach, Lucas the Elder (1472–1553). Luther's neighbor and friend, Cranach had a workshop in Wittenberg where he was a jack-of-all-trades, specializing in painting. He made numerous paintings of key Reformation figures and also illustrated many printed materials with woodcuts.

Cruciger, Casper (1504–1548). Theologian sympathetic to the Reformation and friend of Luther.

Dürer, Albrecht (1471–1528). Painter, artist and "Renaissance Man" very much impressed by Luther. German cultural hero.

Eck, Johann (1486–1543). Papal delegate sent to "deal" with the Luther situation. Eck debated Luther in a highly anticipated contest at Leipzig in 1519. Their debate centered on the question of which authority was higher—the Bible or the church.

Erasmus of Rotterdam (1469–1536). "Humanist" scholar and worldly man. Living in Holland, Erasmus was sympathetic in principle with Luther but never officially sided with the Reformation. His "The Freedom of the Will" was lambasted by Luther. In producing a better edition of the New Testament in Greek and in writing "In Praise of Folly," which ridiculed the sad state of the church, Erasmus was viewed as having "laid the egg of the Reformation, which Luther hatched."

Frederick III (Frederick the Wise, 1465–1525). Elector of Saxony, gifted statesman and prince in Saxony. Frederick, his brother John, and his nephew John Frederick were all protective of Luther and resisted on both theological and political grounds Rome's attempts to confine the Reformation.

George of Saxony (1471–1539). Duke of Saxony who was at first tolerant of Luther's reforms but then became greatly opposed to them. George was very theologically aware and hoped for a council to be convened that would "decide" the Lutheran question. He ruled the part of Saxony not controlled by the Electors.

Grumbach, Argula von (1492–1554). German noblewoman who read Luther's translation of the Bible and became a coworker with him in the Reformation. She wrote a letter to Catholic authorities in Bavaria (a strongly Catholic land), using passages from Scripture to defend the cause of reform.

Hausmann, Nicholas (1478–1538). Friend of Luther, pastor in Zwickau from 1521, court chaplain in Dessau from 1532, and pastor in Freiburg from 1538.

Hus, John (c. 1369-1415). Bohemian priest and reformer of the church burned at the stake at the Council of Constance for his views. Luther had assumed he was a heretic but came to see him as a forerunner in objecting to abuses in the church.

Hutten, Ulrich von (1488–1523). German knight who was also a poet. This supporter of Luther acted as a bridge to humanists fond of poetry but skeptical of the brash Luther.

John, Duke of Saxony (1468–1532). Elector (1525–1532), brother of Frederick the Wise, and supporter of Luther throughout his reign as elector. Cautious in developing further, John oversaw the production of the Augsburg Confession at the Imperial Diet in Augsburg in 1530.

John Frederick, Duke of Saxony (1503–1554). Elector (1532–1547), not as gifted as his predecessors, but committed to Reformation cause. Called "The Magnanimous."

Jonas, Justus (1493–1555). Lutheran theologian and leader in Wittenberg.

Julius II (1443–1513). The "fearsome pope" from 1503 to1513 who campaigned militarily across Europe, patronized the arts, and began the building of Saint Peter's in Rome.

Lang, John. Luther's childhood friend and companion, later prior of the monastery in Erfurt.

Leo X (1475–1521). Pope from 1513 to 1521, very ardent opponent of Luther who excommunicated Luther and all those sympathetic to his views.

Link, Wenceslas. Luther's close friend, frequent correspondent, and former prior, he later became an influential evangelical preacher in the important southern German city of Nuremberg.

Luther, Hans. German miner, father of Martin Luther.

Luther, Katherine von Bora (1499–1552). Former nun who married Luther and bore him six children after leaving the convent.

Luther, Margarete Lindemann. Luther's mother, wife of Hans Luther.

Luther, Martin (1483–1546). By now, you should know this man!

Maximilian I (1459–1519). Emperor of the Holy Roman Empire before Charles V, his grandson. Expanded the influence of the

Hapsburg family across Europe, "taking over" Spain and consolidating power in Austria, Hungary, Burgundy, and Holland.

Melanchthon, Philip (1497–1560). Brilliant scholar and professor of New Testament and Greek at Wittenberg. Luther's "right-hand man" and author of the most important theological statement of the Reformation, the Augsburg Confession (1530). Very cautious and politic, Melanchthon often frustrated Luther by his careful, plodding pace.

Moritz, Duke of Saxony (1521–1553). Elector from 1547 to 53, he turned on the evangelical cause to fight with Charles V in the Schmalkaldic War but then returned to the Protestants at the end of his life.

Müntzer, Thomas (ca. 1488–1525). Religious leader in the countryside, Müntzer embraced an experiential theology that led the Holy Spirit to work wonders in people's hearts. Led peasants in a revolt against nobility and died in aftermath of battle.

Paul III (1468–1549). Pope from 1534 to 1549, he convened of Council of Trent, called to settle questions raised by the Reformation.

Philip, Landgrave of Hesse (1504–1567). Supporter of the evangelical cause, he was a count situated strategically between Protestant Saxony and Catholic lands to the south. He was a leader of the Schmalkaldic League, a group of Protestant princes united for military self-defense. He was married to Christine of Saxony, forever ill and a heavy drinker, and thus married another woman. When Luther was asked to "bless" Philip's bigamy, he consented, and the Reformation lost some moral high ground.

Spalatin, George (1484–1545). Lawyer and chancellor for the electors of Saxony and chief negotiator in many political disputes with Rome.

Stauptiz, Johann (1460–1524). Luther's confessor and friend. Staupitz was in charge of Luther's monastic order, the Augustinian hermits, and encouraged Luther in biblical study.

Tetzel, John (1465–1519). Dominican monk, famous seller of indulgences, and, by this work, fundraiser for the church.

Walther, Johann (1496–1570). Luther's friend and the court musician in Torgau.

Zwingli, Ulrich (1484–1531). Leader of reformation in Zurich, disputed with Luther on many issues, especially on sacraments. Died leading his troops in battle against imperial (Catholic) forces.

Index of Names

Index of Subjects

Index of Martin Luther's Published Writings